EDENSZERO

7

I KNOW YOU CAN KEEP PRESSING ON

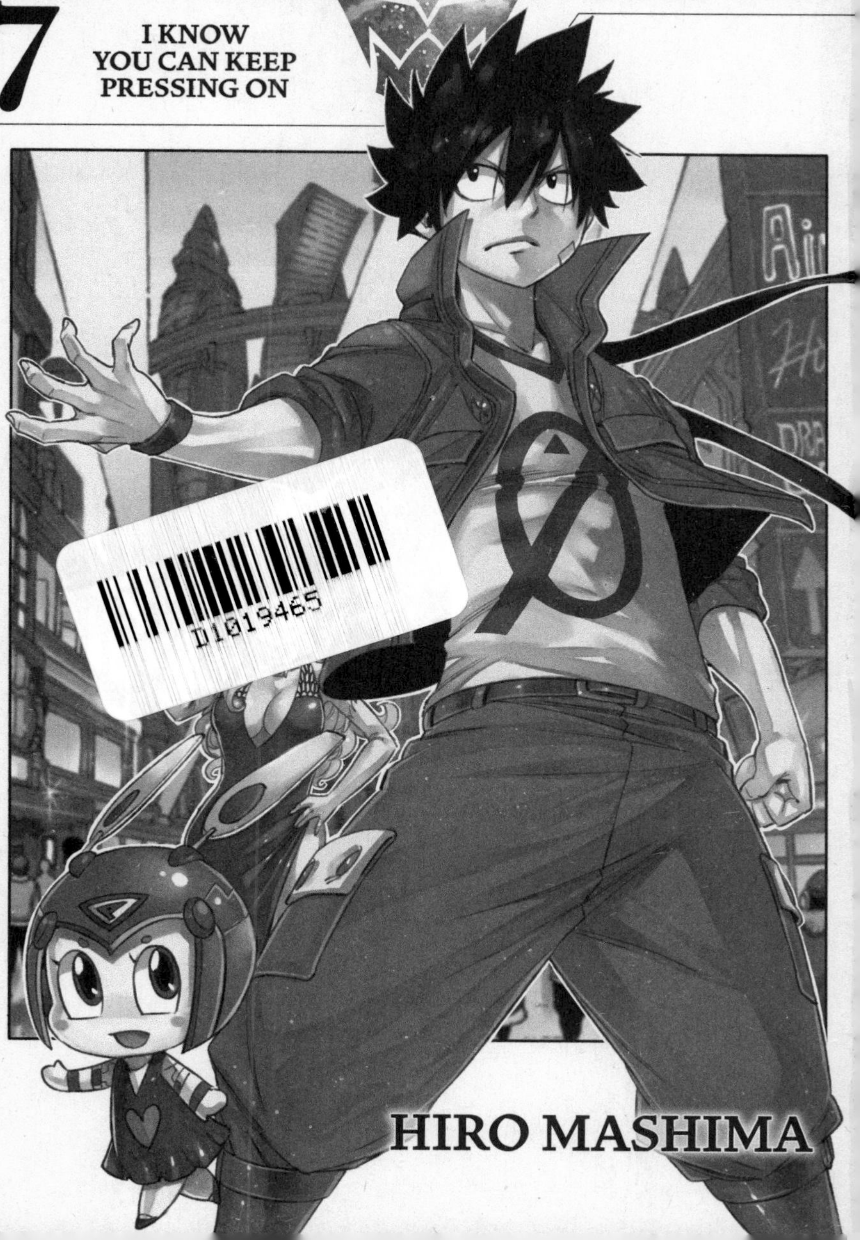

HIRO MASHIMA

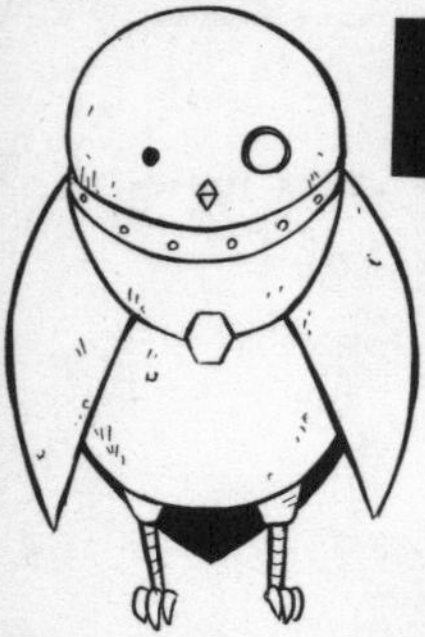

EDENS ZERO 7

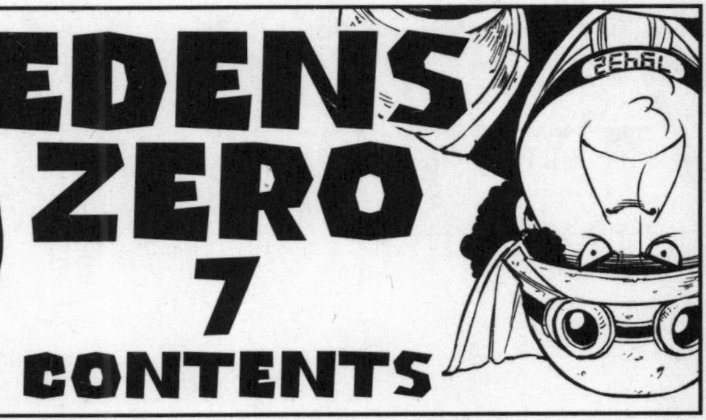

CONTENTS

EDENS ZERO

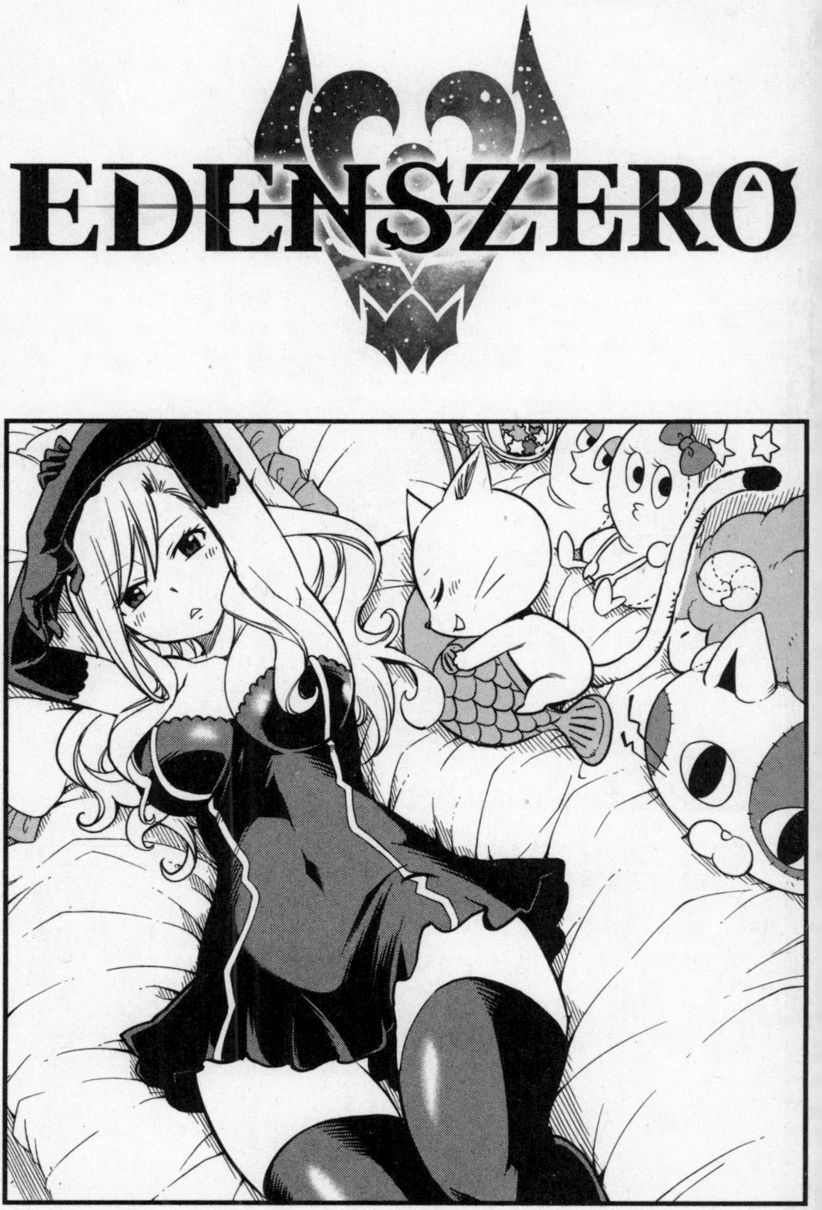

CHAPTER 51: STONES

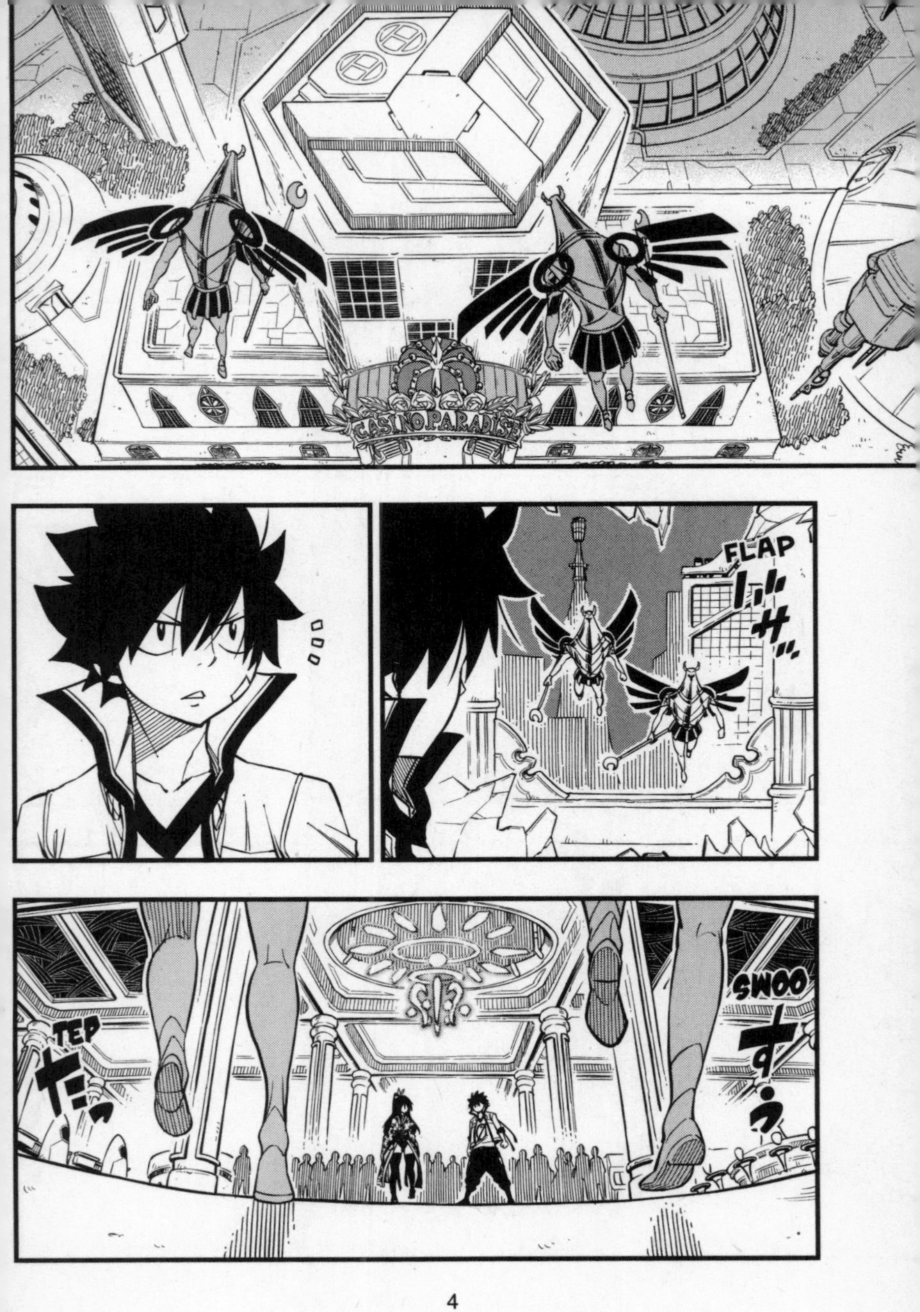
CASINO PARADISE
FLAP
SWOO
TEP

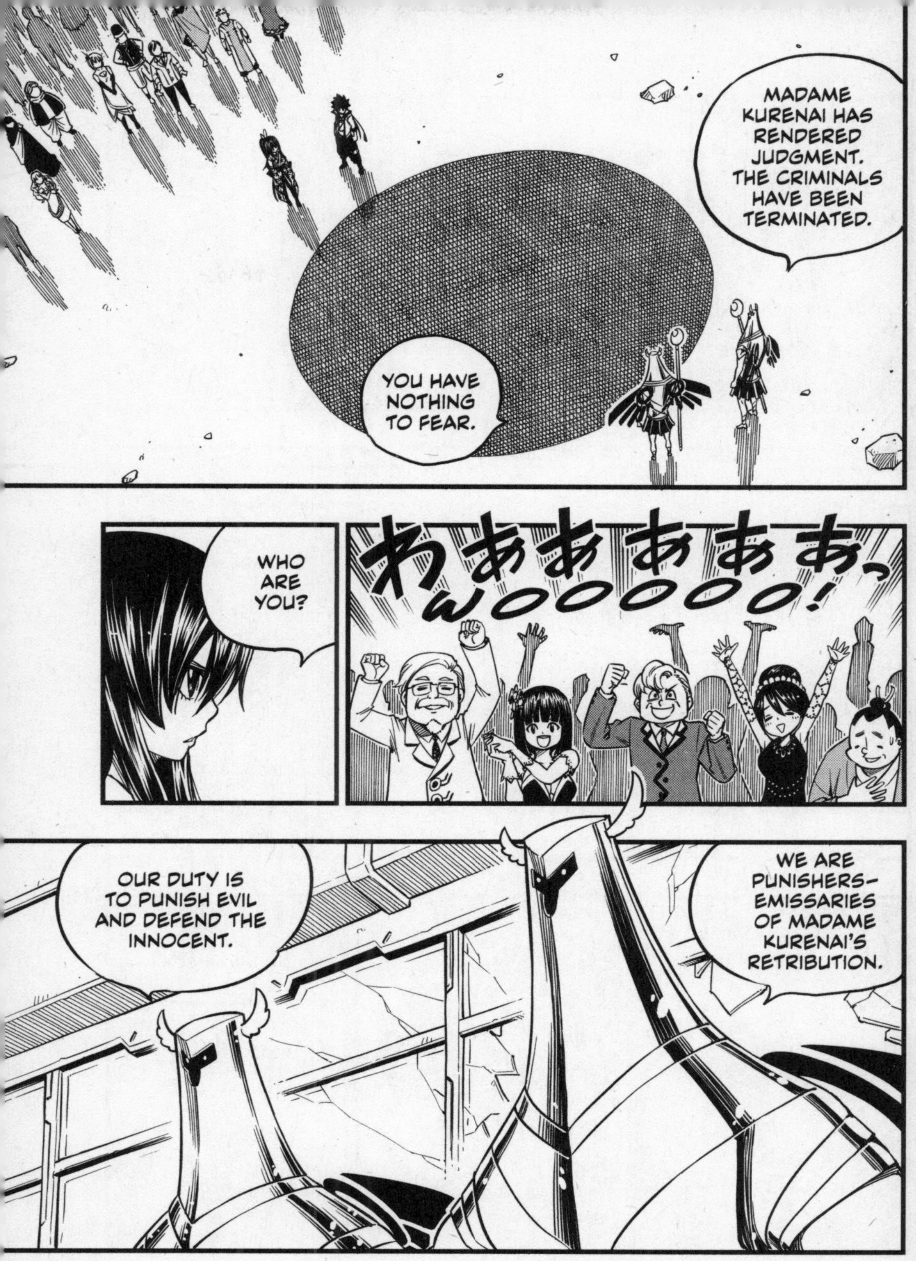
MADAME KURENAI HAS RENDERED JUDGMENT. THE CRIMINALS HAVE BEEN TERMINATED.
YOU HAVE NOTHING TO FEAR.
わあああああっ
WOOOOOO!
WHO ARE YOU?
WE ARE PUNISHERS— EMISSARIES OF MADAME KURENAI'S RETRIBUTION.
OUR DUTY IS TO PUNISH EVIL AND DEFEND THE INNOCENT.

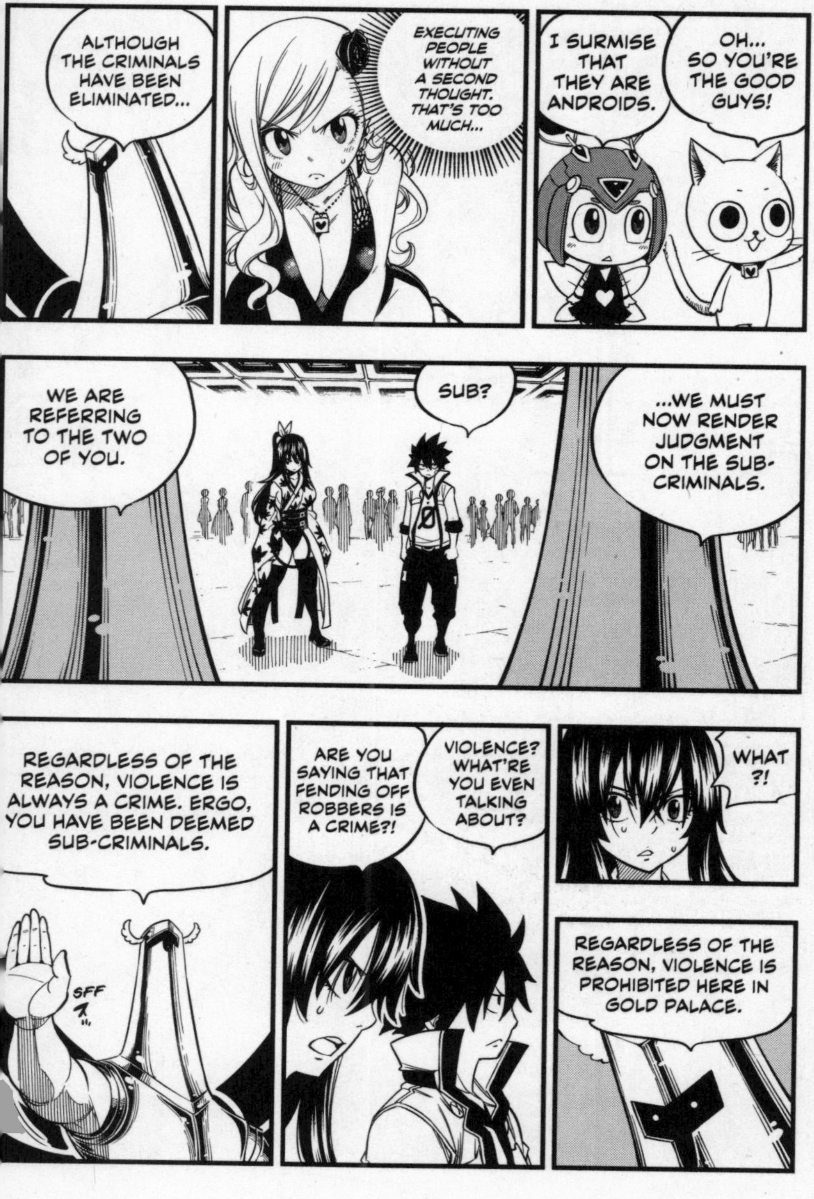
OH... SO YOU'RE THE GOOD GUYS!
I SURMISE THAT THEY ARE ANDROIDS.
EXECUTING PEOPLE WITHOUT A SECOND THOUGHT. THAT'S TOO MUCH...
ALTHOUGH THE CRIMINALS HAVE BEEN ELIMINATED...
...WE MUST NOW RENDER JUDGMENT ON THE SUB-CRIMINALS.
SUB?
WE ARE REFERRING TO THE TWO OF YOU.
WHAT ?!
REGARDLESS OF THE REASON, VIOLENCE IS PROHIBITED HERE IN GOLD PALACE.
VIOLENCE? WHAT'RE YOU EVEN TALKING ABOUT?
ARE YOU SAYING THAT FENDING OFF ROBBERS IS A CRIME?!
REGARDLESS OF THE REASON, VIOLENCE IS ALWAYS A CRIME. ERGO, YOU HAVE BEEN DEEMED SUB-CRIMINALS.
SFF

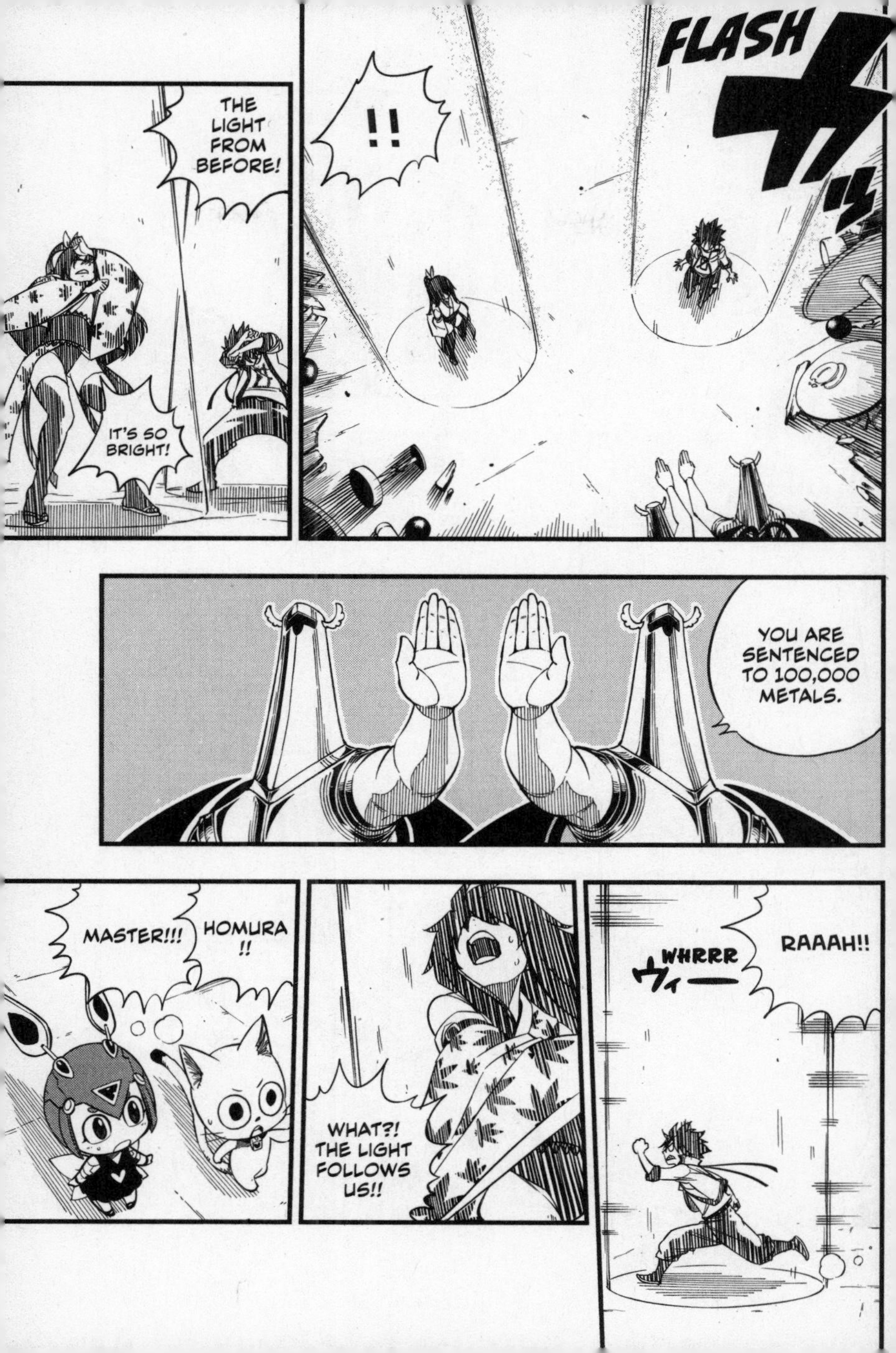
FLASH
!!
THE LIGHT FROM BEFORE!
IT'S SO BRIGHT!
YOU ARE SENTENCED TO 100,000 METALS.
RAAAH!!
WHRRR
WHAT?! THE LIGHT FOLLOWS US!!
HOMURA!!
MASTER!!!

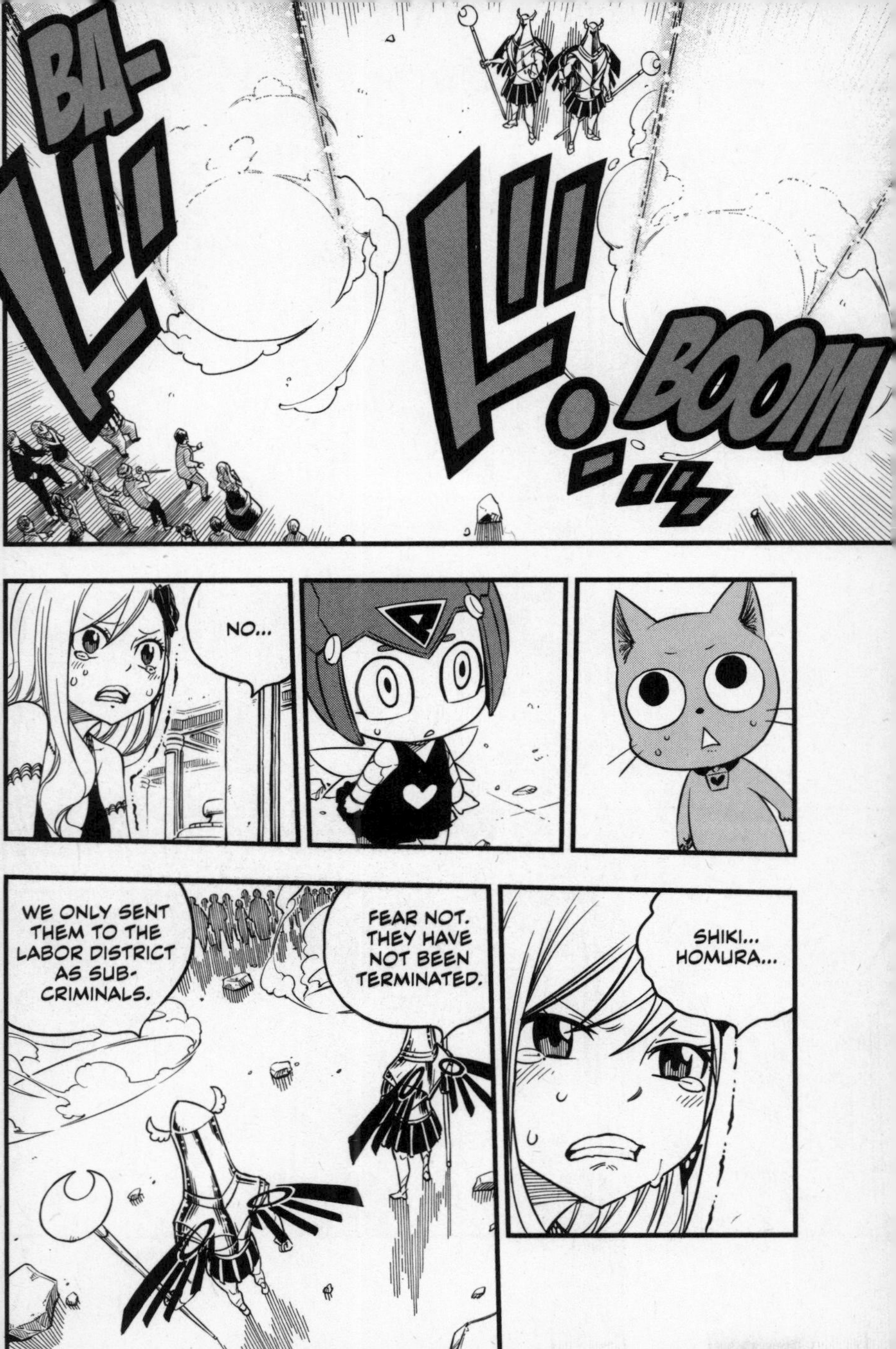
BA-
BOOM
NO...
SHIKI... HOMURA...
FEAR NOT. THEY HAVE NOT BEEN TERMINATED.
WE ONLY SENT THEM TO THE LABOR DISTRICT AS SUB-CRIMINALS.

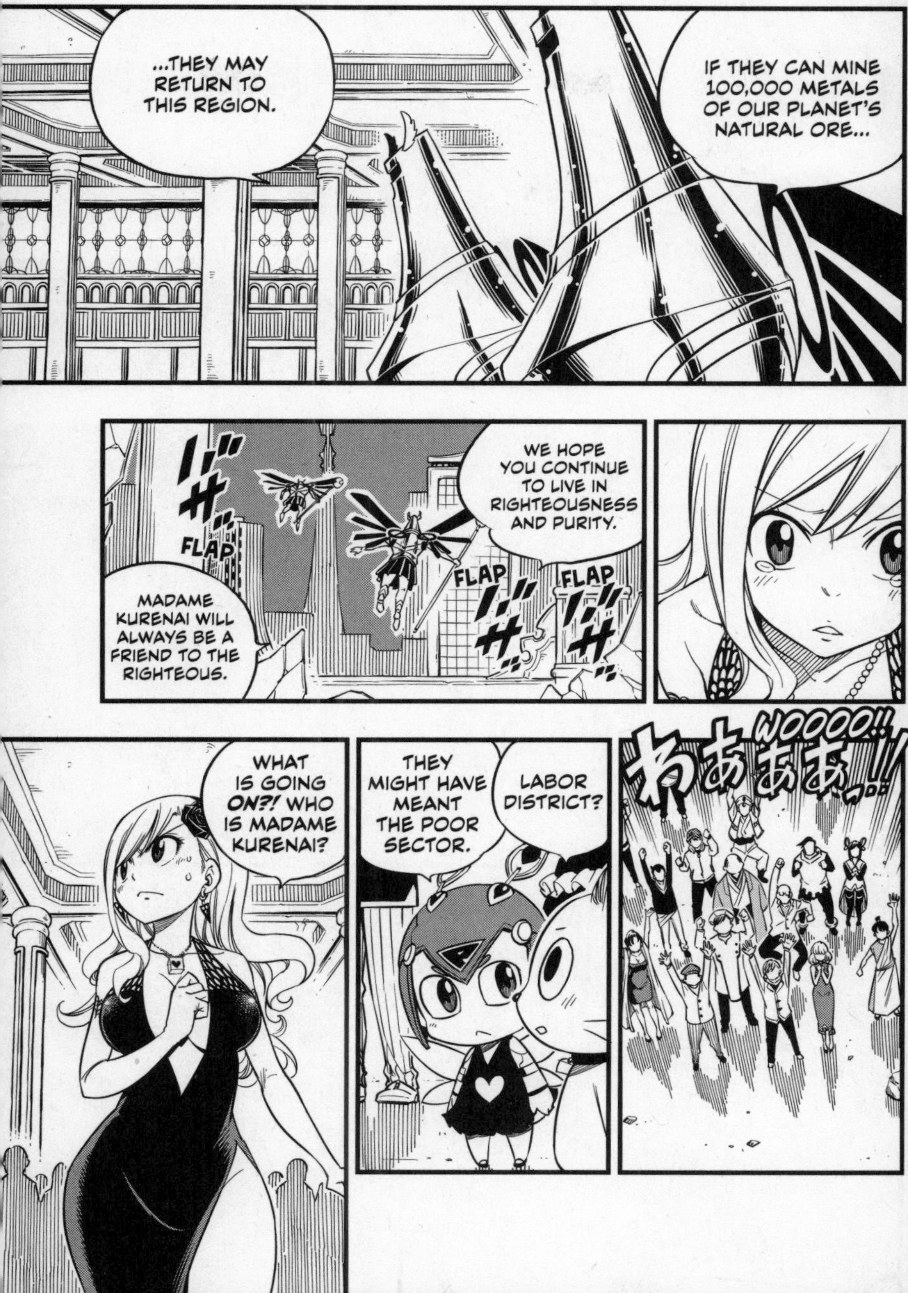

IF THEY CAN MINE 100,000 METALS OF OUR PLANET'S NATURAL ORE...
...THEY MAY RETURN TO THIS REGION.
WE HOPE YOU CONTINUE TO LIVE IN RIGHTEOUSNESS AND PURITY.
FLAP
FLAP
FLAP
MADAME KURENAI WILL ALWAYS BE A FRIEND TO THE RIGHTEOUS.
わあああ!!
WOOOO!!
LABOR DISTRICT?
THEY MIGHT HAVE MEANT THE POOR SECTOR.
WHAT IS GOING *ON?!* WHO IS MADAME KURENAI?

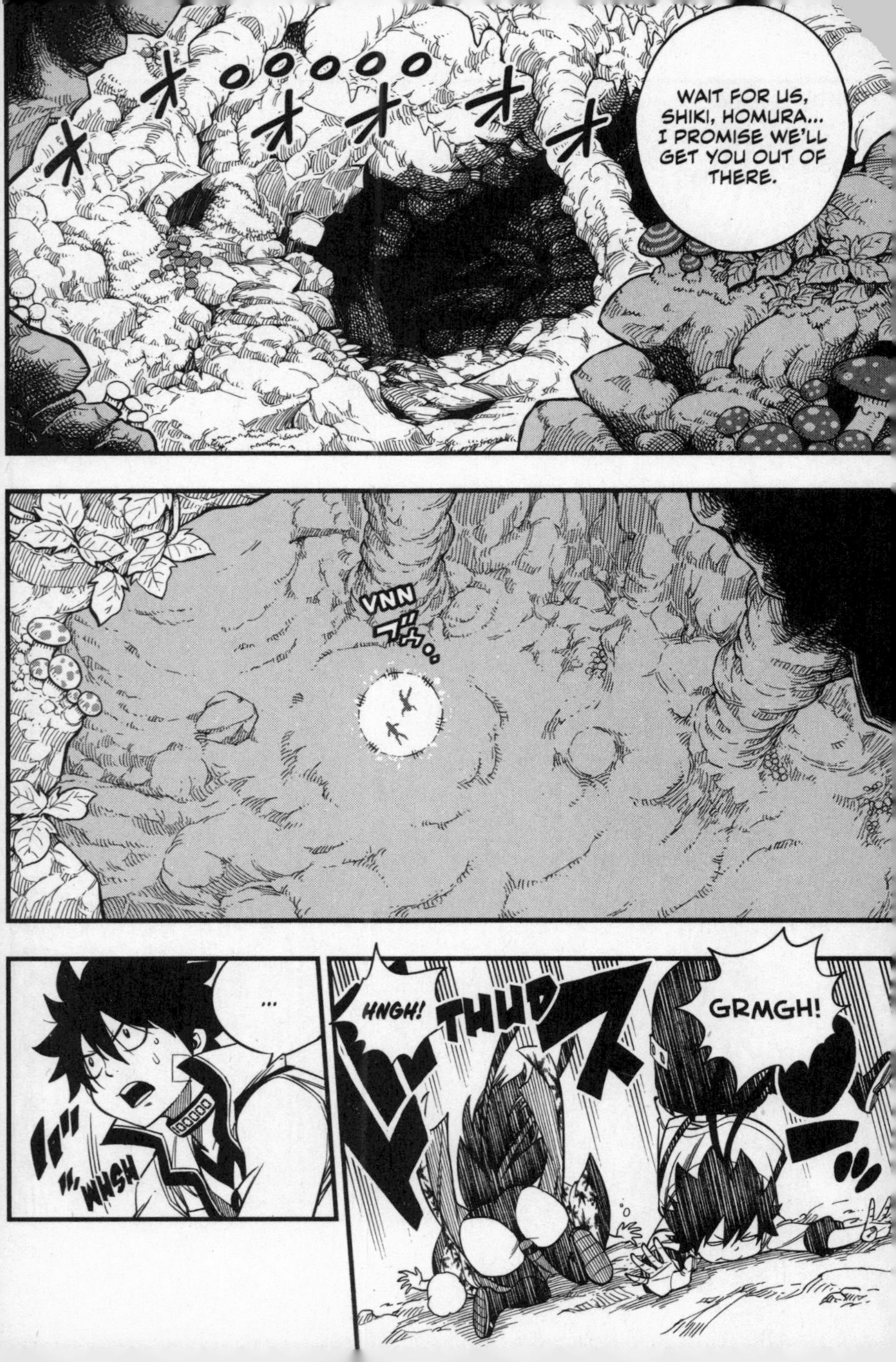

WAIT FOR US, SHIKI, HOMURA... I PROMISE WE'LL GET YOU OUT OF THERE.
OOOOOO
VNN
GRMGH!
HNGH!
THUD
...
WHSH

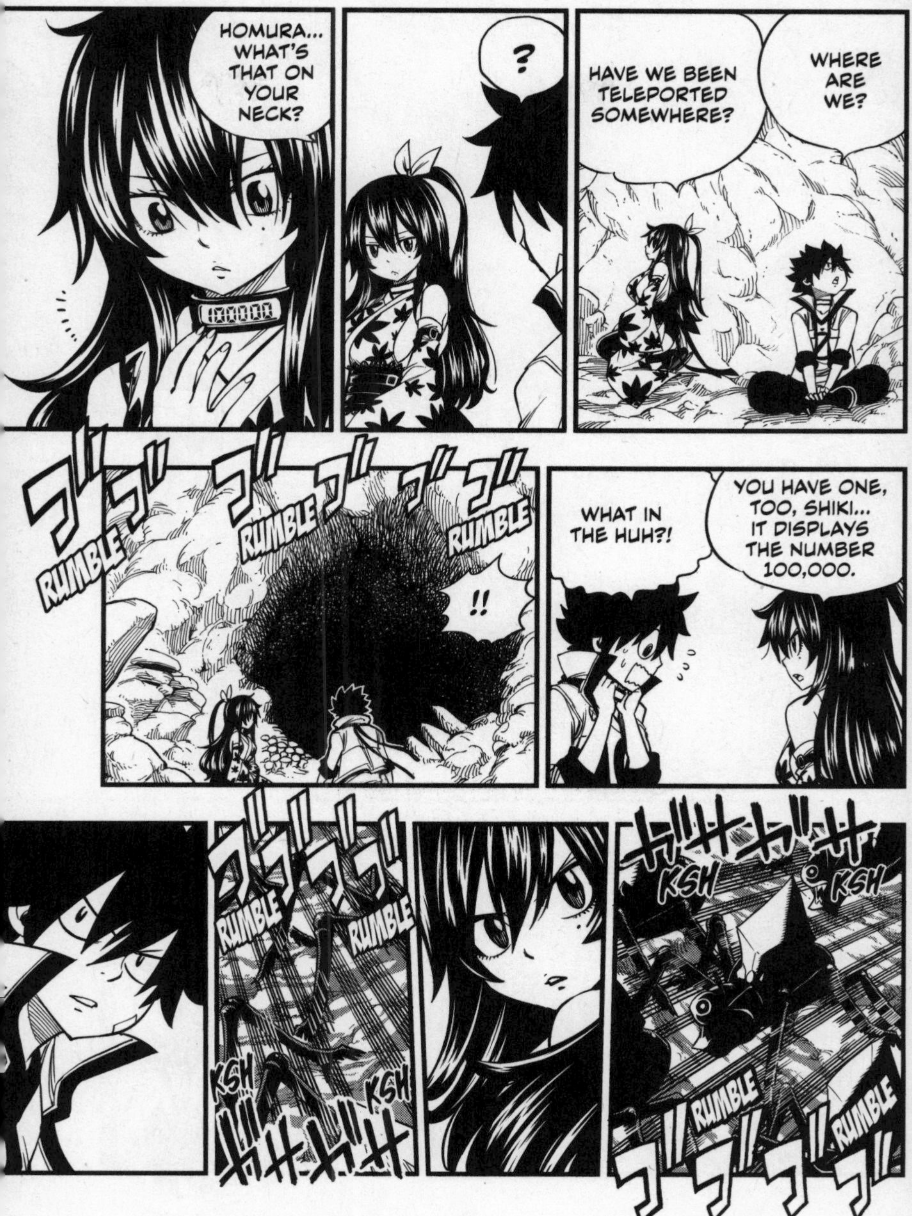
WHERE ARE WE?
HAVE WE BEEN TELEPORTED SOMEWHERE?
?
HOMURA... WHAT'S THAT ON YOUR NECK?
YOU HAVE ONE, TOO, SHIKI... IT DISPLAYS THE NUMBER 100,000.
WHAT IN THE HUH?!
RUMBLE
RUMBLE
RUMBLE
RUMBLE
!!
KSH
KSH
RUMBLE
RUMBLE
RUMBLE
RUMBLE
KSH
KSH

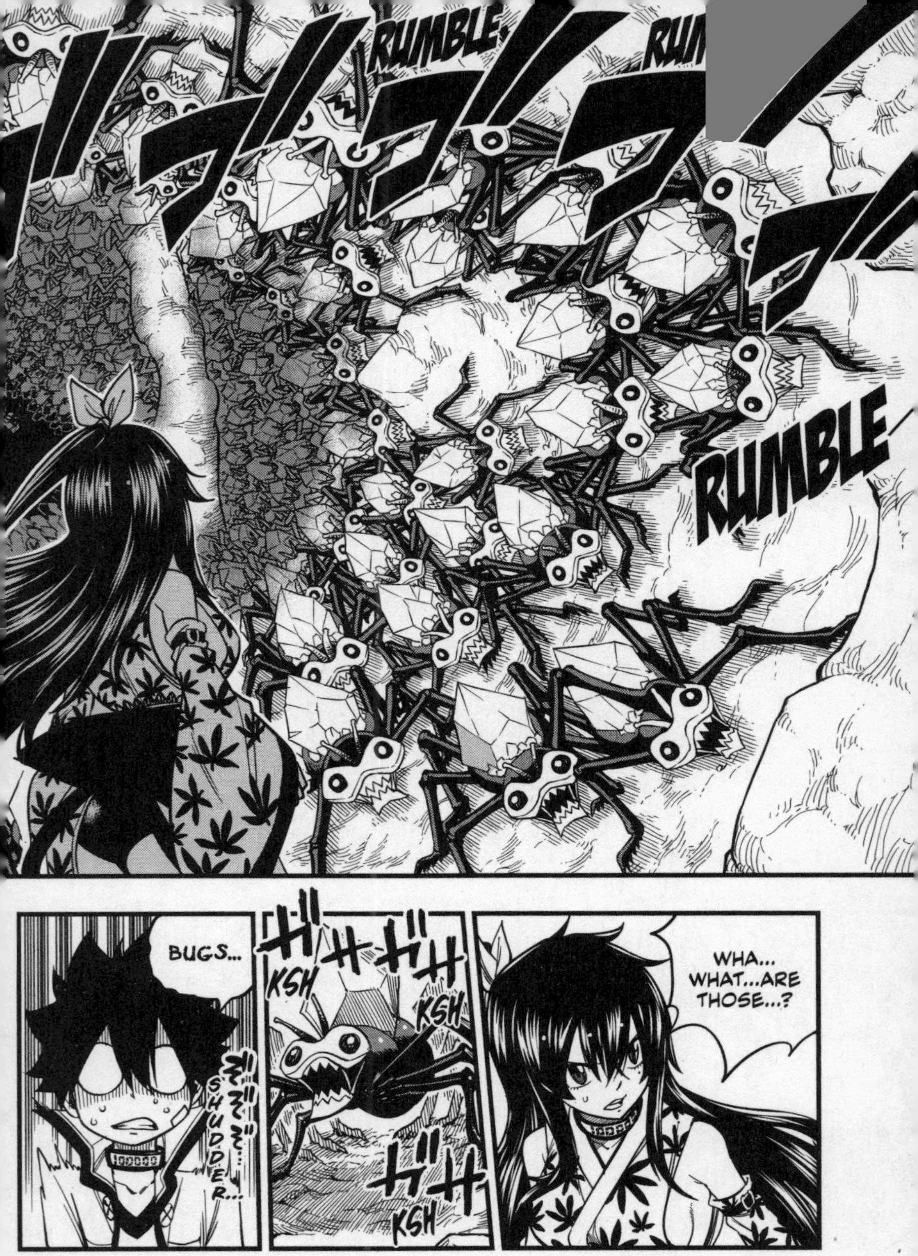
RUM
RUMBLE,
RUMBLE
WHA... WHAT...ARE THOSE...?
KSH
KSH
KSH
BUGS...
SHUDDER...

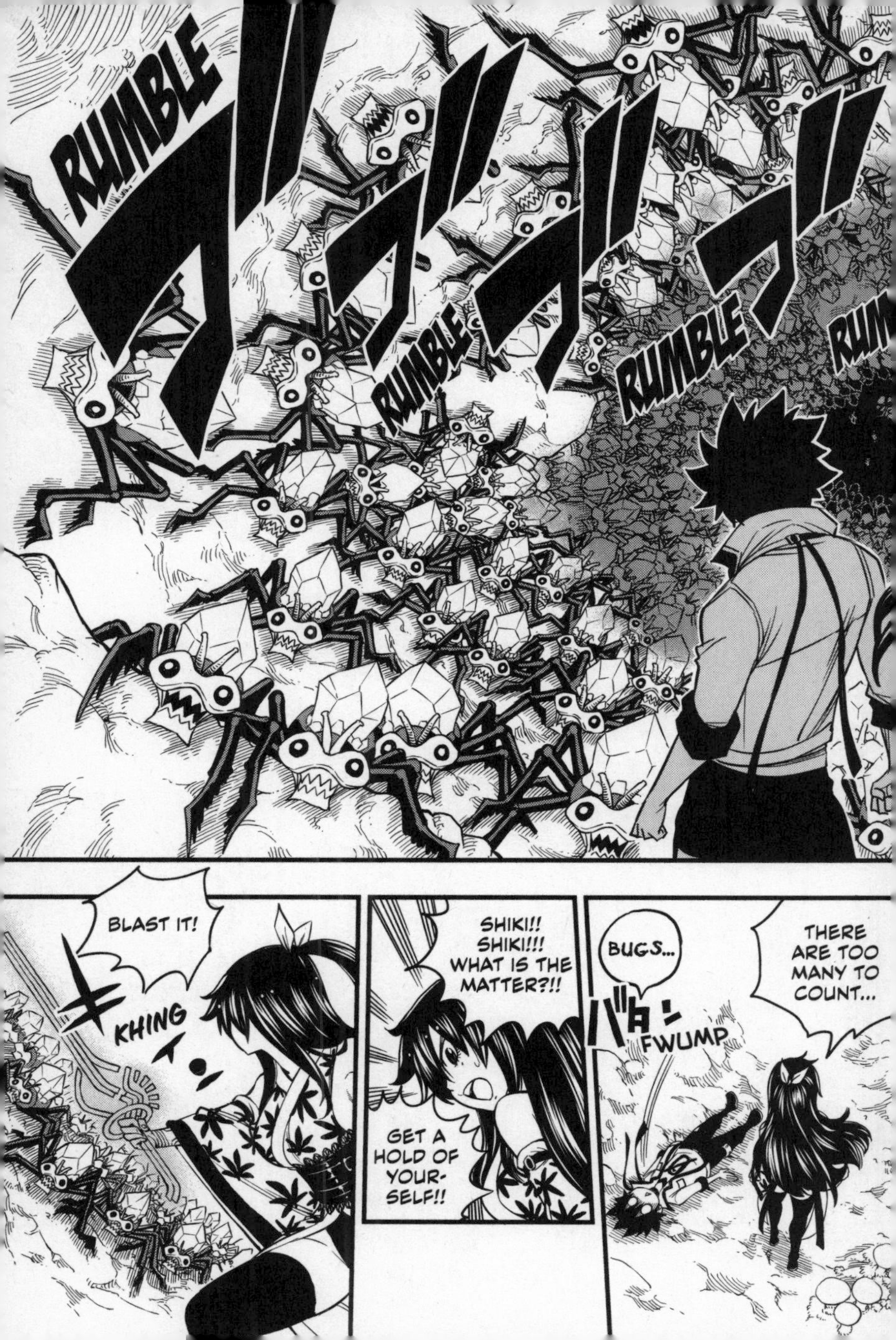
RUMBLE
RUMBLE
RUMBLE
THERE ARE TOO MANY TO COUNT...
BUGS...
FWUMP
SHIKI!! SHIKI!!! WHAT IS THE MATTER?!!
GET A HOLD OF YOUR-SELF!!
BLAST IT!
KHING

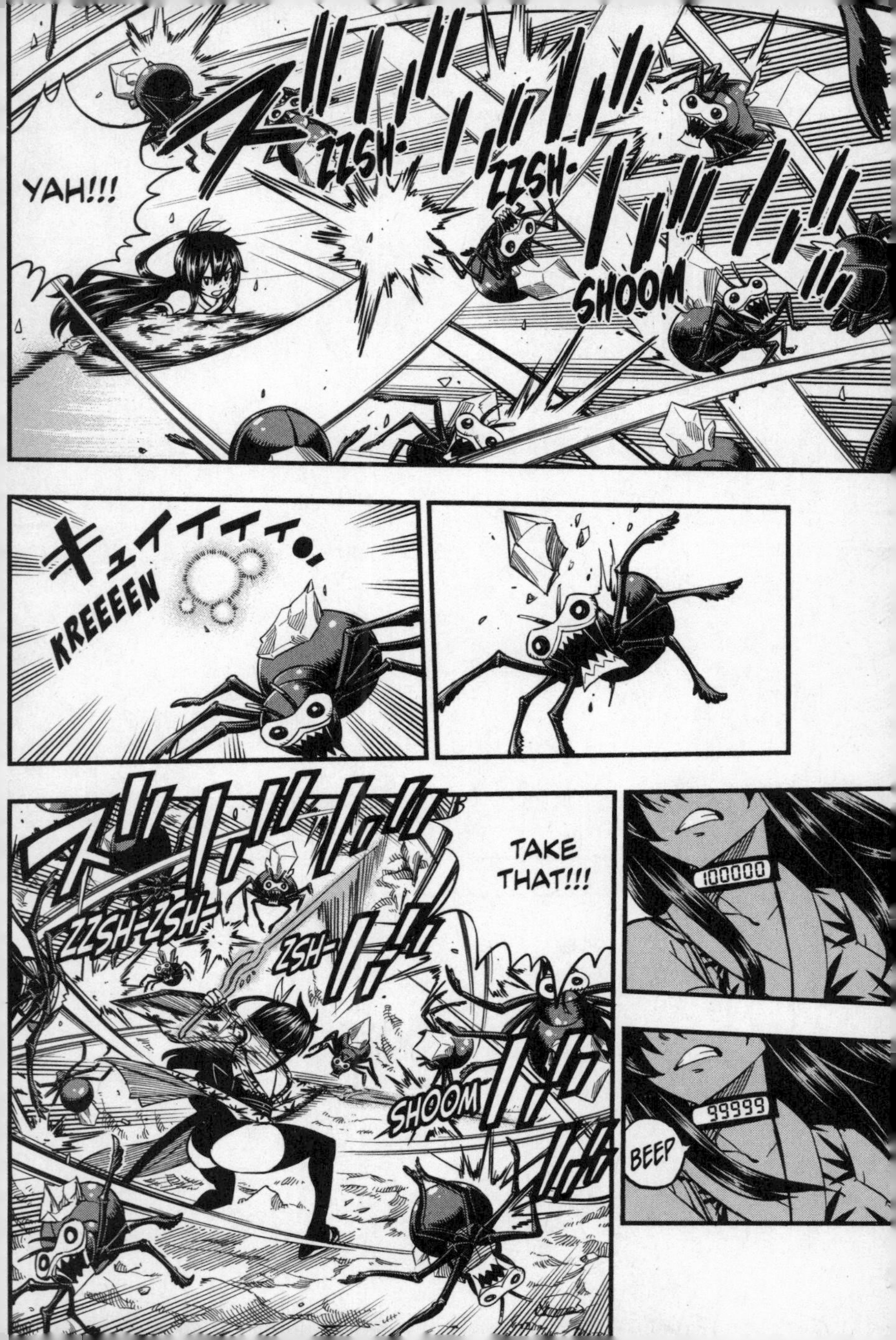
ZZSH
ZZSH
SHOOM
YAH!!!
キュイイイイ
KREEEEN
100000
99999
BEEP
TAKE THAT!!!
ZZSH-ZSH-
ZSH-
SHOOM

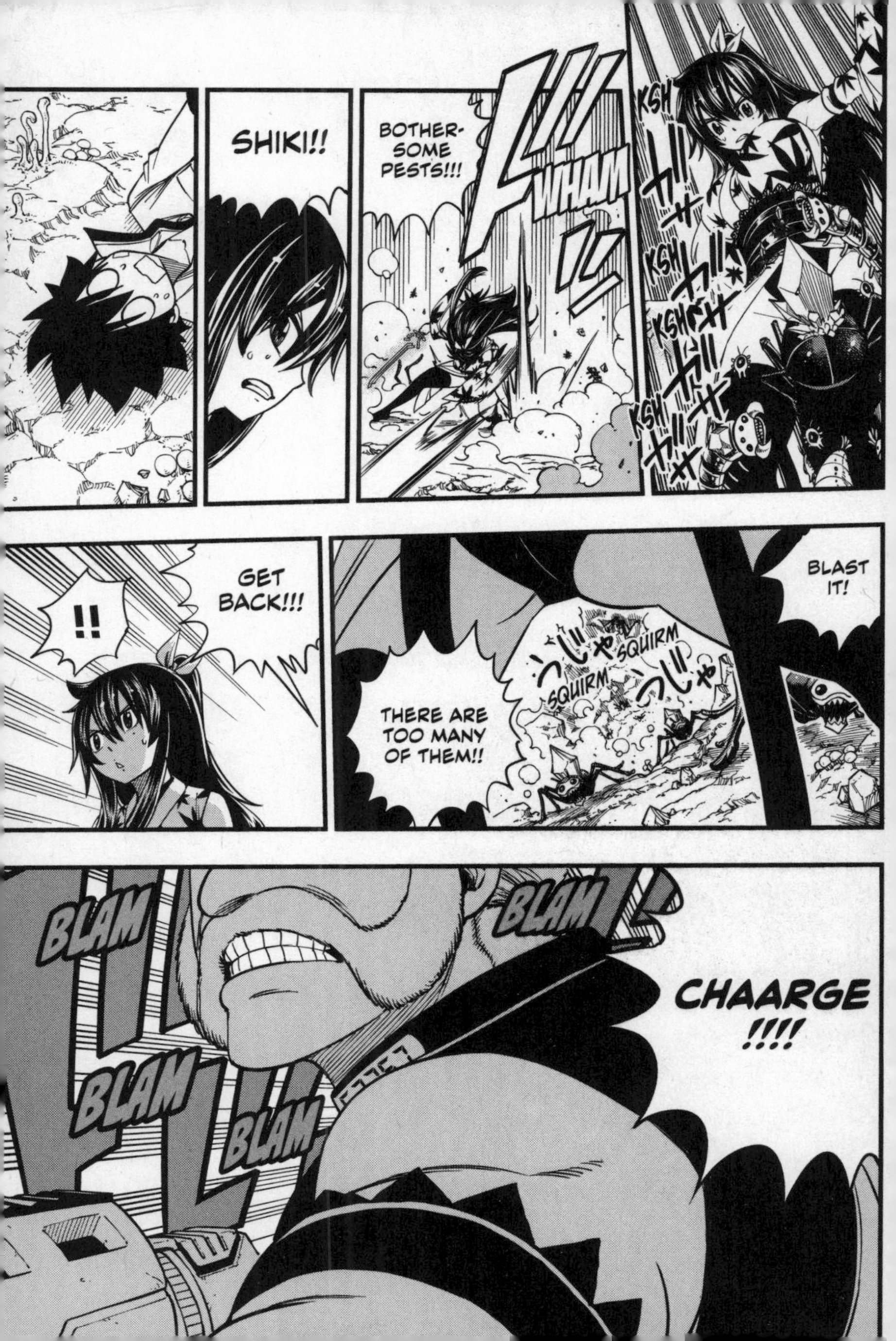
KSH
KSH
KSH
KSH
WHAM
BOTHER-SOME PESTS!!!
SHIKI!!
BLAST IT!
SQUIRM
SQUIRM
THERE ARE TOO MANY OF THEM!!
GET BACK!!!
!!
CHAARGE!!!!
BLAM
BLAM
BLAM
BLAM

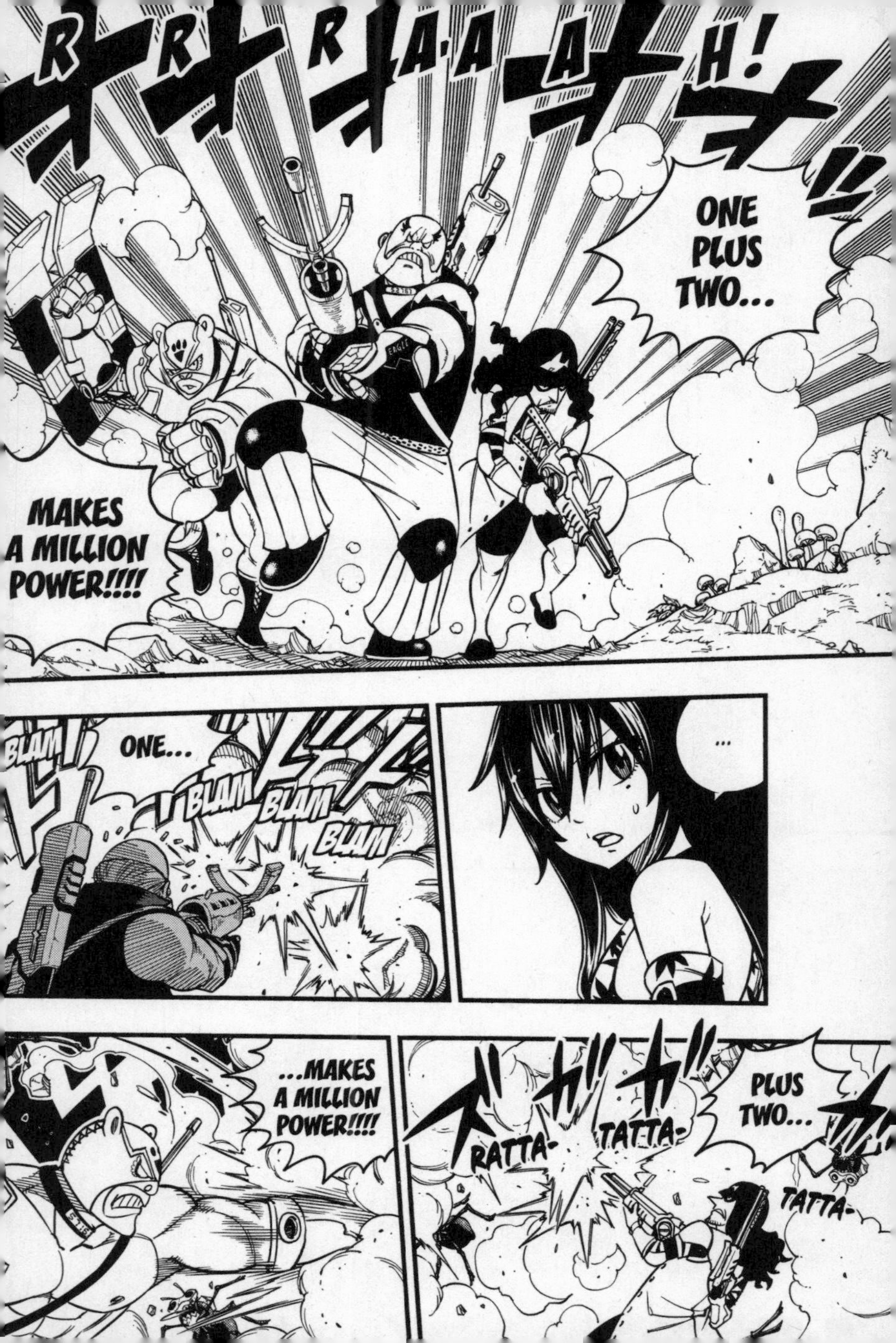
RRRA-A-AH!
ONE PLUS TWO...
MAKES A MILLION POWER!!!!
...
BLAM
ONE...
BLAM
BLAM
BLAM
PLUS TWO...
TATTA-
TATTA-
RATTA-
...MAKES A MILLION POWER!!!!

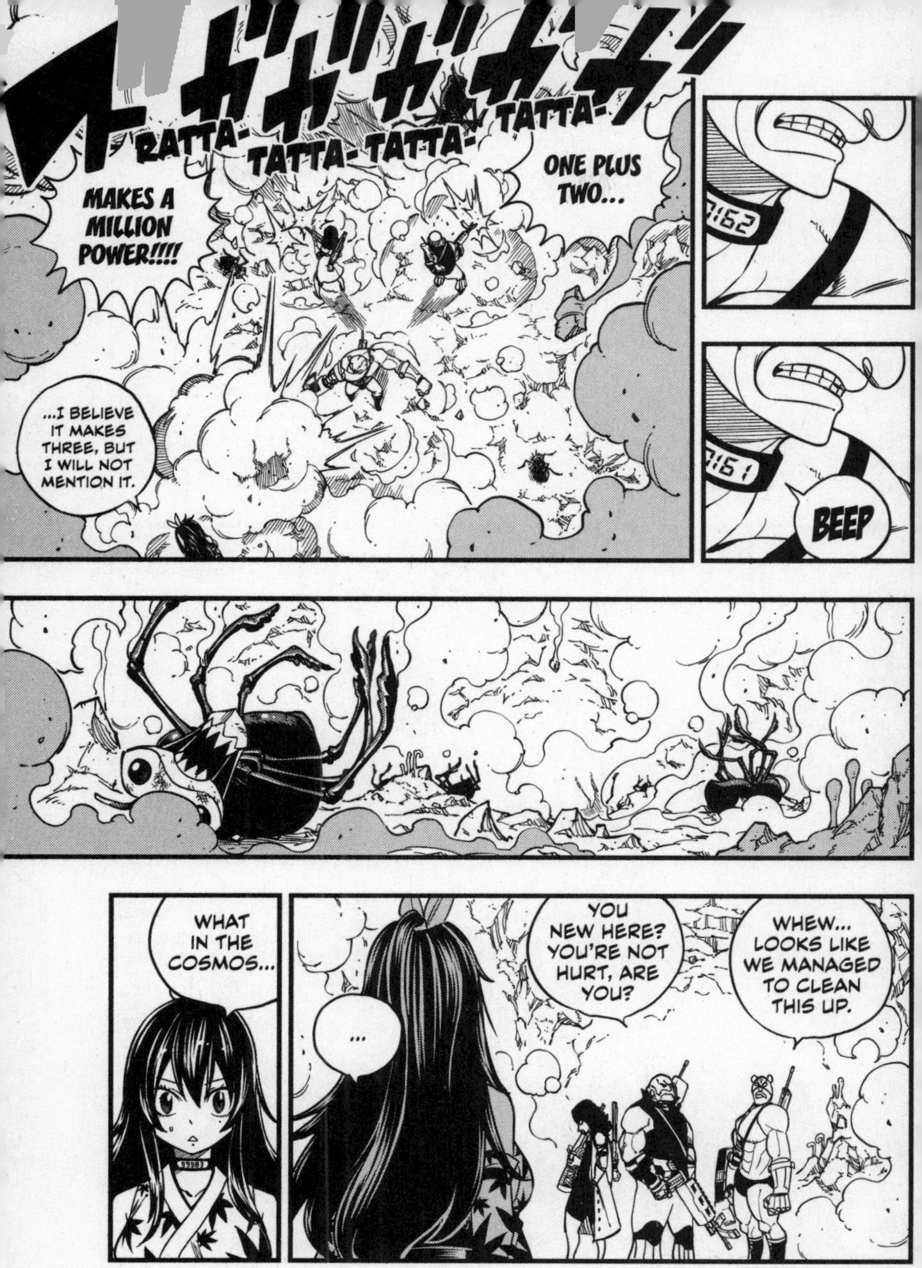
7162
7161
BEEP
RATTA-TATTA-TATTA-TATTA-
ONE PLUS TWO...
MAKES A MILLION POWER!!!!
...I BELIEVE IT MAKES THREE, BUT I WILL NOT MENTION IT.
WHEW... LOOKS LIKE WE MANAGED TO CLEAN THIS UP.
YOU NEW HERE? YOU'RE NOT HURT, ARE YOU?
...
WHAT IN THE COSMOS...

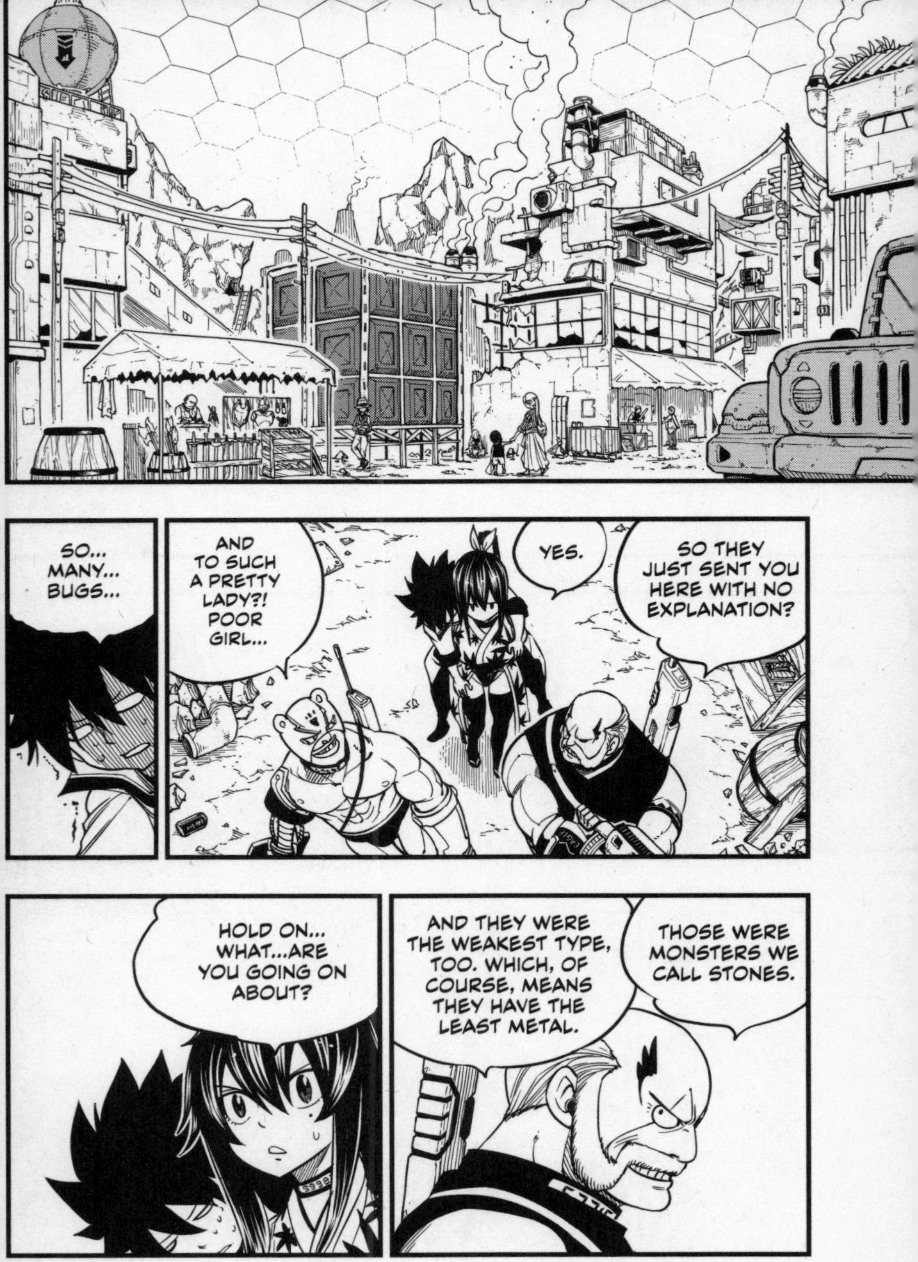
SO THEY JUST SENT YOU HERE WITH NO EXPLANATION?
YES.
AND TO SUCH A PRETTY LADY?! POOR GIRL...
SO... MANY... BUGS...
THOSE WERE MONSTERS WE CALL STONES.
AND THEY WERE THE WEAKEST TYPE, TOO. WHICH, OF COURSE, MEANS THEY HAVE THE LEAST METAL.
HOLD ON... WHAT...ARE YOU GOING ON ABOUT?

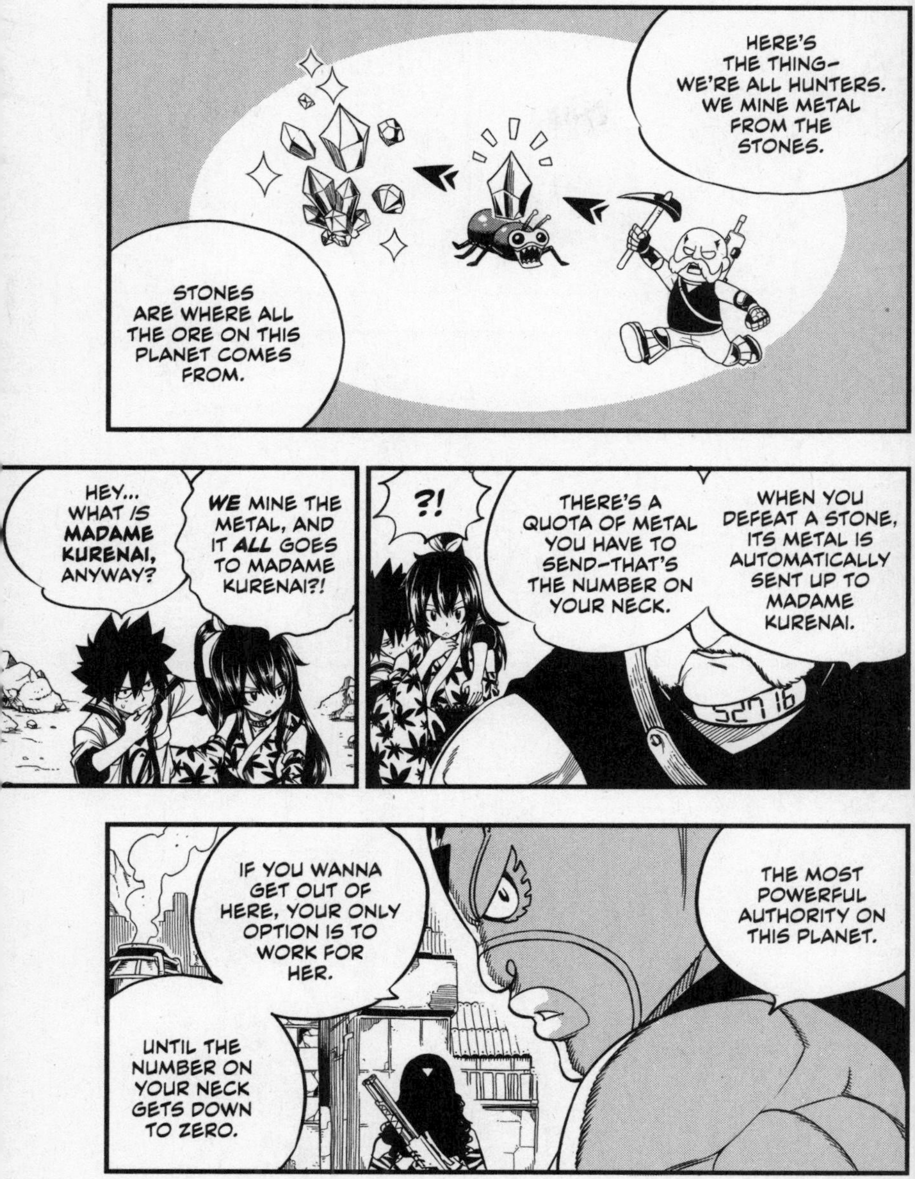
HERE'S THE THING– WE'RE ALL HUNTERS. WE MINE METAL FROM THE STONES.
STONES ARE WHERE ALL THE ORE ON THIS PLANET COMES FROM.
WHEN YOU DEFEAT A STONE, ITS METAL IS AUTOMATICALLY SENT UP TO MADAME KURENAI.
THERE'S A QUOTA OF METAL YOU HAVE TO SEND–THAT'S THE NUMBER ON YOUR NECK.
?!
WE MINE THE METAL, AND IT *ALL* GOES TO MADAME KURENAI?!
HEY... WHAT *IS* **MADAME KURENAI,** ANYWAY?
THE MOST POWERFUL AUTHORITY ON THIS PLANET.
IF YOU WANNA GET OUT OF HERE, YOUR ONLY OPTION IS TO WORK FOR HER.
UNTIL THE NUMBER ON YOUR NECK GETS DOWN TO ZERO.

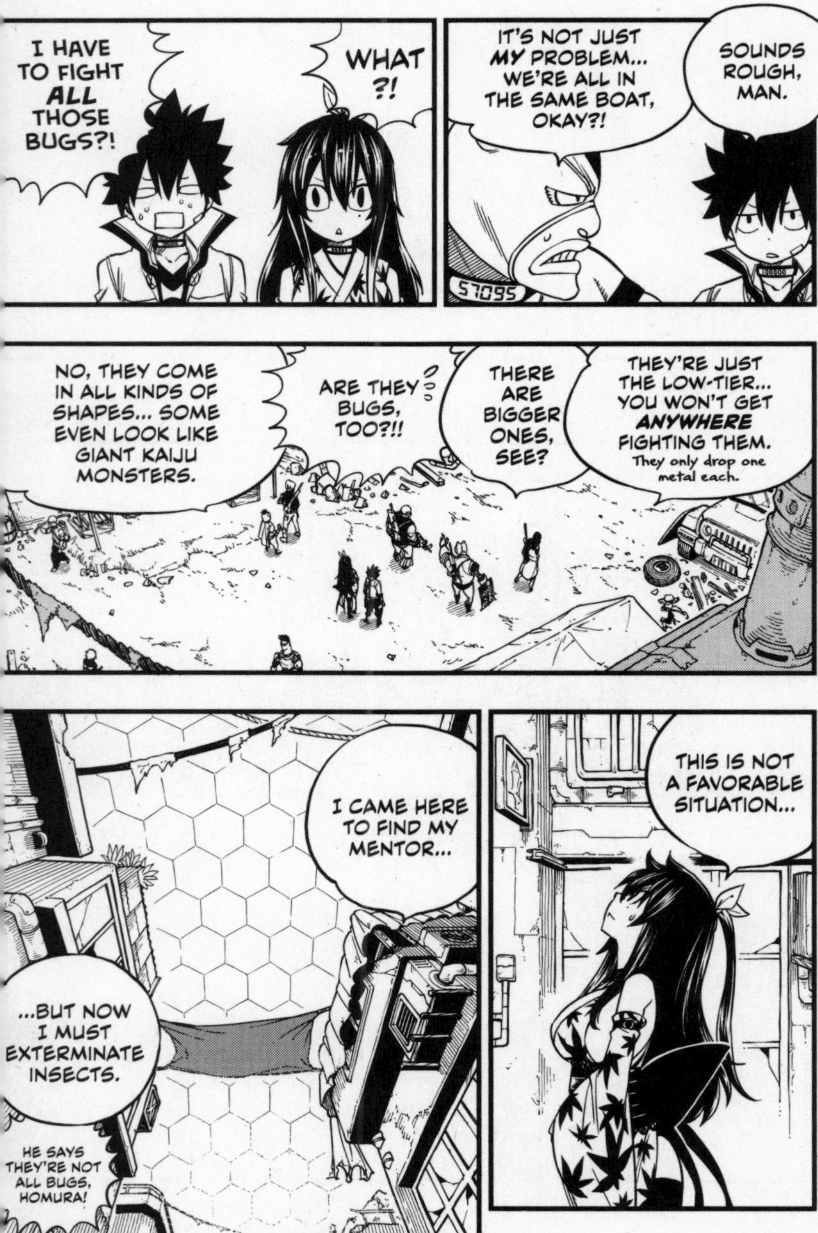
SOUNDS ROUGH, MAN.
IT'S NOT JUST *MY* PROBLEM... WE'RE ALL IN THE SAME BOAT, OKAY?!
57095
WHAT ?!
I HAVE TO FIGHT *ALL* THOSE BUGS?!
THEY'RE JUST THE LOW-TIER... YOU WON'T GET *ANYWHERE* FIGHTING THEM.
They only drop one metal each.
THERE ARE BIGGER ONES, SEE?
ARE THEY BUGS, TOO?!!
NO, THEY COME IN ALL KINDS OF SHAPES... SOME EVEN LOOK LIKE GIANT KAIJU MONSTERS.
THIS IS NOT A FAVORABLE SITUATION...
I CAME HERE TO FIND MY MENTOR...
...BUT NOW I MUST EXTERMINATE INSECTS.
HE SAYS THEY'RE NOT ALL BUGS, HOMURA!

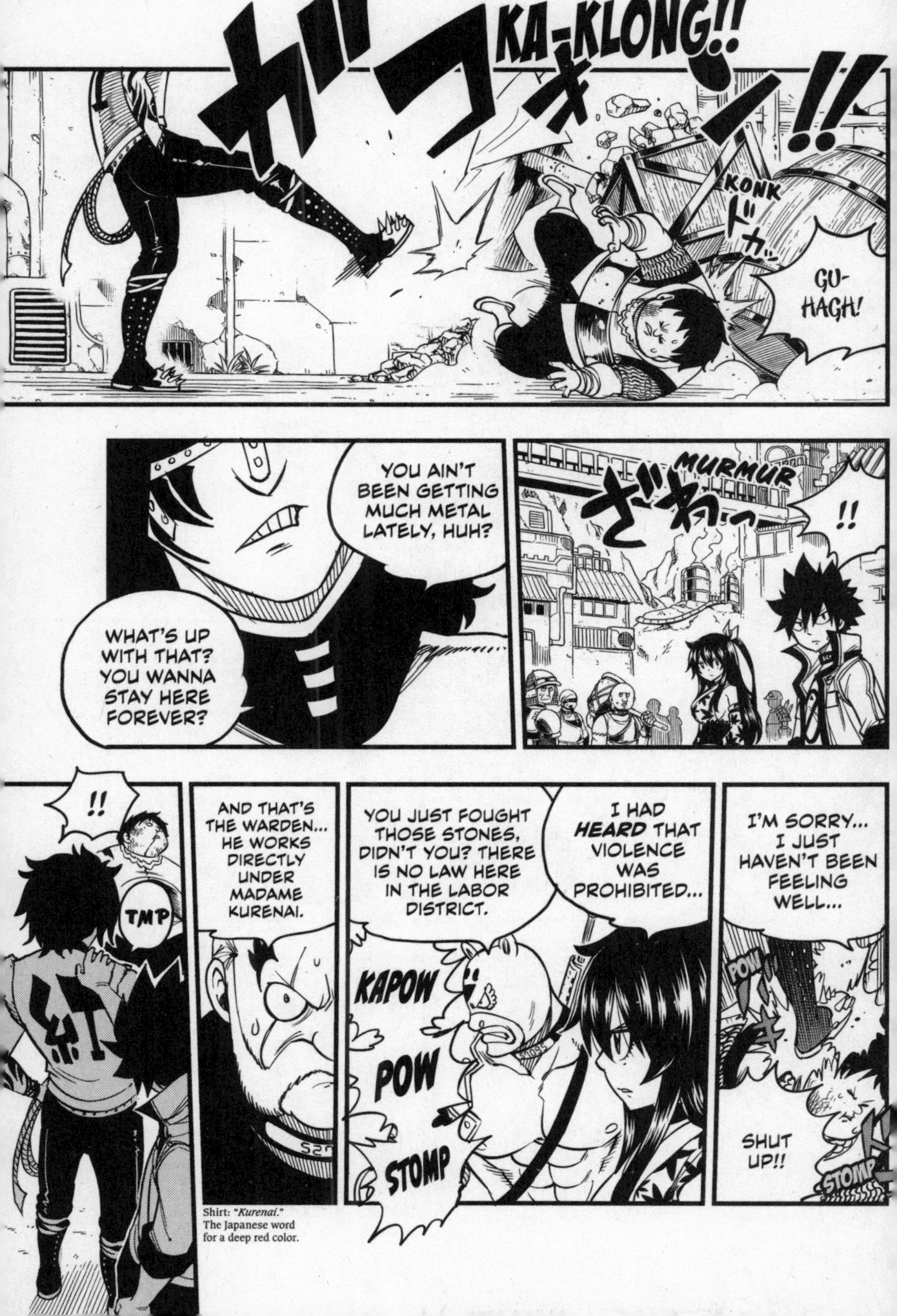
KA-KLONG!!
KONK
GU-HAGH!
MURMUR
!!
YOU AIN'T BEEN GETTING MUCH METAL LATELY, HUH?
WHAT'S UP WITH THAT? YOU WANNA STAY HERE FOREVER?
I'M SORRY... I JUST HAVEN'T BEEN FEELING WELL...
POW
SHUT UP!!
STOMP
I HAD *HEARD* THAT VIOLENCE WAS PROHIBITED...
YOU JUST FOUGHT THOSE STONES, DIDN'T YOU? THERE IS NO LAW HERE IN THE LABOR DISTRICT.
KAPOW
POW
STOMP
AND THAT'S THE WARDEN... HE WORKS DIRECTLY UNDER MADAME KURENAI.
!!
TMP

Shirt: "*Kurenai.*" The Japanese word for a deep red color.

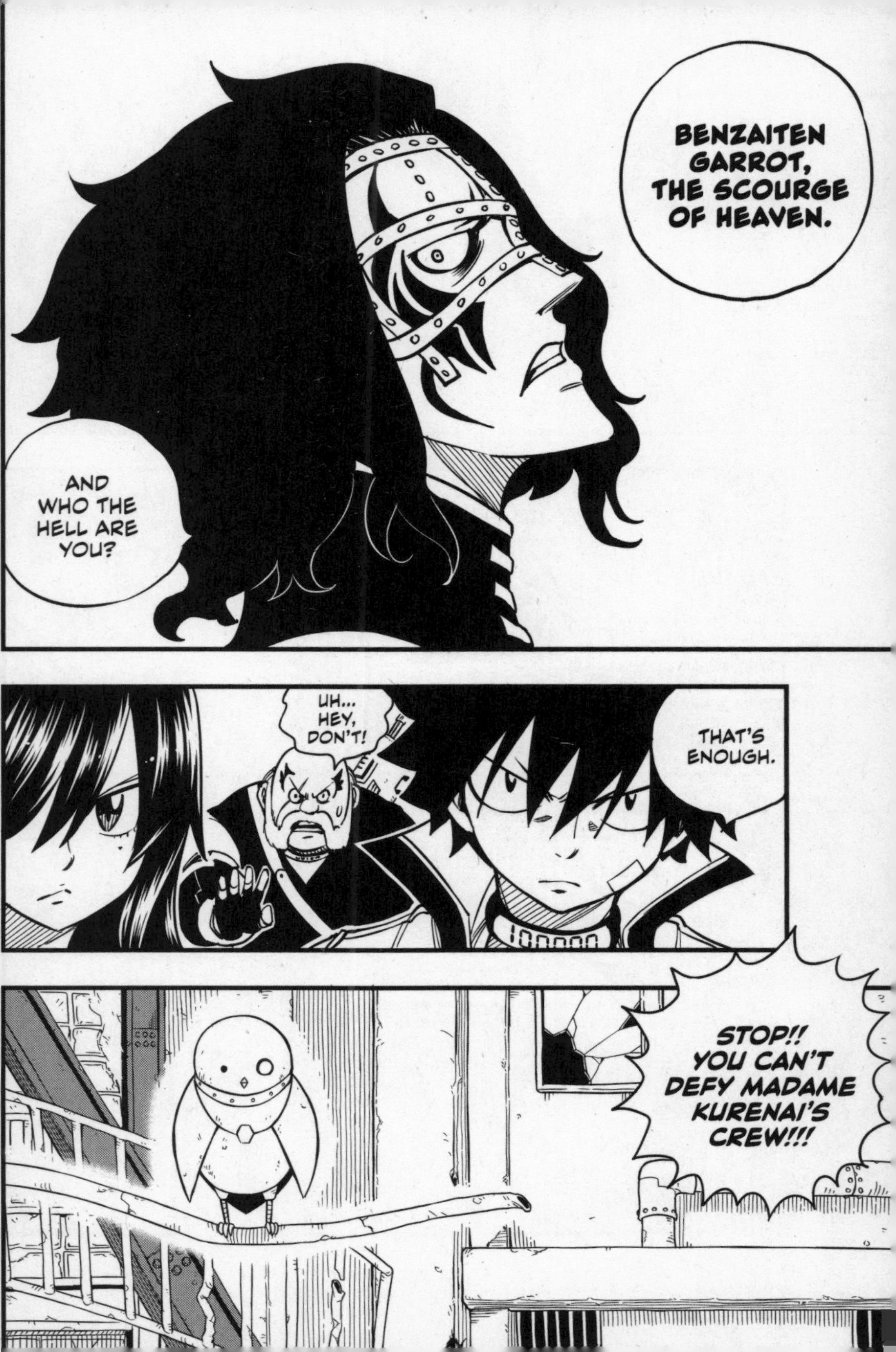
BENZAITEN GARROT, THE SCOURGE OF HEAVEN.
AND WHO THE HELL ARE YOU?
THAT'S ENOUGH.
UH... HEY, DON'T!
STOP!! YOU CAN'T DEFY MADAME KURENAI'S CREW!!!

EDENS ZERO

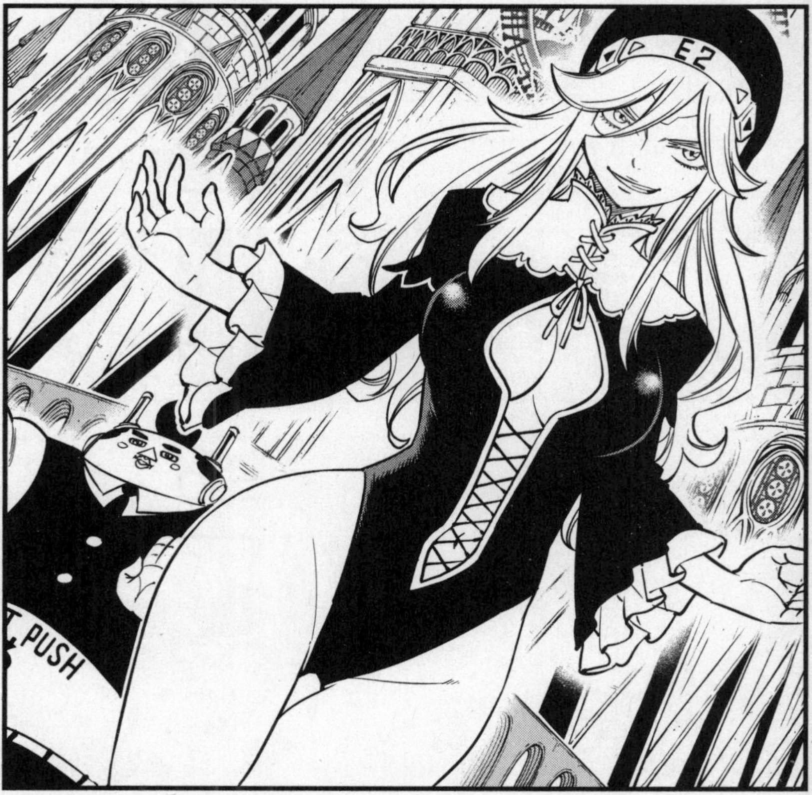
E2
PUSH

CHAPTER 52: KURENAI'S GAUNTLET

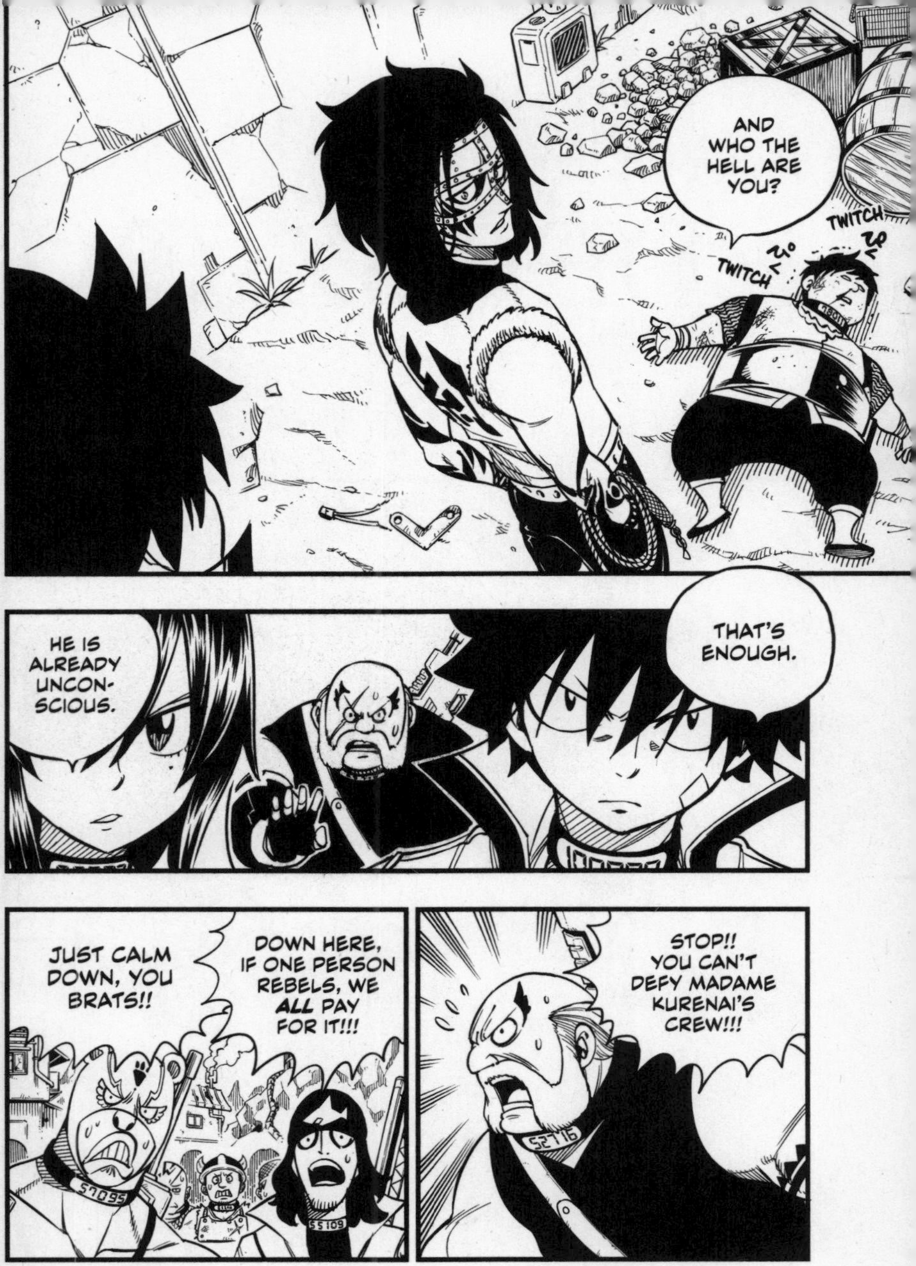
AND WHO THE HELL ARE YOU?
TWITCH
TWITCH
THAT'S ENOUGH.
HE IS ALREADY UNCON-SCIOUS.
STOP!! YOU CAN'T DEFY MADAME KURENAI'S CREW!!!
DOWN HERE, IF ONE PERSON REBELS, WE ALL PAY FOR IT!!!
JUST CALM DOWN, YOU BRATS!!

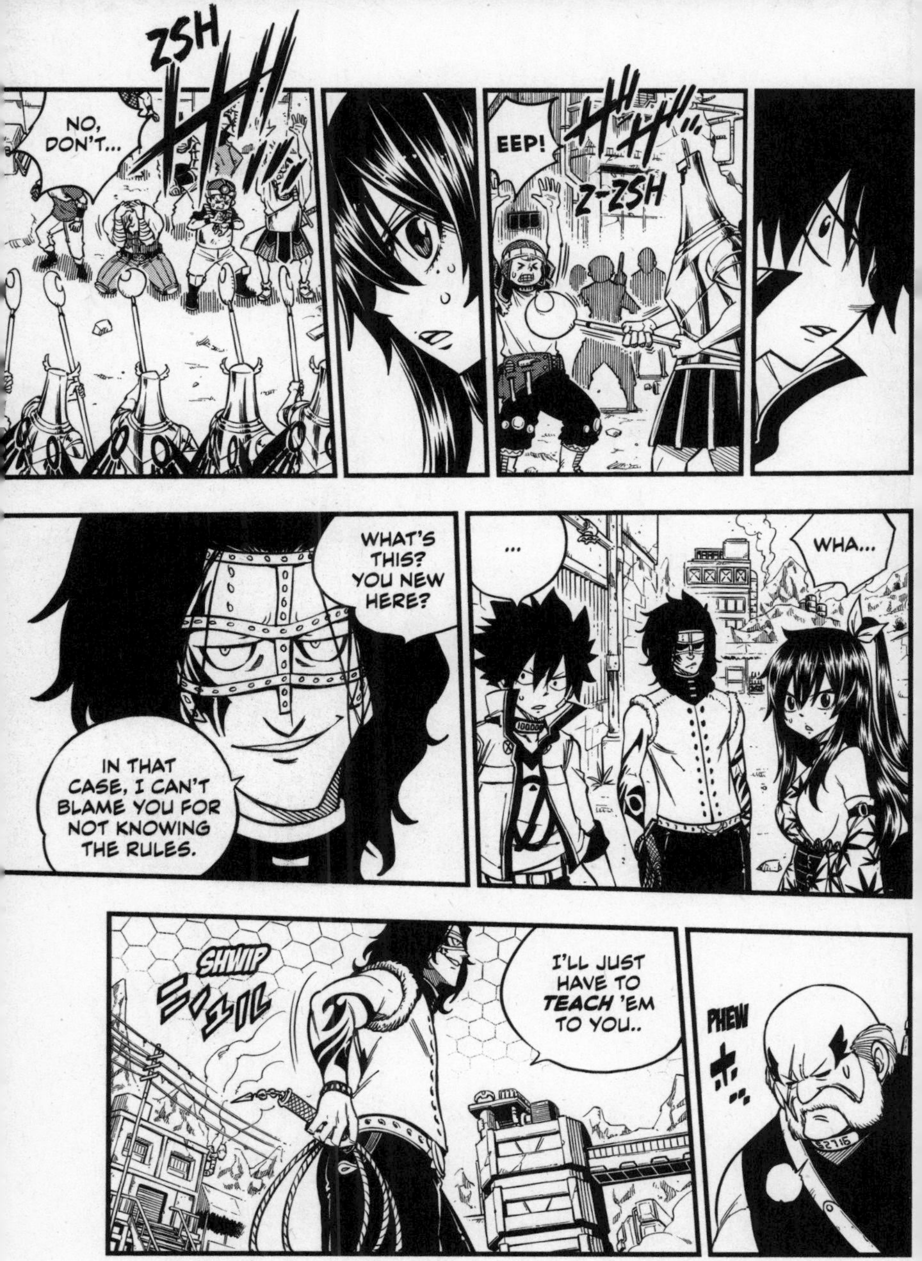
EEP!
Z-ZSH
ZSH
NO, DON'T...
WHA...
...
WHAT'S THIS? YOU NEW HERE?
IN THAT CASE, I CAN'T BLAME YOU FOR NOT KNOWING THE RULES.
PHEW
I'LL JUST HAVE TO *TEACH* 'EM TO YOU..
SHWIP

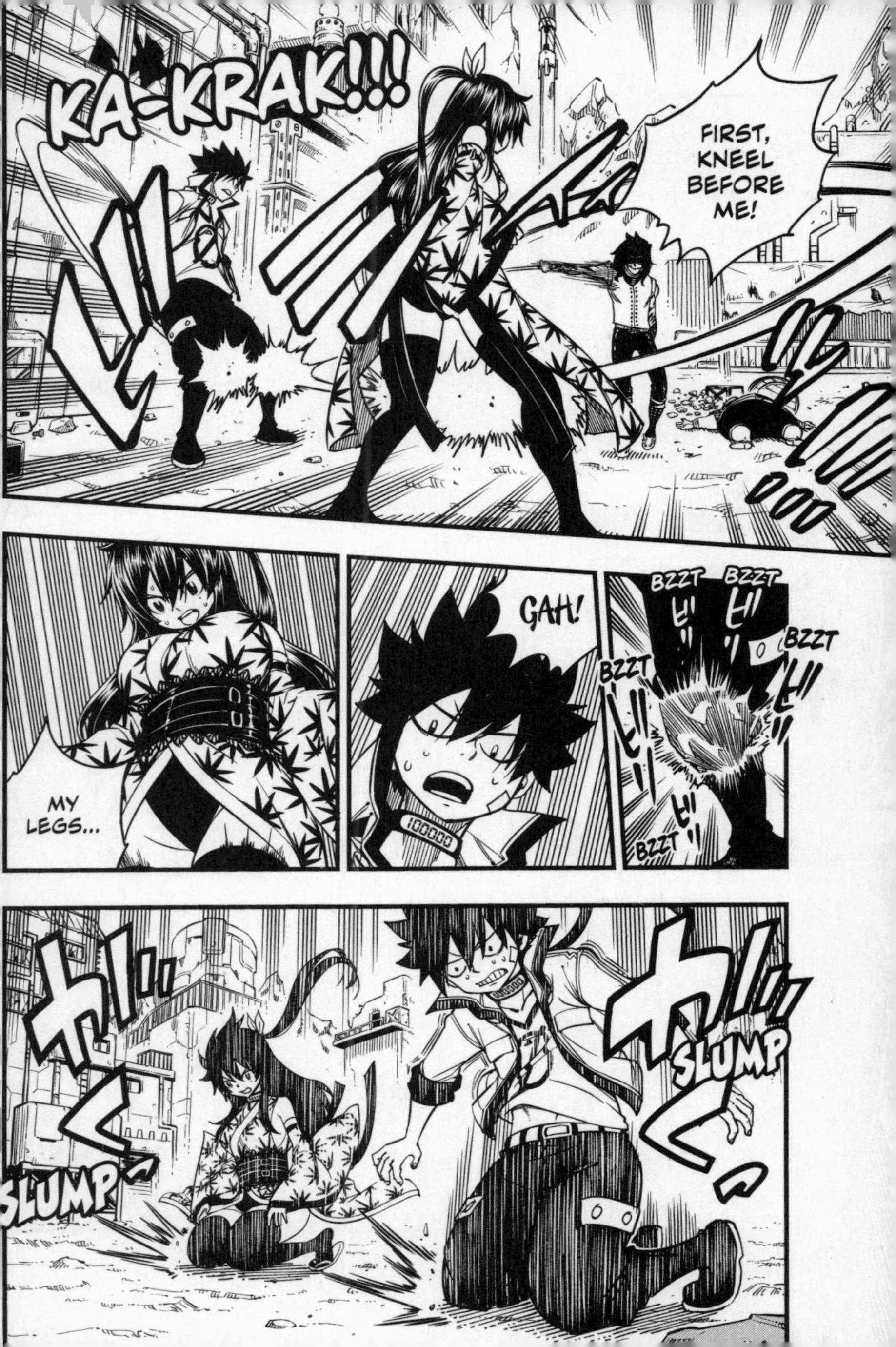
FIRST, KNEEL BEFORE ME!
KA-KRAK!!!
BZZT
BZZT
BZZT
BZZT
BZZT
GAH!
MY LEGS...
SLUMP
SLUMP

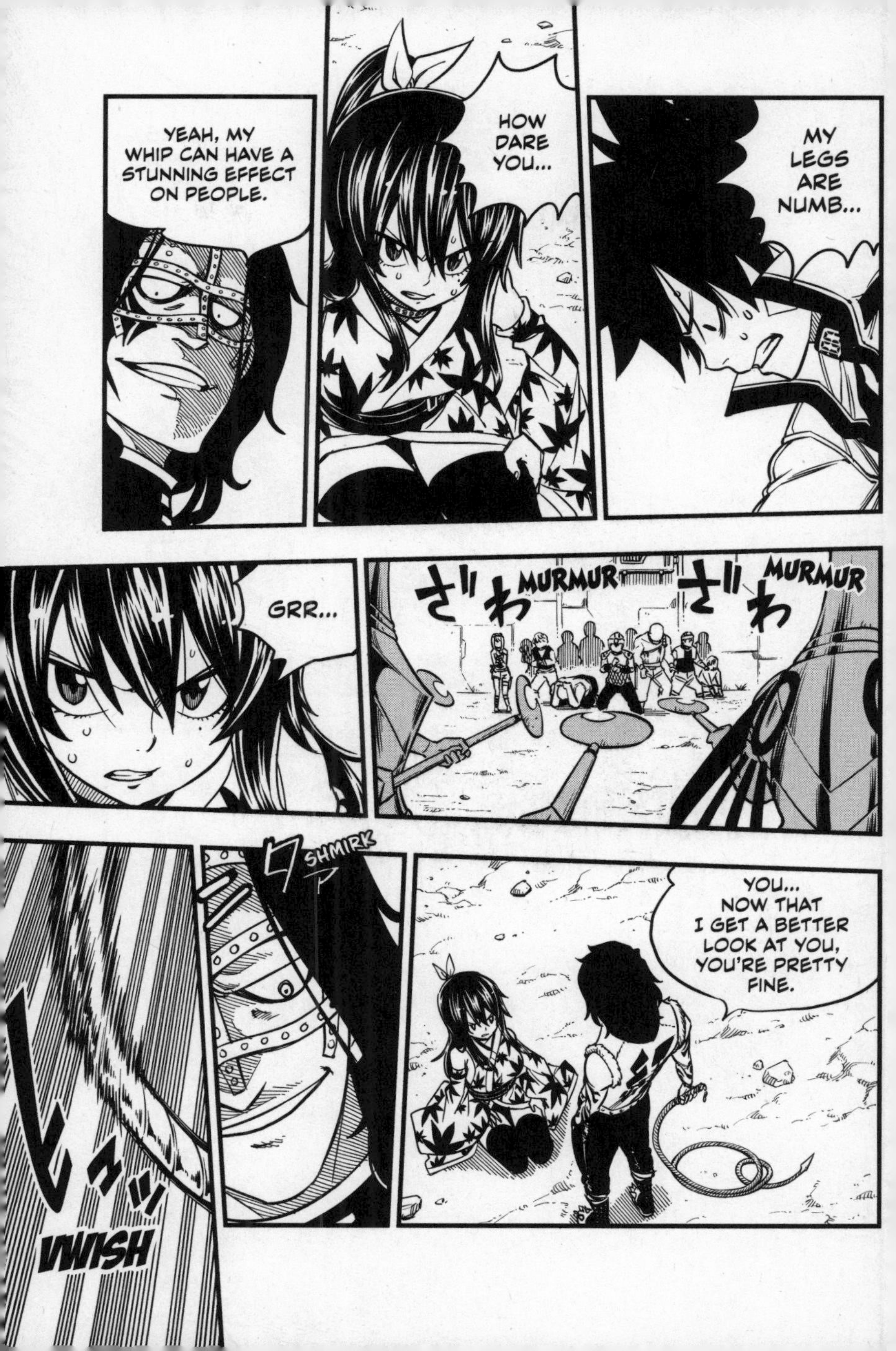
MY LEGS ARE NUMB...
HOW DARE YOU...
YEAH, MY WHIP CAN HAVE A STUNNING EFFECT ON PEOPLE.
ざわ MURMUR
ざわ MURMUR
GRR...
YOU... NOW THAT I GET A BETTER LOOK AT YOU, YOU'RE PRETTY FINE.
SHMIRK
VWISH

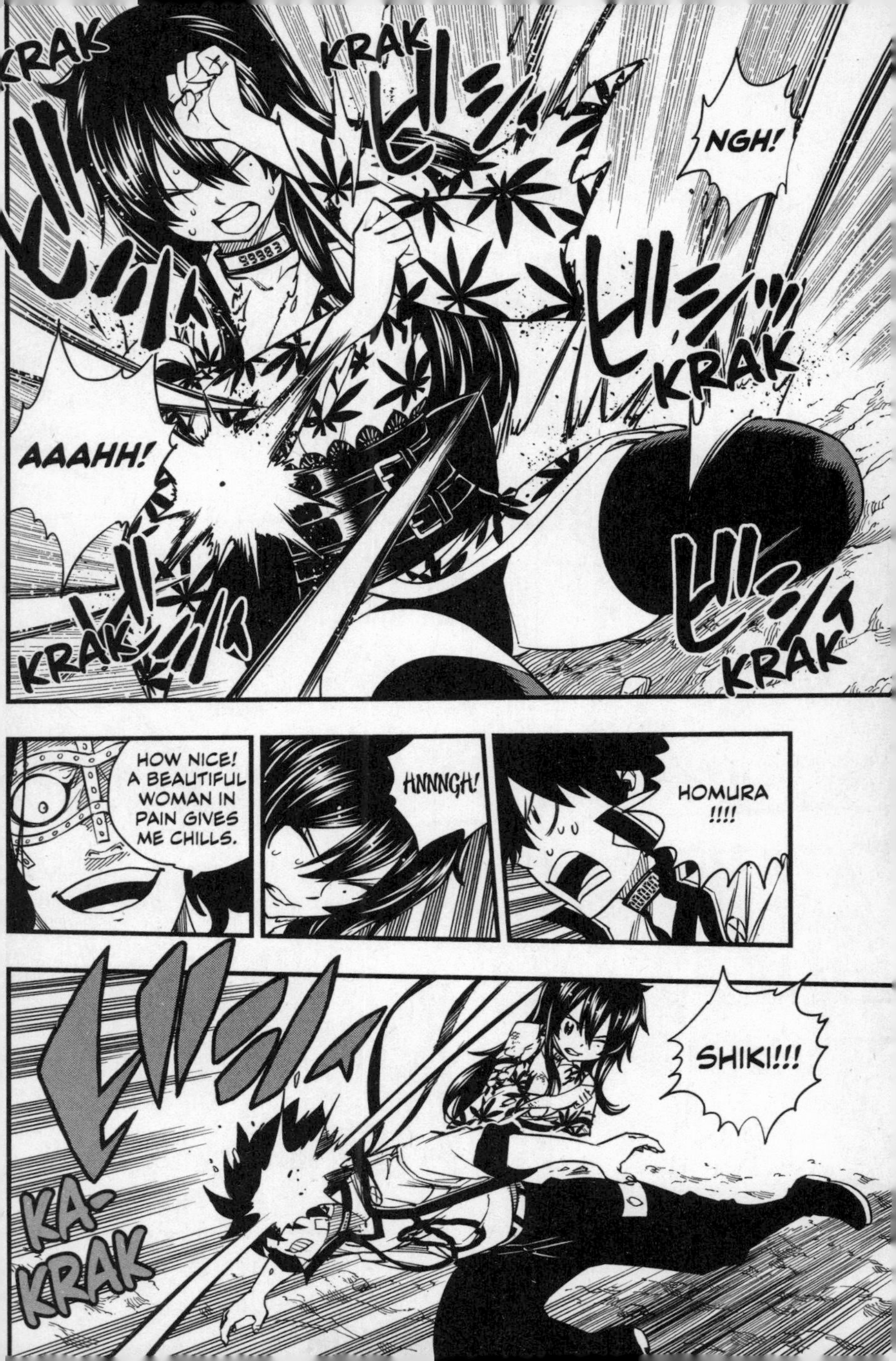
NGH!
KRAK
KRAK
KRAK
AAAHH!
KRAK
KRAK
HOMURA !!!!
HNNNGH!
HOW NICE! A BEAUTIFUL WOMAN IN PAIN GIVES ME CHILLS.
SHIKI!!!
KA-KRAK

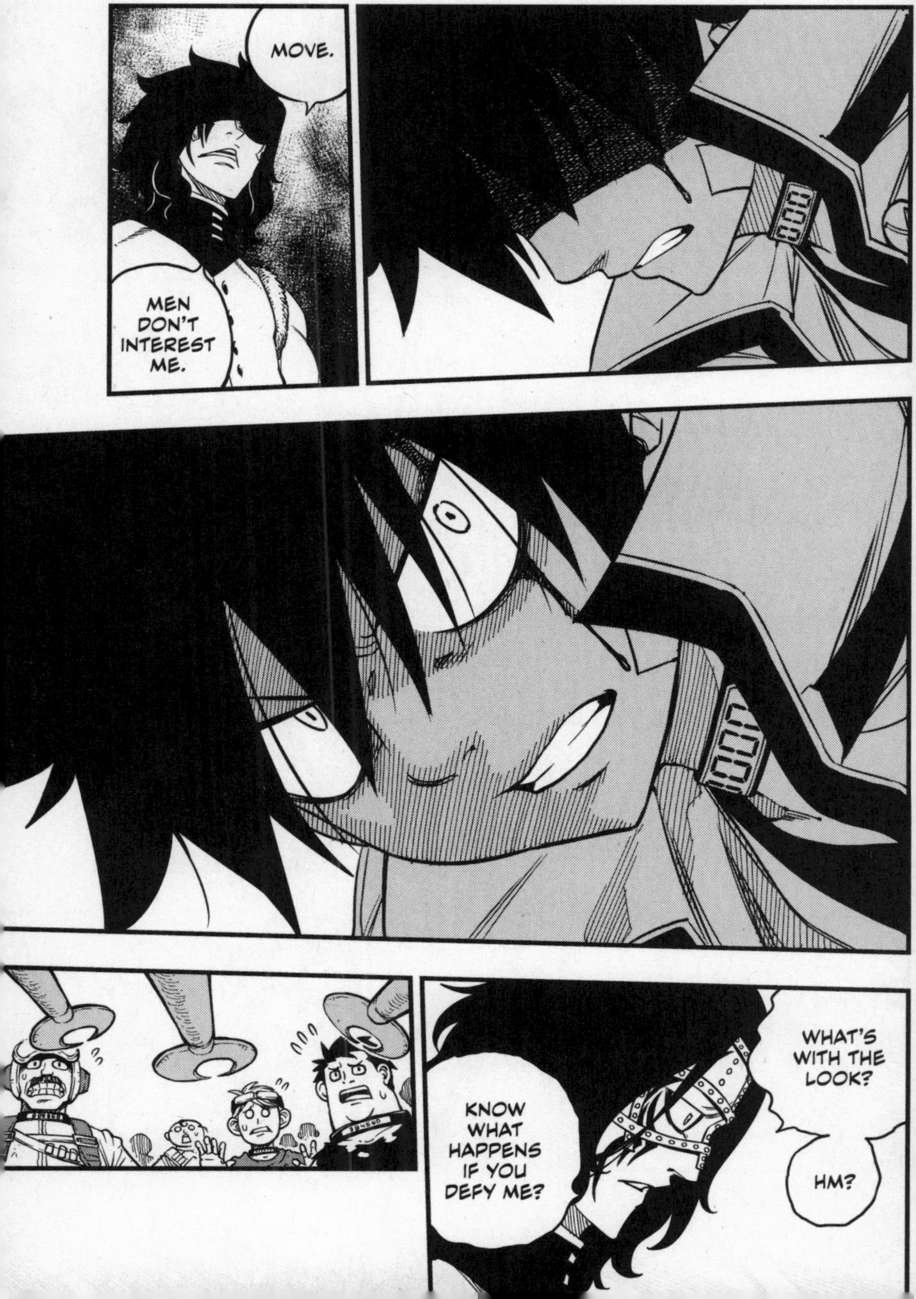
MOVE.
MEN DON'T INTEREST ME.
WHAT'S WITH THE LOOK?
HM?
KNOW WHAT HAPPENS IF YOU DEFY ME?

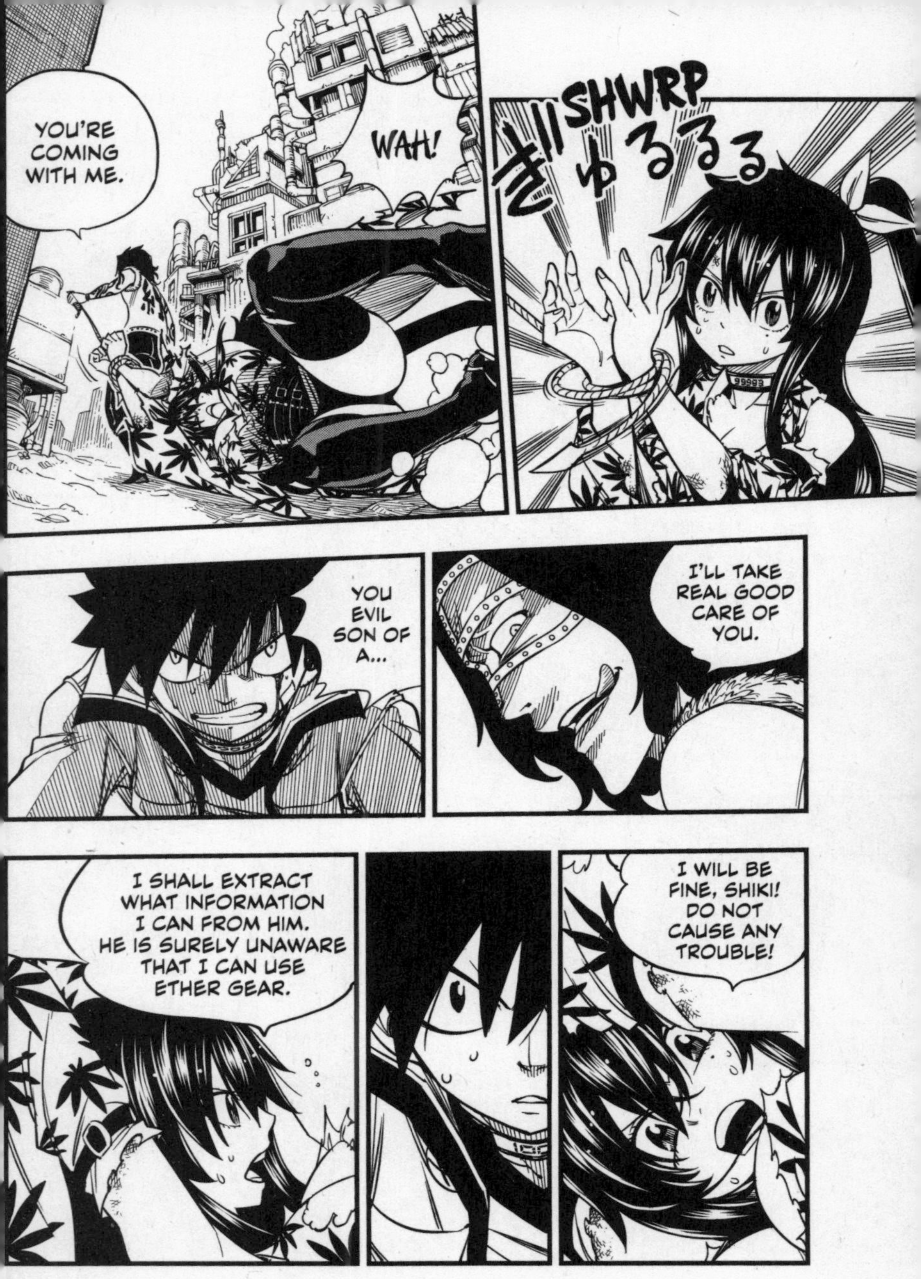
SHWRP
きゅるるる
WAH!
YOU'RE COMING WITH ME.
I'LL TAKE REAL GOOD CARE OF YOU.
YOU EVIL SON OF A...
I WILL BE FINE, SHIKI! DO NOT CAUSE ANY TROUBLE!
I SHALL EXTRACT WHAT INFORMATION I CAN FROM HIM. HE IS SURELY UNAWARE THAT I CAN USE ETHER GEAR.

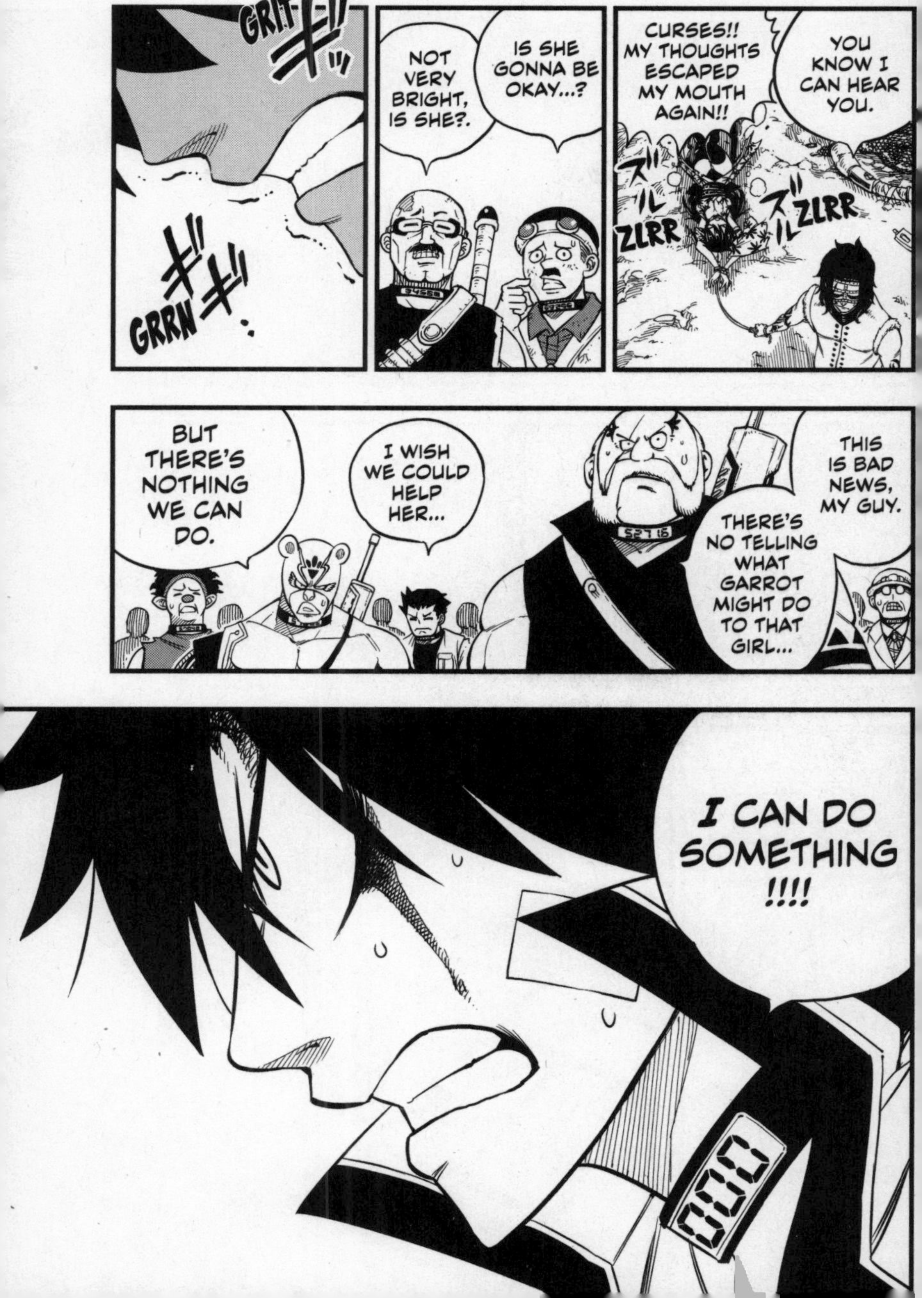
YOU KNOW I CAN HEAR YOU.
CURSES!! MY THOUGHTS ESCAPED MY MOUTH AGAIN!!
ZLRR
ZLRR
IS SHE GONNA BE OKAY...?
NOT VERY BRIGHT, IS SHE?.
GRIT
GRRN
THIS IS BAD NEWS, MY GUY.
THERE'S NO TELLING WHAT GARROT MIGHT DO TO THAT GIRL...
I WISH WE COULD HELP HER...
BUT THERE'S NOTHING WE CAN DO.
I CAN DO SOMETHING !!!!

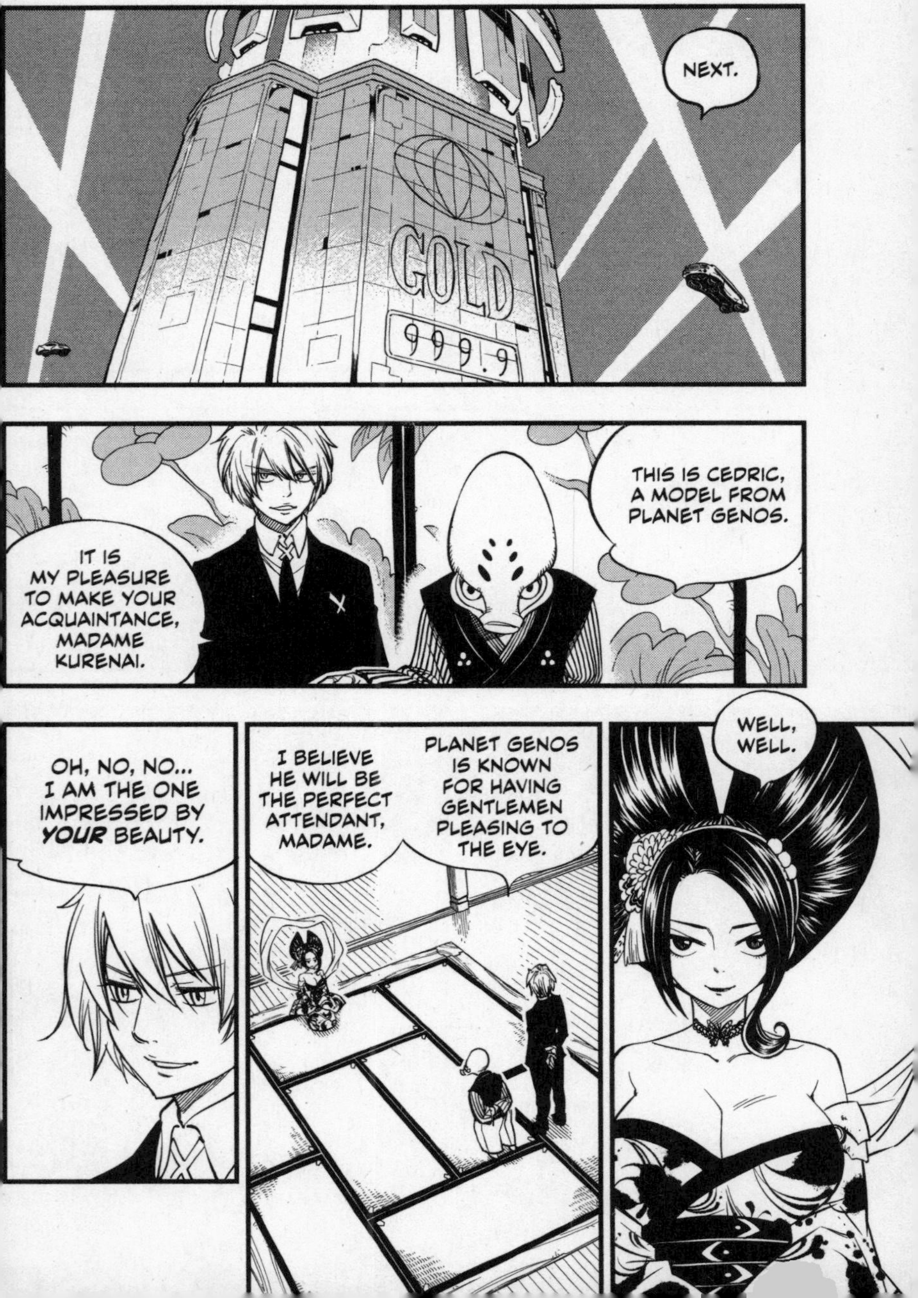
NEXT.
GOLD
999.9
THIS IS CEDRIC, A MODEL FROM PLANET GENOS.
IT IS MY PLEASURE TO MAKE YOUR ACQUAINTANCE, MADAME KURENAI.
WELL, WELL.
PLANET GENOS IS KNOWN FOR HAVING GENTLEMEN PLEASING TO THE EYE.
I BELIEVE HE WILL BE THE PERFECT ATTENDANT, MADAME.
OH, NO, NO... I AM THE ONE IMPRESSED BY ***YOUR*** BEAUTY.

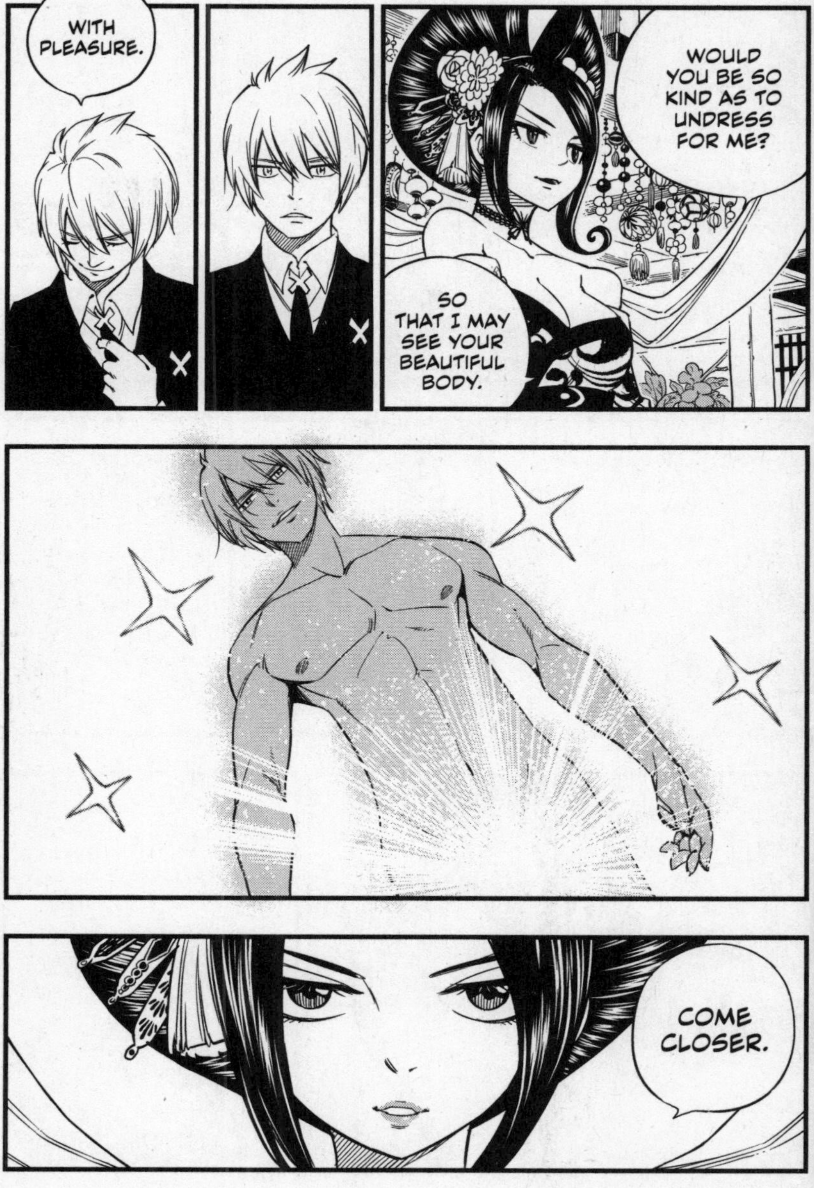
WOULD YOU BE SO KIND AS TO UNDRESS FOR ME?
SO THAT I MAY SEE YOUR BEAUTIFUL BODY.
WITH PLEASURE.
COME CLOSER.

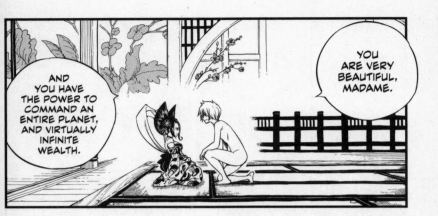

YOU ARE VERY BEAUTIFUL, MADAME.
AND YOU HAVE THE POWER TO COMMAND AN ENTIRE PLANET, AND VIRTUALLY INFINITE WEALTH.
I WOULD DO ANYTHING TO BE YOUR ATTENDANT.
ANY-THING?
YES. IF YOU WISH IT... I CAN KEEP YOU WARM ON LONELY NIGHTS.
FSH
WHAT DO YOU THINK OF HIM, MADAME KURENAI? IN ADDITION TO BEING A MODEL, HE IS ALSO A CERTIFIED BUTLER.
I DISAP-PROVE.
WHAT?

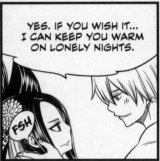

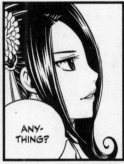

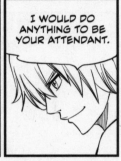

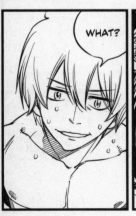

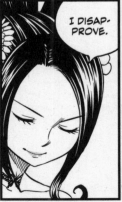

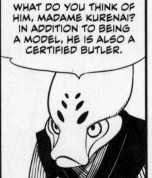

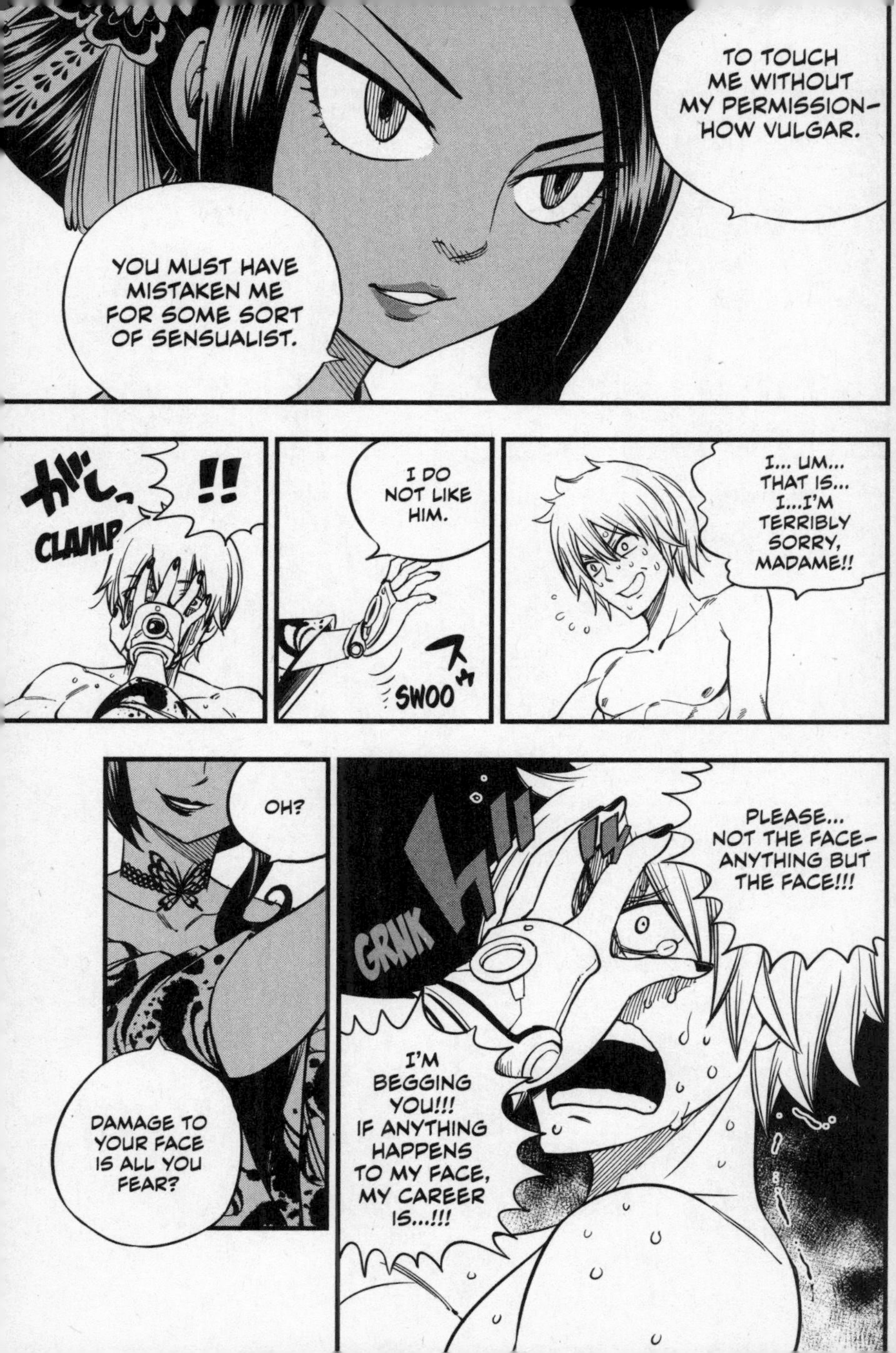
TO TOUCH ME WITHOUT MY PERMISSION— HOW VULGAR.
YOU MUST HAVE MISTAKEN ME FOR SOME SORT OF SENSUALIST.
I... UM... THAT IS... I...I'M TERRIBLY SORRY, MADAME!!
I DO NOT LIKE HIM.
SWOO
!!
CLAMP
PLEASE... NOT THE FACE— ANYTHING BUT THE FACE!!!
GRNK
I'M BEGGING YOU!!! IF ANYTHING HAPPENS TO MY FACE, MY CAREER IS...!!!
OH?
DAMAGE TO YOUR FACE IS ALL YOU FEAR?

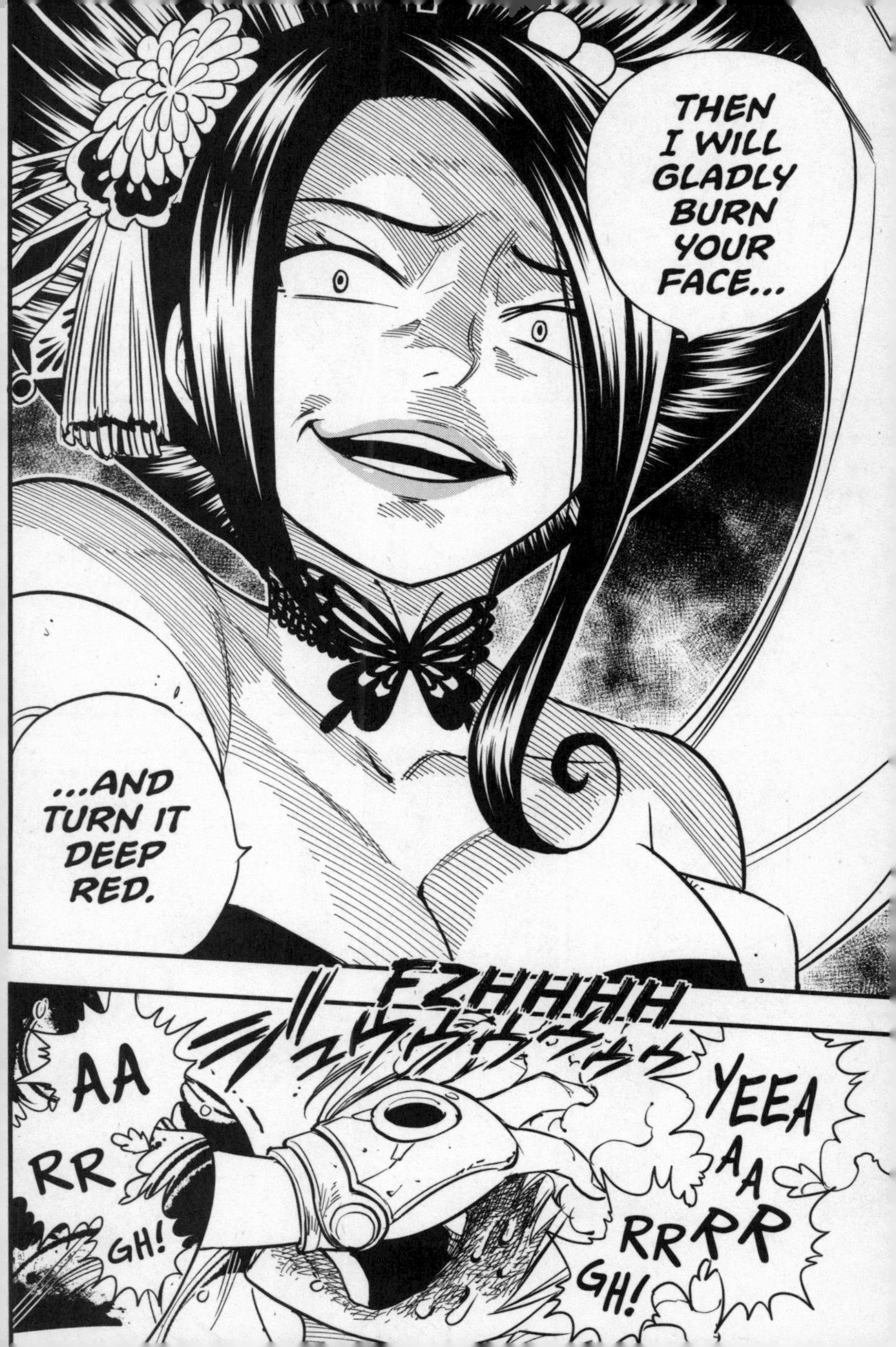
THEN I WILL GLADLY BURN YOUR FACE...
...AND TURN IT DEEP RED.
FZHHHHH
YEEAAARRRRRGH!
AARRGH!

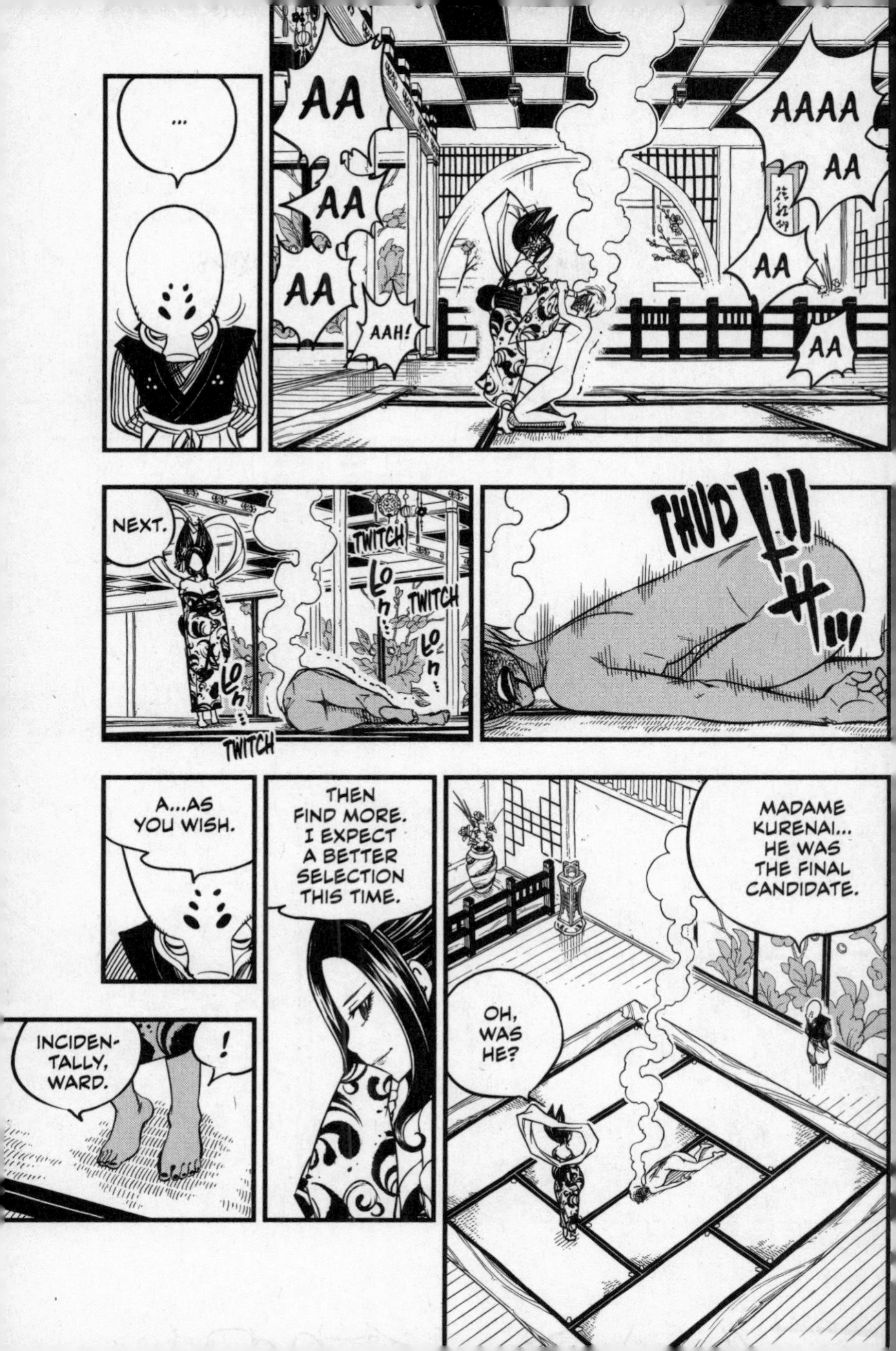
AAAA
AA
AA
AA
AA
AA
AA
AAH!
...
THUD!!!
NEXT.
TWITCH
TWITCH
TWITCH
MADAME KURENAI... HE WAS THE FINAL CANDIDATE.
OH, WAS HE?
THEN FIND MORE. I EXPECT A BETTER SELECTION THIS TIME.
A...AS YOU WISH.
!
INCIDEN-TALLY, WARD.

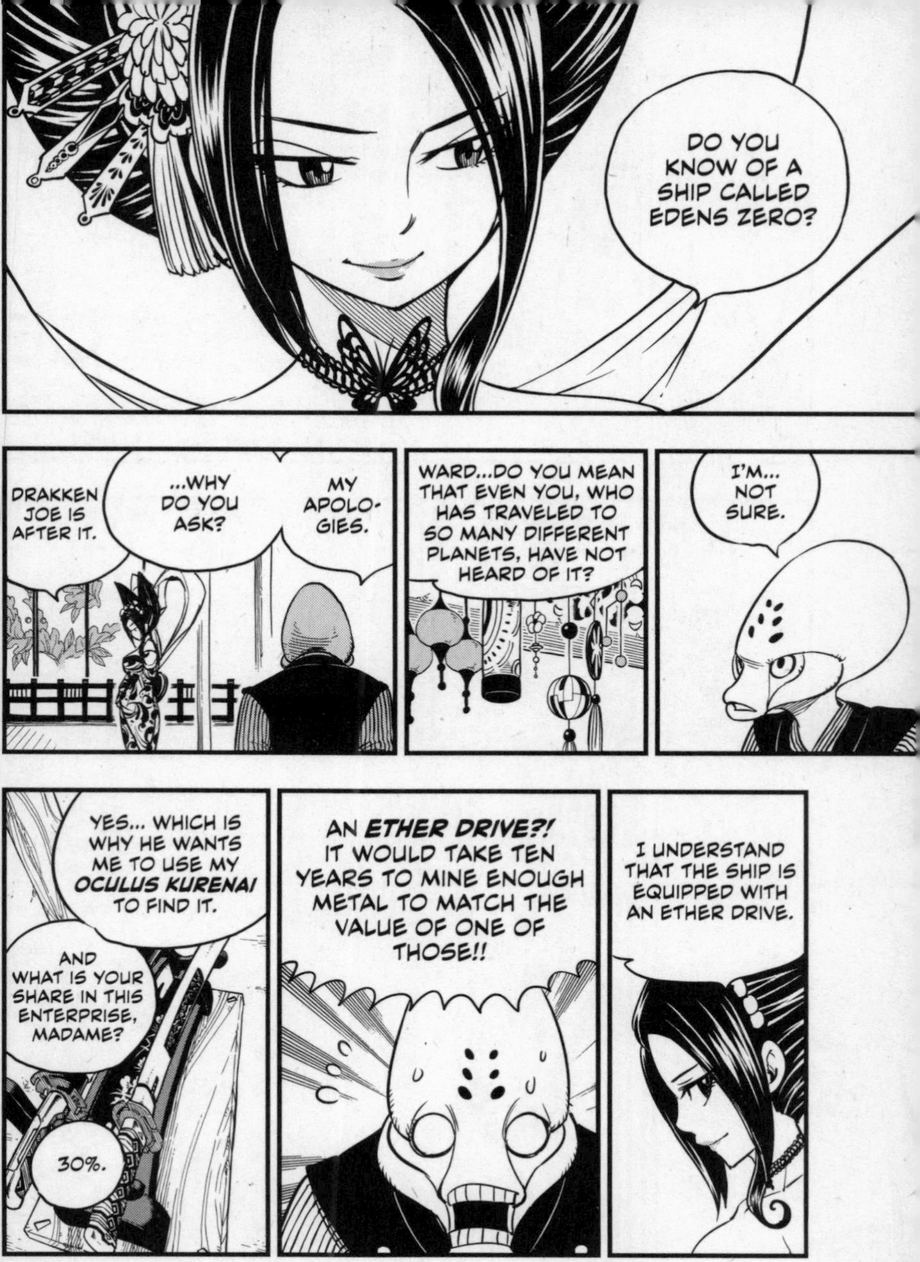

DO YOU KNOW OF A SHIP CALLED EDENS ZERO?
I'M... NOT SURE.
WARD...DO YOU MEAN THAT EVEN YOU, WHO HAS TRAVELED TO SO MANY DIFFERENT PLANETS, HAVE NOT HEARD OF IT?
MY APOLOGIES.
...WHY DO YOU ASK?
DRAKKEN JOE IS AFTER IT.
I UNDERSTAND THAT THE SHIP IS EQUIPPED WITH AN ETHER DRIVE.
AN *ETHER DRIVE?!* IT WOULD TAKE TEN YEARS TO MINE ENOUGH METAL TO MATCH THE VALUE OF ONE OF THOSE!!
YES... WHICH IS WHY HE WANTS ME TO USE MY ***OCULUS KURENAI*** TO FIND IT.
AND WHAT IS YOUR SHARE IN THIS ENTERPRISE, MADAME?
30%.

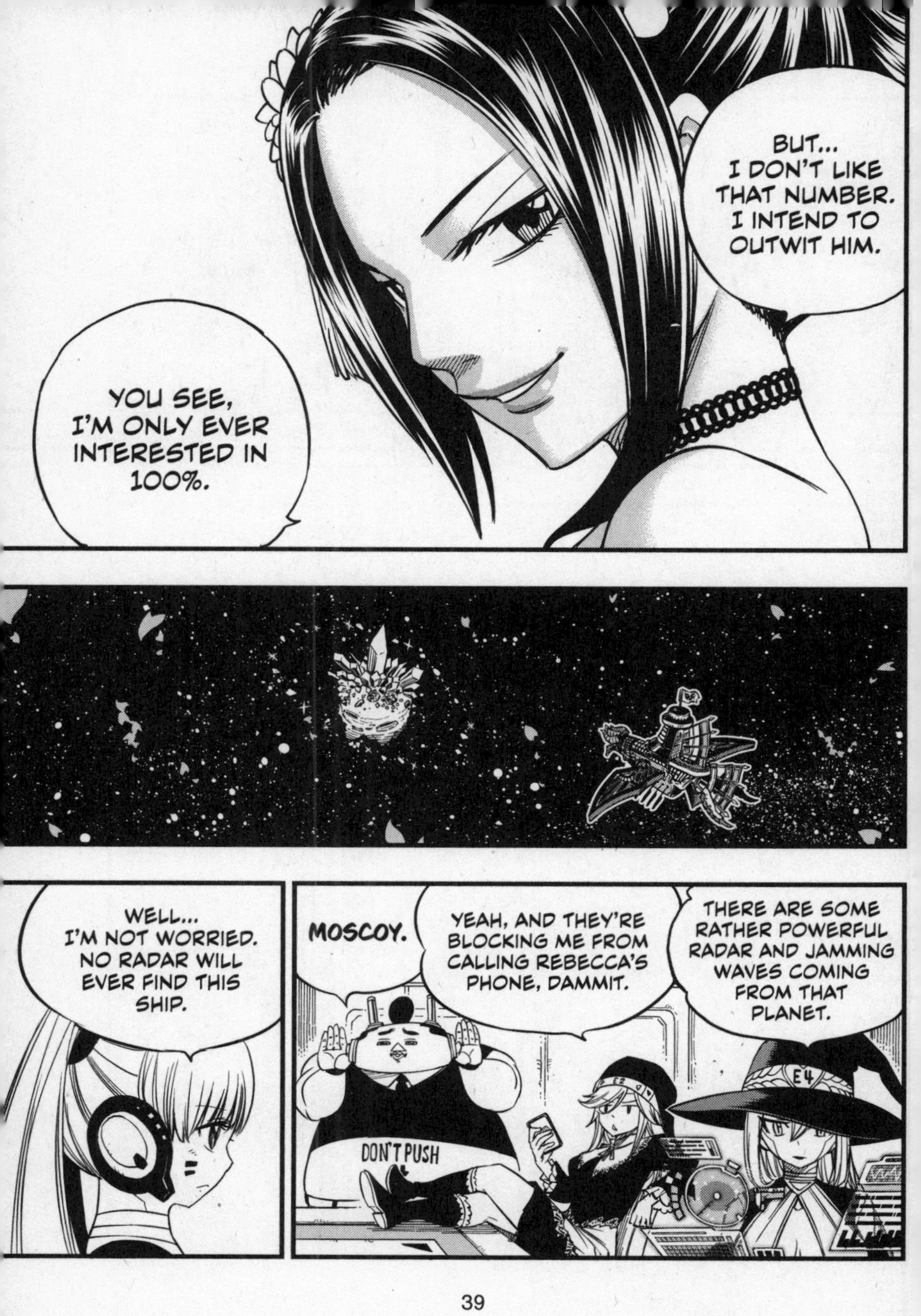
BUT... I DON'T LIKE THAT NUMBER. I INTEND TO OUTWIT HIM.
YOU SEE, I'M ONLY EVER INTERESTED IN 100%.
THERE ARE SOME RATHER POWERFUL RADAR AND JAMMING WAVES COMING FROM THAT PLANET.
YEAH, AND THEY'RE BLOCKING ME FROM CALLING REBECCA'S PHONE, DAMMIT.
MOSCOY.
DON'T PUSH
WELL... I'M NOT WORRIED. NO RADAR WILL EVER FIND THIS SHIP.

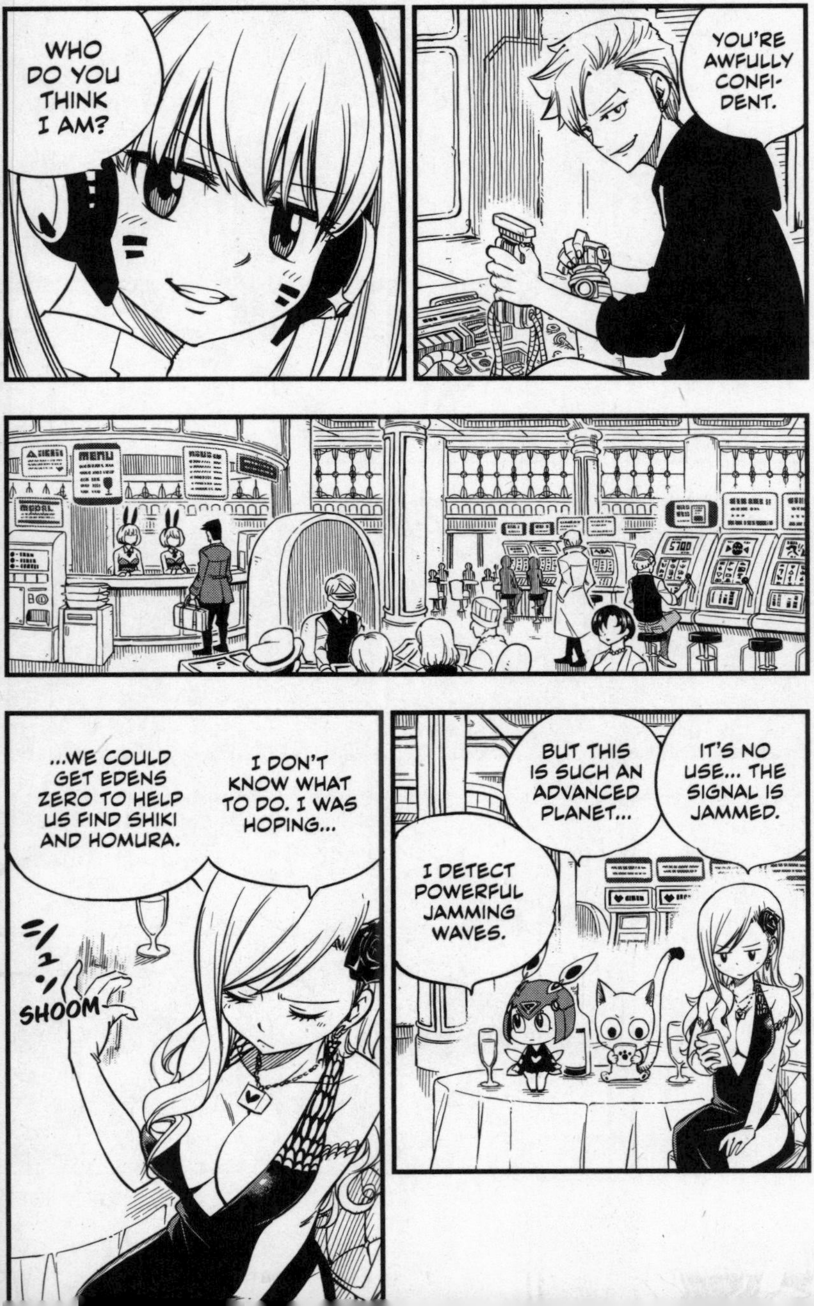
YOU'RE AWFULLY CONFI-DENT.
WHO DO YOU THINK I AM?
IT'S NO USE... THE SIGNAL IS JAMMED.
BUT THIS IS SUCH AN ADVANCED PLANET...
I DETECT POWERFUL JAMMING WAVES.
I DON'T KNOW WHAT TO DO. I WAS HOPING...
...WE COULD GET EDENS ZERO TO HELP US FIND SHIKI AND HOMURA.
SHOOM

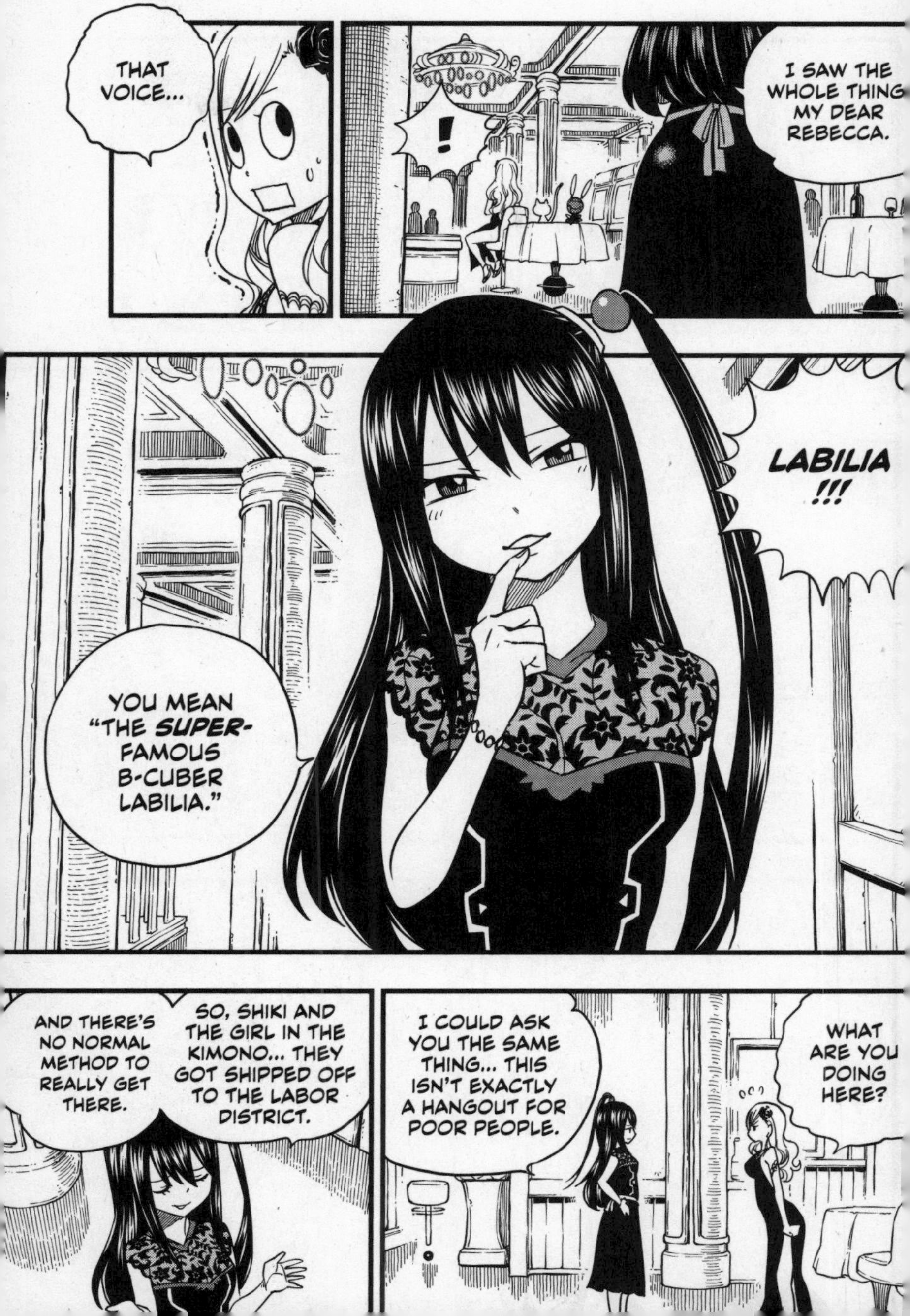

I SAW THE WHOLE THING MY DEAR REBECCA.
!
THAT VOICE...
LABILIA !!!
YOU MEAN "THE SUPER-FAMOUS B-CUBER LABILIA."
WHAT ARE YOU DOING HERE?
I COULD ASK YOU THE SAME THING... THIS ISN'T EXACTLY A HANGOUT FOR POOR PEOPLE.
SO, SHIKI AND THE GIRL IN THE KIMONO... THEY GOT SHIPPED OFF TO THE LABOR DISTRICT.
AND THERE'S NO NORMAL METHOD TO REALLY GET THERE.

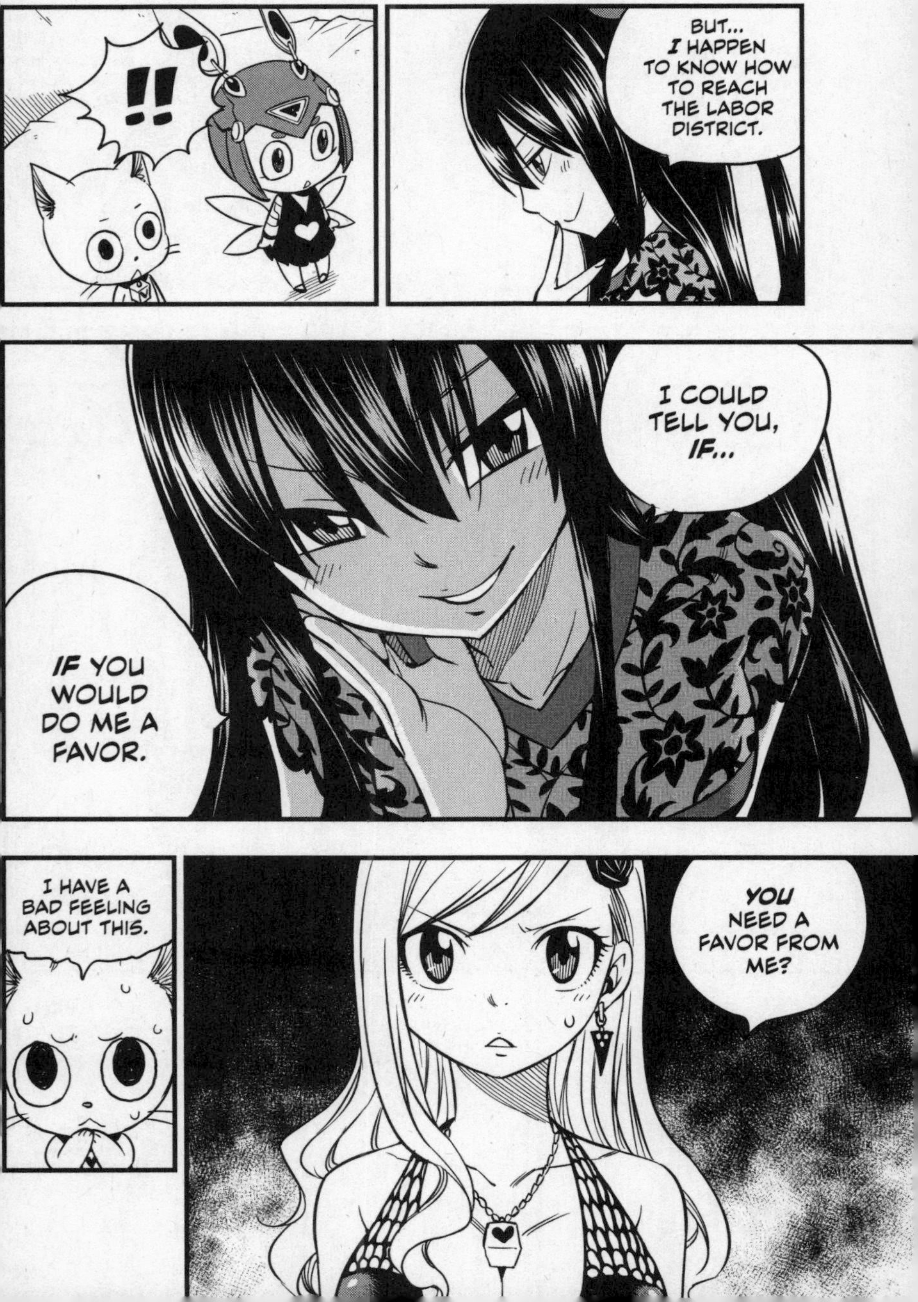
BUT... I HAPPEN TO KNOW HOW TO REACH THE LABOR DISTRICT.
!!
I COULD TELL YOU, IF...
IF YOU WOULD DO ME A FAVOR.
YOU NEED A FAVOR FROM ME?
I HAVE A BAD FEELING ABOUT THIS.

EDENS ZERO

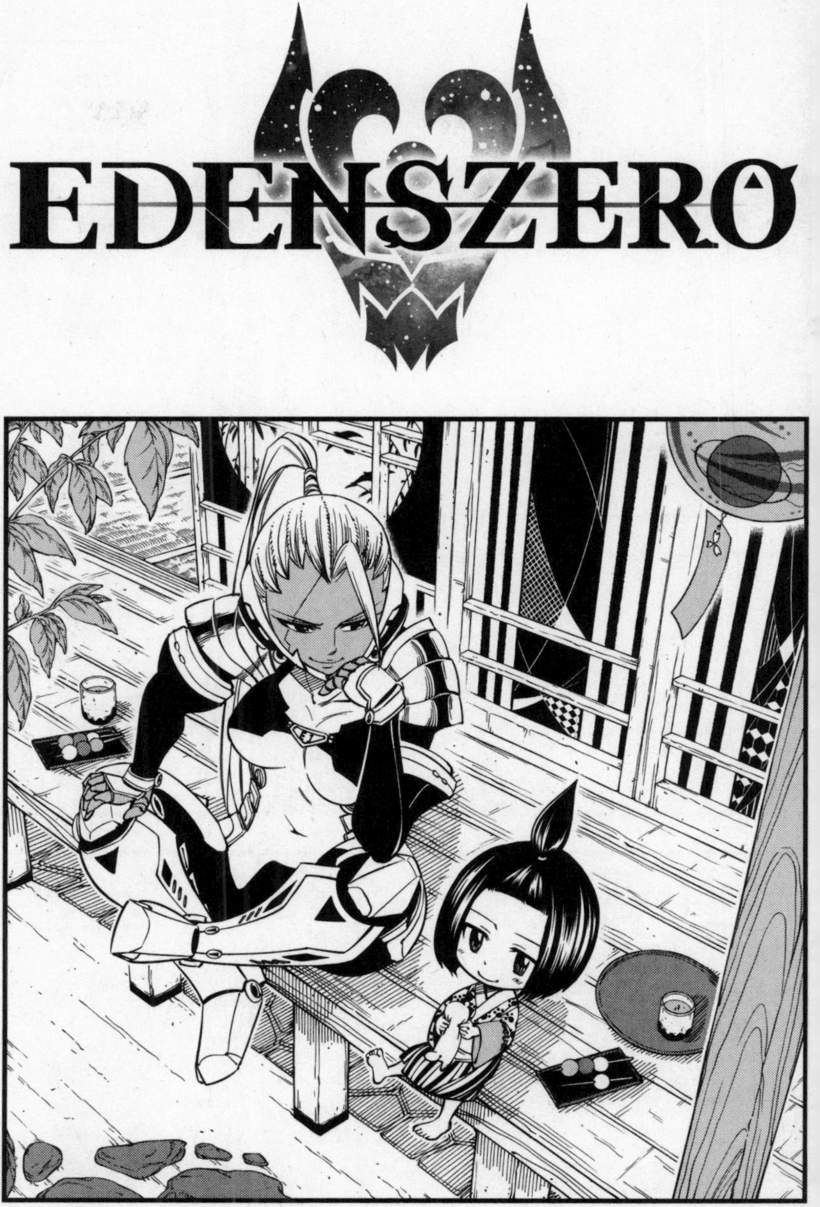

CHAPTER 53: WIBBLE WOBBLE RUBY BOBBLE

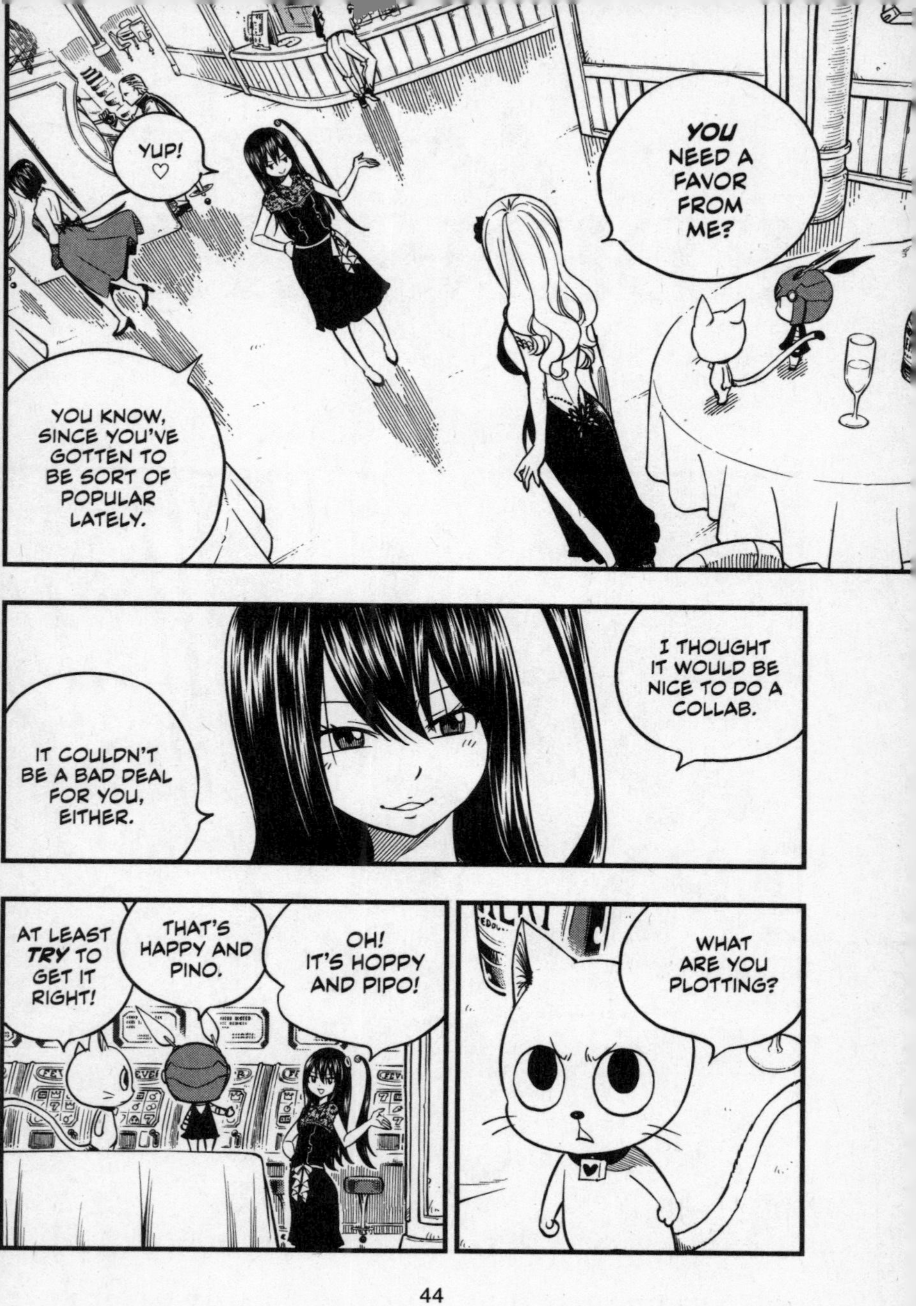
YOU NEED A FAVOR FROM ME?
YUP! ♡
YOU KNOW, SINCE YOU'VE GOTTEN TO BE SORT OF POPULAR LATELY.
I THOUGHT IT WOULD BE NICE TO DO A COLLAB.
IT COULDN'T BE A BAD DEAL FOR YOU, EITHER.
WHAT ARE YOU PLOTTING?
OH! IT'S HOPPY AND PIPO!
THAT'S HAPPY AND PINO.
AT LEAST TRY TO GET IT RIGHT!

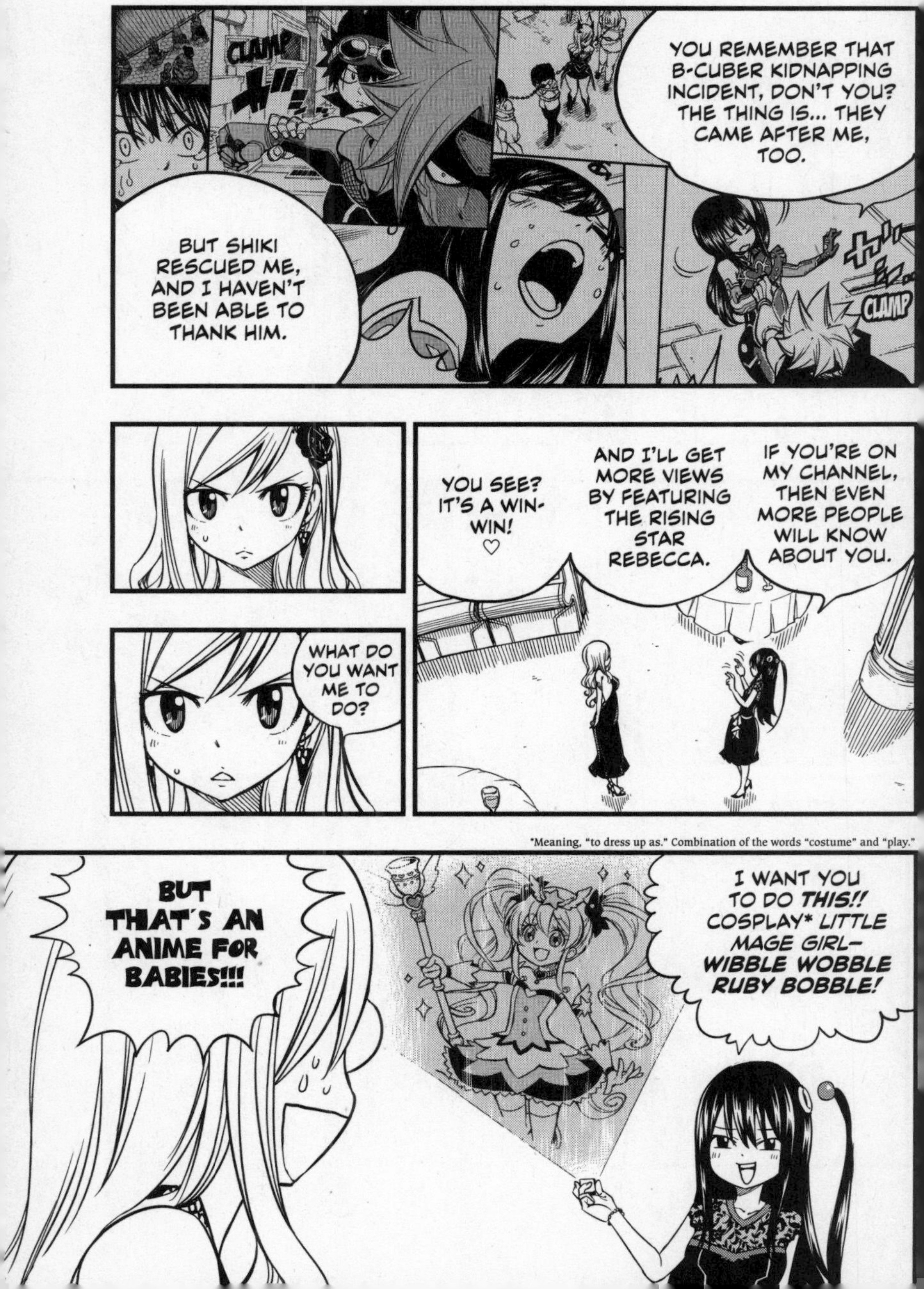
YOU REMEMBER THAT B-CUBER KIDNAPPING INCIDENT, DON'T YOU? THE THING IS... THEY CAME AFTER ME, TOO.
CLAMP
BUT SHIKI RESCUED ME, AND I HAVEN'T BEEN ABLE TO THANK HIM.
CLAMP
IF YOU'RE ON MY CHANNEL, THEN EVEN MORE PEOPLE WILL KNOW ABOUT YOU.
AND I'LL GET MORE VIEWS BY FEATURING THE RISING STAR REBECCA.
YOU SEE? IT'S A WIN-WIN! ♡
WHAT DO YOU WANT ME TO DO?
I WANT YOU TO DO *THIS!!* COSPLAY* *LITTLE MAGE GIRL— WIBBLE WOBBLE RUBY BOBBLE!*
BUT THAT'S AN ANIME FOR BABIES!!!

*Meaning, "to dress up as." Combination of the words "costume" and "play."

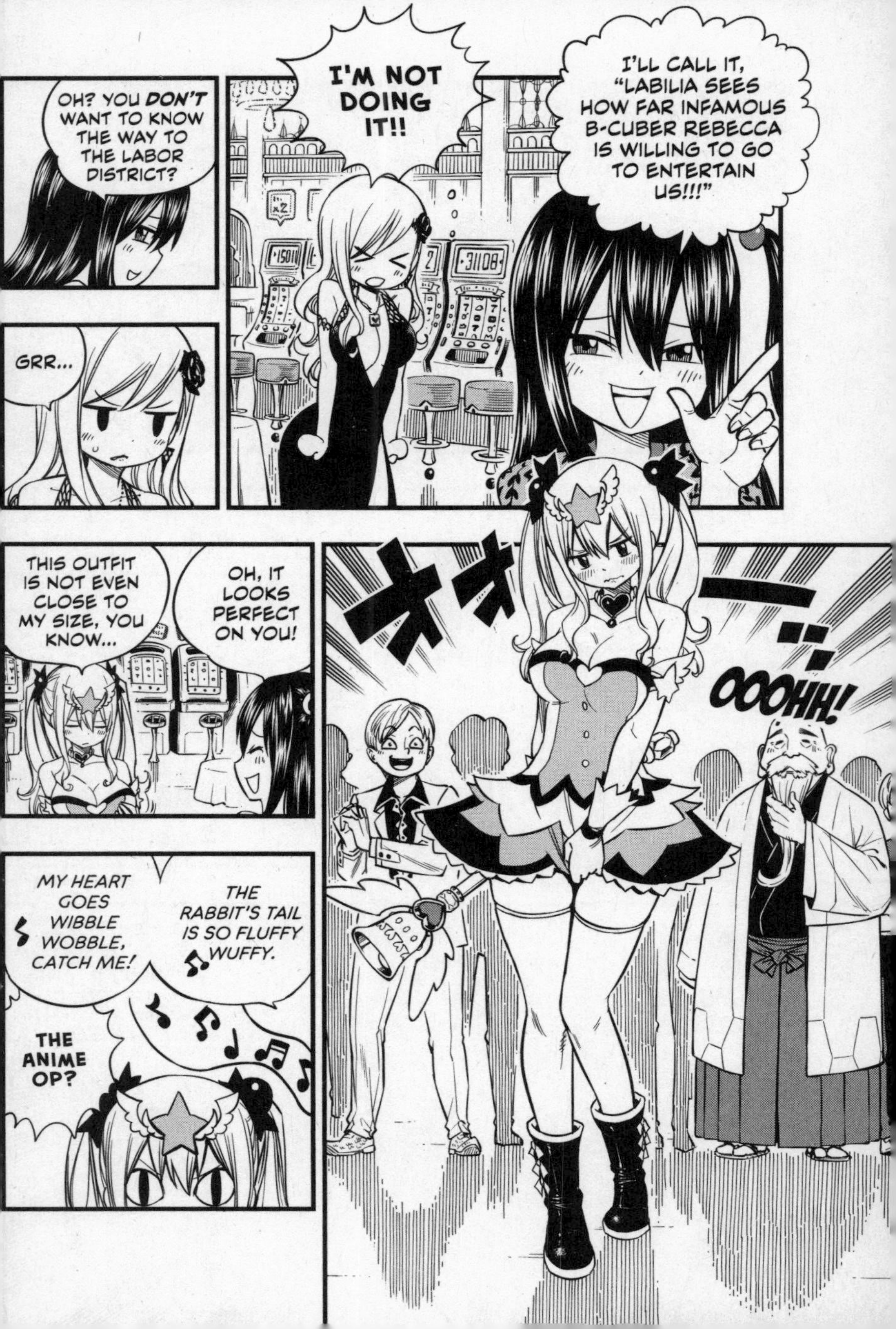
I'LL CALL IT, "LABILIA SEES HOW FAR INFAMOUS B-CUBER REBECCA IS WILLING TO GO TO ENTERTAIN US!!!"
I'M NOT DOING IT!!
OH? YOU DON'T WANT TO KNOW THE WAY TO THE LABOR DISTRICT?
GRR...
オオーーッ
OOOHH!
OH, IT LOOKS PERFECT ON YOU!
THIS OUTFIT IS NOT EVEN CLOSE TO MY SIZE, YOU KNOW...
THE RABBIT'S TAIL IS SO FLUFFY WUFFY.
MY HEART GOES WIBBLE WOBBLE, CATCH ME!
THE ANIME OP?

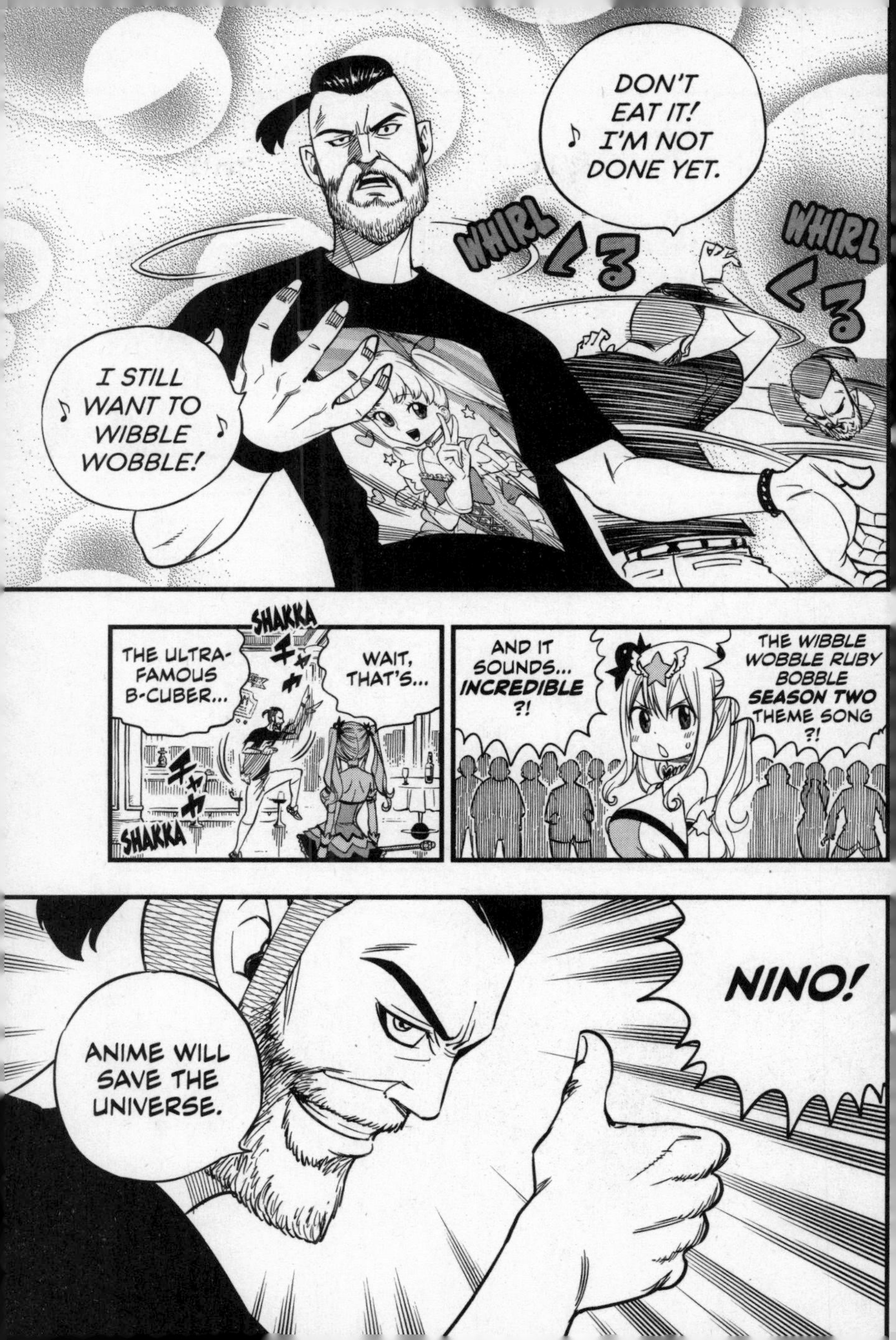
♪ DON'T EAT IT! I'M NOT DONE YET.
WHIRL くる
WHIRL くる
I STILL ♪ WANT TO WIBBLE WOBBLE! ♪
THE WIBBLE WOBBLE RUBY BOBBLE **SEASON TWO** THEME SONG ?!
AND IT SOUNDS... ***INCREDIBLE*** ?!
WAIT, THAT'S...
SHAKKA
THE ULTRA-FAMOUS B-CUBER...
SHAKKA
NINO!
ANIME WILL SAVE THE UNIVERSE.

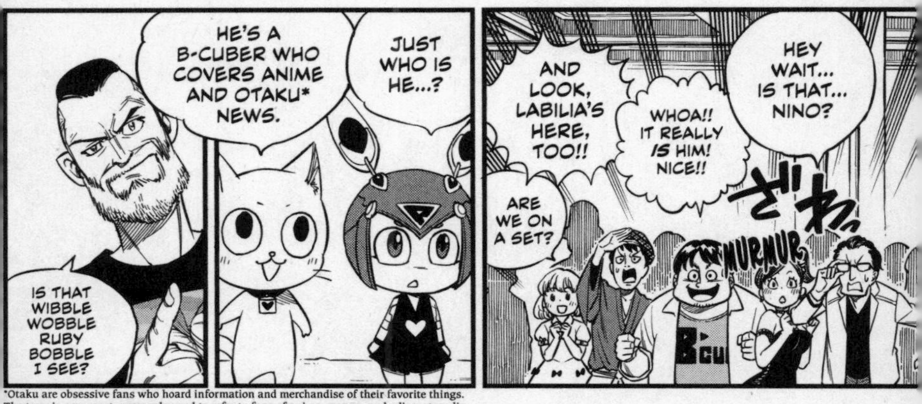
HEY WAIT... IS THAT... NINO?
WHOA!! IT REALLY IS HIM! NICE!!
AND LOOK, LABILIA'S HERE, TOO!!
ARE WE ON A SET?
ざわ
MURMUR
JUST WHO IS HE...?
HE'S A B-CUBER WHO COVERS ANIME AND OTAKU* NEWS.
IS THAT WIBBLE WOBBLE RUBY BOBBLE I SEE?

*Otaku are obsessive fans who hoard information and merchandise of their favorite things. The term is now most commonly used to refer to fans of anime, manga, and adjacent media.

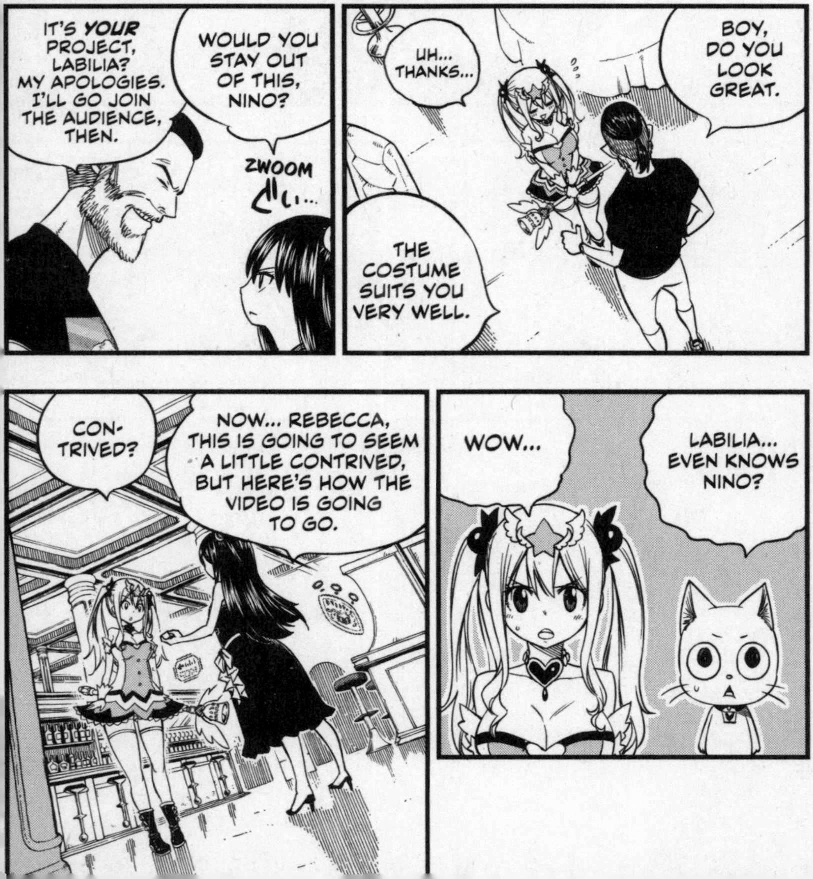
BOY, DO YOU LOOK GREAT.
UH... THANKS...
THE COSTUME SUITS YOU VERY WELL.
WOULD YOU STAY OUT OF THIS, NINO?
IT'S YOUR PROJECT, LABILIA? MY APOLOGIES. I'LL GO JOIN THE AUDIENCE, THEN.
ZWOOM
LABILIA... EVEN KNOWS NINO?
WOW...
NOW... REBECCA, THIS IS GOING TO SEEM A LITTLE CONTRIVED, BUT HERE'S HOW THE VIDEO IS GOING TO GO.
CON-TRIVED?

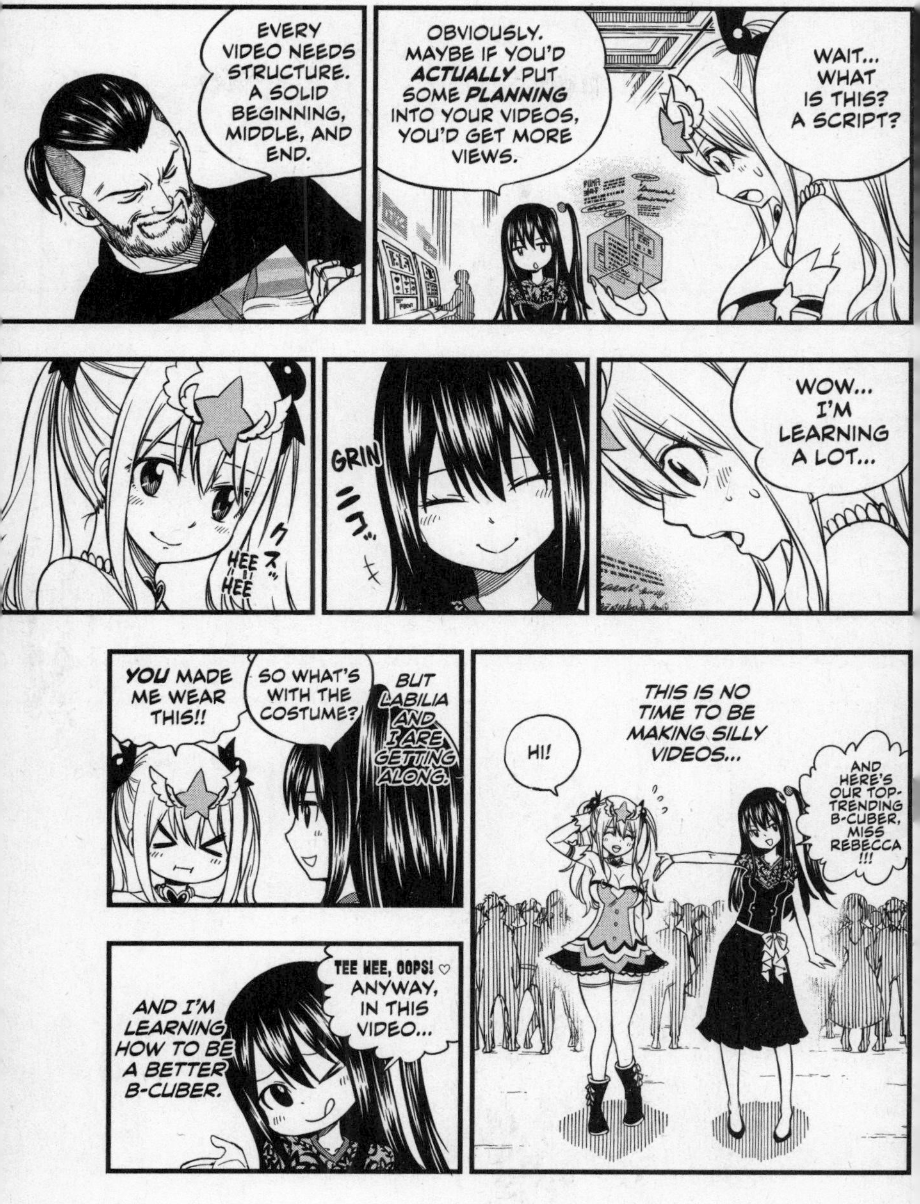
WAIT... WHAT IS THIS? A SCRIPT?
OBVIOUSLY. MAYBE IF YOU'D ACTUALLY PUT SOME PLANNING INTO YOUR VIDEOS, YOU'D GET MORE VIEWS.
EVERY VIDEO NEEDS STRUCTURE. A SOLID BEGINNING, MIDDLE, AND END.
WOW... I'M LEARNING A LOT...
GRIN
ニコッ
クスッ
HEE HEE
AND HERE'S OUR TOP-TRENDING B-CUBER, MISS REBECCA!!!
HI!
THIS IS NO TIME TO BE MAKING SILLY VIDEOS...
BUT LABILIA AND I ARE GETTING ALONG.
SO WHAT'S WITH THE COSTUME?
YOU MADE ME WEAR THIS!!
TEE HEE, OOPS! ♡ ANYWAY, IN THIS VIDEO...
AND I'M LEARNING HOW TO BE A BETTER B-CUBER.

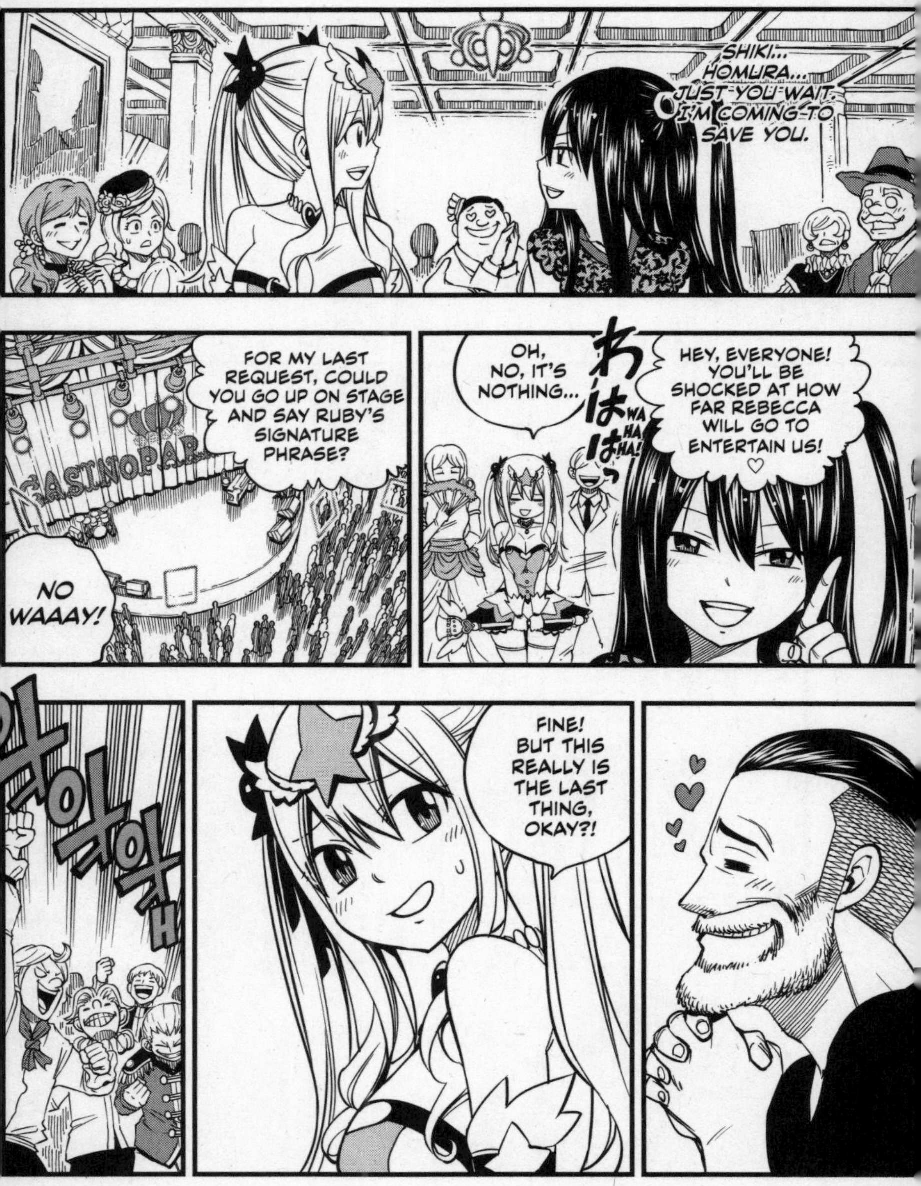
SHIKI... HOMURA... JUST YOU WAIT. I'M COMING TO SAVE YOU.
HEY, EVERYONE! YOU'LL BE SHOCKED AT HOW FAR REBECCA WILL GO TO ENTERTAIN US! ♡
わははっ
WA HA HA!
OH, NO, IT'S NOTHING...
FOR MY LAST REQUEST, COULD YOU GO UP ON STAGE AND SAY RUBY'S SIGNATURE PHRASE?
NO WAAAY!
FINE! BUT THIS REALLY IS THE LAST THING, OKAY?!

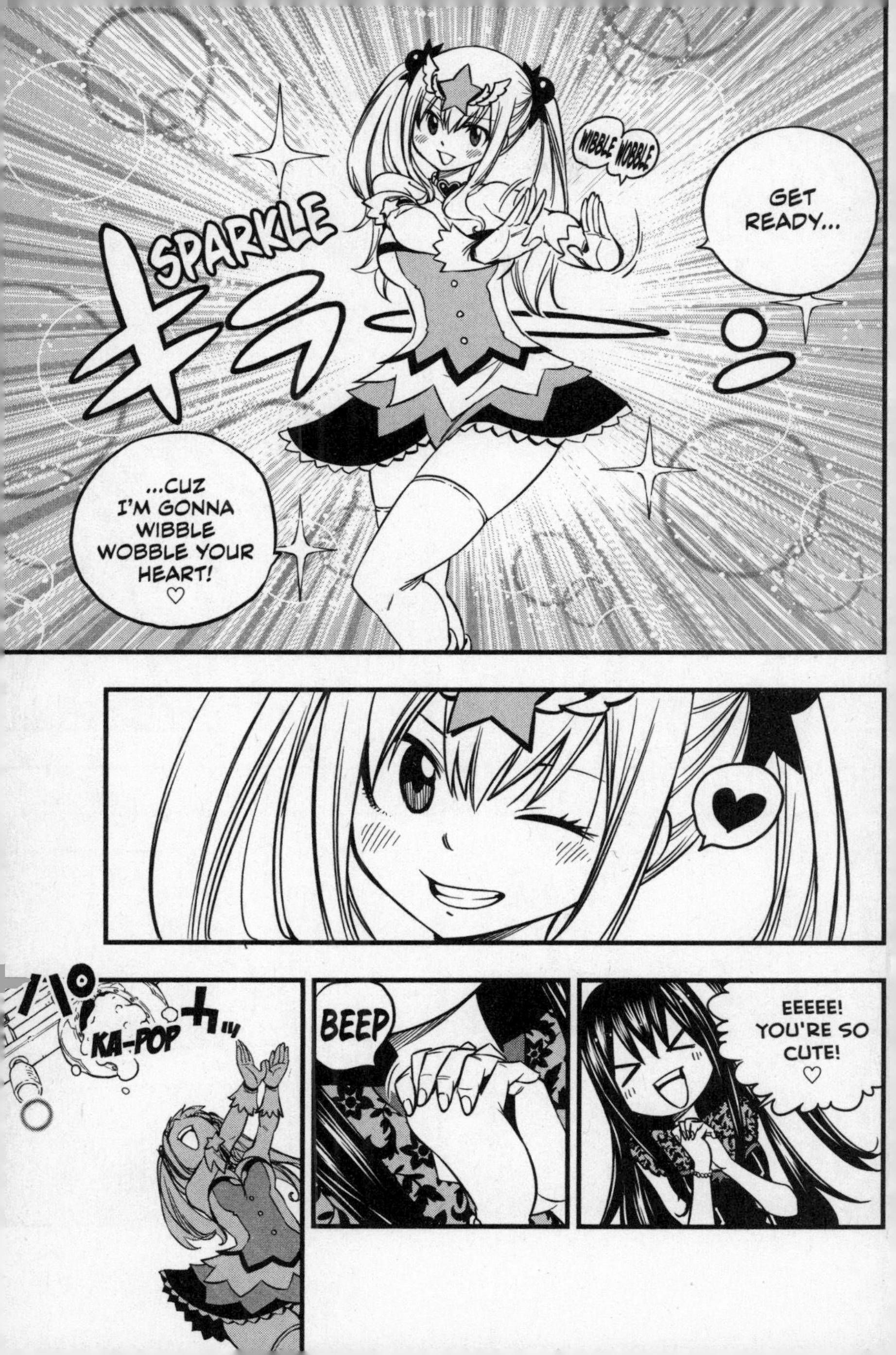
GET READY...
WIBBLE WOBBLE
SPARKLE
...CUZ I'M GONNA WIBBLE WOBBLE YOUR HEART! ♡
EEEEE! YOU'RE SO CUTE! ♡
BEEP
KA-POP

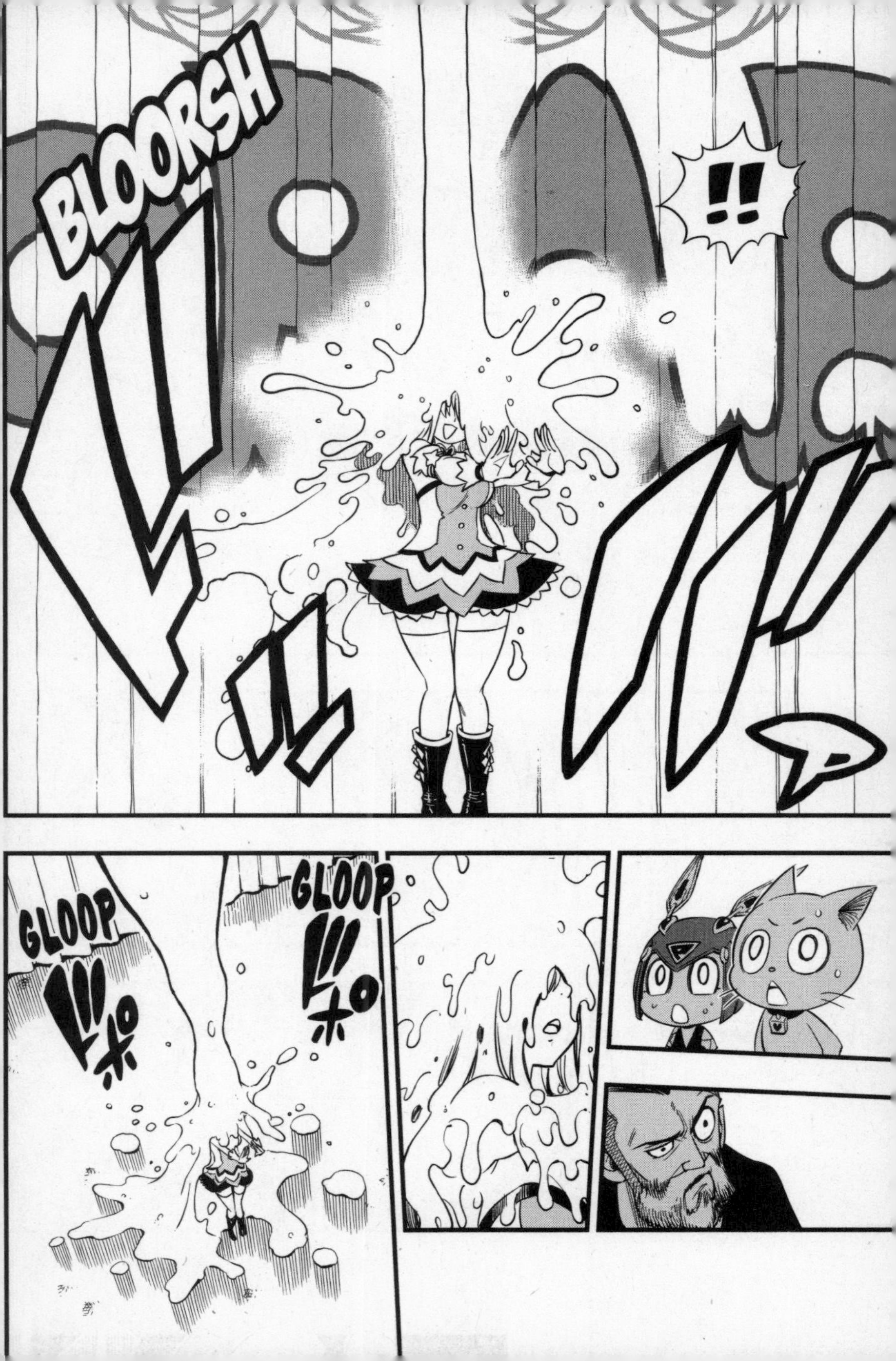
!!
BLOORSH
GLOOP
GLOOP

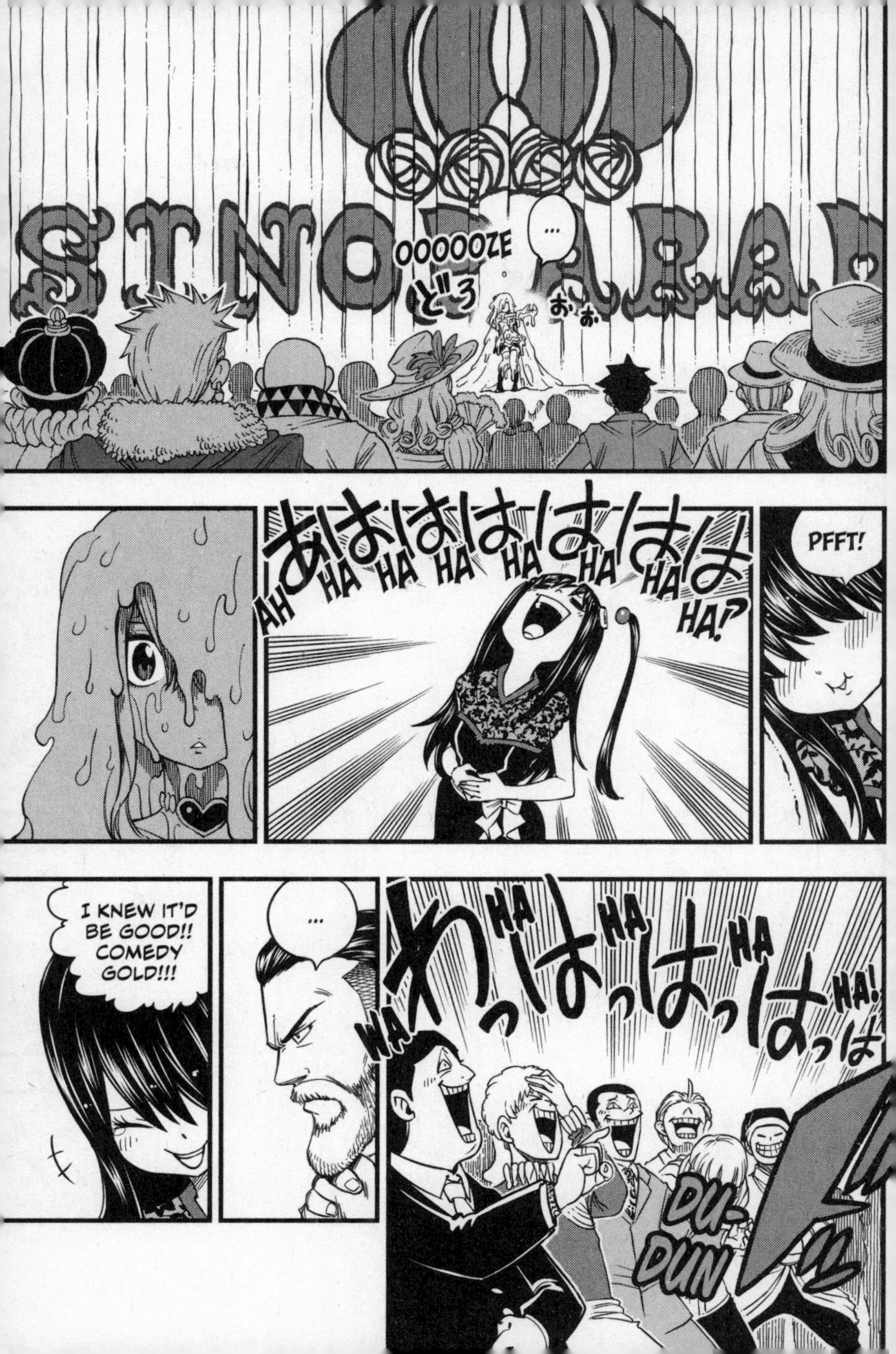
...
OOOOOOZE
どろ
おぉ
PFFT!
AH HA HA HA HA HA HA HA!?
あはははははは
HA HA HA HA HA!
わっはっはっはっは
DU-DUN
...
I KNEW IT'D BE GOOD!! COMEDY GOLD!!!

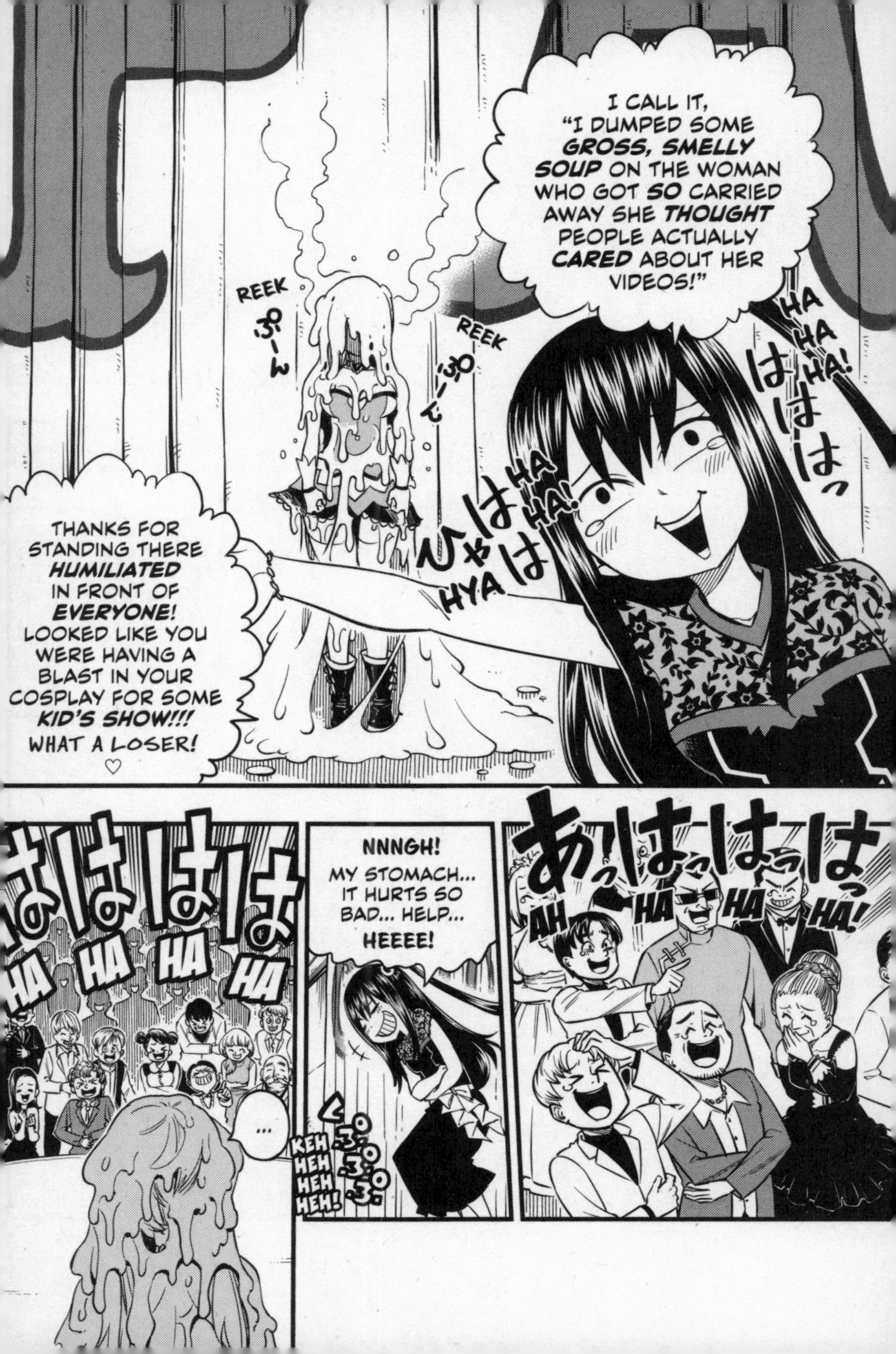
I CALL IT, "I DUMPED SOME GROSS, SMELLY SOUP ON THE WOMAN WHO GOT SO CARRIED AWAY SHE THOUGHT PEOPLE ACTUALLY CARED ABOUT HER VIDEOS!"
HA HA HA!
はははっ
HYA HA HA!
ひゃははは
REEK
ぷ～ん
REEK
ぷ～ん
THANKS FOR STANDING THERE HUMILIATED IN FRONT OF EVERYONE! LOOKED LIKE YOU WERE HAVING A BLAST IN YOUR COSPLAY FOR SOME KID'S SHOW!!! WHAT A LOSER! ♡
あっはっはっはっ
AH HA HA HA!
NNNGH! MY STOMACH... IT HURTS SO BAD... HELP... HEEEE!
KEH HEH HEH HEH!
くっ3333
あははは
HA HA HA HA
...

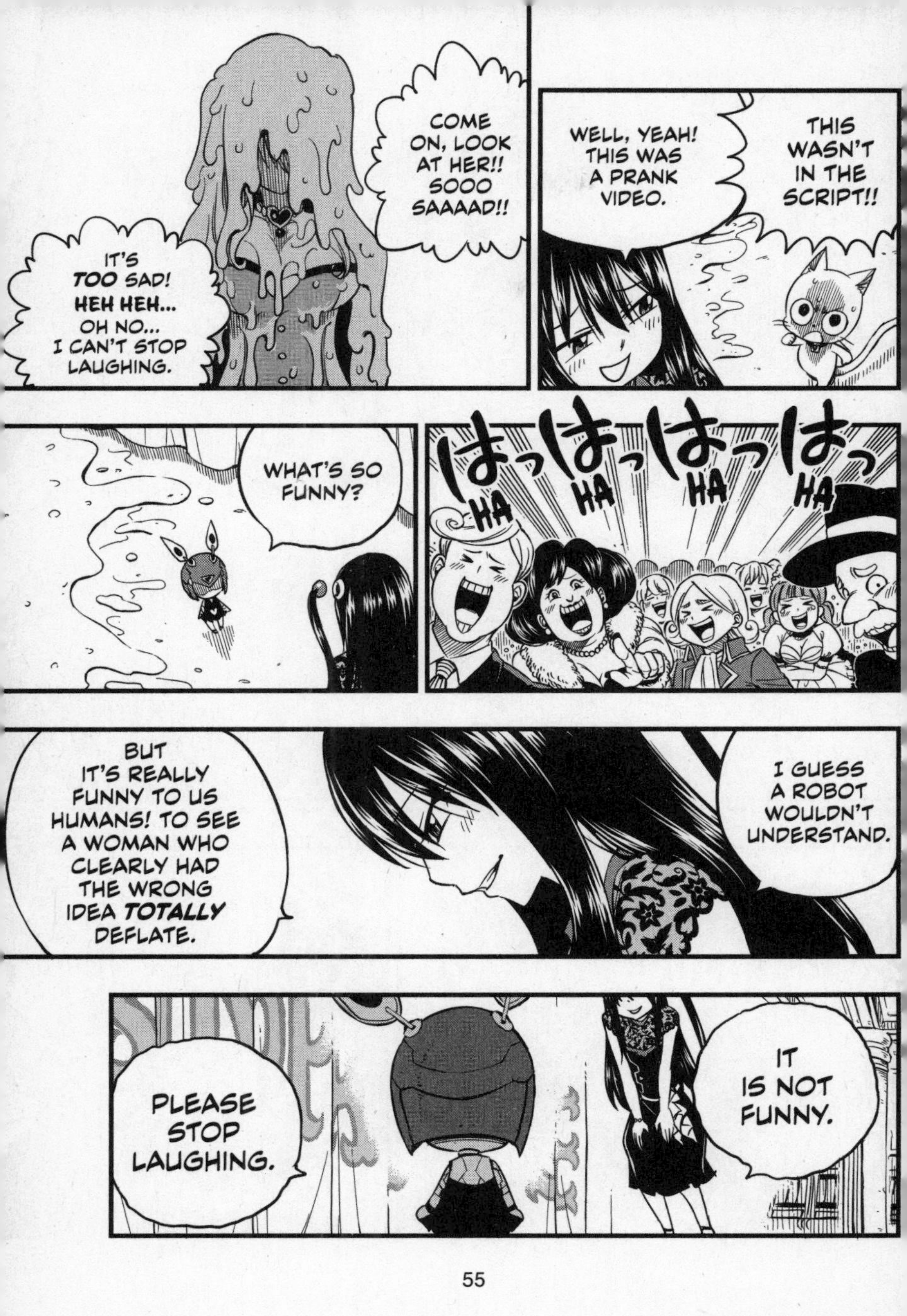
THIS WASN'T IN THE SCRIPT!!
WELL, YEAH! THIS WAS A PRANK VIDEO.
COME ON, LOOK AT HER!! SOOO SAAAAD!!
IT'S *TOO* SAD! **HEH HEH...** OH NO... I CAN'T STOP LAUGHING.
はっはっはっはっ
HA HA HA HA
WHAT'S SO FUNNY?
I GUESS A ROBOT WOULDN'T UNDERSTAND.
BUT IT'S REALLY FUNNY TO US HUMANS! TO SEE A WOMAN WHO CLEARLY HAD THE WRONG IDEA ***TOTALLY*** DEFLATE.
IT IS NOT FUNNY.
PLEASE STOP LAUGHING.

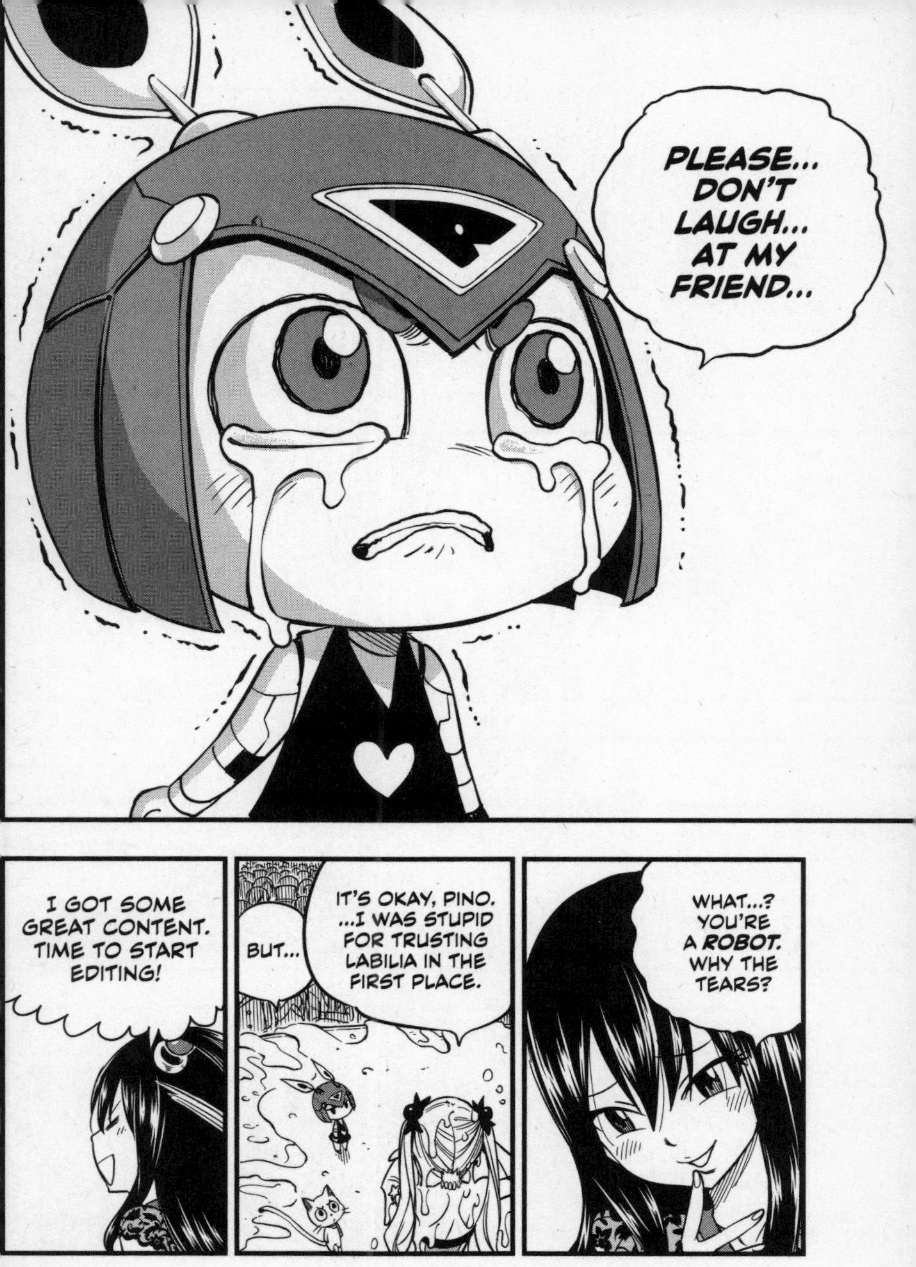
PLEASE... DON'T LAUGH... AT MY FRIEND...
WHAT...? YOU'RE A *ROBOT.* WHY THE TEARS?
IT'S OKAY, PINO. ...I WAS STUPID FOR TRUSTING LABILIA IN THE FIRST PLACE.
BUT...
I GOT SOME GREAT CONTENT. TIME TO START EDITING!

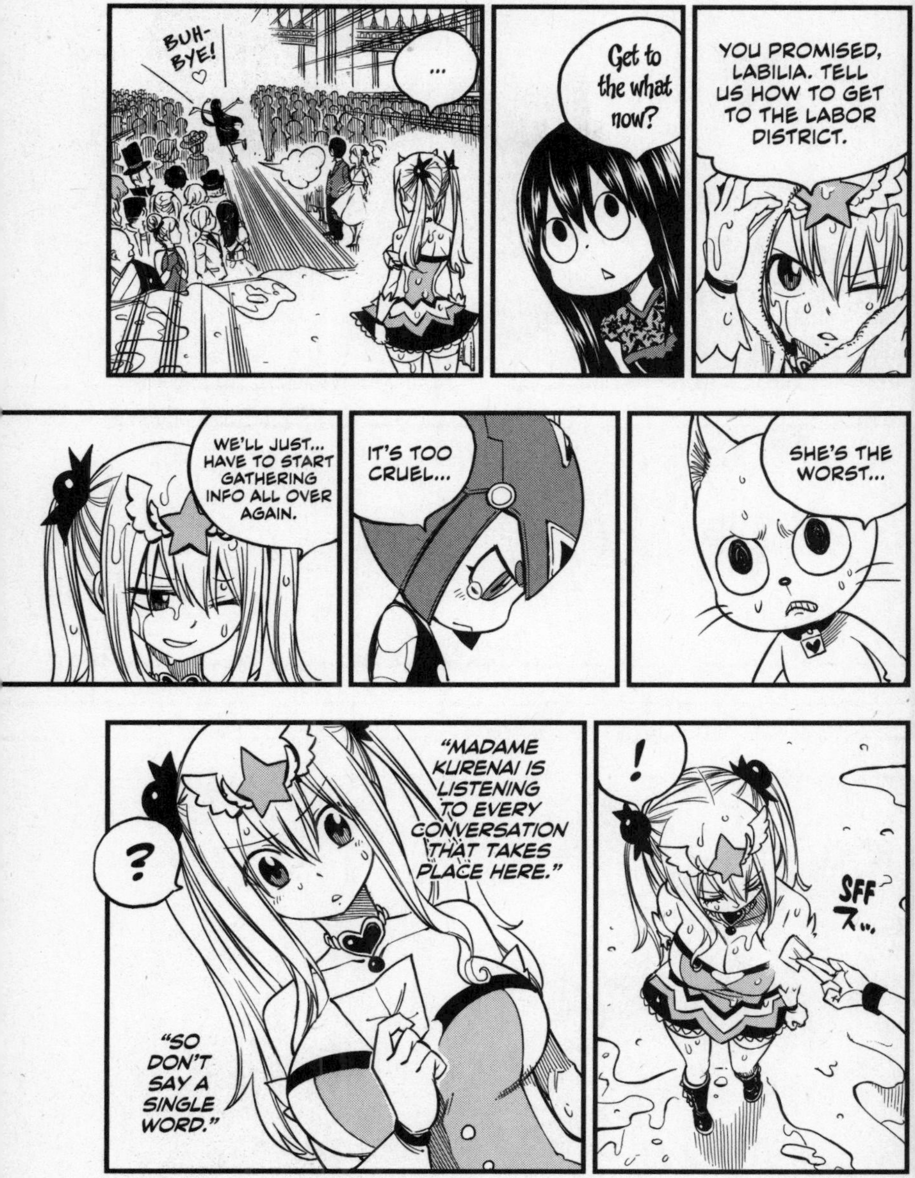
YOU PROMISED, LABILIA. TELL US HOW TO GET TO THE LABOR DISTRICT.
Get to the what now?
...
BUH-BYE! ♡
SHE'S THE WORST...
IT'S TOO CRUEL...
WE'LL JUST... HAVE TO START GATHERING INFO ALL OVER AGAIN.
!
SFF
ス..
"MADAME KURENAI IS LISTENING TO EVERY CONVERSATION THAT TAKES PLACE HERE."
?
"SO DON'T SAY A SINGLE WORD."

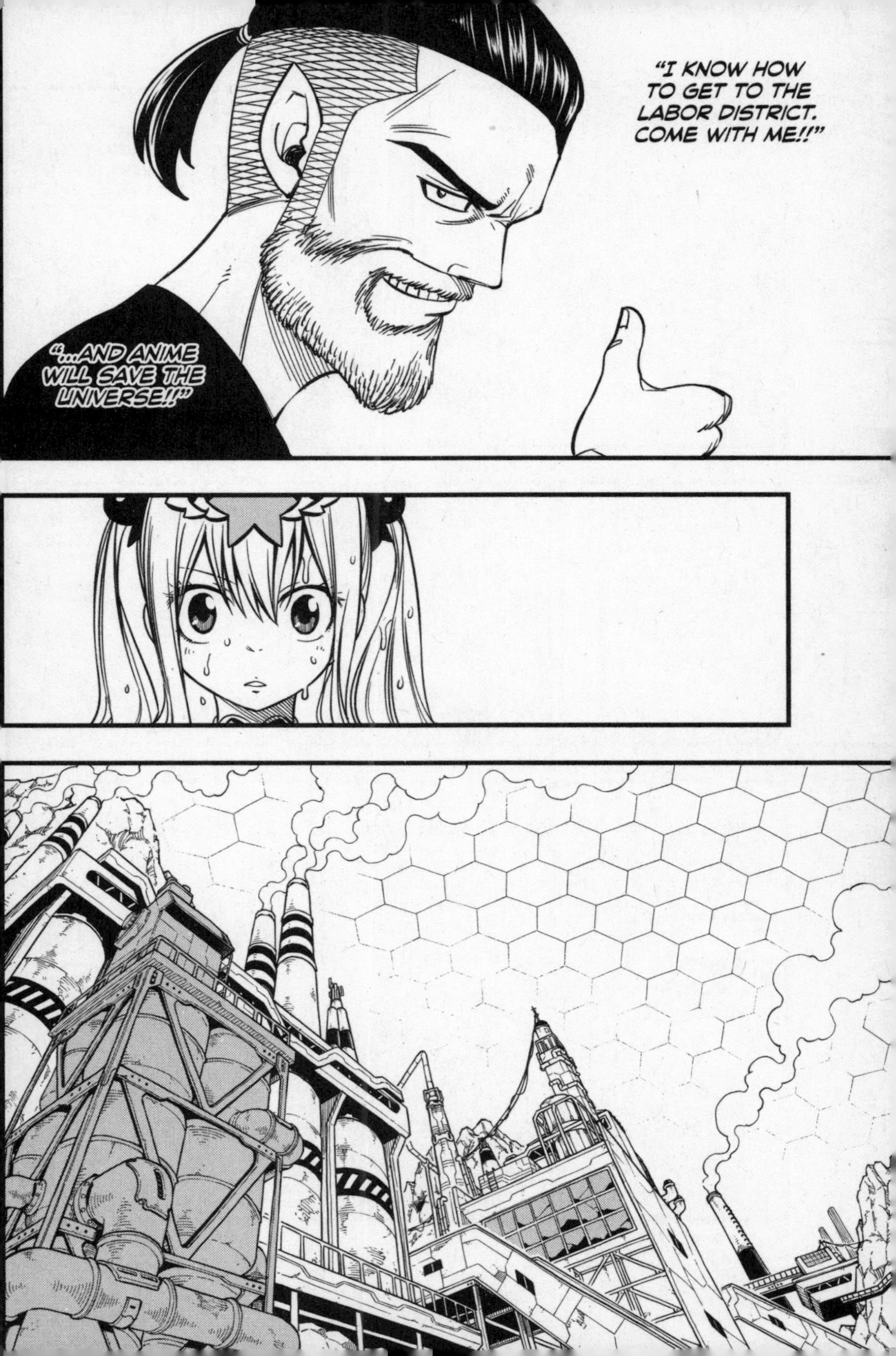
"I KNOW HOW TO GET TO THE LABOR DISTRICT. COME WITH ME!!"
"...AND ANIME WILL SAVE THE UNIVERSE!!"

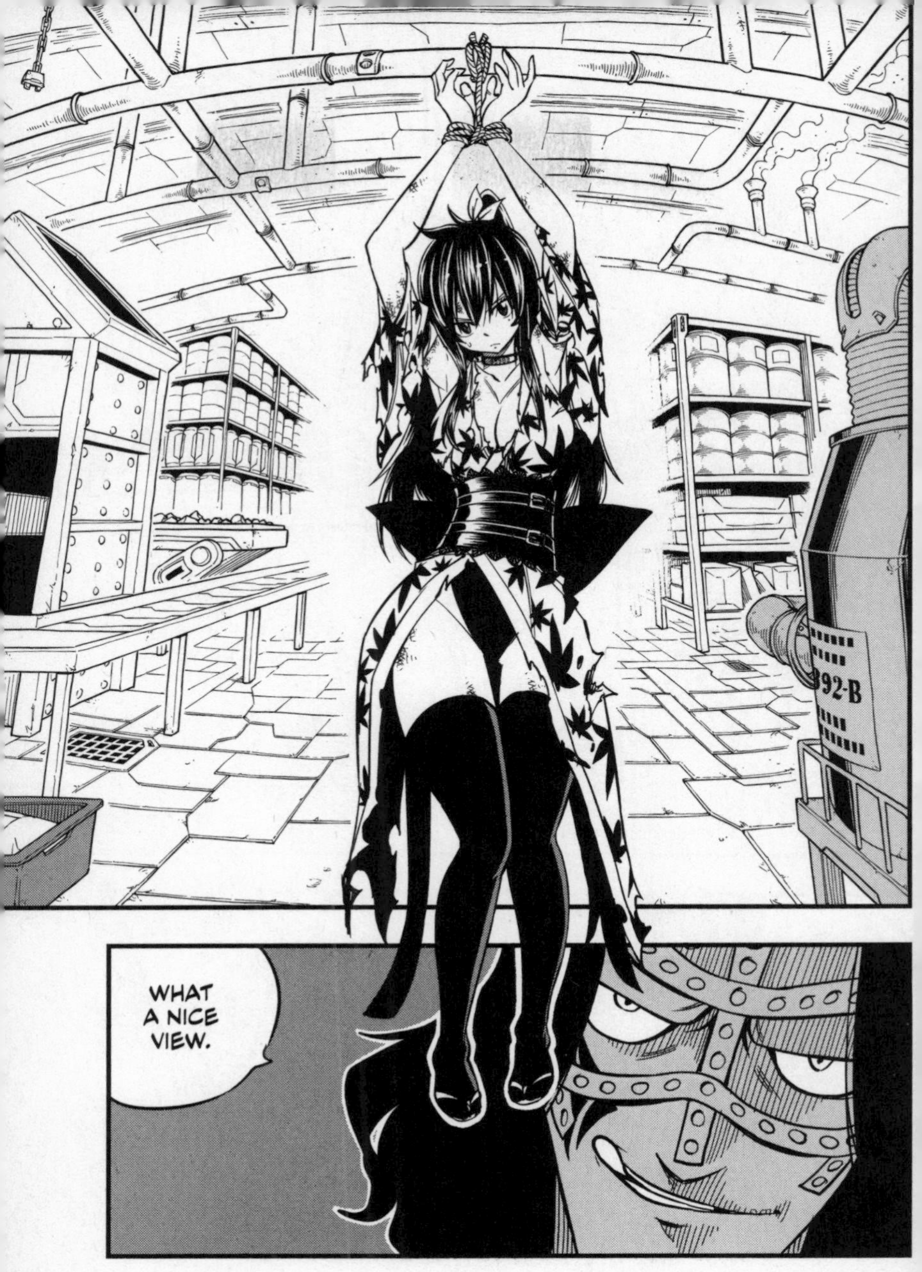
WHAT A NICE VIEW.

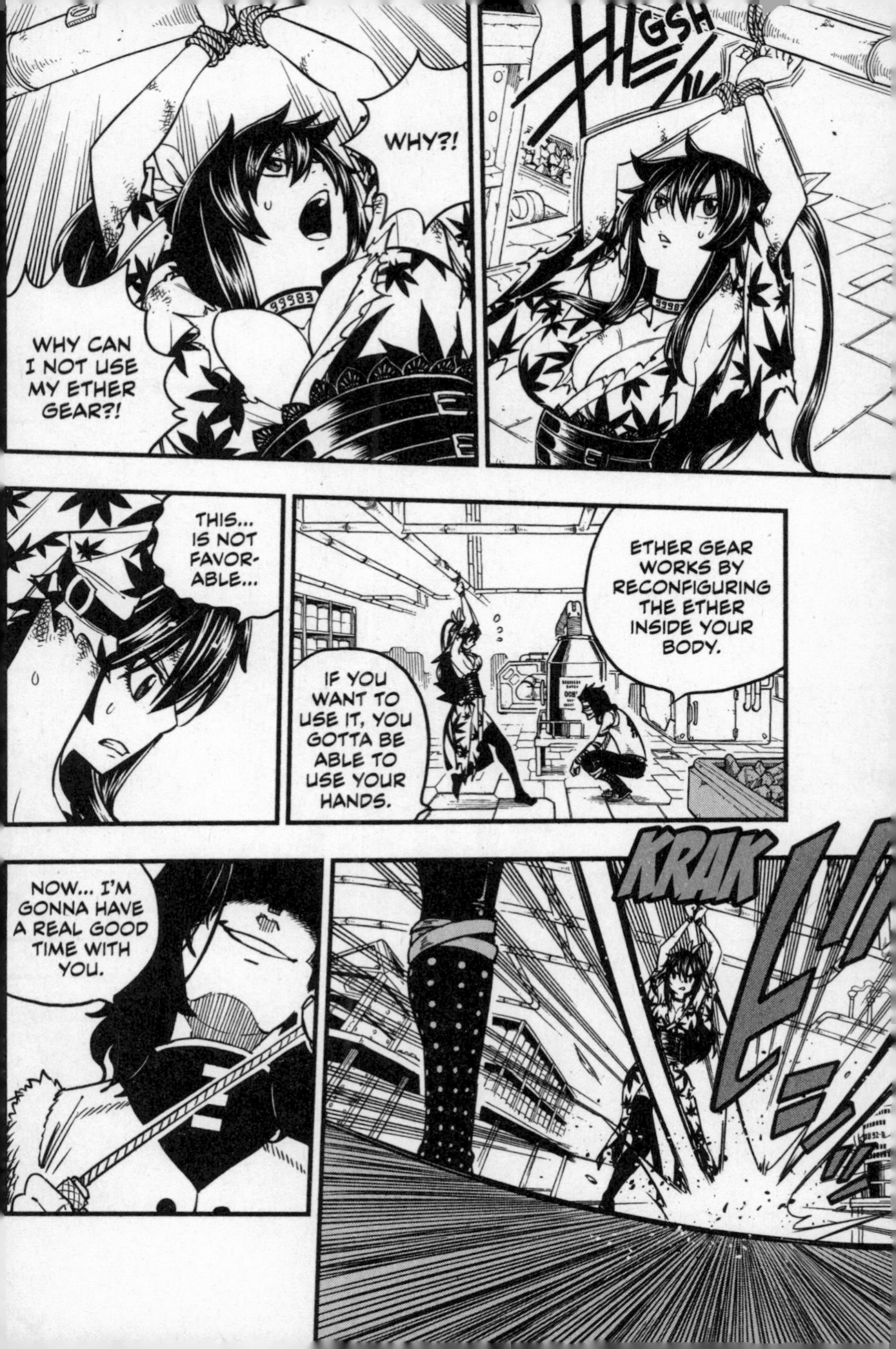
GSH
WHY?!
WHY CAN I NOT USE MY ETHER GEAR?!
ETHER GEAR WORKS BY RECONFIGURING THE ETHER INSIDE YOUR BODY.
IF YOU WANT TO USE IT, YOU GOTTA BE ABLE TO USE YOUR HANDS.
THIS... IS NOT FAVORABLE...
KRAK
NOW... I'M GONNA HAVE A REAL GOOD TIME WITH YOU.

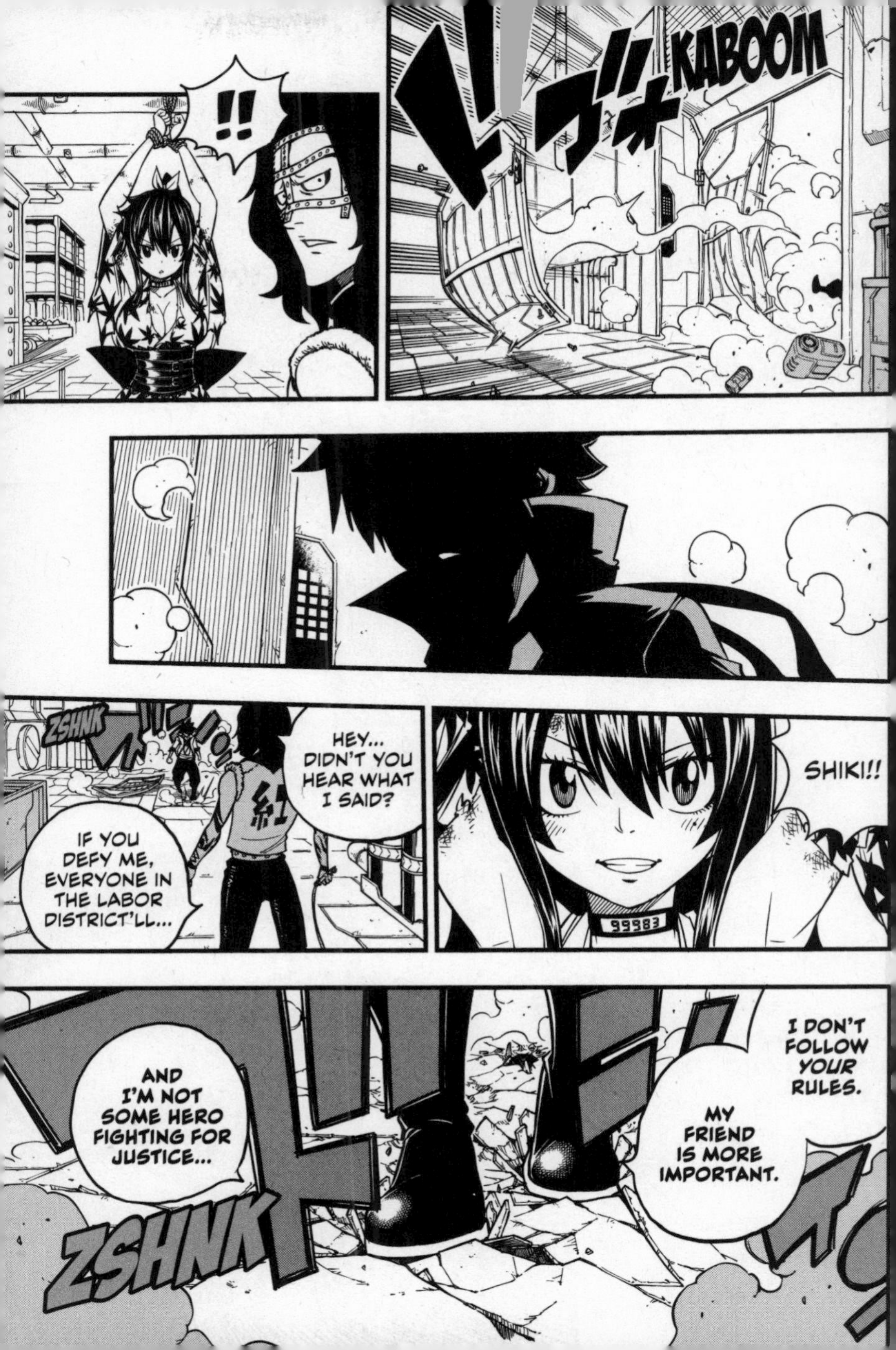
KABOOM
!!
SHIKI!!
99983
HEY... DIDN'T YOU HEAR WHAT I SAID?
ZSHNK
IF YOU DEFY ME, EVERYONE IN THE LABOR DISTRICT'LL...
I DON'T FOLLOW YOUR RULES.
MY FRIEND IS MORE IMPORTANT.
AND I'M NOT SOME HERO FIGHTING FOR JUSTICE...
ZSHNK

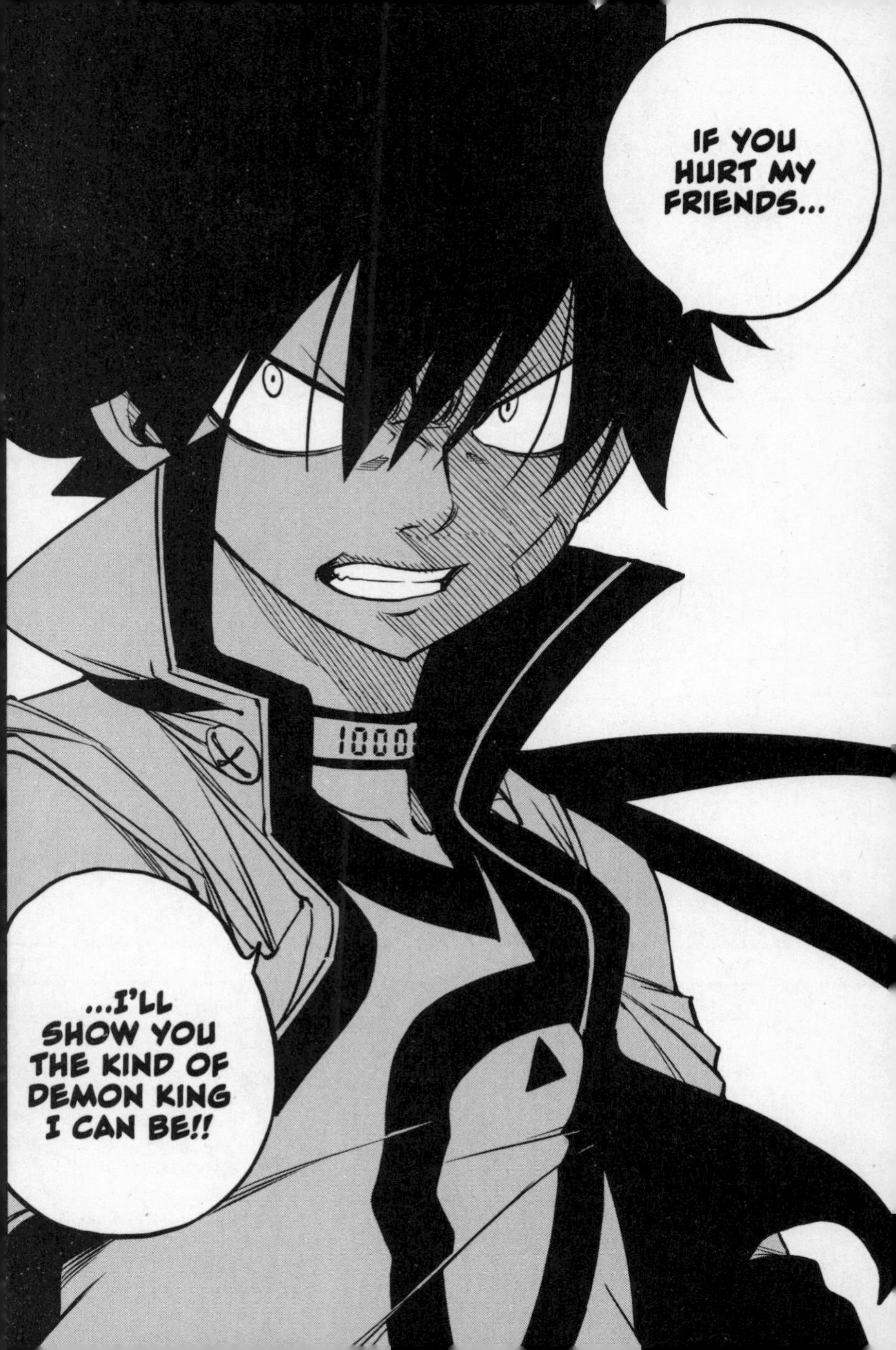
IF YOU HURT MY FRIENDS...
1000
...I'LL SHOW YOU THE KIND OF DEMON KING I CAN BE!!

EDENS ZERO

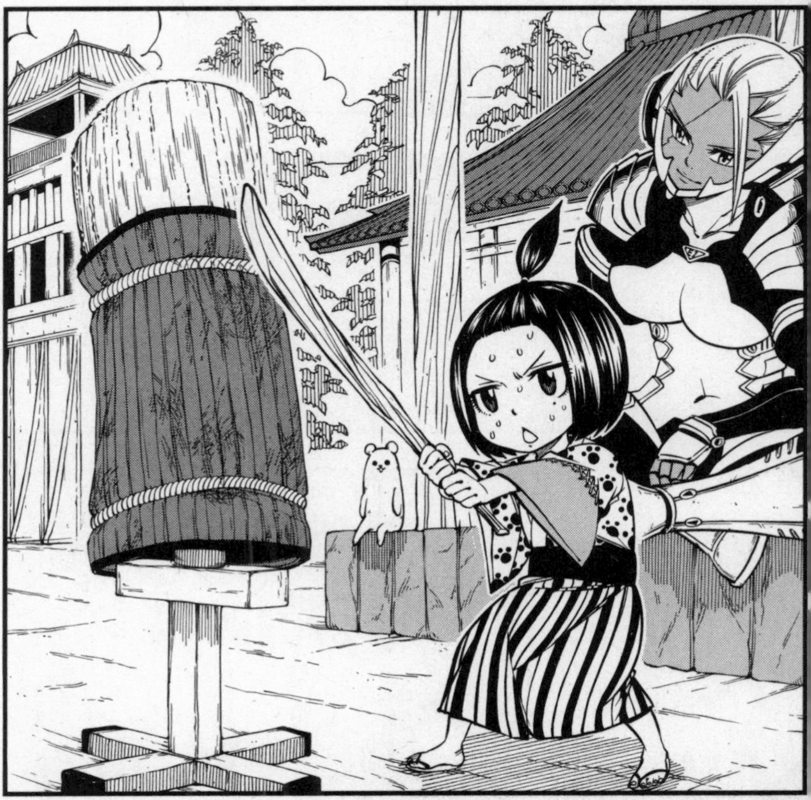

CHAPTER 54: THE TRUTH IS IN THE CUBE

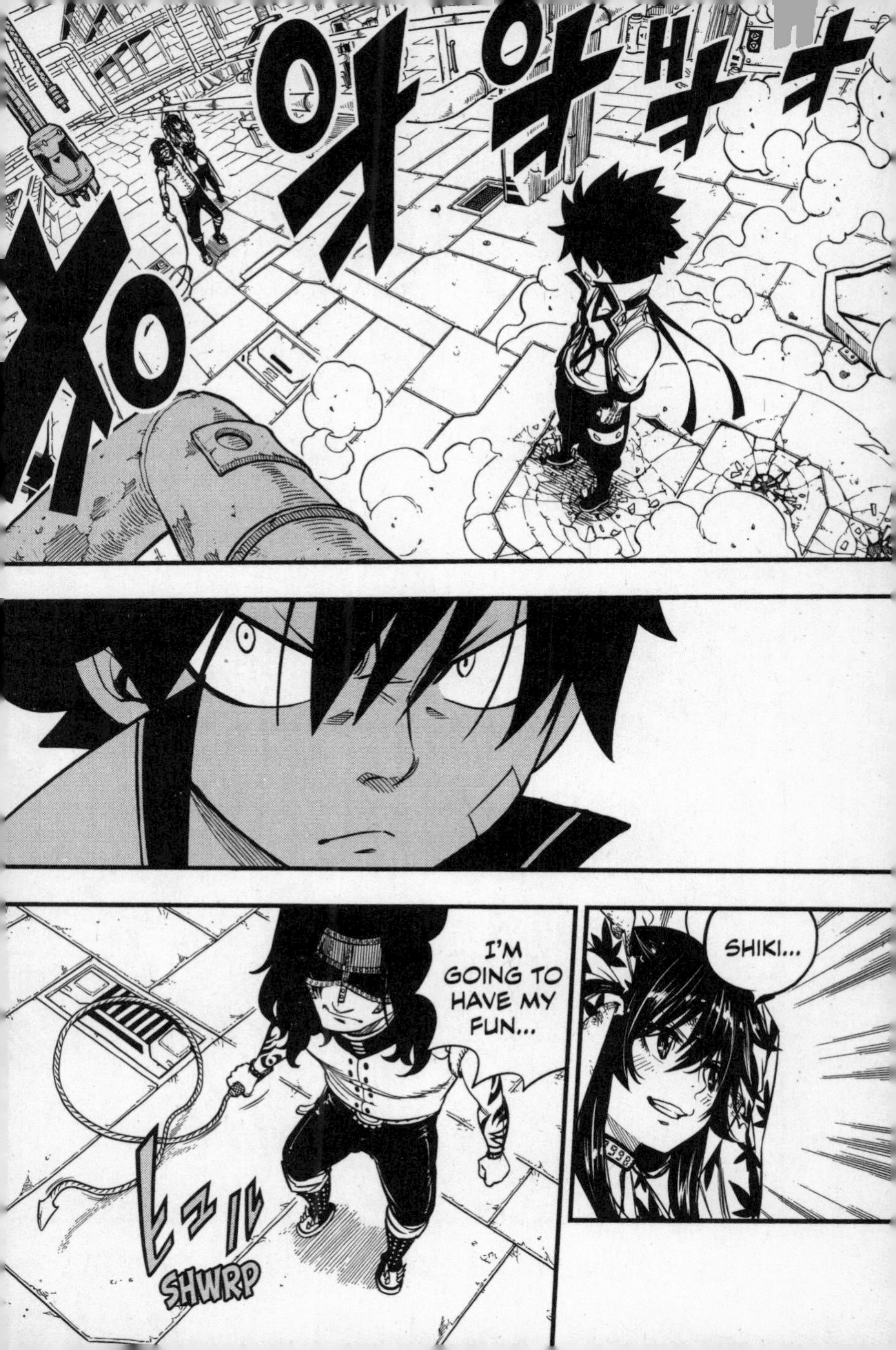
SHIKI...
I'M GOING TO HAVE MY FUN...
SHWRP

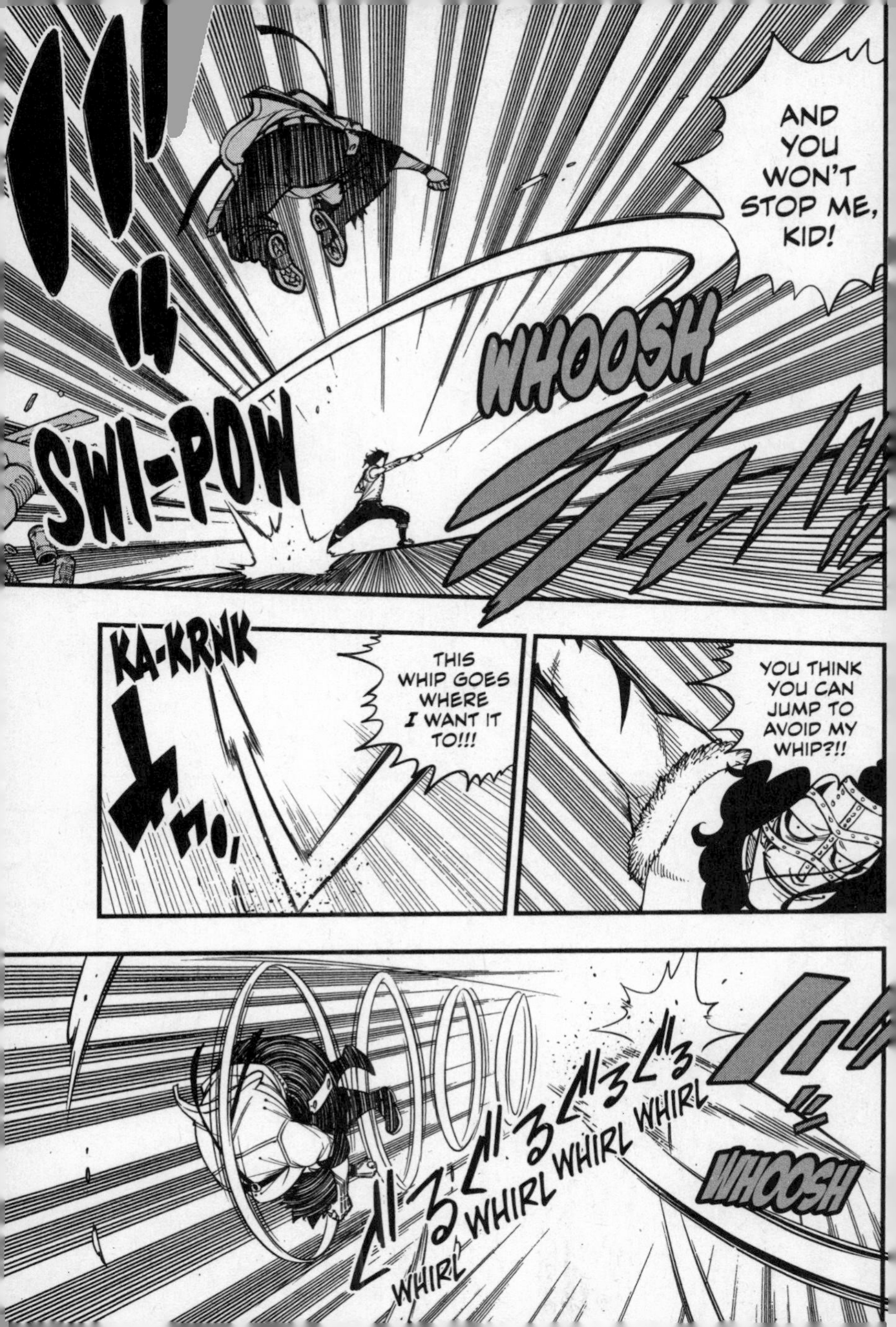
AND YOU WON'T STOP ME, KID!
WHOOSH
SWI-POW
YOU THINK YOU CAN JUMP TO AVOID MY WHIP?!!
KA-KRNK
THIS WHIP GOES WHERE I WANT IT TO!!!
WHOOSH
WHIRL WHIRL WHIRL WHIRL WHIRL

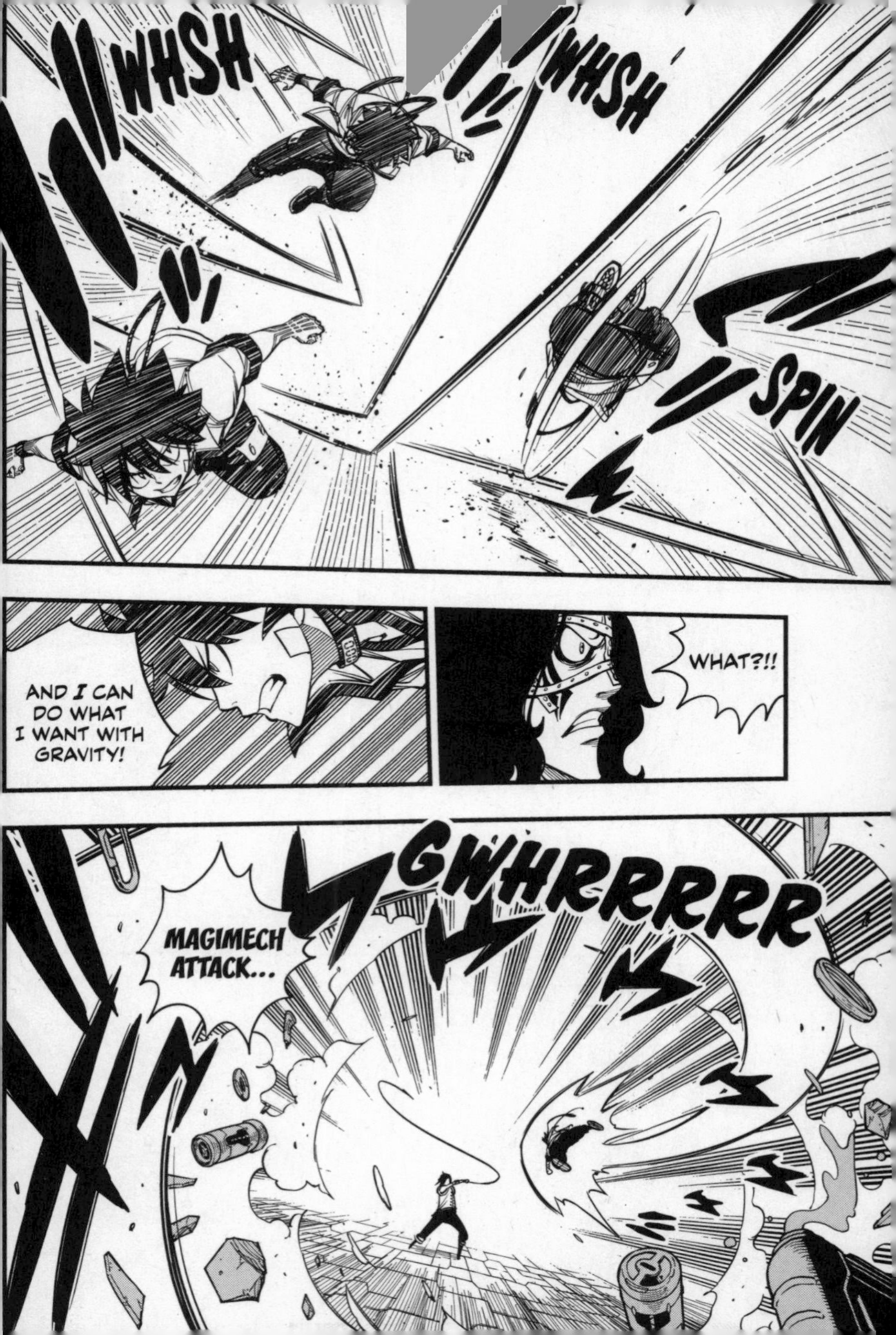
WHSH
SPIN
WHSH
WHAT?!!
AND I CAN DO WHAT I WANT WITH GRAVITY!
GWHRRRRR
MAGIMECH ATTACK...

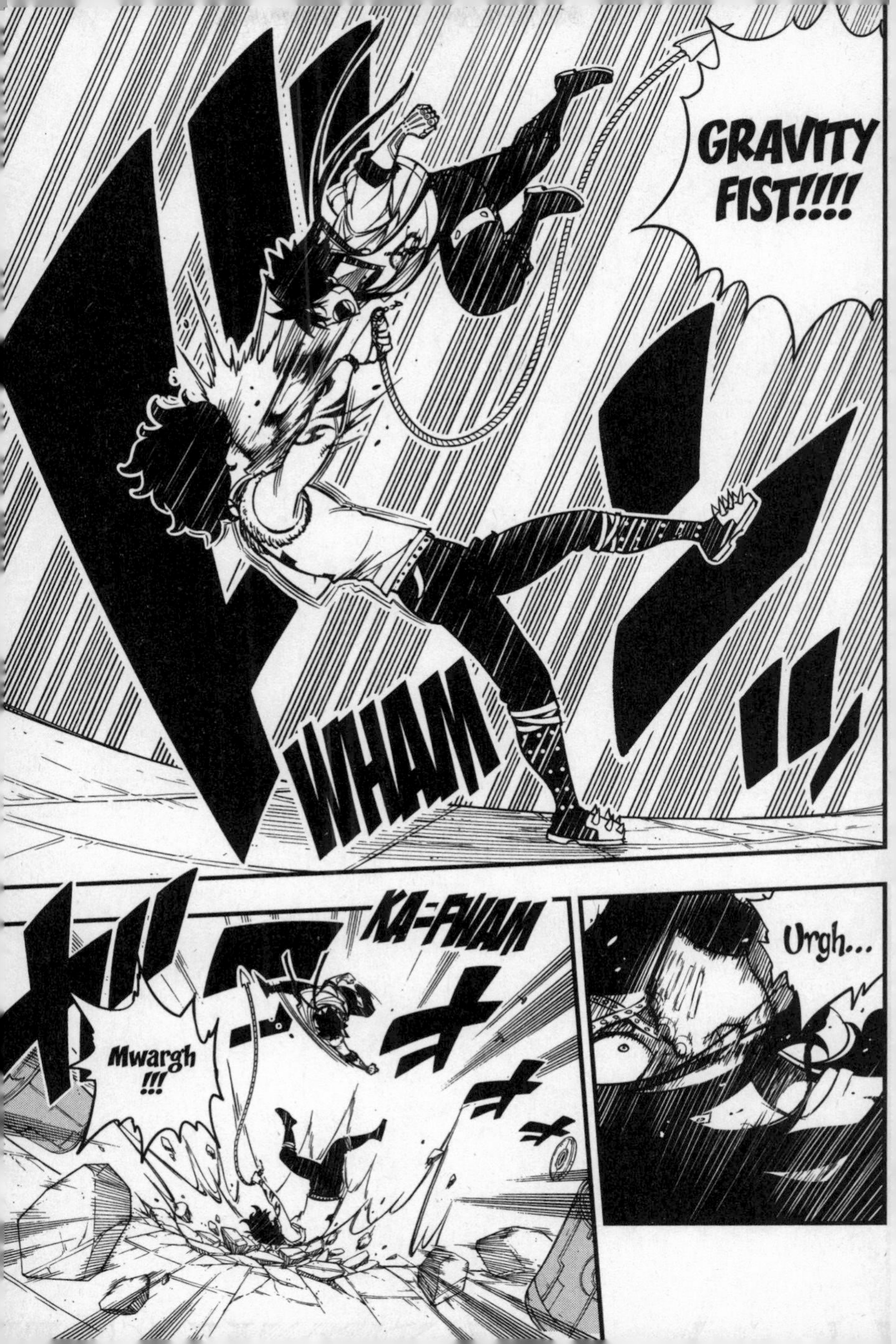
GRAVITY FIST!!!!
WHAM
Urgh...
KA-FWAM
Mwargh!!!

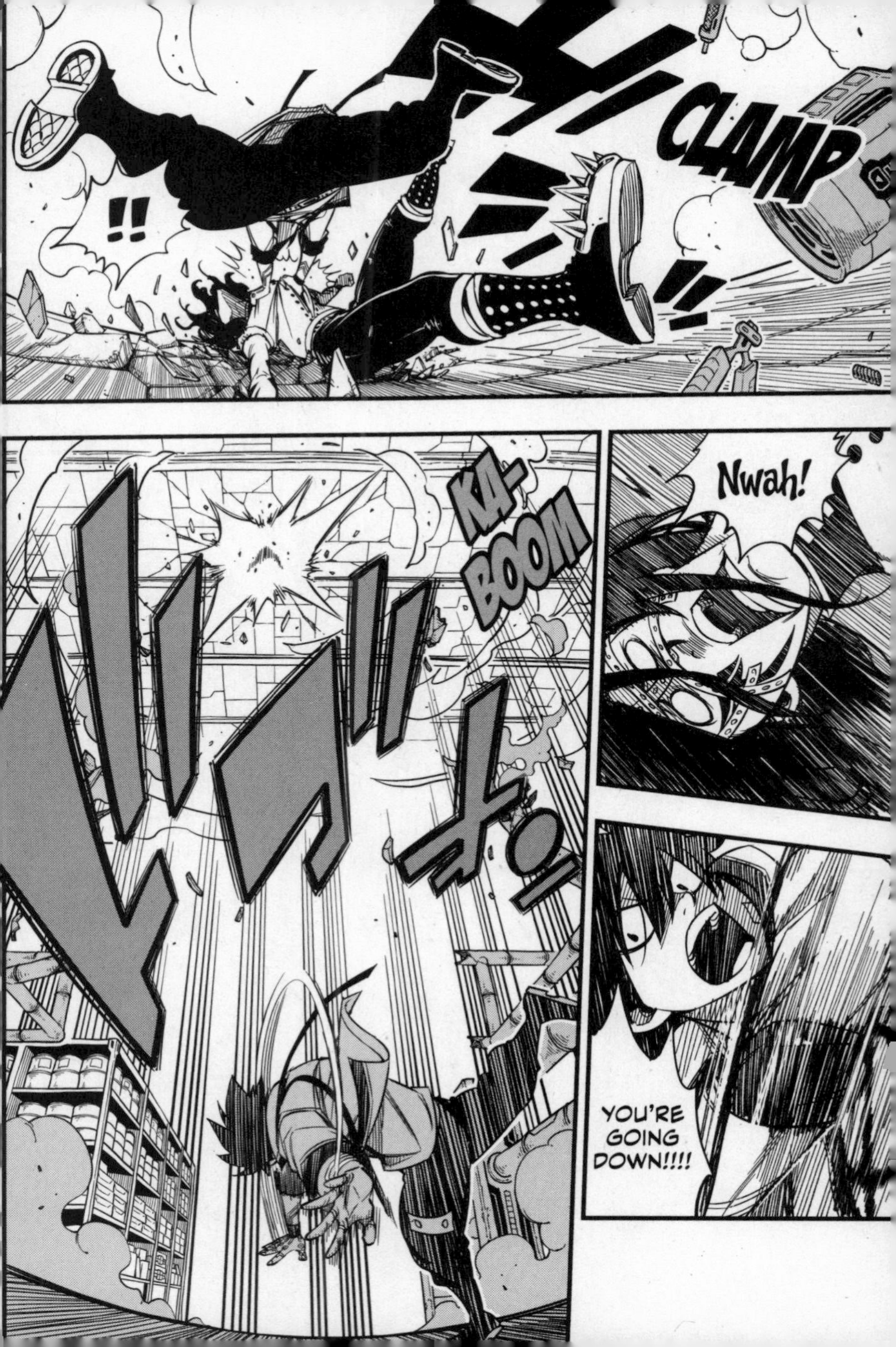
CLAMP
!!
Nwah!
YOU'RE GOING DOWN!!!!
KA-BOOM

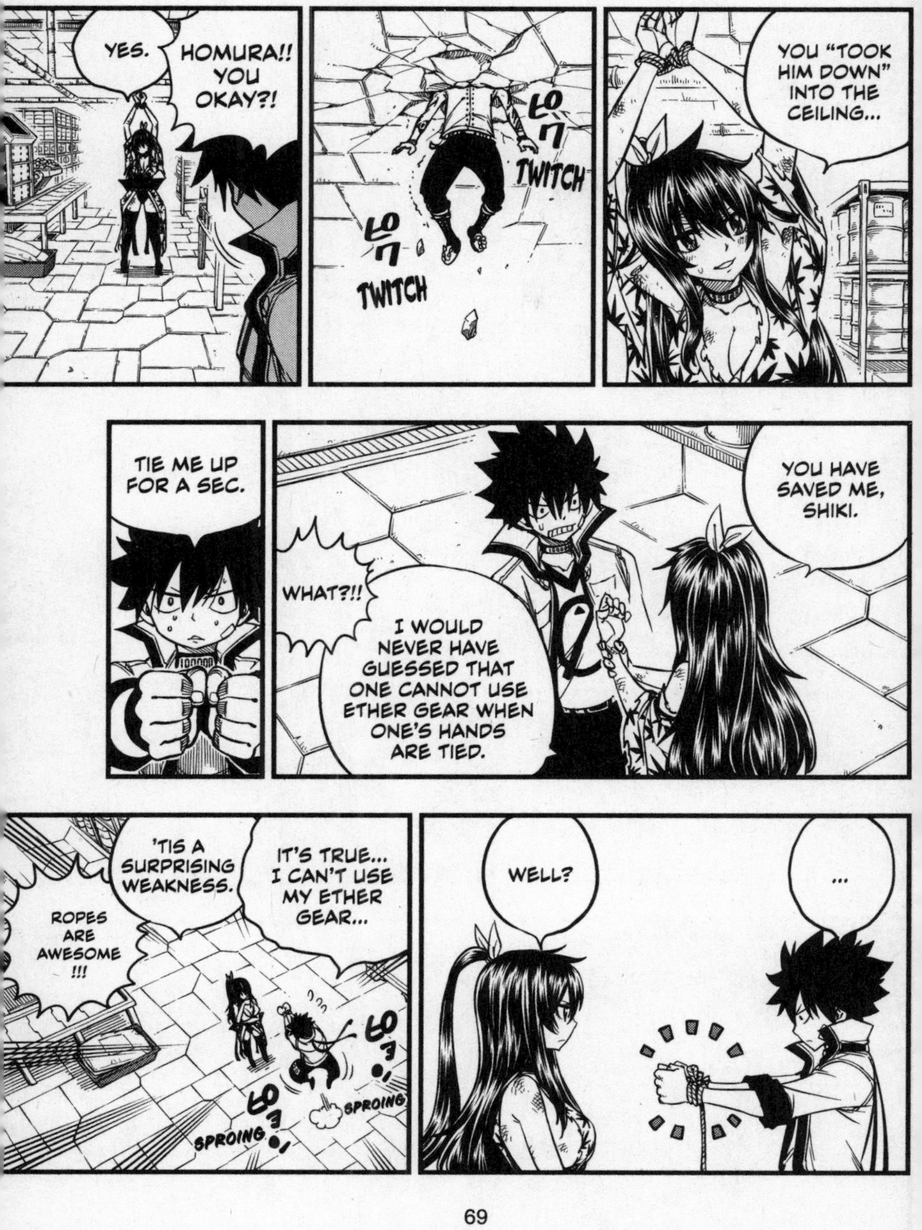
YOU "TOOK HIM DOWN" INTO THE CEILING...
ピク
TWITCH
ピク
TWITCH
HOMURA!! YOU OKAY?!
YES.
YOU HAVE SAVED ME, SHIKI.
WHAT?!!
I WOULD NEVER HAVE GUESSED THAT ONE CANNOT USE ETHER GEAR WHEN ONE'S HANDS ARE TIED.
TIE ME UP FOR A SEC.
...
WELL?
IT'S TRUE... I CAN'T USE MY ETHER GEAR...
'TIS A SURPRISING WEAKNESS.
ROPES ARE AWESOME !!!
ピョーン
SPROING
ピョーン
SPROING

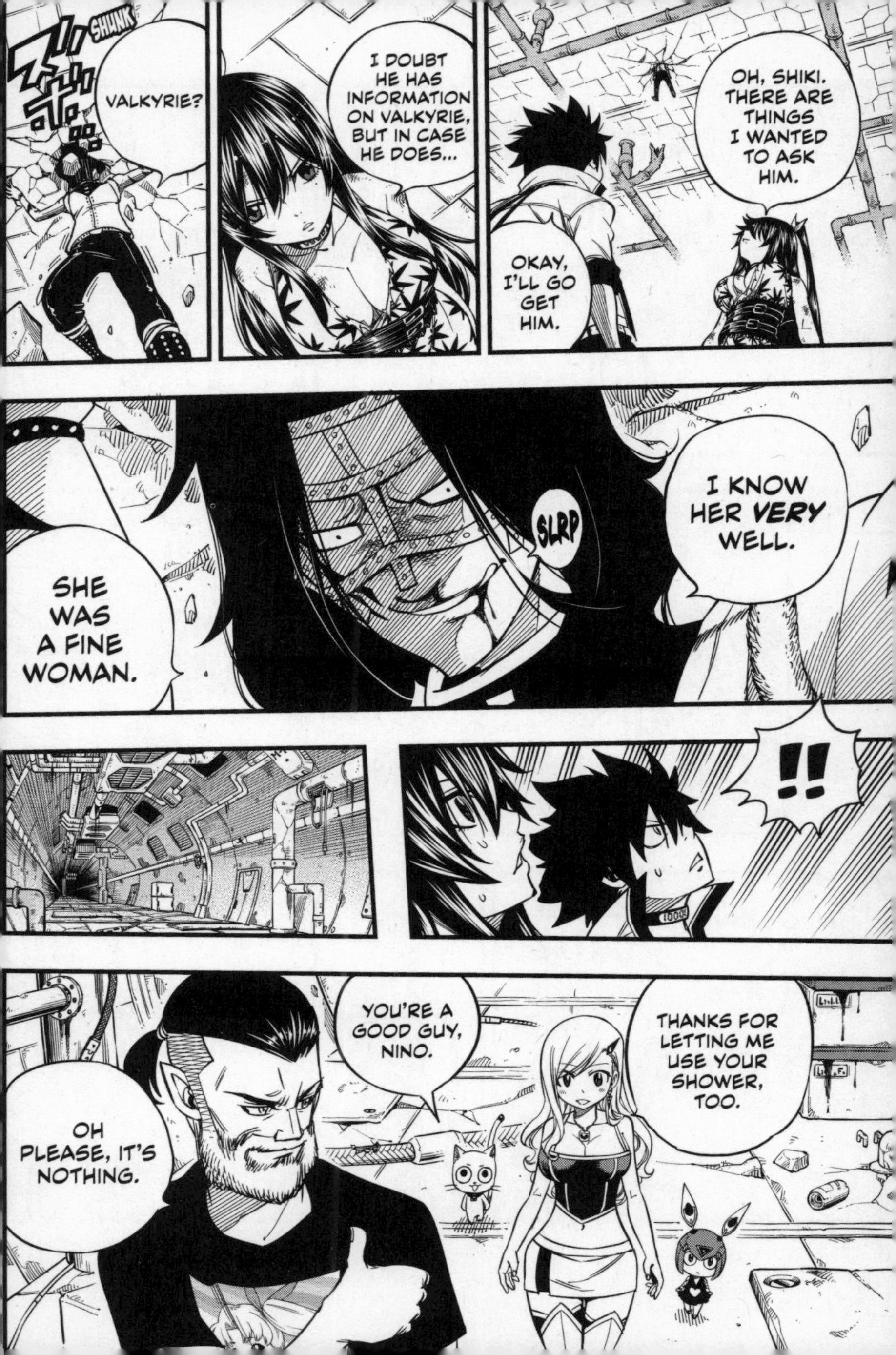
OH, SHIKI. THERE ARE THINGS I WANTED TO ASK HIM.
OKAY, I'LL GO GET HIM.
I DOUBT HE HAS INFORMATION ON VALKYRIE, BUT IN CASE HE DOES...
SHUNK
VALKYRIE?
I KNOW HER **VERY** WELL.
SLRP
SHE WAS A FINE WOMAN.
!!
THANKS FOR LETTING ME USE YOUR SHOWER, TOO.
YOU'RE A GOOD GUY, NINO.
OH PLEASE, IT'S NOTHING.

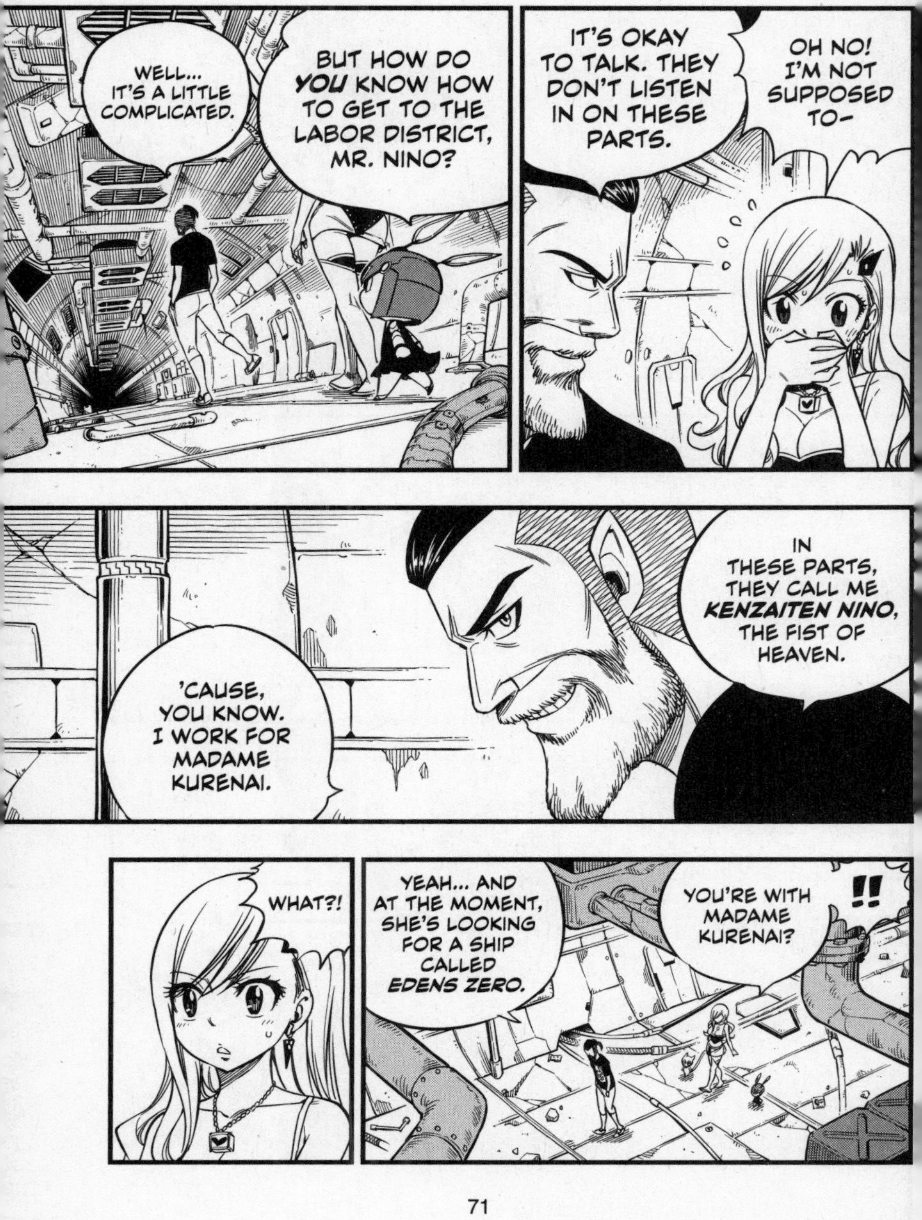
OH NO! I'M NOT SUPPOSED TO-
IT'S OKAY TO TALK. THEY DON'T LISTEN IN ON THESE PARTS.
BUT HOW DO *YOU* KNOW HOW TO GET TO THE LABOR DISTRICT, MR. NINO?
WELL... IT'S A LITTLE COMPLICATED.
IN THESE PARTS, THEY CALL ME *KENZAITEN NINO*, THE FIST OF HEAVEN.
'CAUSE, YOU KNOW. I WORK FOR MADAME KURENAI.
!!
YOU'RE WITH MADAME KURENAI?
YEAH... AND AT THE MOMENT, SHE'S LOOKING FOR A SHIP CALLED *EDENS ZERO.*
WHAT?!

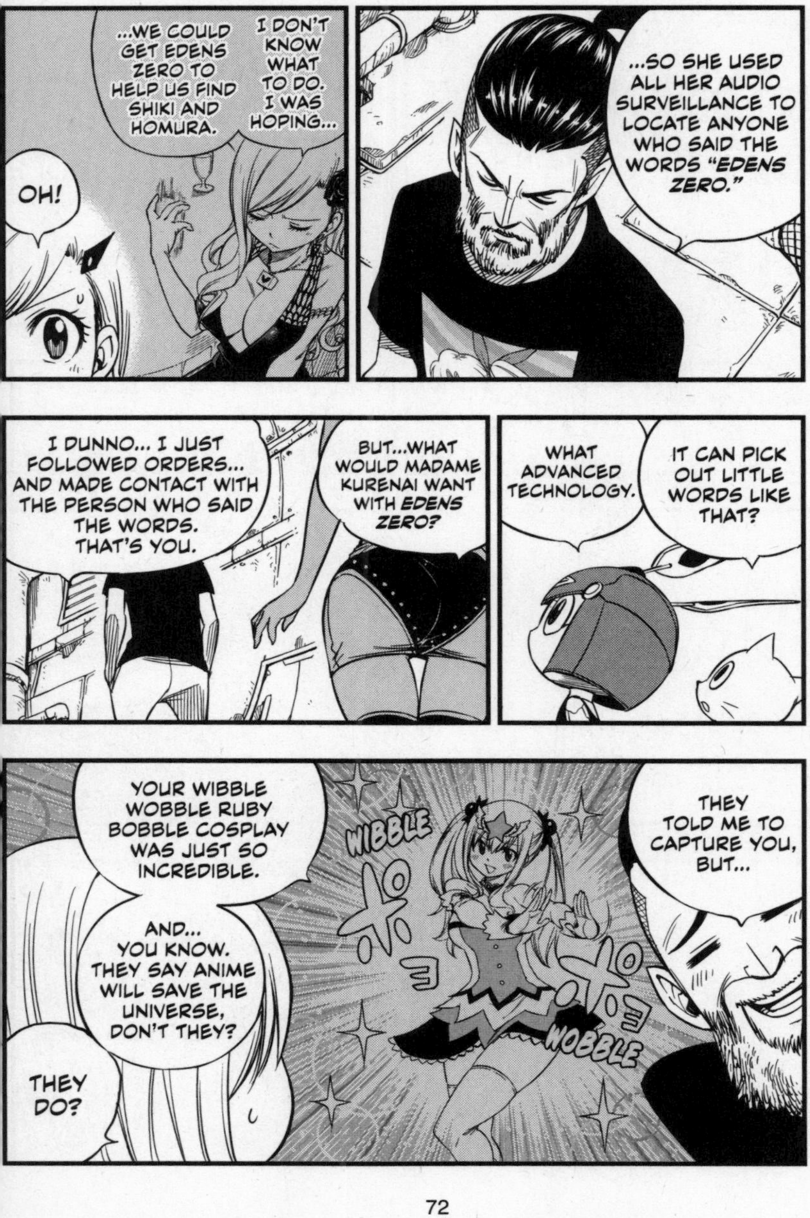
...SO SHE USED ALL HER AUDIO SURVEILLANCE TO LOCATE ANYONE WHO SAID THE WORDS "EDENS ZERO."
I DON'T KNOW WHAT TO DO. I WAS HOPING...
...WE COULD GET EDENS ZERO TO HELP US FIND SHIKI AND HOMURA.
OH!
IT CAN PICK OUT LITTLE WORDS LIKE THAT?
WHAT ADVANCED TECHNOLOGY.
BUT...WHAT WOULD MADAME KURENAI WANT WITH *EDENS ZERO?*
I DUNNO... I JUST FOLLOWED ORDERS... AND MADE CONTACT WITH THE PERSON WHO SAID THE WORDS. THAT'S YOU.
THEY TOLD ME TO CAPTURE YOU, BUT...
WIBBLE
YOUR WIBBLE WOBBLE RUBY BOBBLE COSPLAY WAS JUST SO INCREDIBLE.
AND... YOU KNOW. THEY SAY ANIME WILL SAVE THE UNIVERSE, DON'T THEY?
WOBBLE
THEY DO?

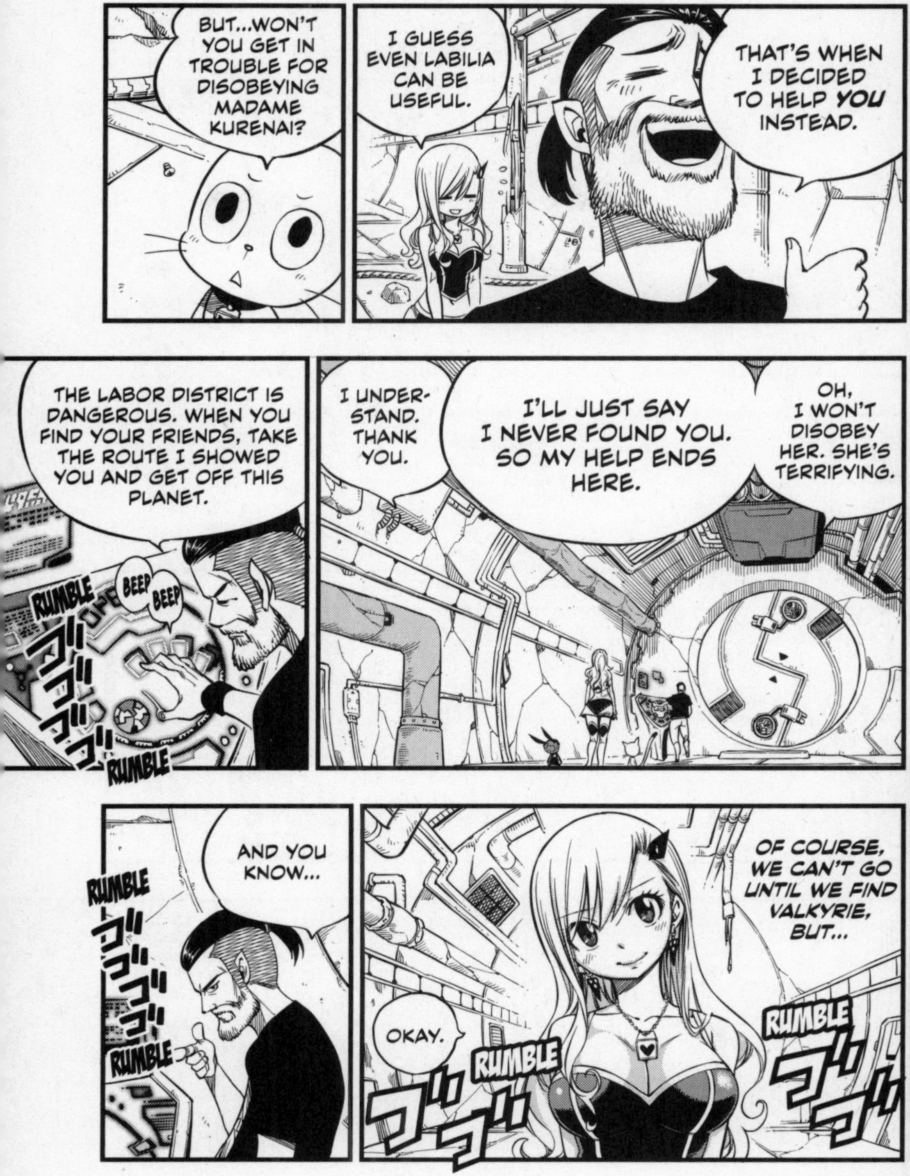
THAT'S WHEN I DECIDED TO HELP *YOU* INSTEAD.
I GUESS EVEN LABILIA CAN BE USEFUL.
BUT...WON'T YOU GET IN TROUBLE FOR DISOBEYING MADAME KURENAI?
OH, I WON'T DISOBEY HER. SHE'S TERRIFYING.
I'LL JUST SAY I NEVER FOUND YOU. SO MY HELP ENDS HERE.
I UNDER-STAND. THANK YOU.
THE LABOR DISTRICT IS DANGEROUS. WHEN YOU FIND YOUR FRIENDS, TAKE THE ROUTE I SHOWED YOU AND GET OFF THIS PLANET.
BEEP
BEEP
RUMBLE
RUMBLE
OF COURSE, WE CAN'T GO UNTIL WE FIND VALKYRIE, BUT...
OKAY.
RUMBLE
RUMBLE
AND YOU KNOW...
RUMBLE
RUMBLE

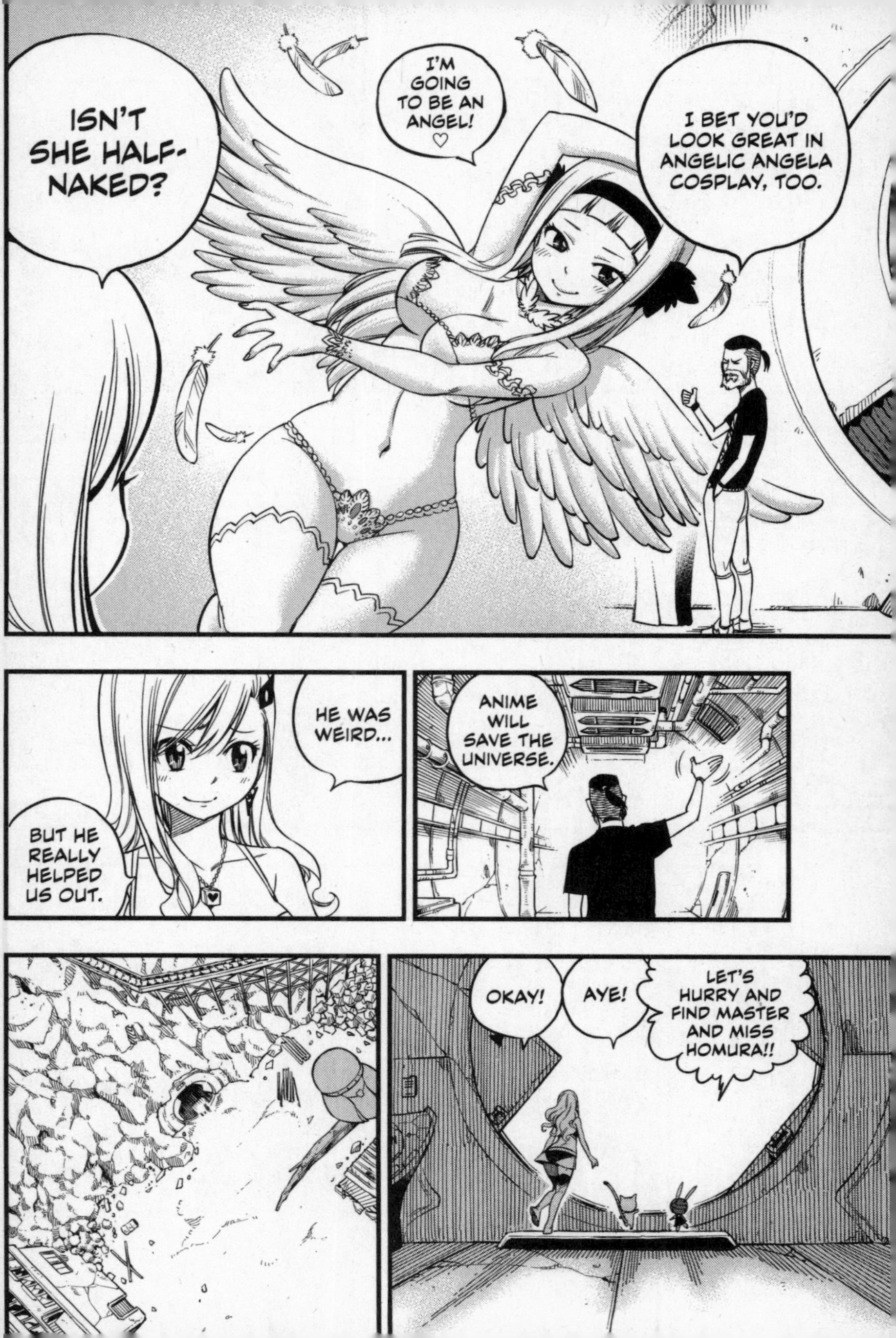
I BET YOU'D LOOK GREAT IN ANGELIC ANGELA COSPLAY, TOO.
I'M GOING TO BE AN ANGEL! ♡
ISN'T SHE HALF-NAKED?
ANIME WILL SAVE THE UNIVERSE.
HE WAS WEIRD...
BUT HE REALLY HELPED US OUT.
LET'S HURRY AND FIND MASTER AND MISS HOMURA!!
AYE!
OKAY!

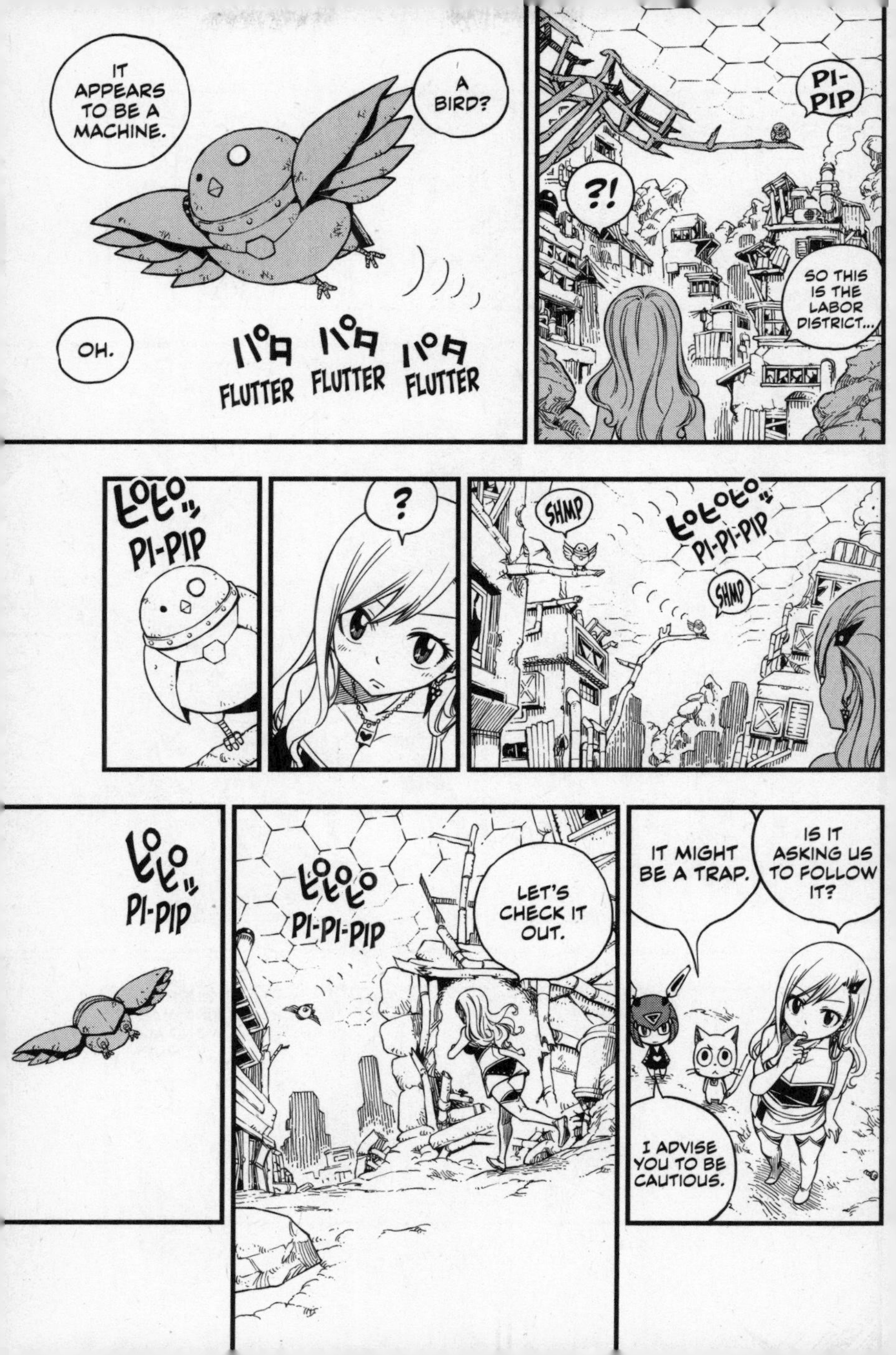
PI-PIP
?!
SO THIS IS THE LABOR DISTRICT...
A BIRD?
IT APPEARS TO BE A MACHINE.
OH.
パタ FLUTTER
パタ FLUTTER
パタ FLUTTER
SHMP
PI-PI-PIP
SHMP
?
PI-PIP
IS IT ASKING US TO FOLLOW IT?
IT MIGHT BE A TRAP.
I ADVISE YOU TO BE CAUTIOUS.
LET'S CHECK IT OUT.
PI-PI-PIP
PI-PIP

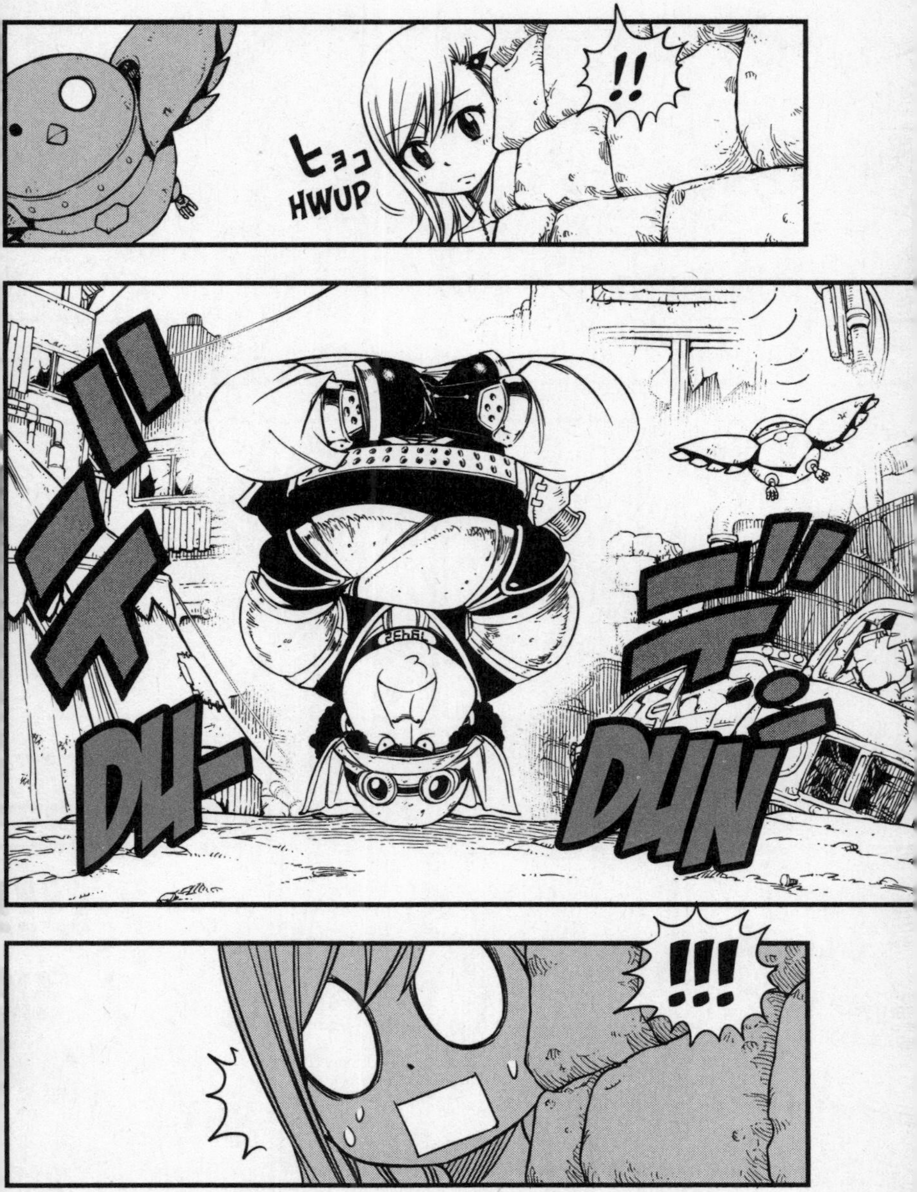
!!
ヒョコ
HWUP
DU-
DUN
!!!

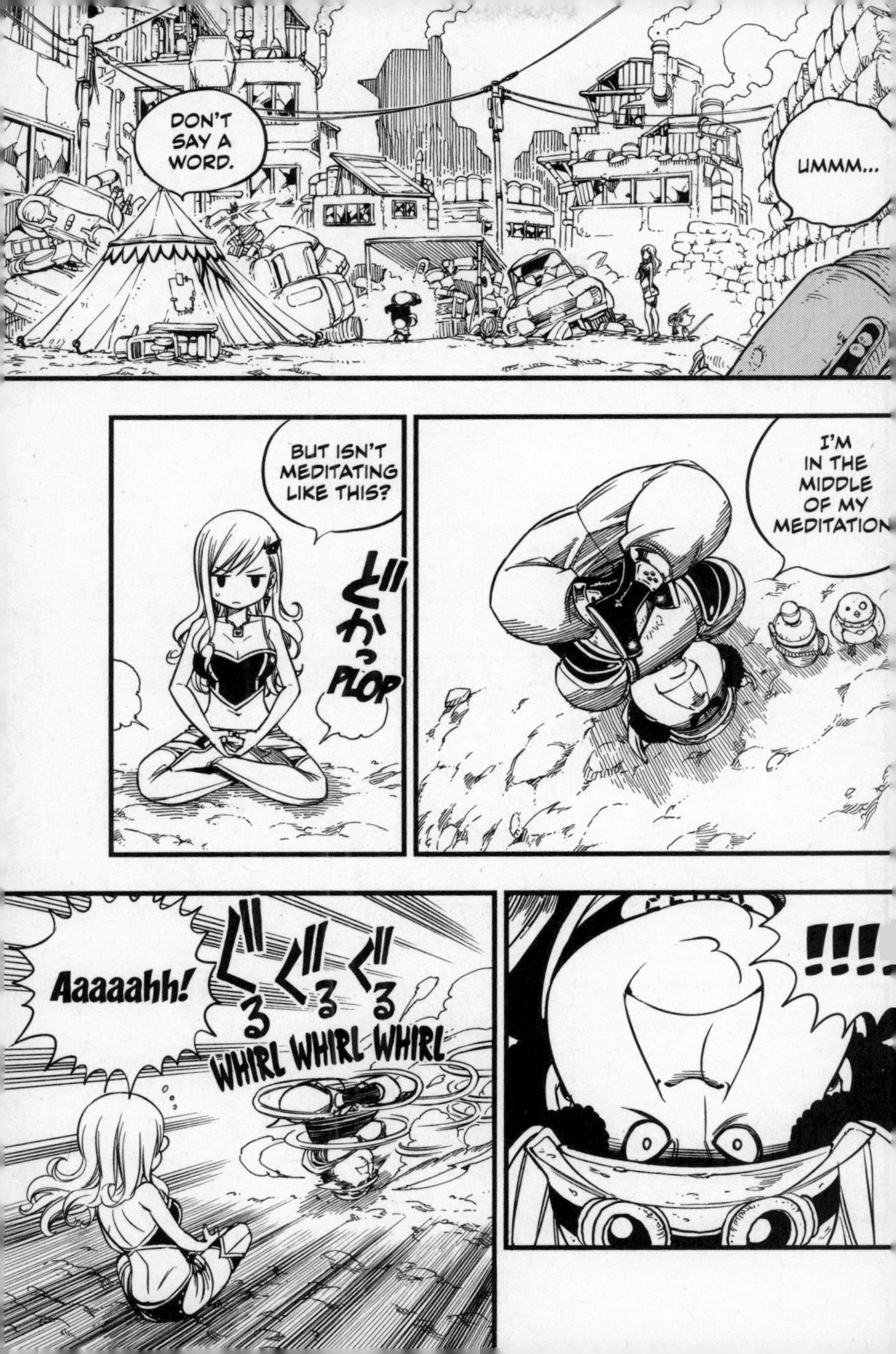
UMMM...
DON'T SAY A WORD.
I'M IN THE MIDDLE OF MY MEDITATION
BUT ISN'T MEDITATING LIKE THIS?
どかっ
PLOP
!!!
Aaaaahh!
ぐるぐるぐる
WHIRL WHIRL WHIRL

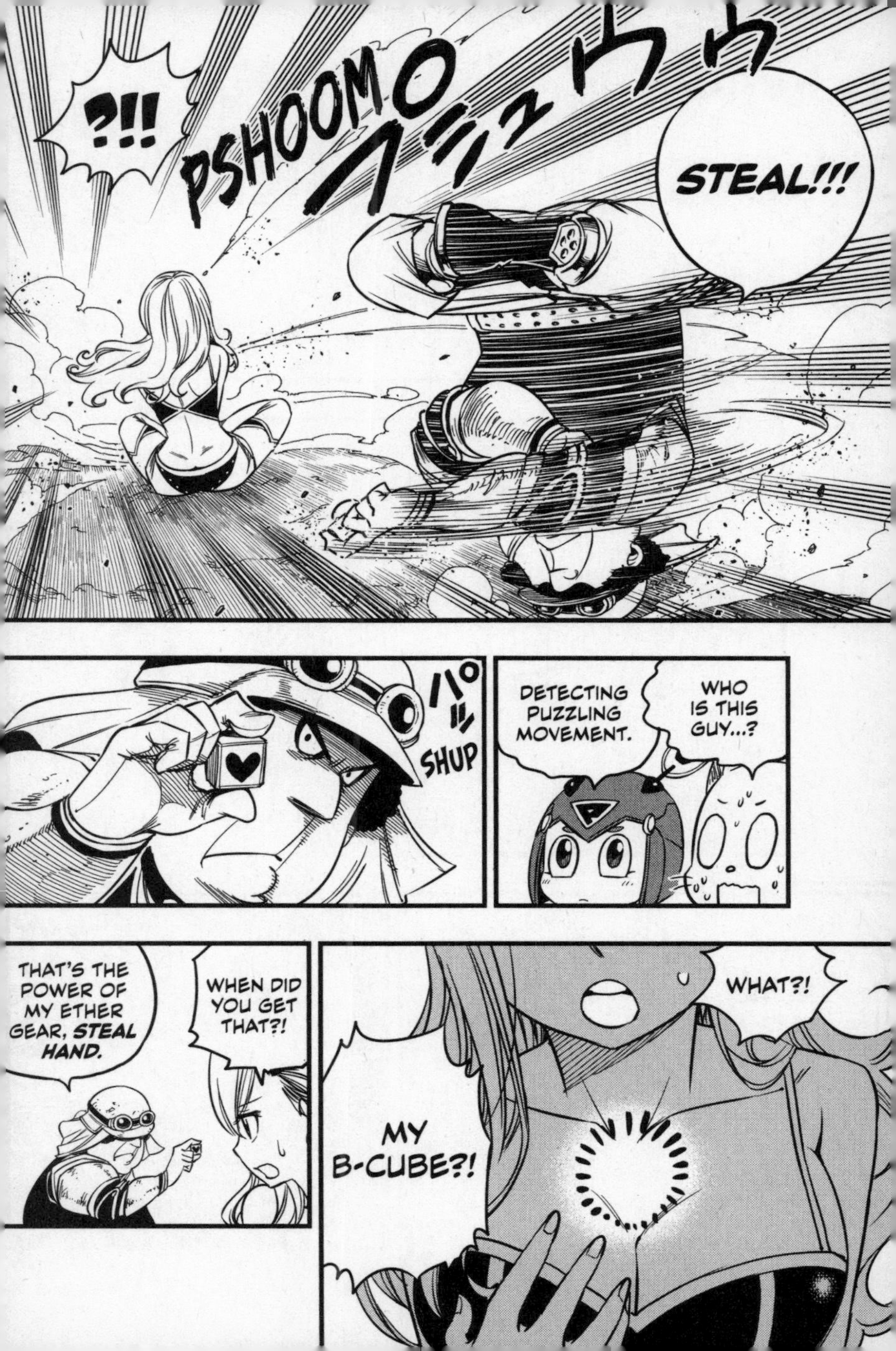
STEAL!!!
PSHOOM
?!!
WHO IS THIS GUY...?
DETECTING PUZZLING MOVEMENT.
SHUP
WHAT?!
MY B-CUBE?!
WHEN DID YOU GET THAT?!
THAT'S THE POWER OF MY ETHER GEAR, STEAL HAND.

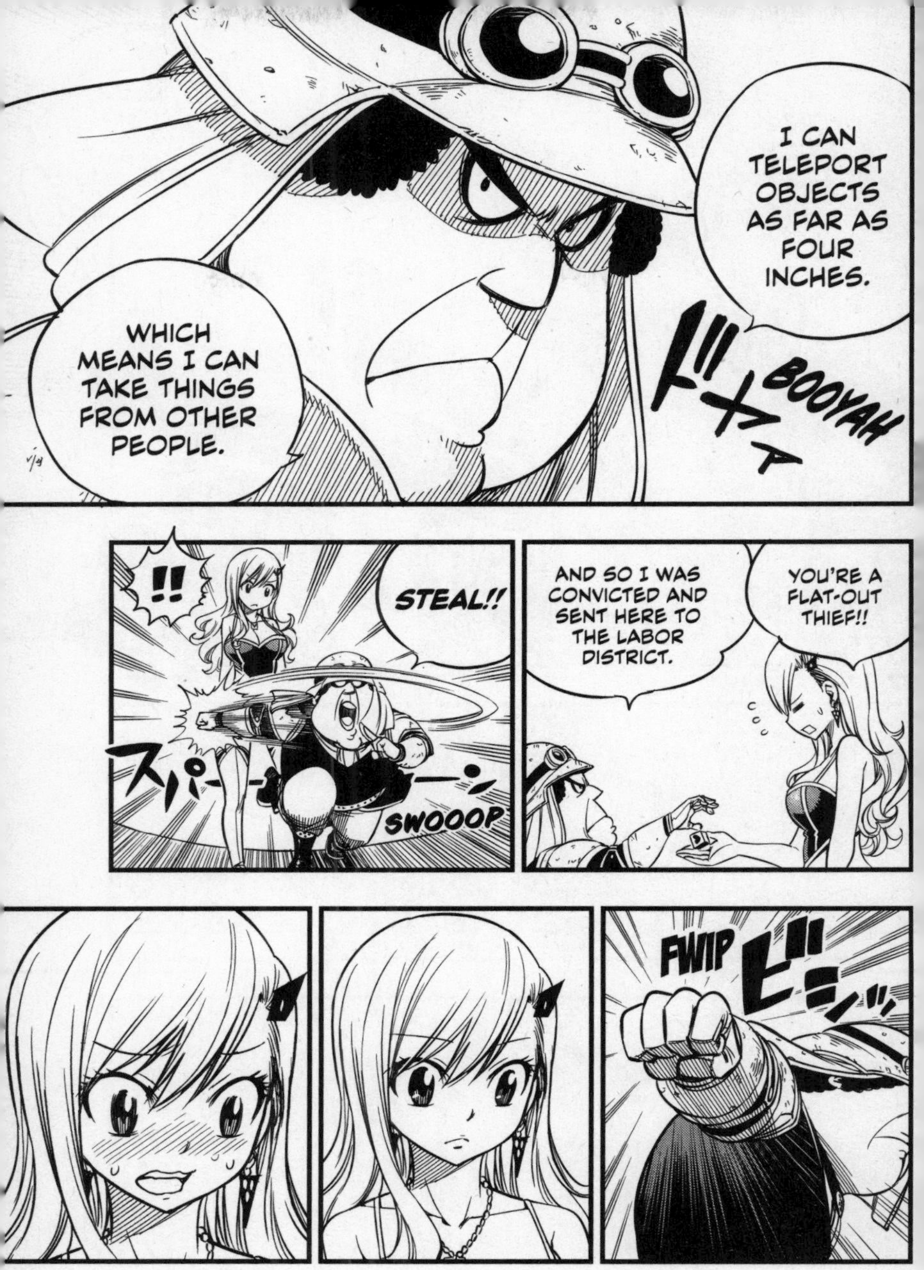
I CAN TELEPORT OBJECTS AS FAR AS FOUR INCHES.
BOOYAH
WHICH MEANS I CAN TAKE THINGS FROM OTHER PEOPLE.
YOU'RE A FLAT-OUT THIEF!!
AND SO I WAS CONVICTED AND SENT HERE TO THE LABOR DISTRICT.
STEAL!!
!!
SWOOOP
FWIP

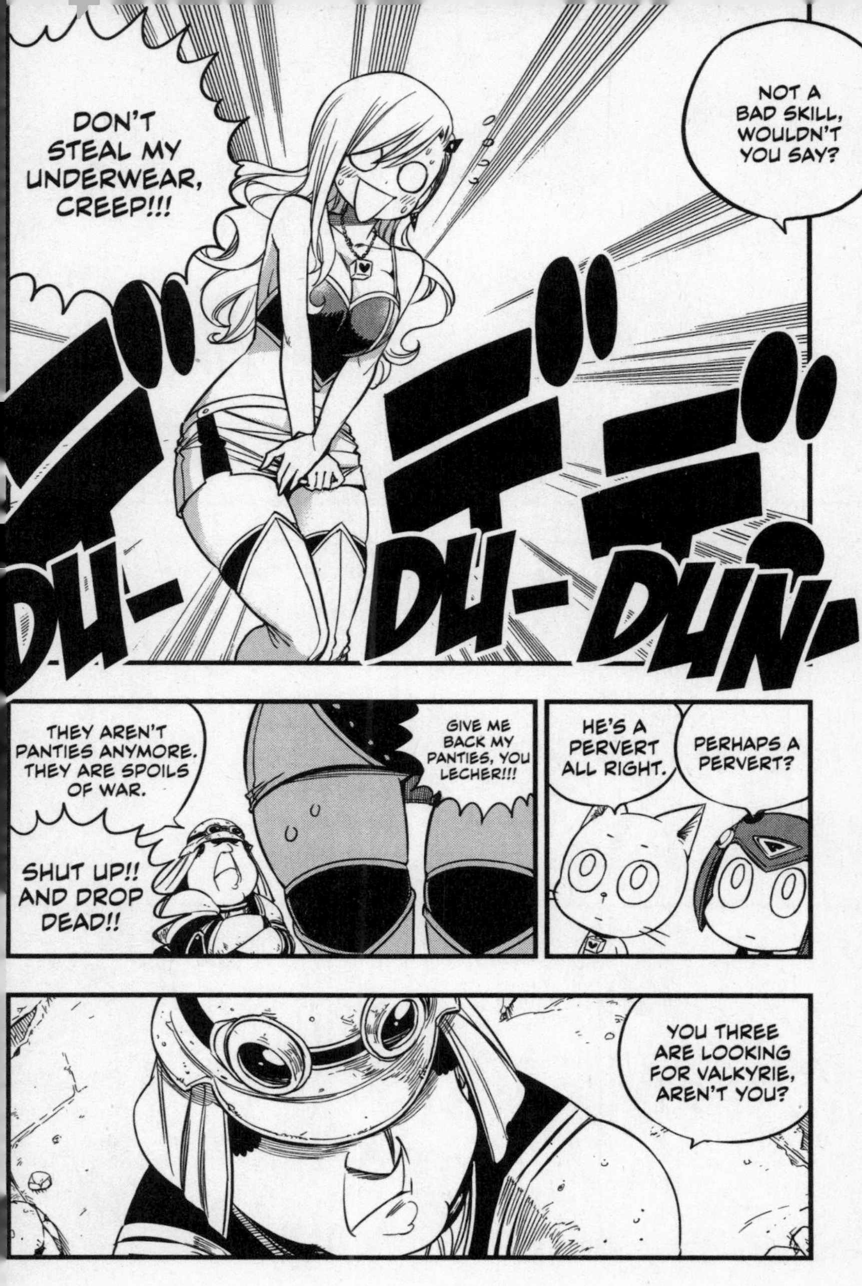
NOT A BAD SKILL, WOULDN'T YOU SAY?
DON'T STEAL MY UNDERWEAR, CREEP!!!
DU-DU-DUN
PERHAPS A PERVERT?
HE'S A PERVERT ALL RIGHT.
GIVE ME BACK MY PANTIES, YOU LECHER!!!
THEY AREN'T PANTIES ANYMORE. THEY ARE SPOILS OF WAR.
SHUT UP!! AND DROP DEAD!!
YOU THREE ARE LOOKING FOR VALKYRIE, AREN'T YOU?

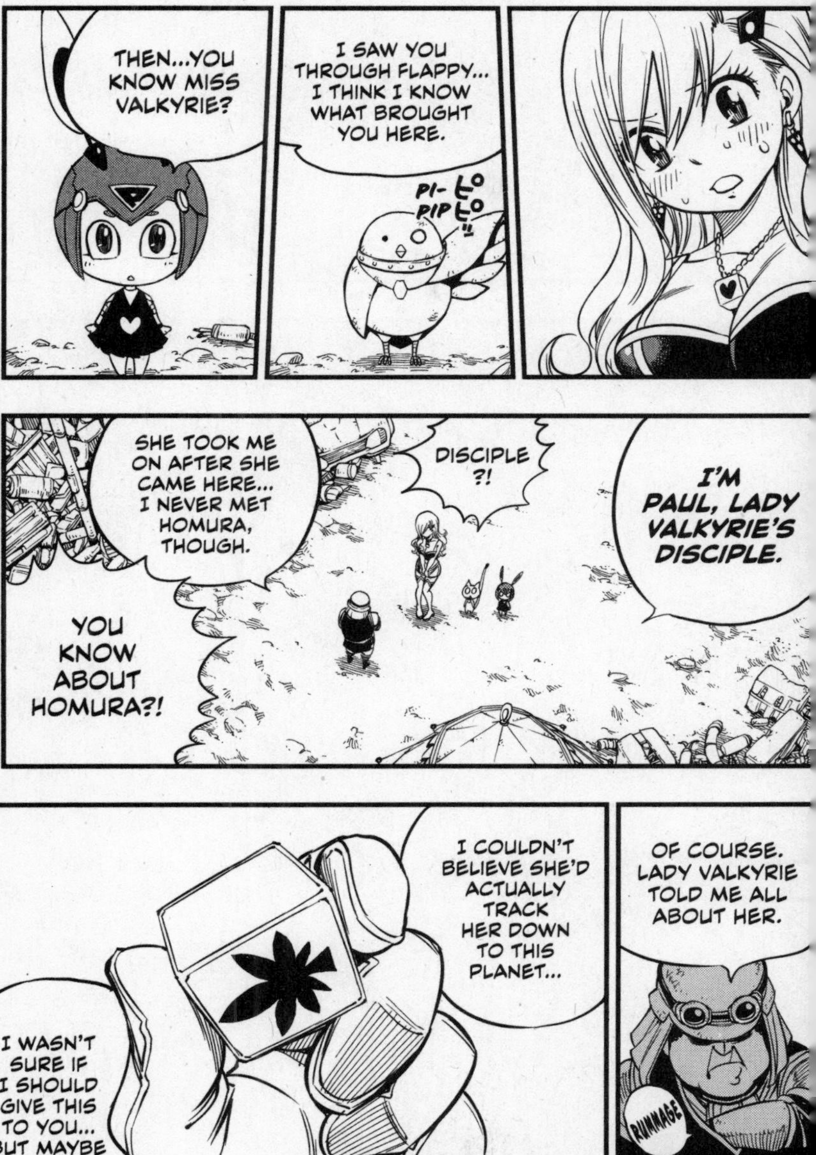
I SAW YOU THROUGH FLAPPY... I THINK I KNOW WHAT BROUGHT YOU HERE.
PI-PIP
THEN...YOU KNOW MISS VALKYRIE?
I'M PAUL, LADY VALKYRIE'S DISCIPLE.
DISCIPLE?!
SHE TOOK ME ON AFTER SHE CAME HERE... I NEVER MET HOMURA, THOUGH.
YOU KNOW ABOUT HOMURA?!
OF COURSE. LADY VALKYRIE TOLD ME ALL ABOUT HER.
RUMMAGE
I COULDN'T BELIEVE SHE'D ACTUALLY TRACK HER DOWN TO THIS PLANET...
I WASN'T SURE IF I SHOULD GIVE THIS TO YOU... BUT MAYBE I SHOULD...

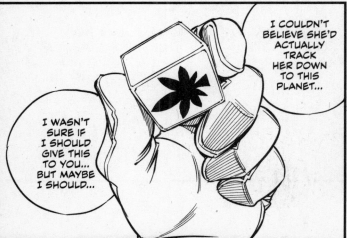

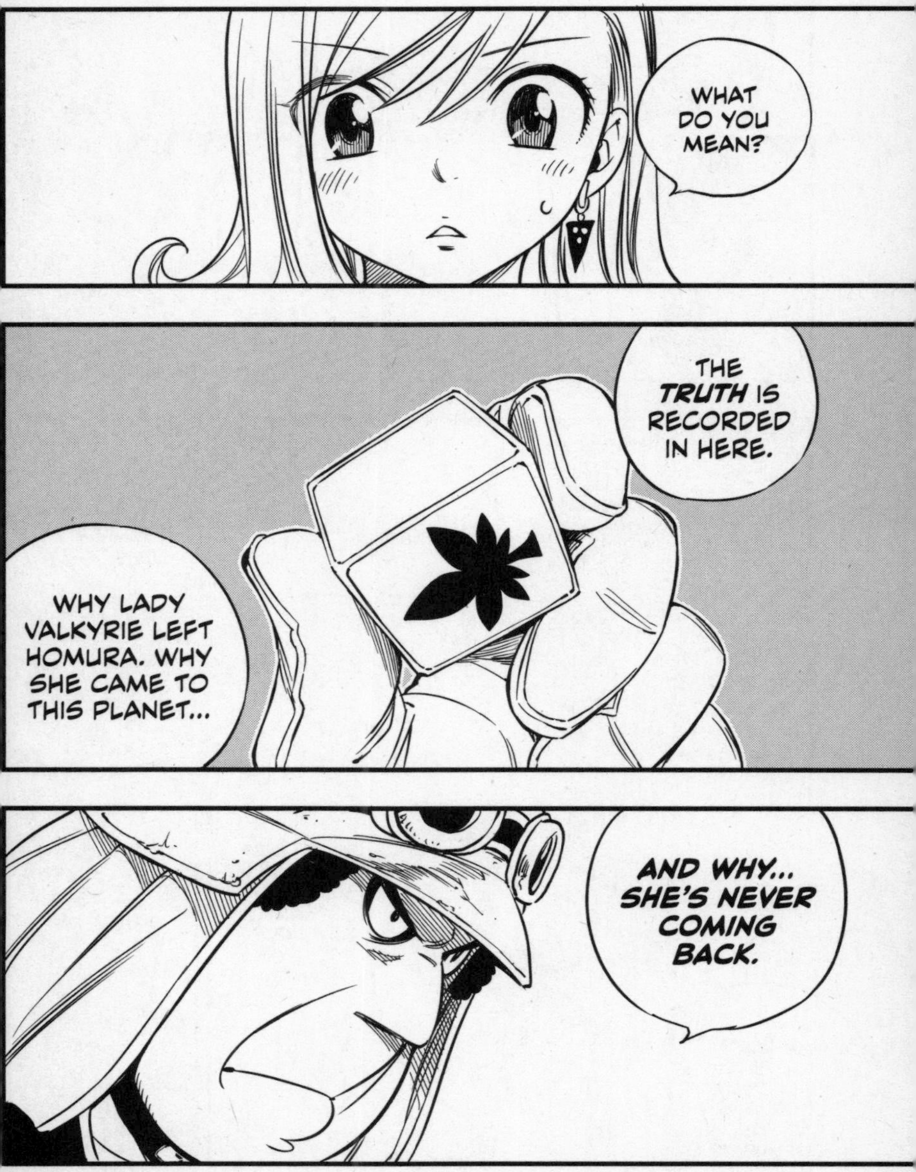
WHAT DO YOU MEAN?
THE *TRUTH* IS RECORDED IN HERE.
WHY LADY VALKYRIE LEFT HOMURA. WHY SHE CAME TO THIS PLANET...
AND WHY... SHE'S NEVER COMING BACK.

EDENS ZERO

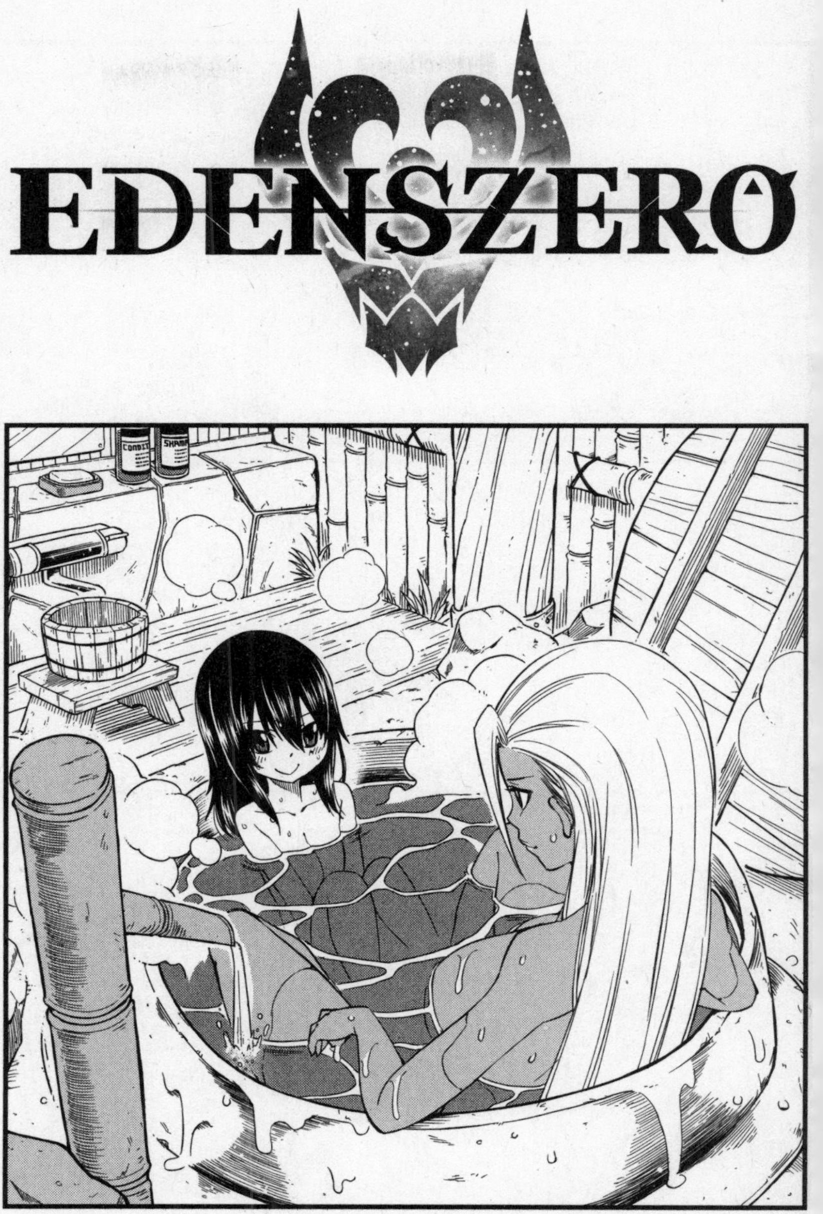

CHAPTER 55: BLACK ROCK

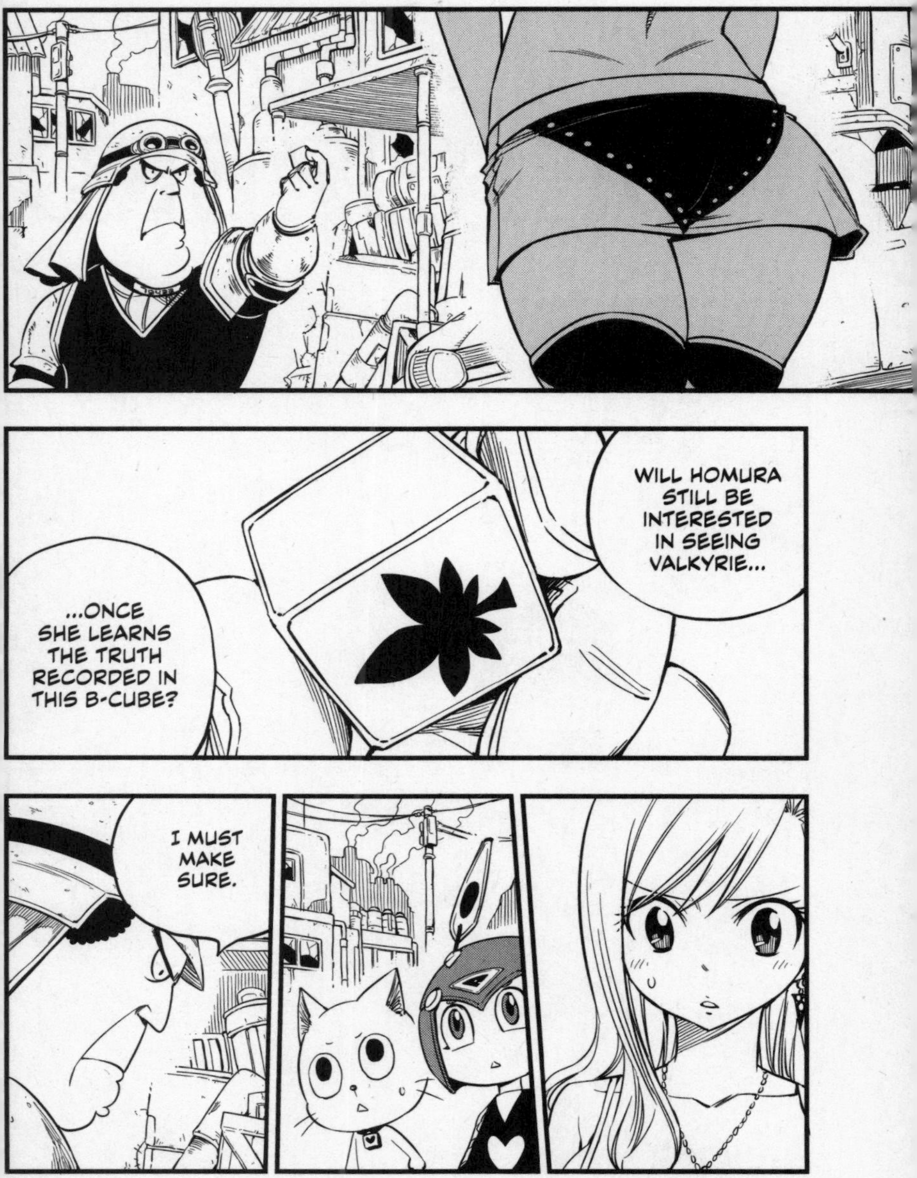
WILL HOMURA STILL BE INTERESTED IN SEEING VALKYRIE...
...ONCE SHE LEARNS THE TRUTH RECORDED IN THIS B-CUBE?
I MUST MAKE SURE.

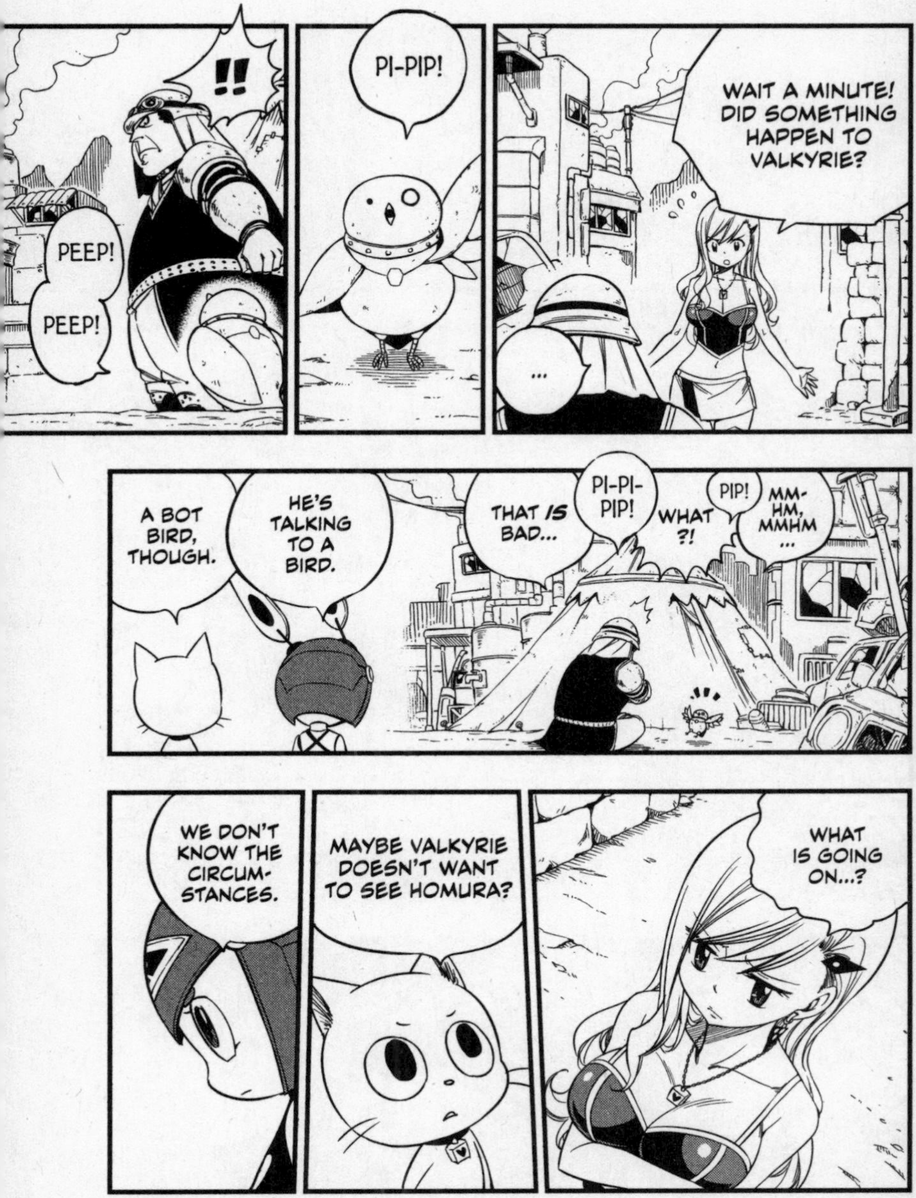
WAIT A MINUTE! DID SOMETHING HAPPEN TO VALKYRIE?
...
PI-PIP!
!!
PEEP!
PEEP!
MM-HM, MMHM ...
PIP!
WHAT ?!
PI-PI-PIP!
THAT *IS* BAD...
HE'S TALKING TO A BIRD.
A BOT BIRD, THOUGH.
WHAT IS GOING ON...?
MAYBE VALKYRIE DOESN'T WANT TO SEE HOMURA?
WE DON'T KNOW THE CIRCUMSTANCES.

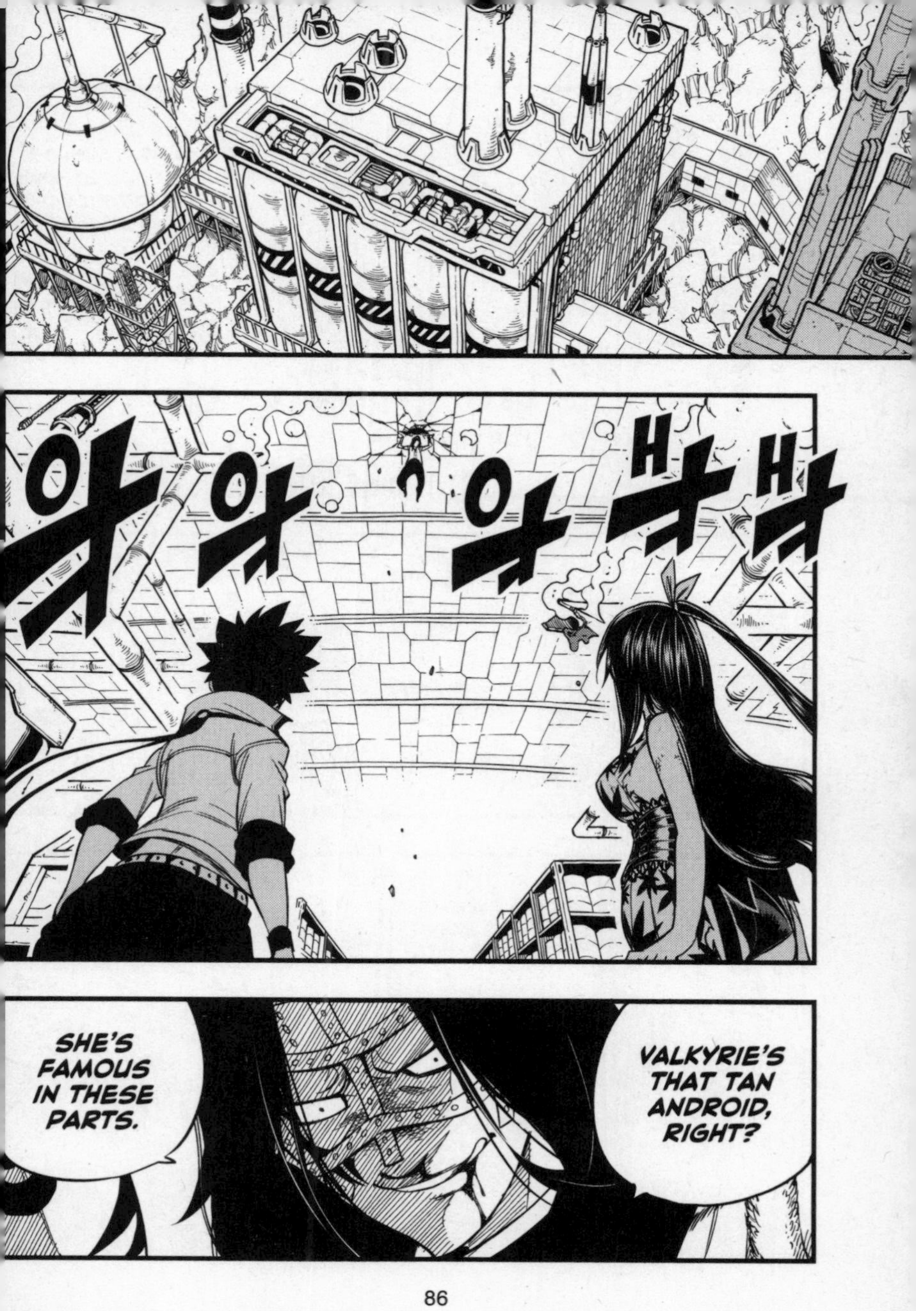
VALKYRIE'S THAT TAN ANDROID, RIGHT?
SHE'S FAMOUS IN THESE PARTS.

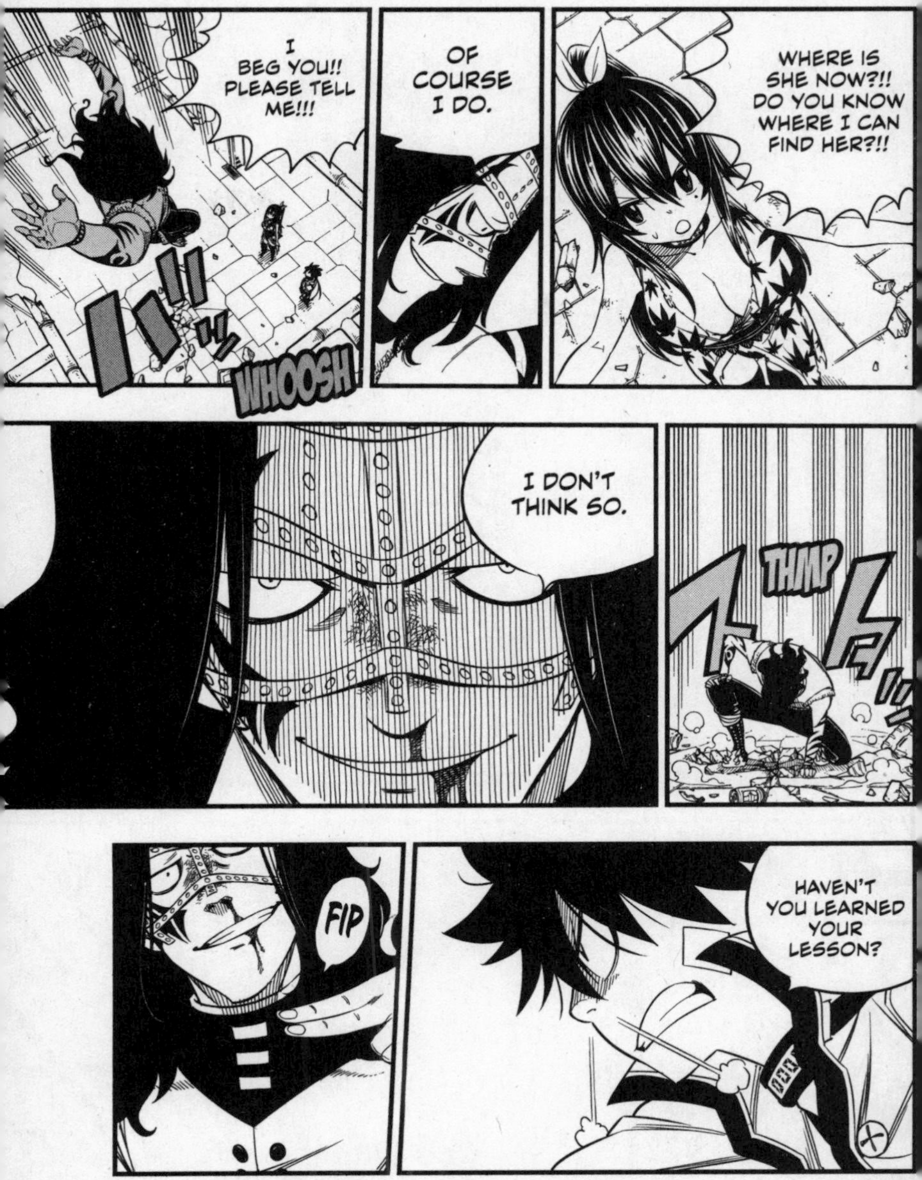
WHERE IS SHE NOW?!! DO YOU KNOW WHERE I CAN FIND HER?!!
OF COURSE I DO.
I BEG YOU!! PLEASE TELL ME!!!
WHOOSH
THMP
I DON'T THINK SO.
HAVEN'T YOU LEARNED YOUR LESSON?
FIP

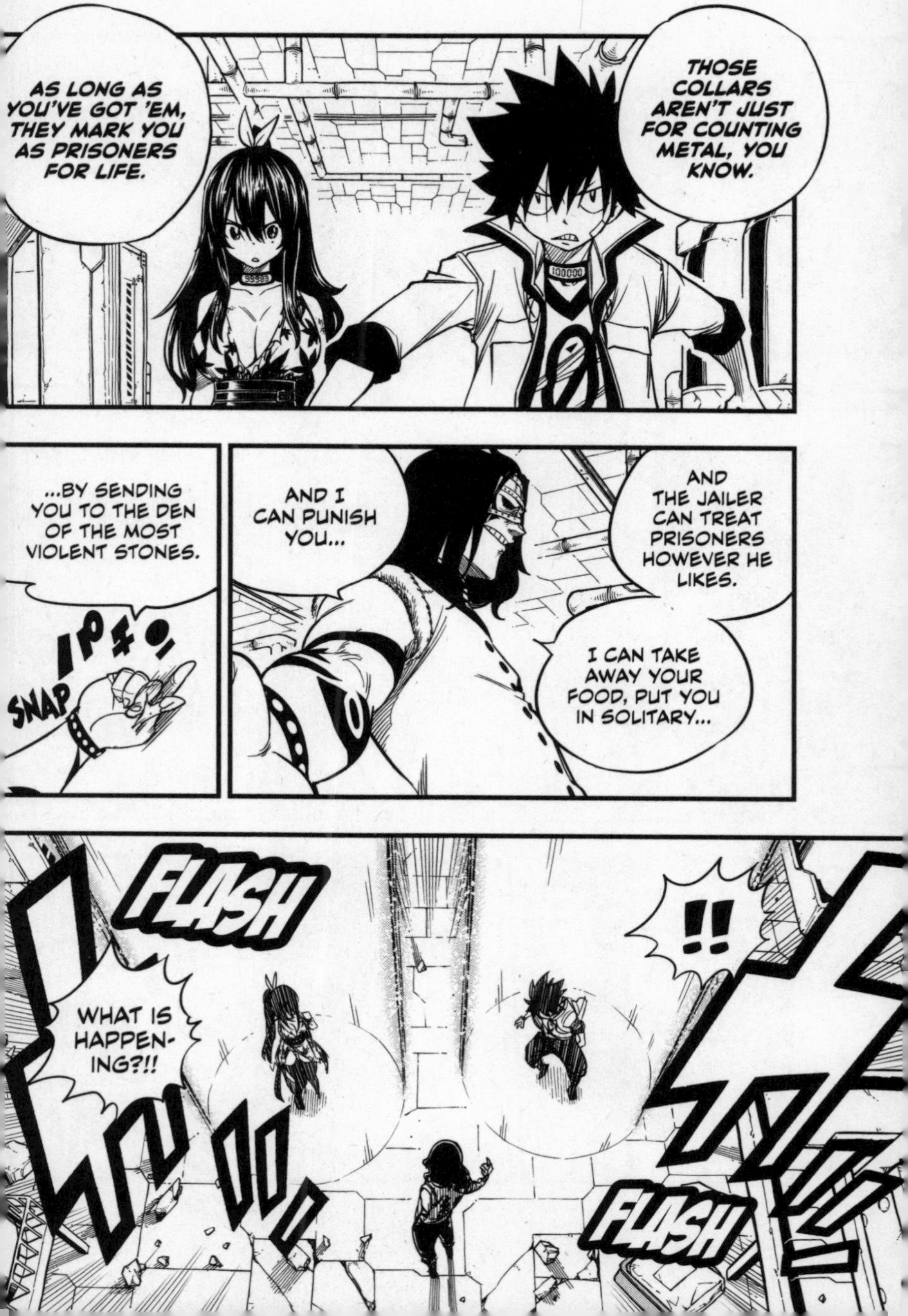
THOSE COLLARS AREN'T JUST FOR COUNTING METAL, YOU KNOW.
AS LONG AS YOU'VE GOT 'EM, THEY MARK YOU AS PRISONERS FOR LIFE.
AND THE JAILER CAN TREAT PRISONERS HOWEVER HE LIKES.
I CAN TAKE AWAY YOUR FOOD, PUT YOU IN SOLITARY...
AND I CAN PUNISH YOU...
...BY SENDING YOU TO THE DEN OF THE MOST VIOLENT STONES.
SNAP
!!
FLASH
WHAT IS HAPPEN-ING?!!
FLASH

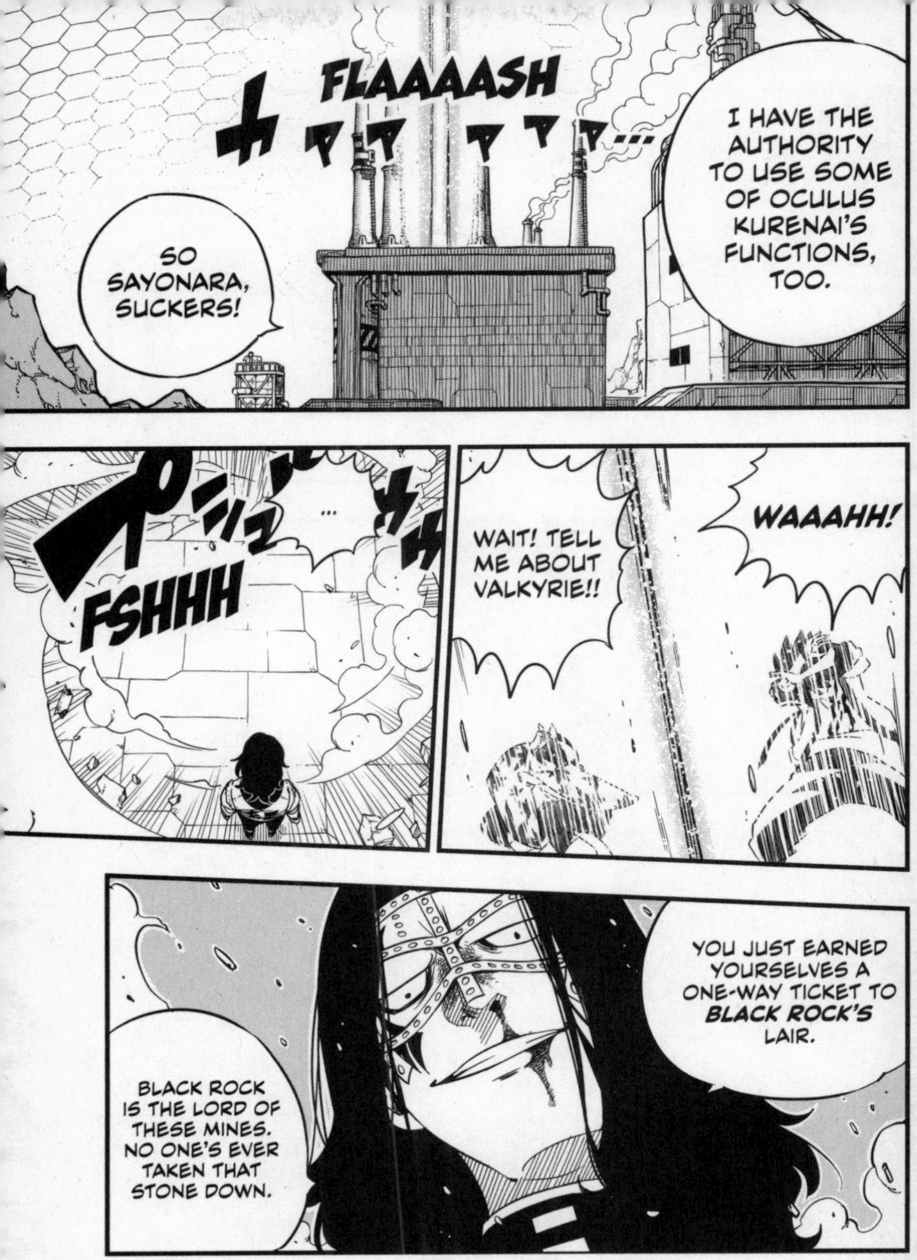
FLAAAASH
I HAVE THE AUTHORITY TO USE SOME OF OCULUS KURENAI'S FUNCTIONS, TOO.
SO SAYONARA, SUCKERS!
WAAAHH!
WAIT! TELL ME ABOUT VALKYRIE!!
...
FSHHH
YOU JUST EARNED YOURSELVES A ONE-WAY TICKET TO BLACK ROCK'S LAIR.
BLACK ROCK IS THE LORD OF THESE MINES. NO ONE'S EVER TAKEN THAT STONE DOWN.

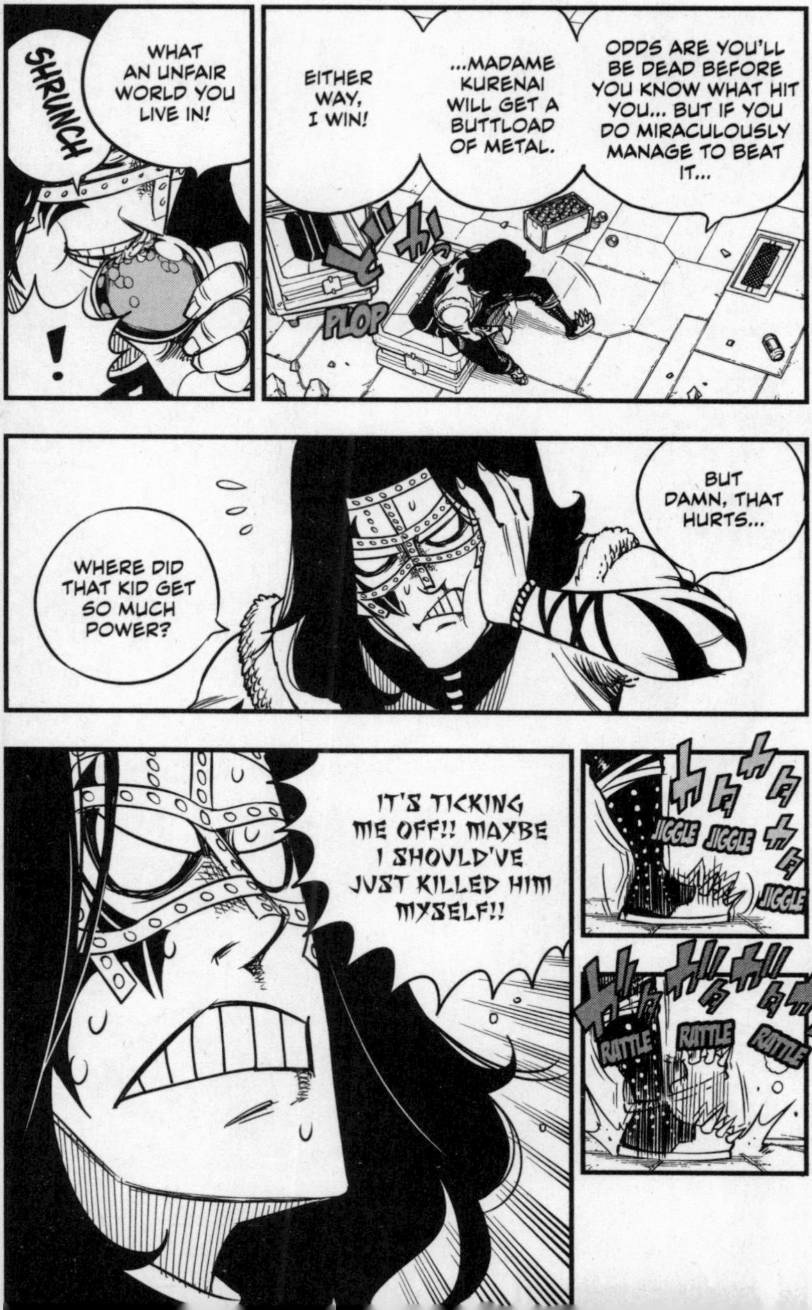
ODDS ARE YOU'LL BE DEAD BEFORE YOU KNOW WHAT HIT YOU... BUT IF YOU DO MIRACULOUSLY MANAGE TO BEAT IT...
...MADAME KURENAI WILL GET A BUTTLOAD OF METAL.
EITHER WAY, I WIN!
PLOP
WHAT AN UNFAIR WORLD YOU LIVE IN!
SHRUNCH
!
BUT DAMN, THAT HURTS...
WHERE DID THAT KID GET SO MUCH POWER?
JIGGLE
JIGGLE
JIGGLE
RATTLE
RATTLE
RATTLE
IT'S TICKING ME OFF!! MAYBE I SHOULD'VE JUST KILLED HIM MYSELF!!

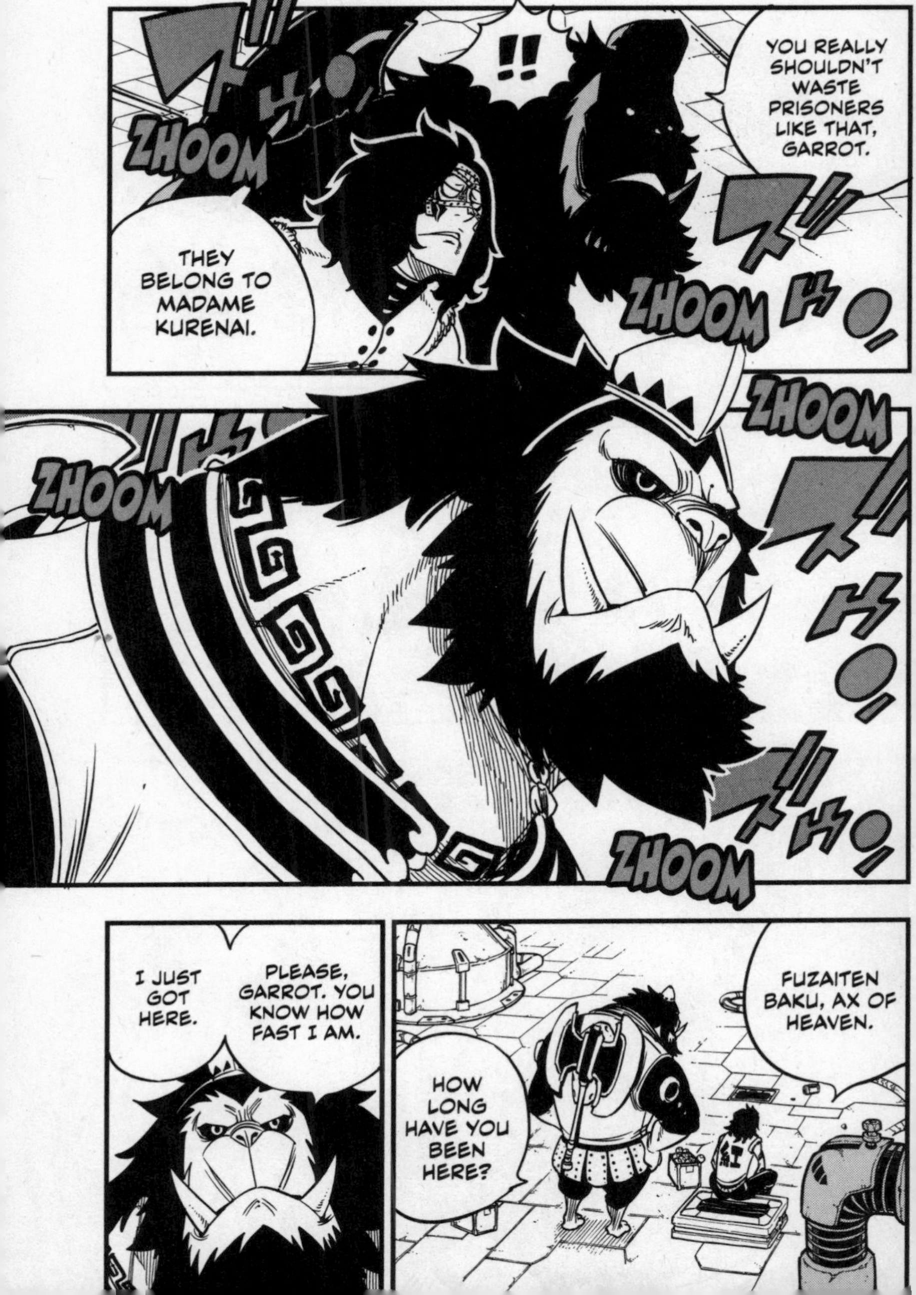
YOU REALLY SHOULDN'T WASTE PRISONERS LIKE THAT, GARROT.
!!
ZHOOM
ZHOOM
THEY BELONG TO MADAME KURENAI.
ZHOOM
ZHOOM
ZHOOM
FUZAITEN BAKU, AX OF HEAVEN.
HOW LONG HAVE YOU BEEN HERE?
PLEASE, GARROT. YOU KNOW HOW FAST I AM.
I JUST GOT HERE.

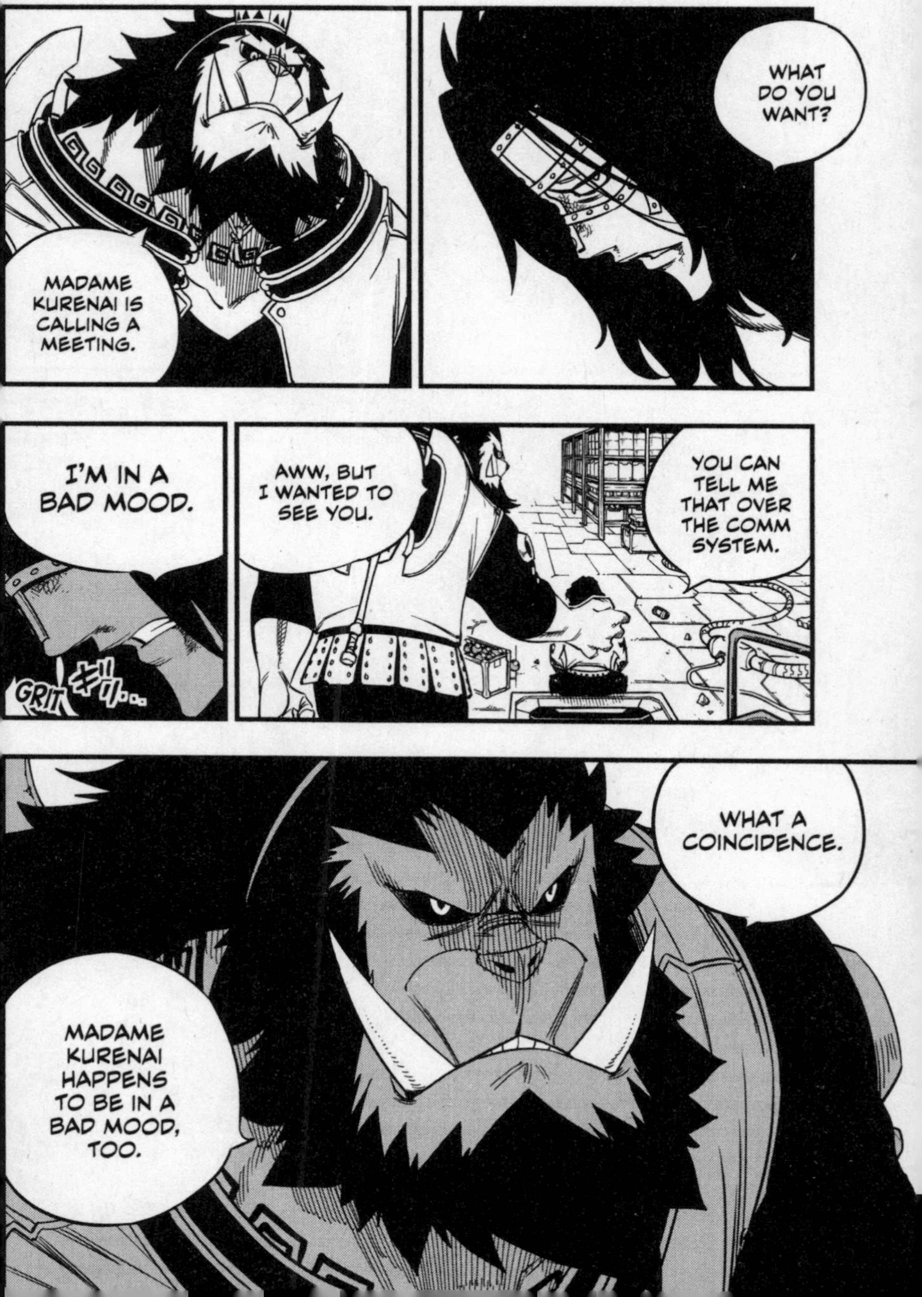
WHAT DO YOU WANT?
MADAME KURENAI IS CALLING A MEETING.
YOU CAN TELL ME THAT OVER THE COMM SYSTEM.
AWW, BUT I WANTED TO SEE YOU.
I'M IN A BAD MOOD.
GRIT
WHAT A COINCIDENCE.
MADAME KURENAI HAPPENS TO BE IN A BAD MOOD, TOO.

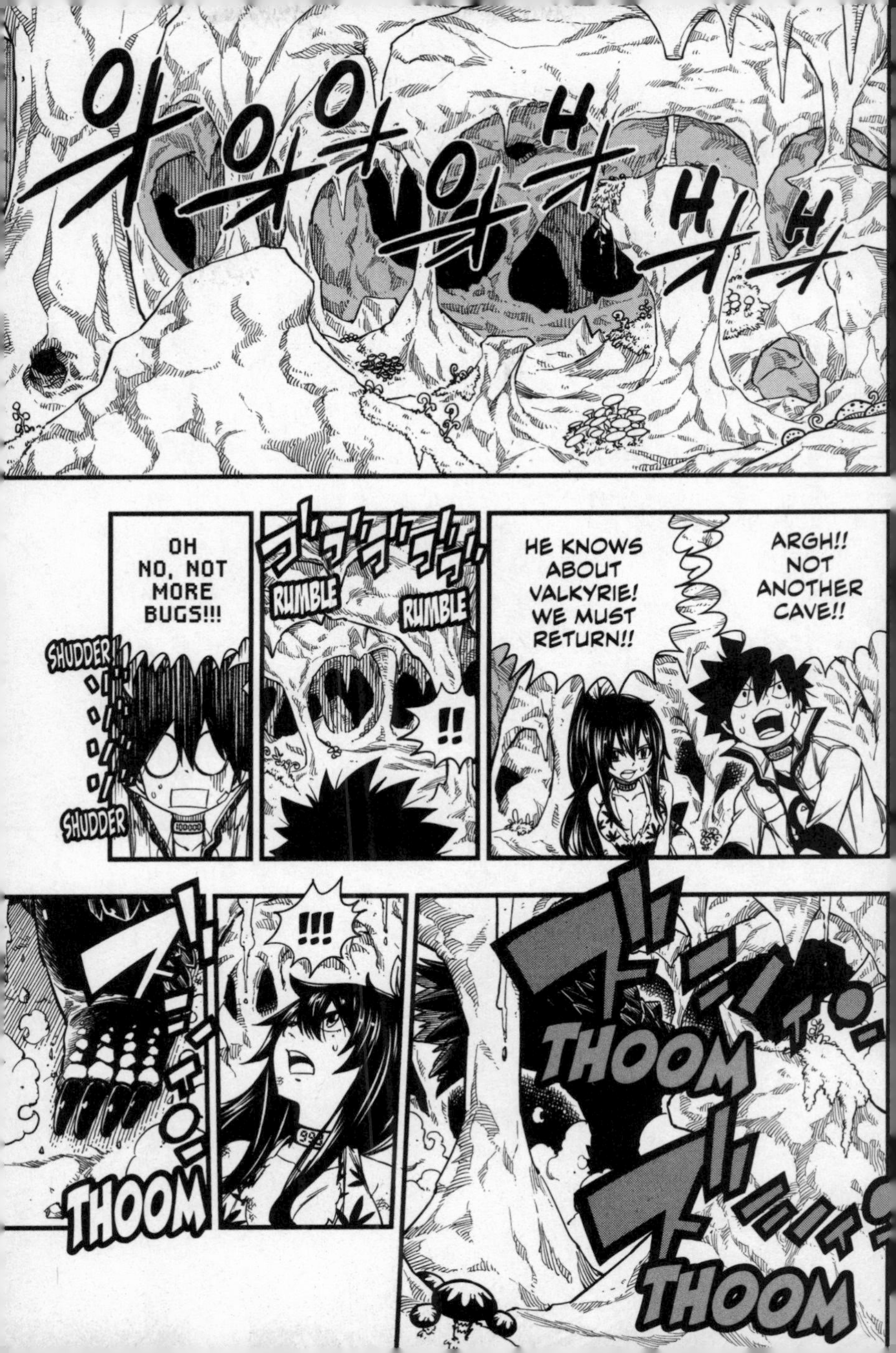
ARGH!! NOT ANOTHER CAVE!!
HE KNOWS ABOUT VALKYRIE! WE MUST RETURN!!
RUMBLE
RUMBLE
!!
OH NO, NOT MORE BUGS!!!
SHUDDER
SHUDDER
THOOM
THOOM
!!!
THOOM

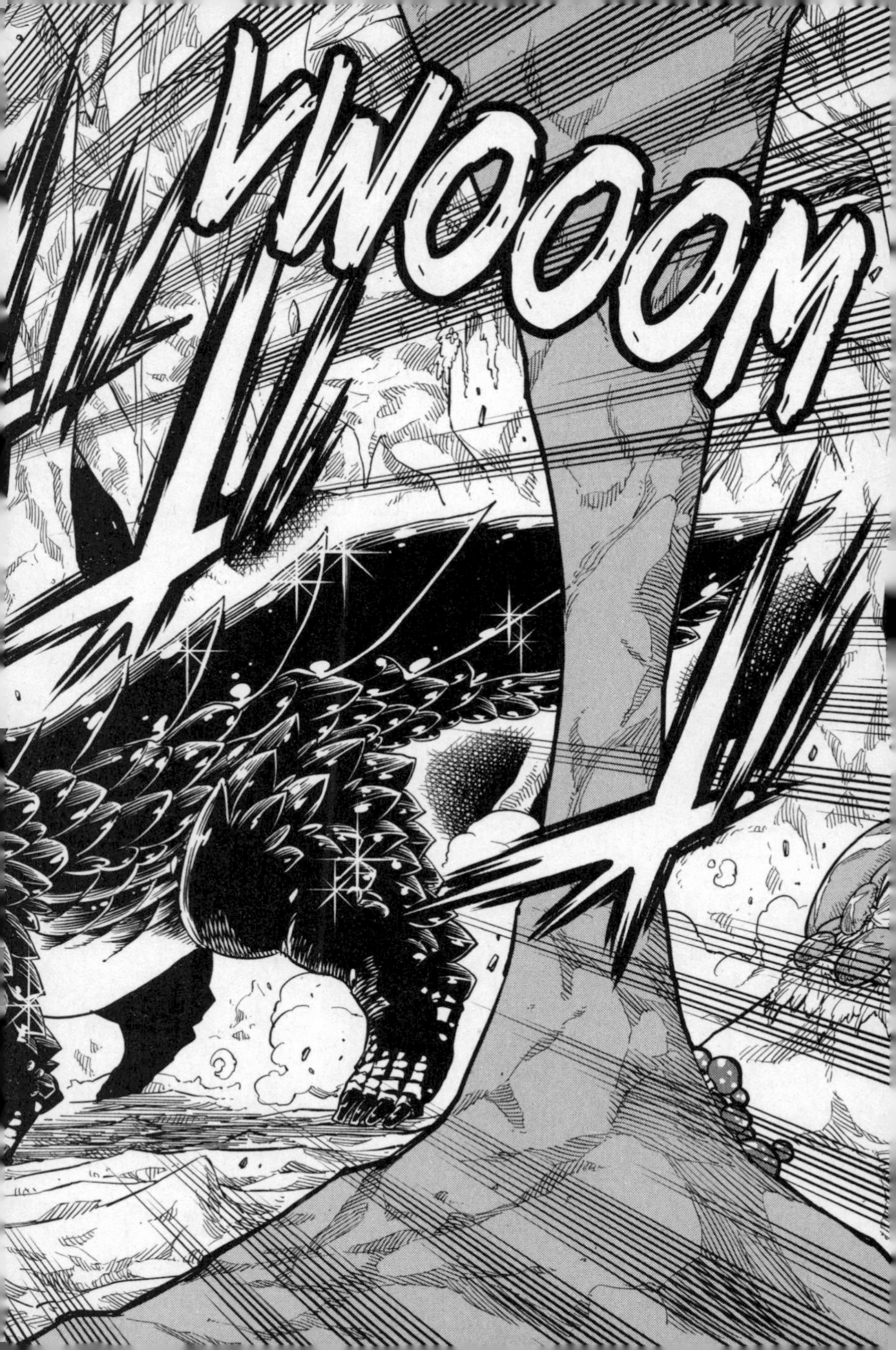
WHOOOM

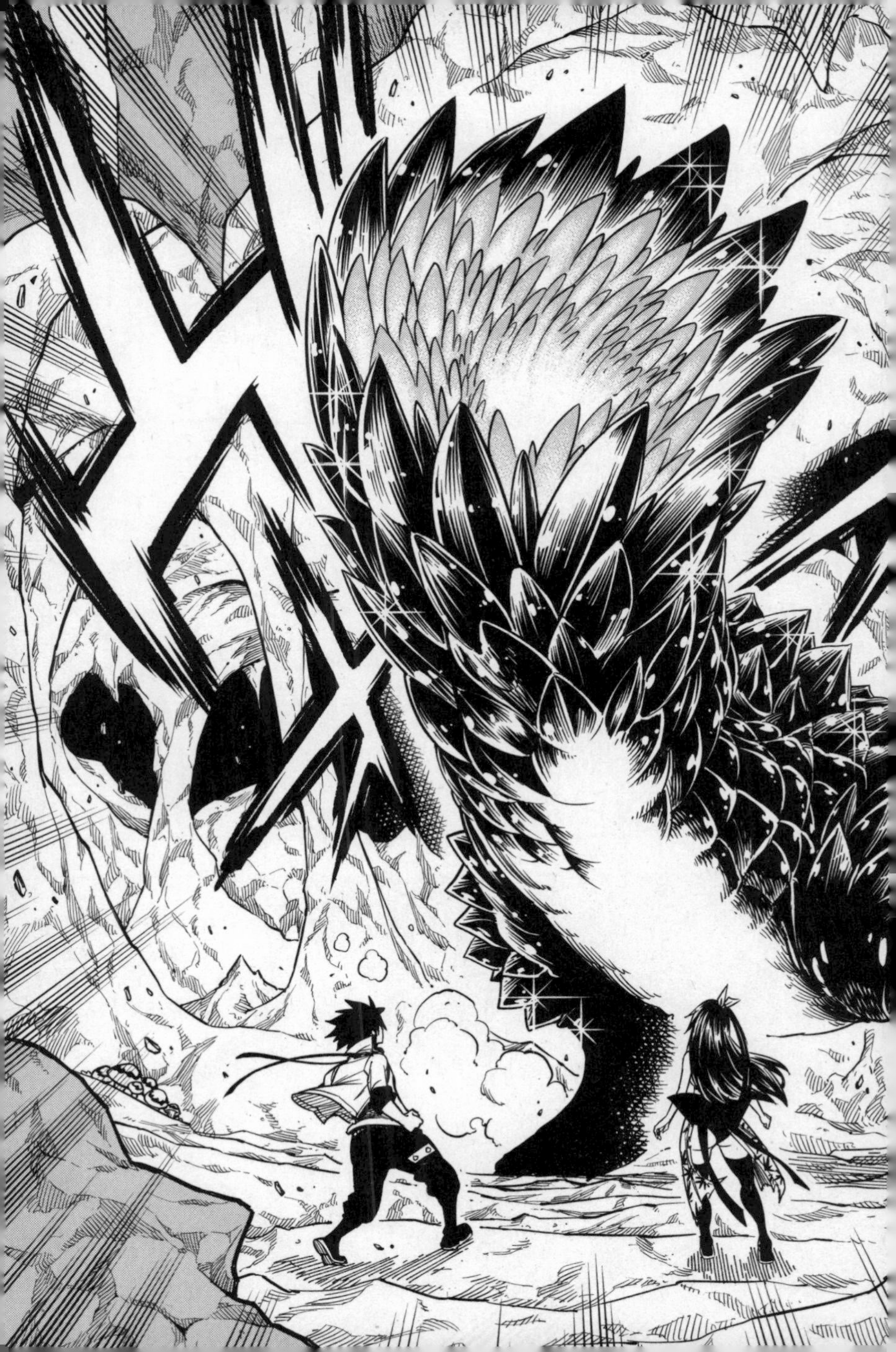

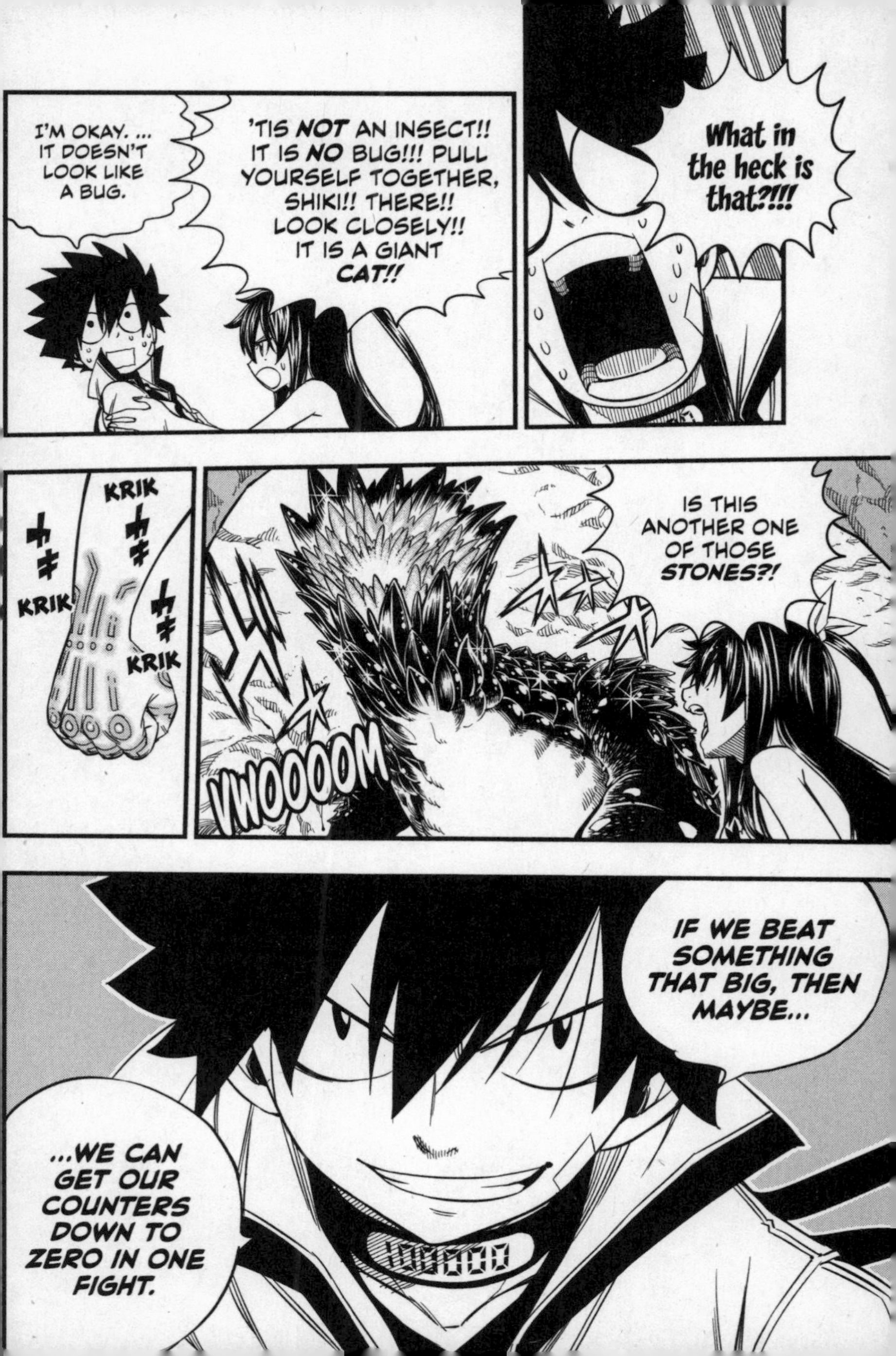
What in the heck is that?!!!
'TIS NOT AN INSECT!! IT IS NO BUG!!! PULL YOURSELF TOGETHER, SHIKI!! THERE!! LOOK CLOSELY!! IT IS A GIANT CAT!!
I'M OKAY. ... IT DOESN'T LOOK LIKE A BUG.
IS THIS ANOTHER ONE OF THOSE STONES?!
VWOOOOM
KRIK
KRIK
KRIK
IF WE BEAT SOMETHING THAT BIG, THEN MAYBE...
...WE CAN GET OUR COUNTERS DOWN TO ZERO IN ONE FIGHT.

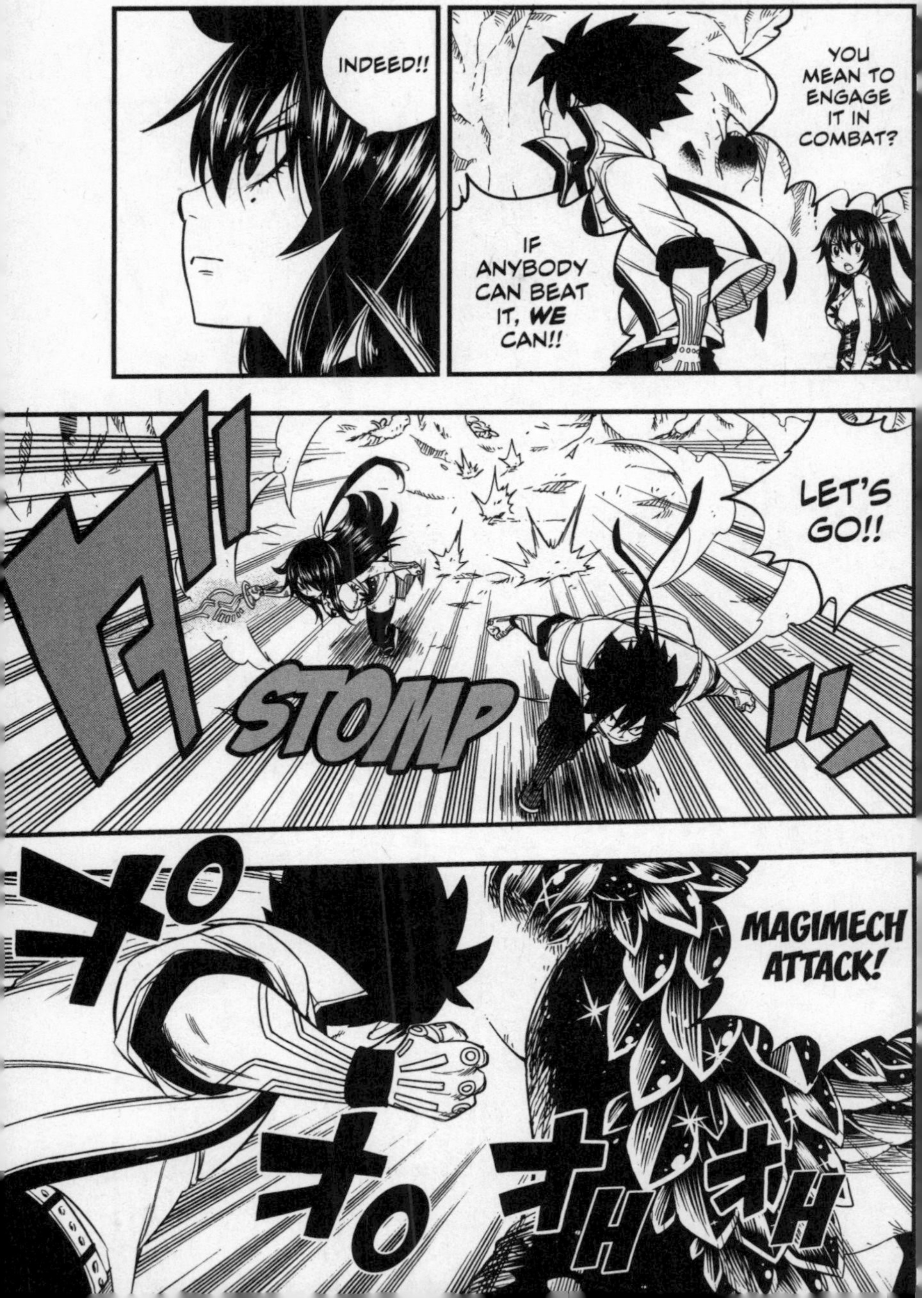
YOU MEAN TO ENGAGE IT IN COMBAT?
IF ANYBODY CAN BEAT IT, WE CAN!!
INDEED!!
LET'S GO!!
STOMP
MAGIMECH ATTACK!

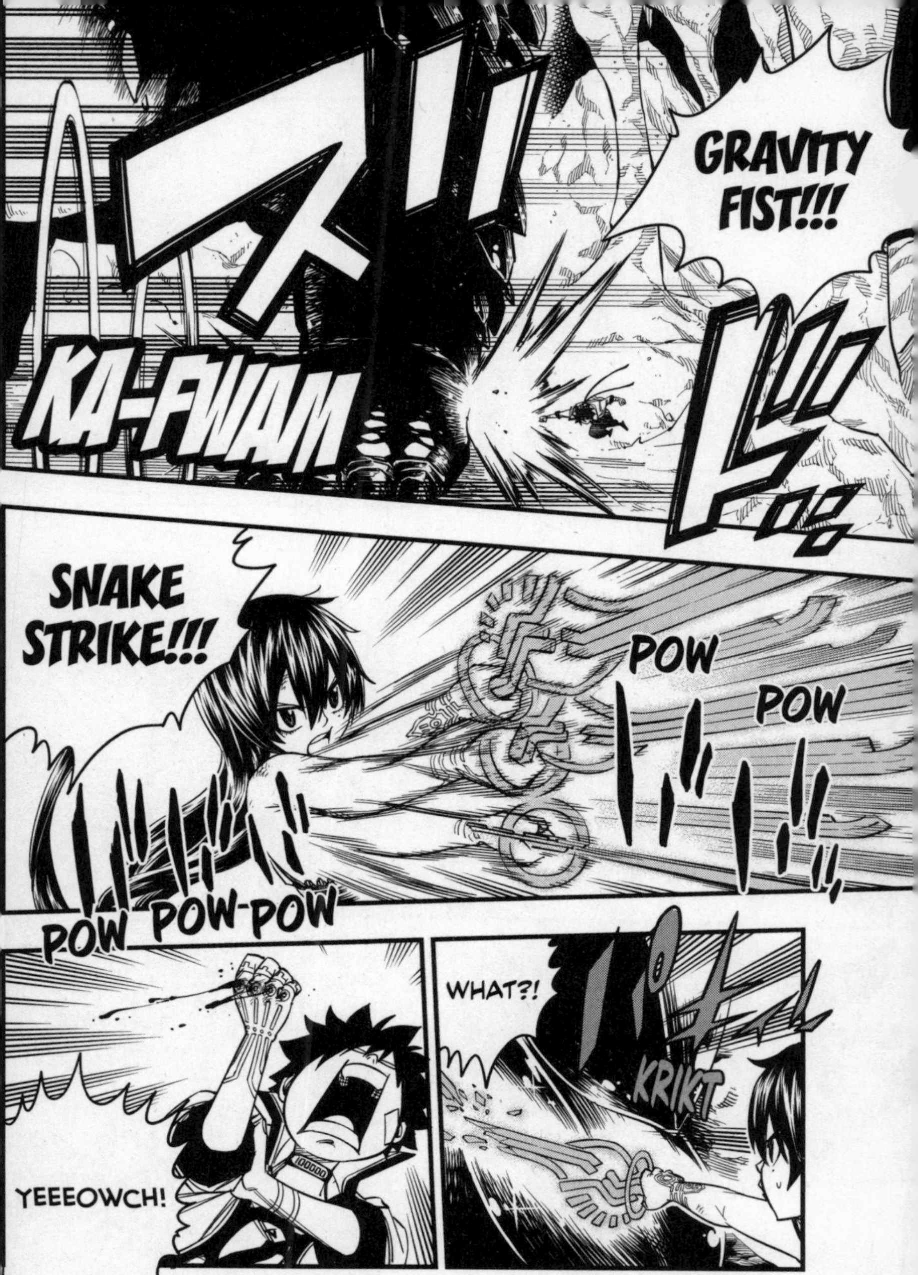
GRAVITY FIST!!!
KA-FWAM
SNAKE STRIKE!!!
POW
POW
POW POW-POW
WHAT?!
KRIKT
YEEEOWCH!

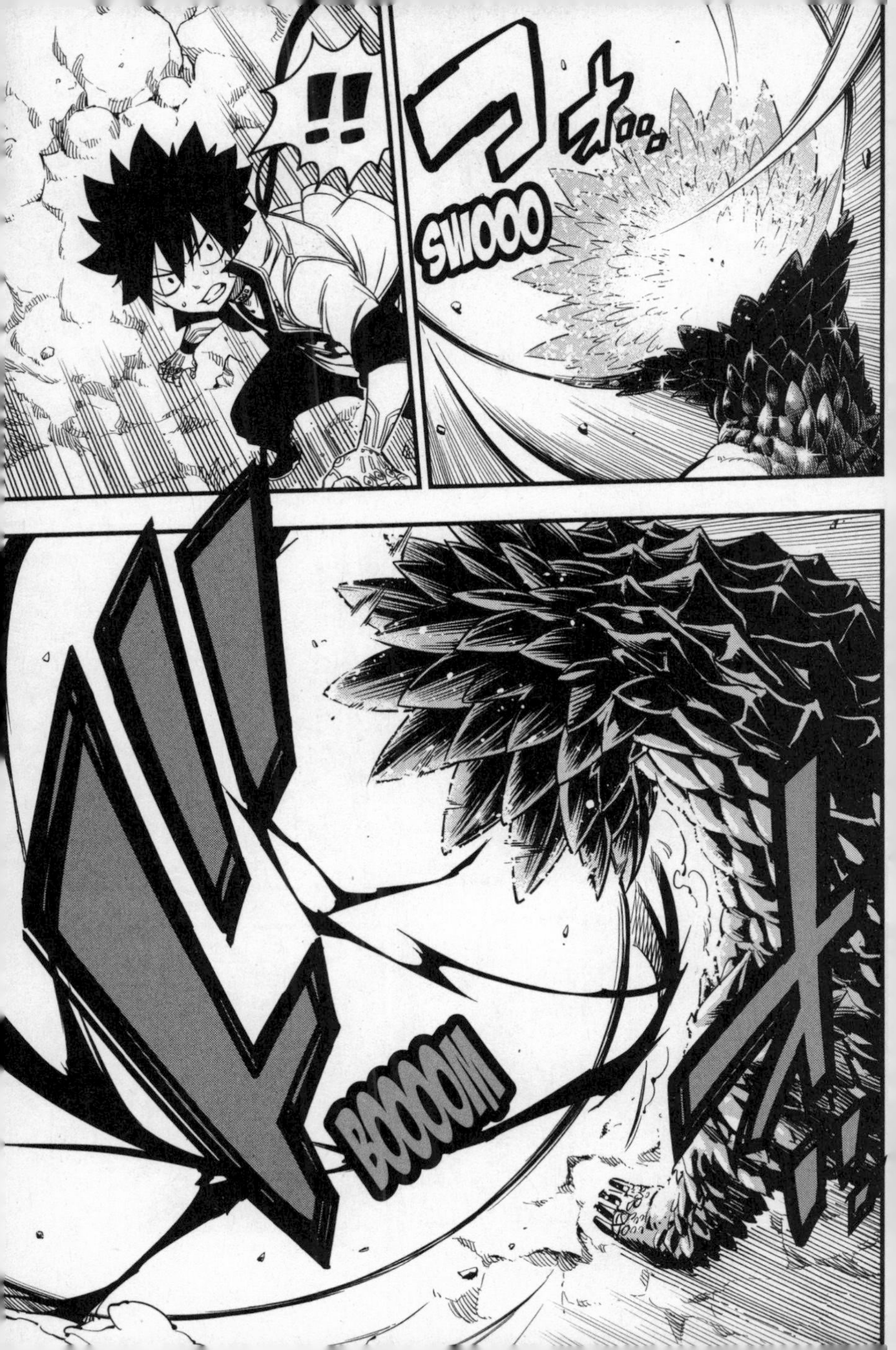
SWOOO
!!
BOOOOM

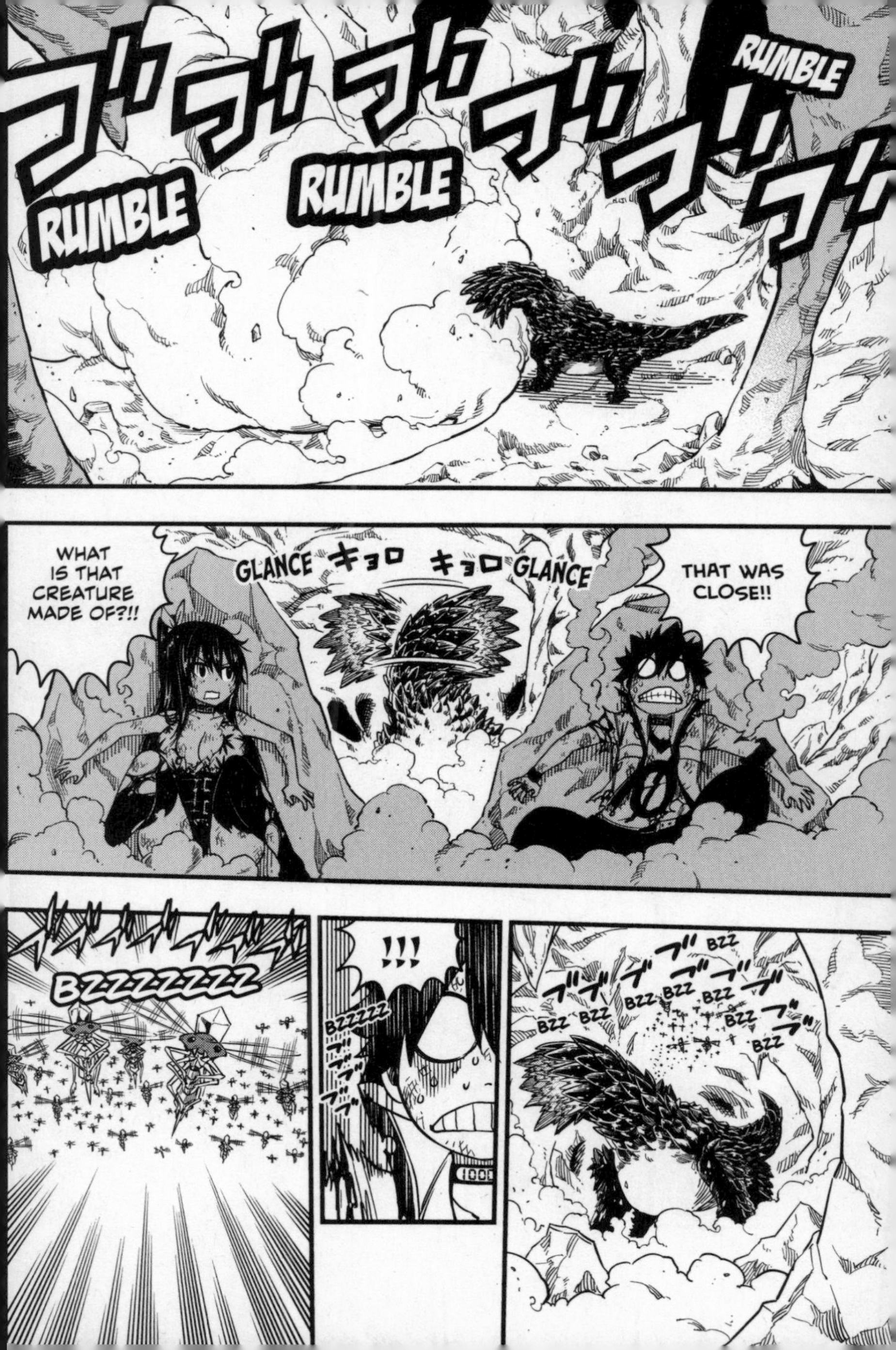
RUMBLE
RUMBLE
RUMBLE
THAT WAS CLOSE!!
GLANCE キョロ
キョロ GLANCE
WHAT IS THAT CREATURE MADE OF?!!
BZZ
BZZ BZZ BZZ
BZZ BZZ BZZ
BZZ
BZZ
!!!
BZZZZZ
BZZZZZZZZ

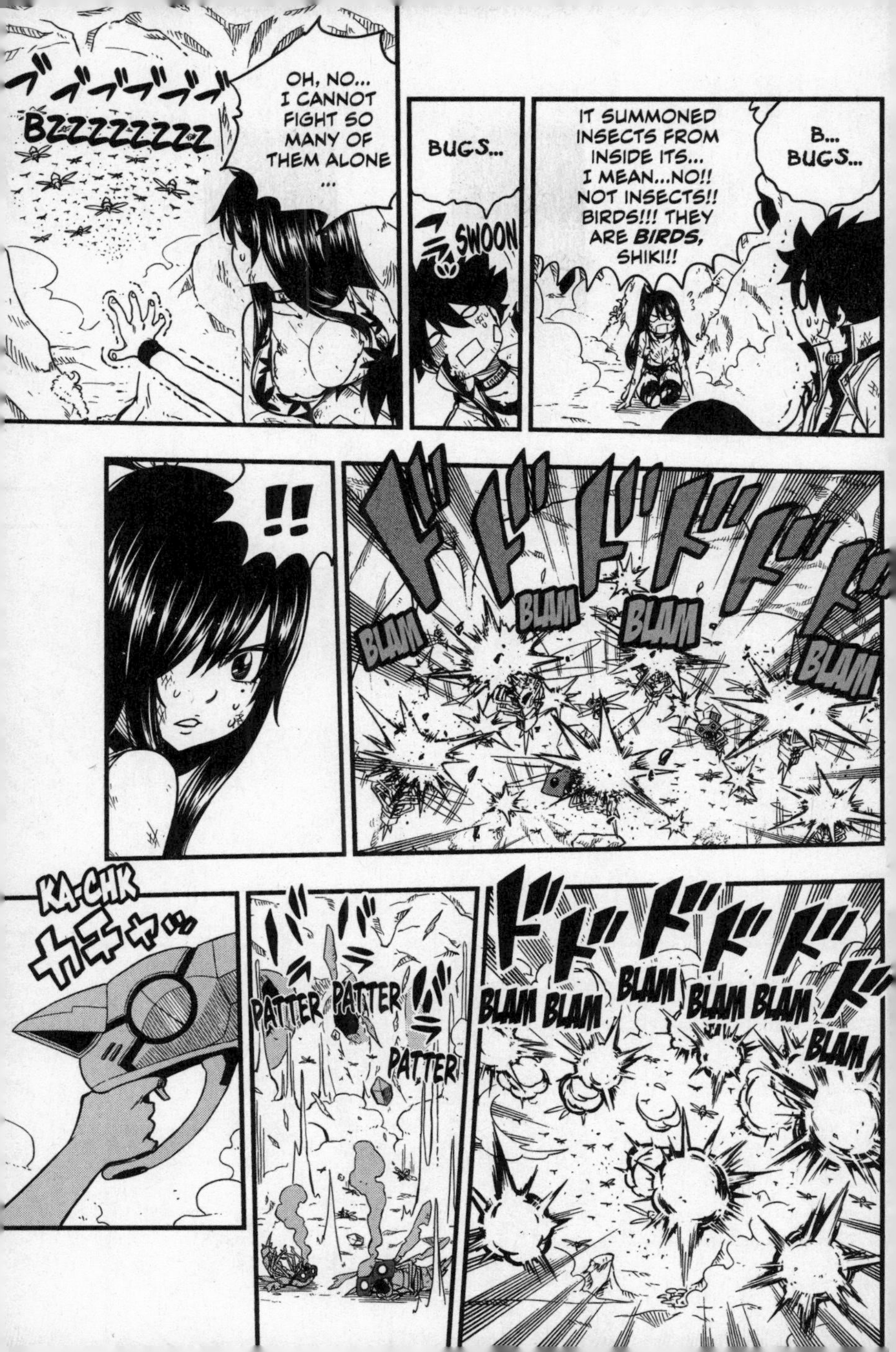
B... BUGS...
IT SUMMONED INSECTS FROM INSIDE ITS... I MEAN...NO!! NOT INSECTS!! BIRDS!!! THEY ARE *BIRDS*, SHIKI!!
BUGS...
SWOON
OH, NO... I CANNOT FIGHT SO MANY OF THEM ALONE ...
BZZZZZZZZZ
BLAM
BLAM
BLAM
BLAM
!!
BLAM
BLAM BLAM
BLAM
BLAM BLAM
BLAM
PATTER
PATTER
PATTER
KA-CHK

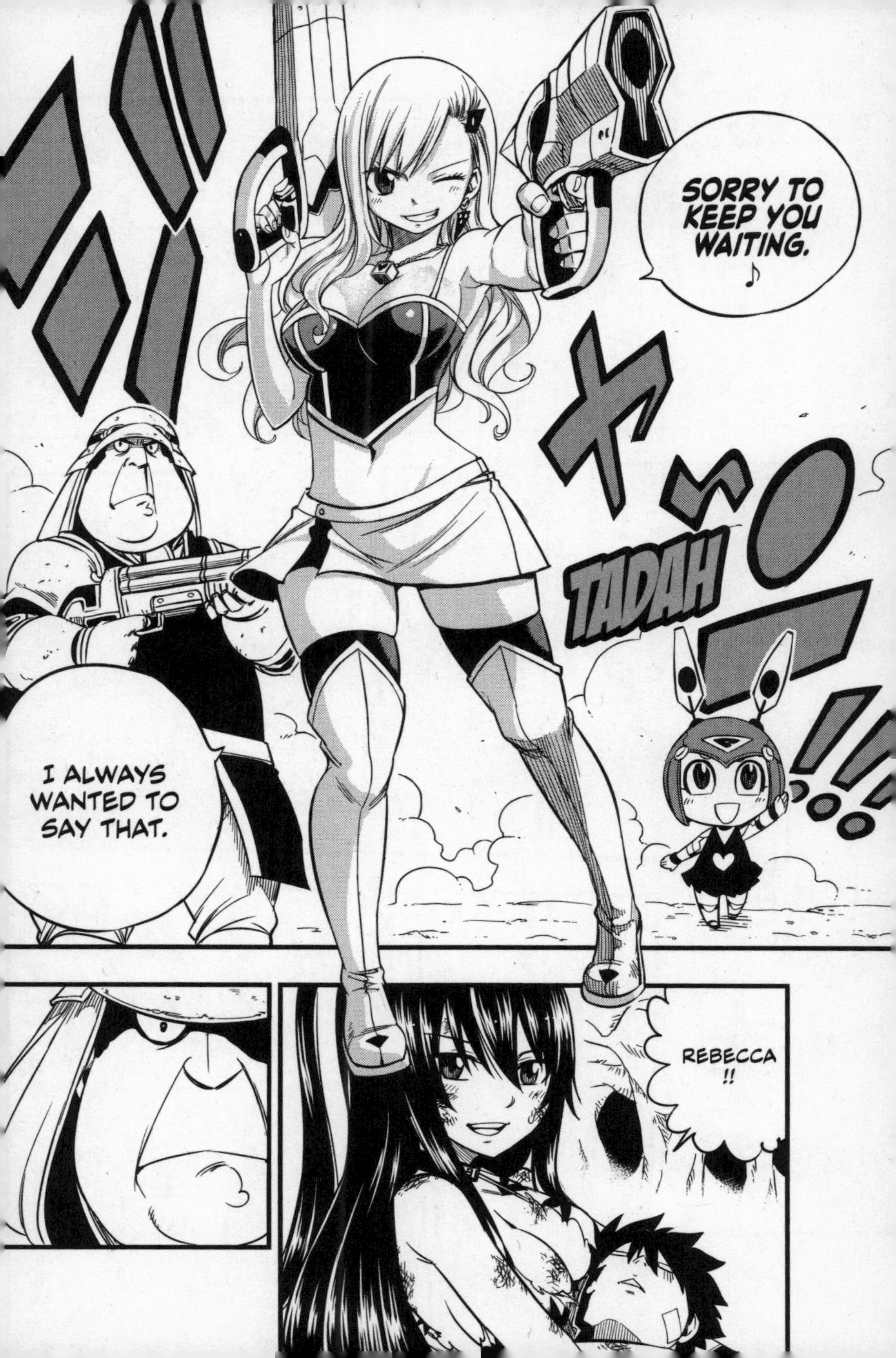
SORRY TO KEEP YOU WAITING. ♪
TADAH
I ALWAYS WANTED TO SAY THAT.
REBECCA !!

EDENS ZERO

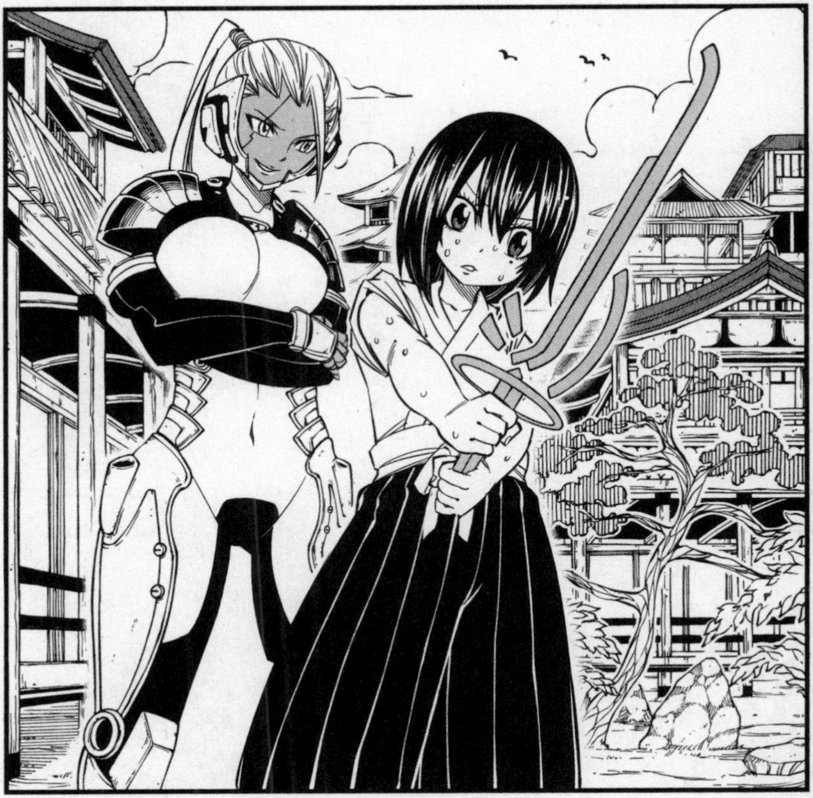

CHAPTER 56: RESET

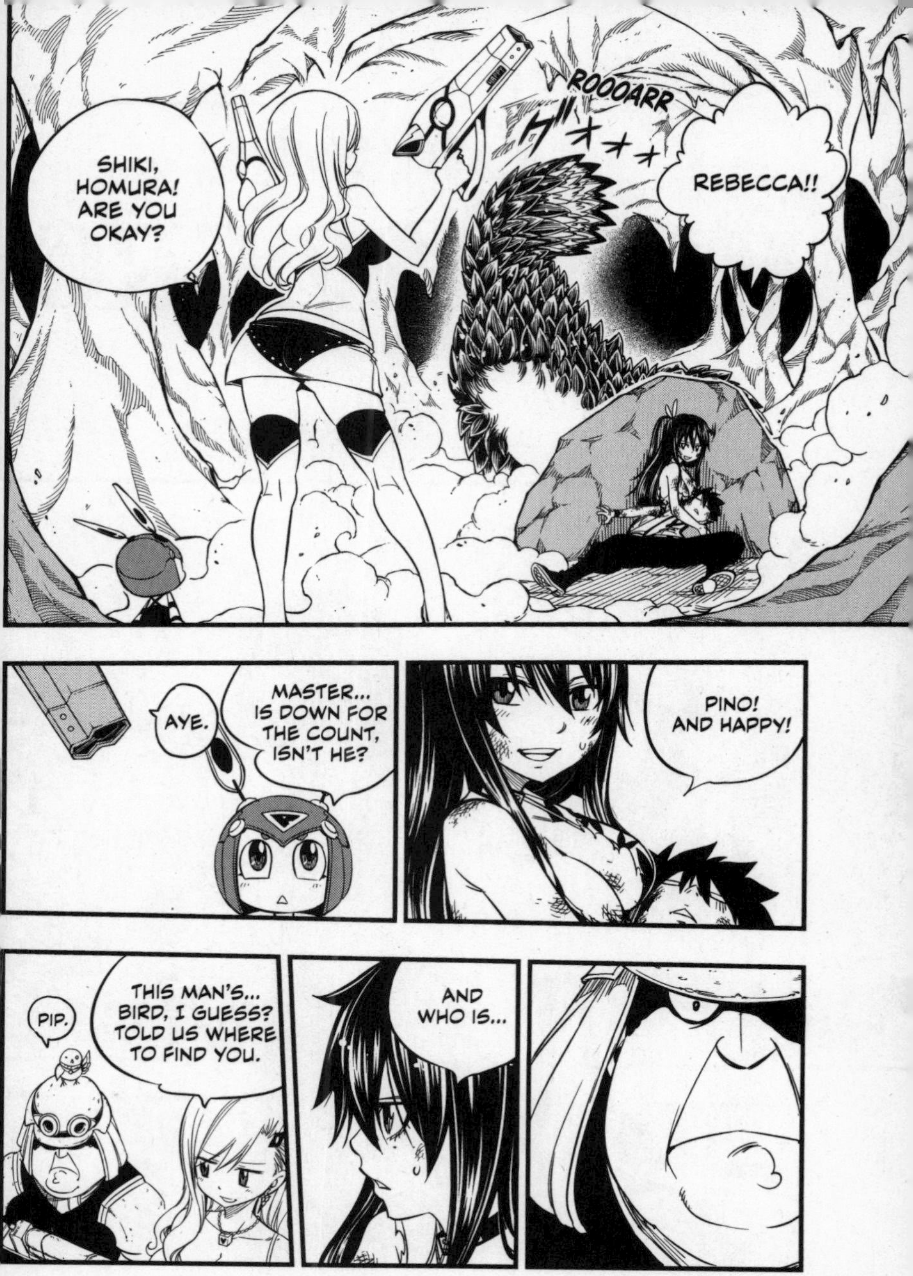
ROOOARR
REBECCA!!
SHIKI, HOMURA! ARE YOU OKAY?
PINO! AND HAPPY!
MASTER... IS DOWN FOR THE COUNT, ISN'T HE?
AYE.
AND WHO IS...
THIS MAN'S... BIRD, I GUESS? TOLD US WHERE TO FIND YOU.
PIP.

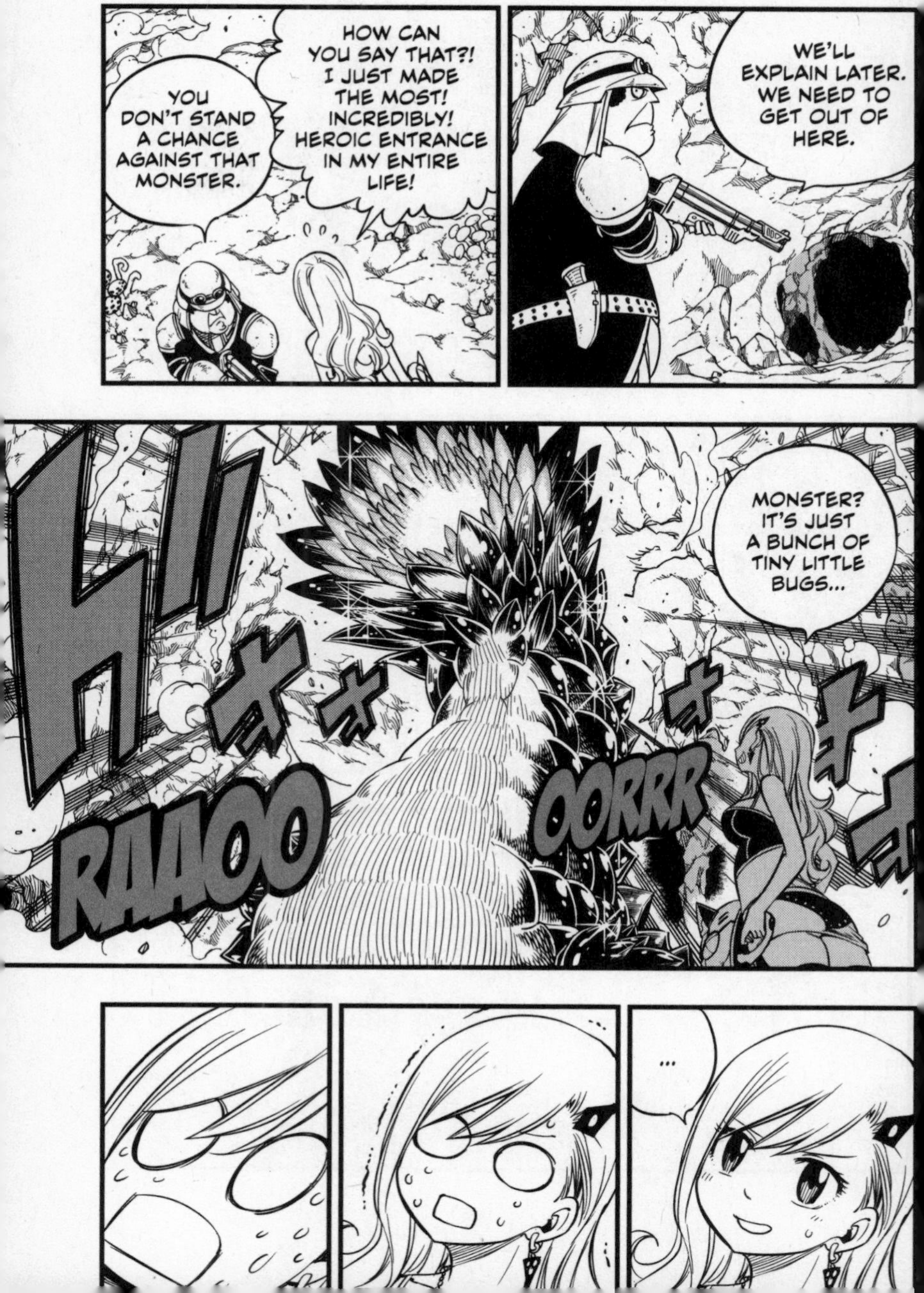
WE'LL EXPLAIN LATER. WE NEED TO GET OUT OF HERE.
HOW CAN YOU SAY THAT?! I JUST MADE THE MOST! INCREDIBLY! HEROIC ENTRANCE IN MY ENTIRE LIFE!
YOU DON'T STAND A CHANCE AGAINST THAT MONSTER.
MONSTER? IT'S JUST A BUNCH OF TINY LITTLE BUGS...
RAAOO OORRR
...

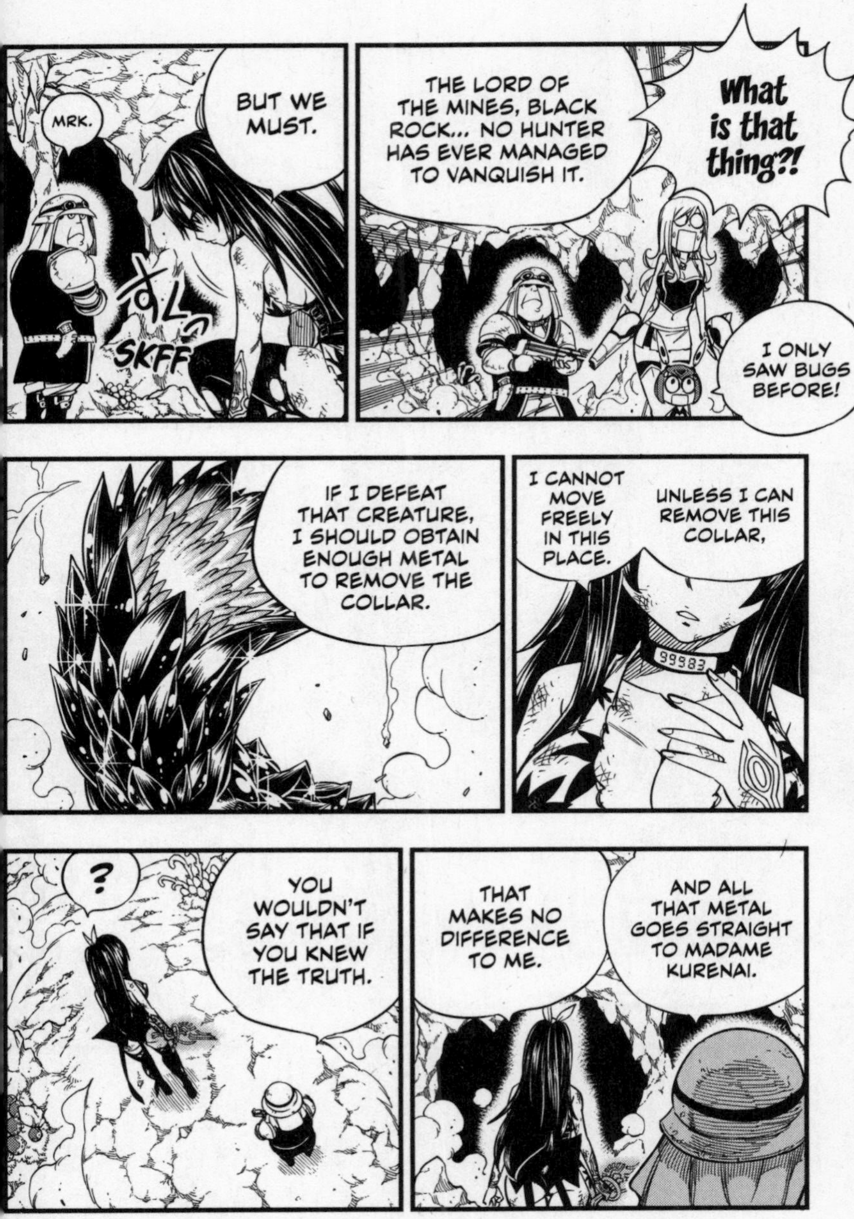
THE LORD OF THE MINES, BLACK ROCK... NO HUNTER HAS EVER MANAGED TO VANQUISH IT.
What is that thing?!
I ONLY SAW BUGS BEFORE!
BUT WE MUST.
MRK.
SKFF
UNLESS I CAN REMOVE THIS COLLAR,
I CANNOT MOVE FREELY IN THIS PLACE.
99983
IF I DEFEAT THAT CREATURE, I SHOULD OBTAIN ENOUGH METAL TO REMOVE THE COLLAR.
AND ALL THAT METAL GOES STRAIGHT TO MADAME KURENAI.
THAT MAKES NO DIFFERENCE TO ME.
?
YOU WOULDN'T SAY THAT IF YOU KNEW THE TRUTH.

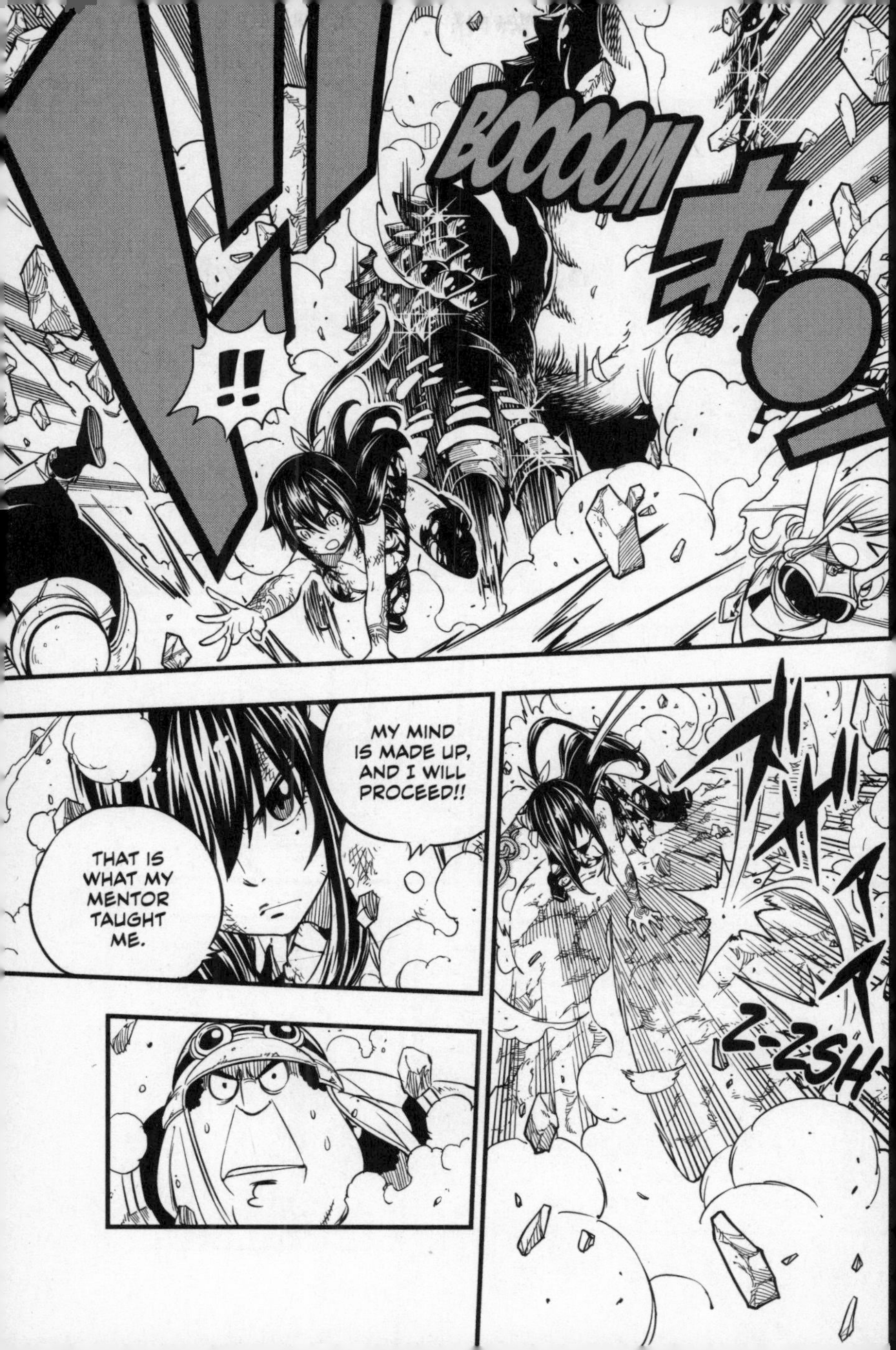
BOOOOM
!!
Z-ZSH
MY MIND IS MADE UP, AND I WILL PROCEED!!
THAT IS WHAT MY MENTOR TAUGHT ME.

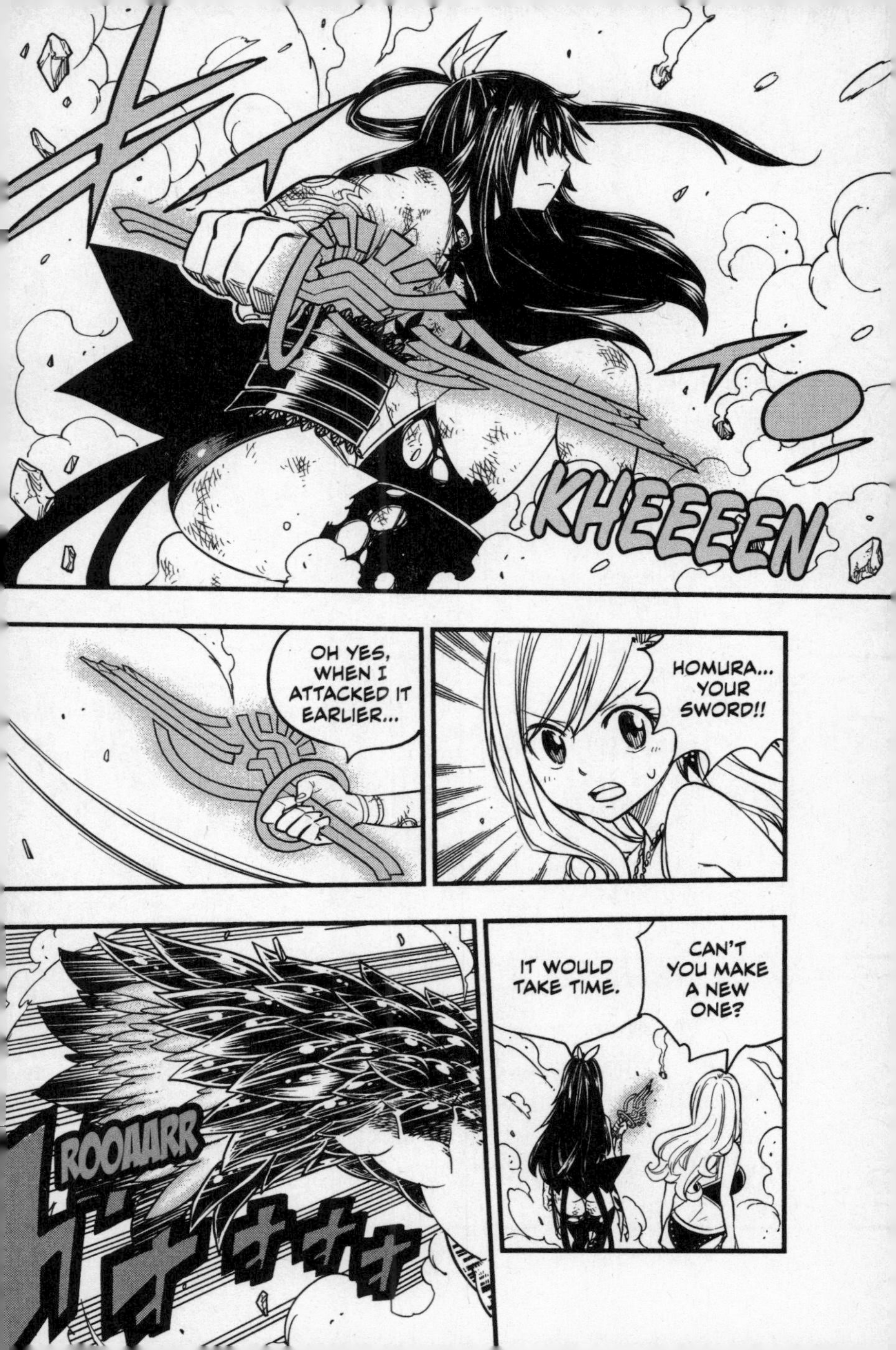
KHEEEEN
HOMURA... YOUR SWORD!!
OH YES, WHEN I ATTACKED IT EARLIER...
CAN'T YOU MAKE A NEW ONE?
IT WOULD TAKE TIME.
ROOAARR

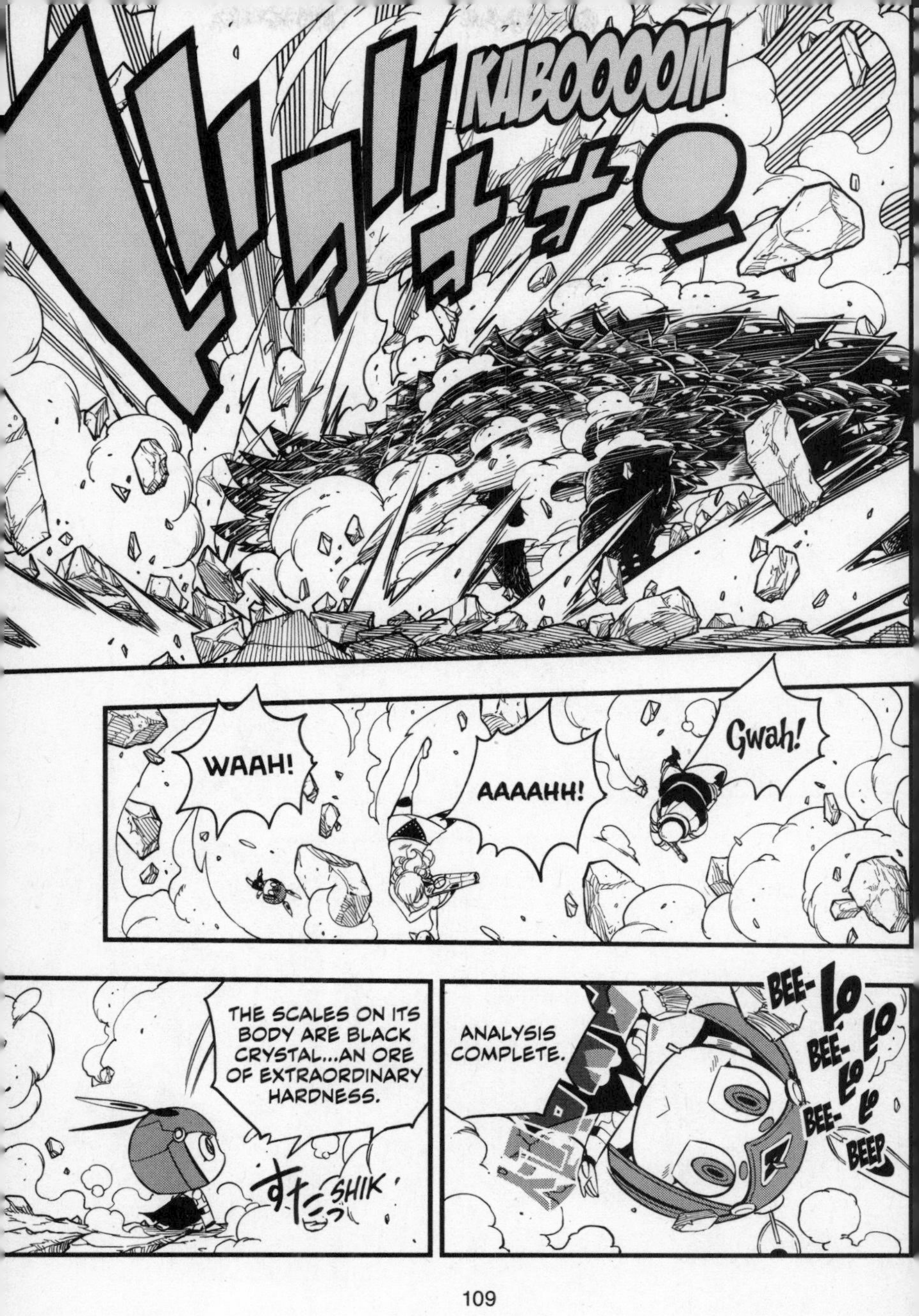
KABOOOOM
Gwah!
AAAAHH!
WAAH!
ANALYSIS COMPLETE.
BEE- BEE- BEE- BEEP
THE SCALES ON ITS BODY ARE BLACK CRYSTAL...AN ORE OF EXTRAORDINARY HARDNESS.
SHIK

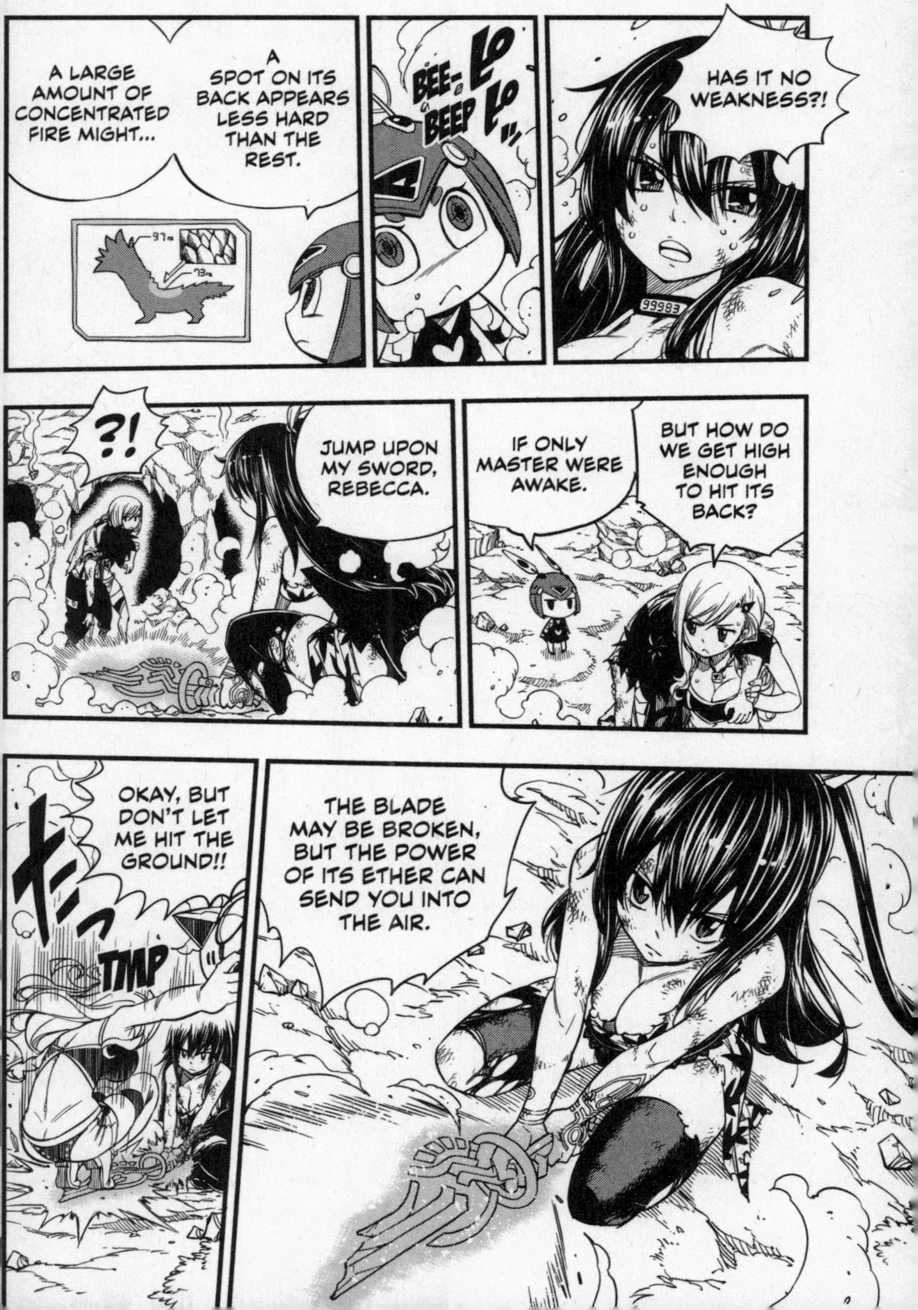
HAS IT NO WEAKNESS?!
99983
BEE-BEEP
LO LO
A SPOT ON ITS BACK APPEARS LESS HARD THAN THE REST.
A LARGE AMOUNT OF CONCENTRATED FIRE MIGHT...
BUT HOW DO WE GET HIGH ENOUGH TO HIT ITS BACK?
IF ONLY MASTER WERE AWAKE.
JUMP UPON MY SWORD, REBECCA.
?!
THE BLADE MAY BE BROKEN, BUT THE POWER OF ITS ETHER CAN SEND YOU INTO THE AIR.
OKAY, BUT DON'T LET ME HIT THE GROUND!!
TMP

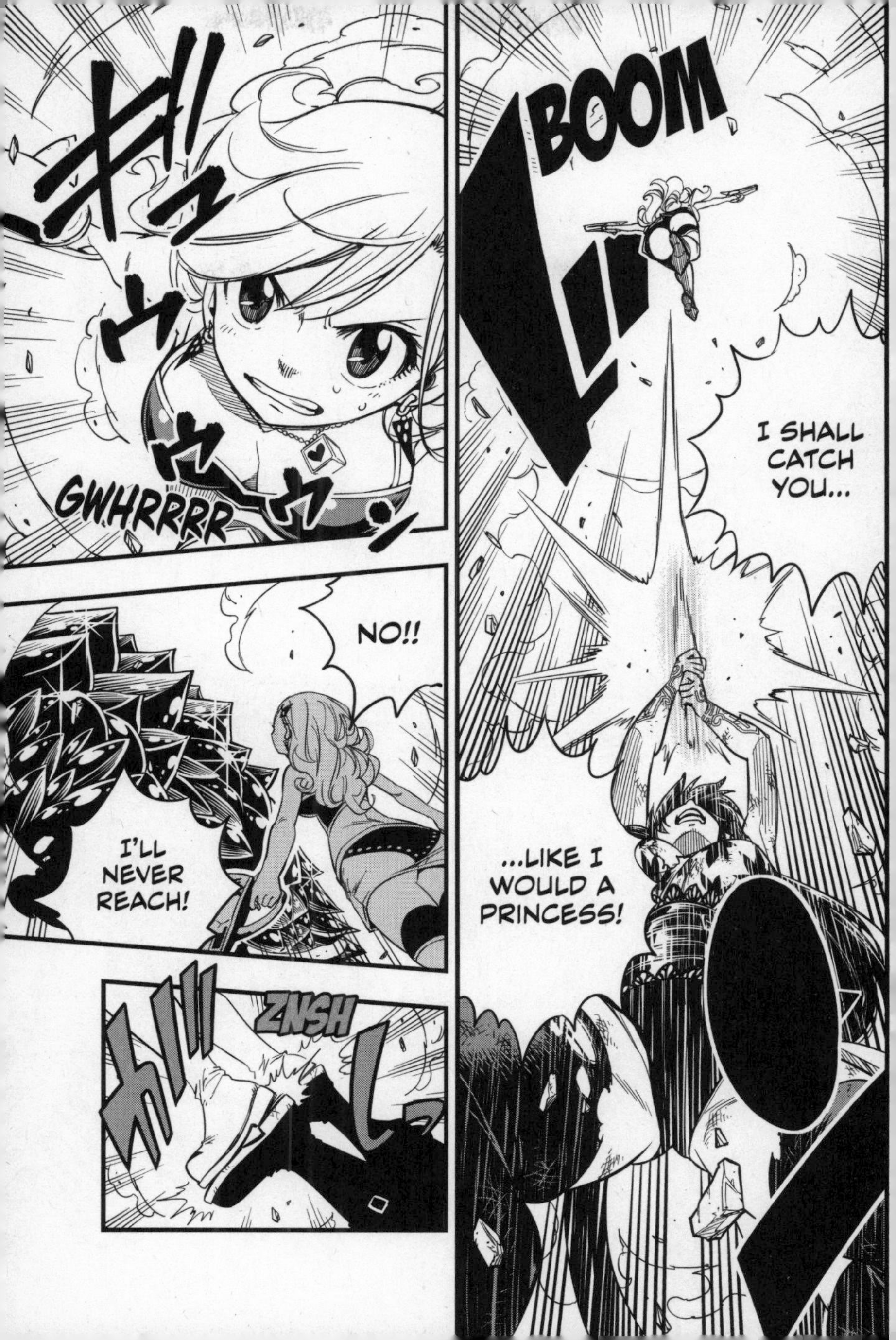
BOOM
I SHALL CATCH YOU...
...LIKE I WOULD A PRINCESS!
GWHRRRR
NO!!
I'LL NEVER REACH!
ZNSH

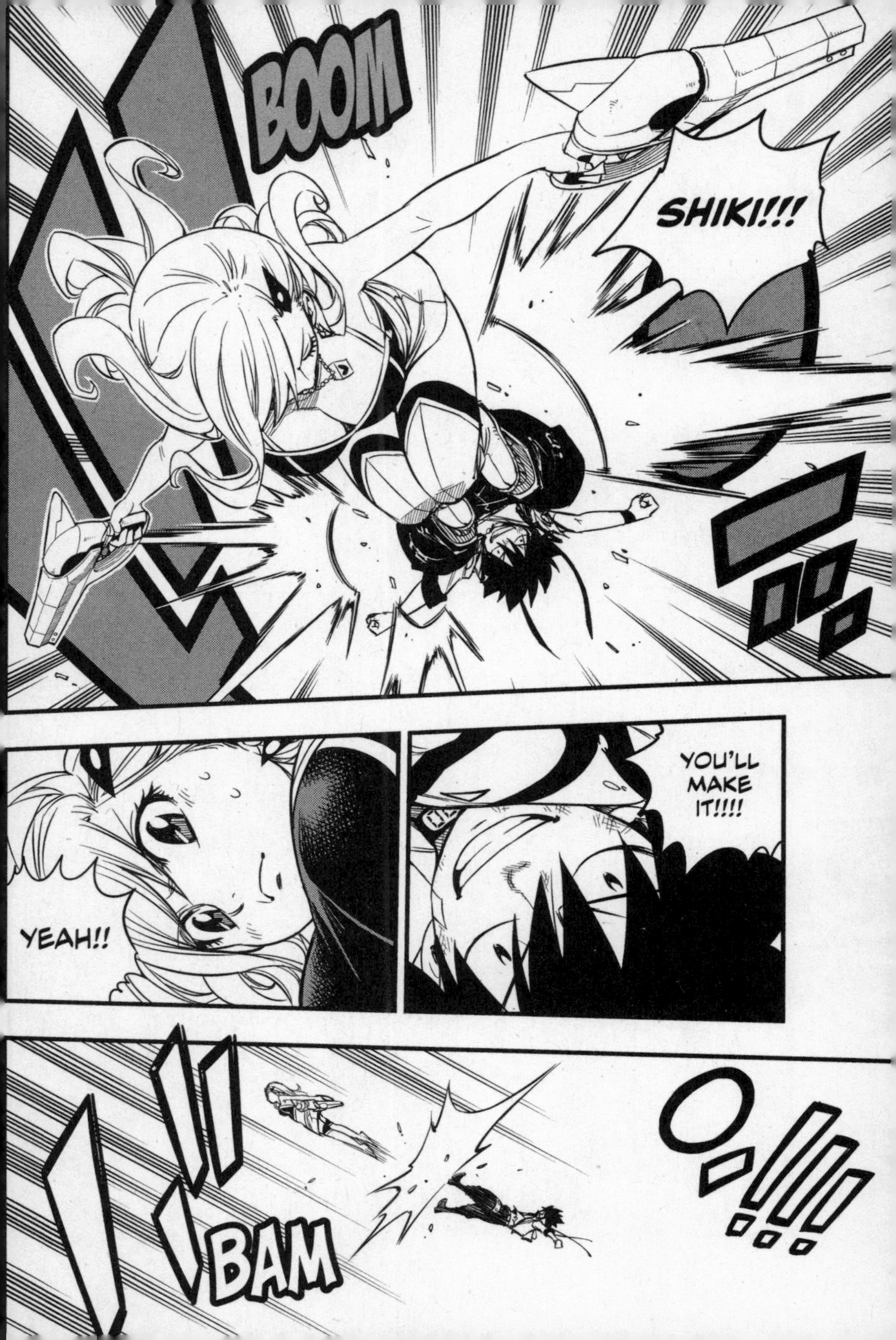
SHIKI!!!
BOOM
YOU'LL MAKE IT!!!!
YEAH!!
BAM

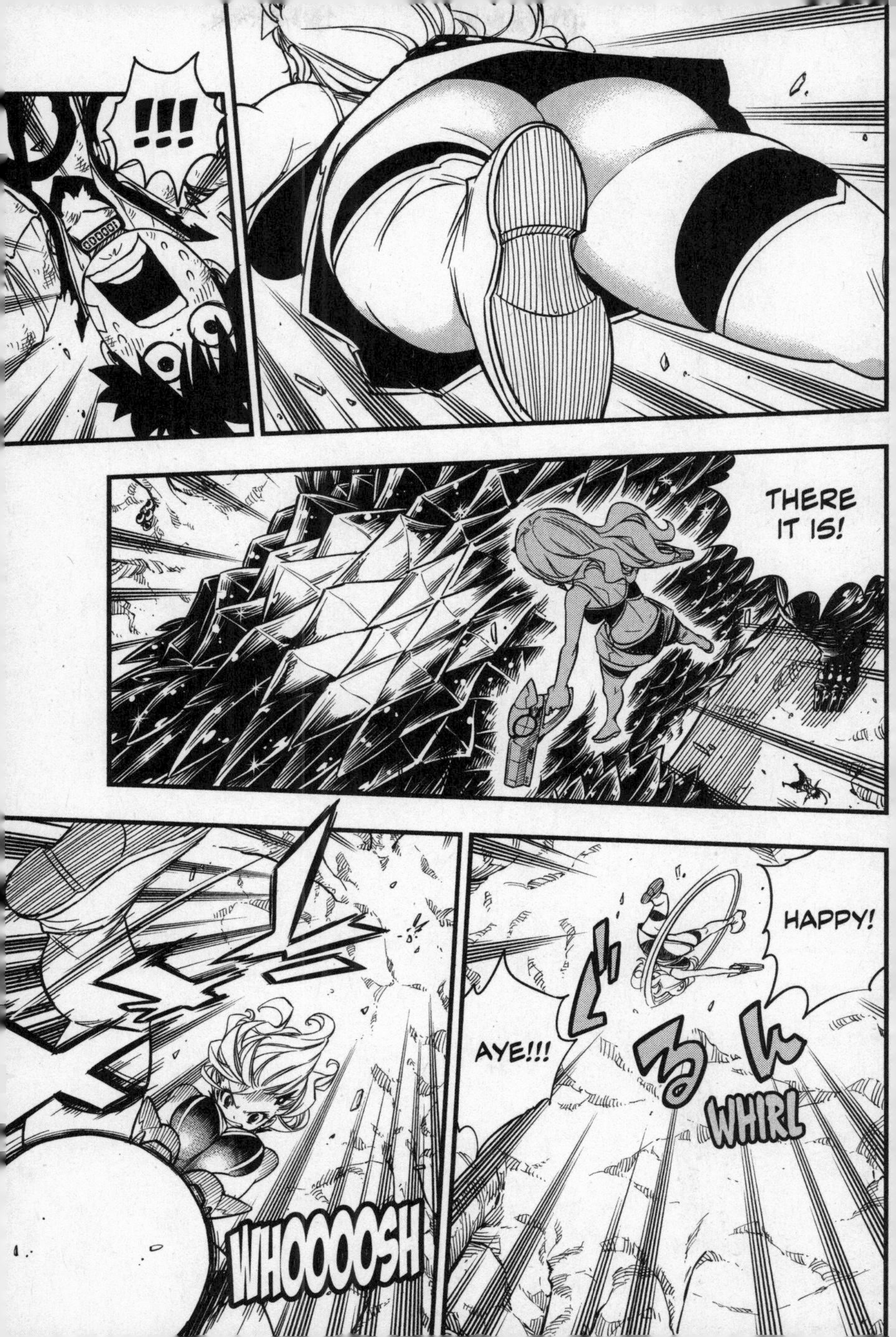
!!!
THERE IT IS!
HAPPY!
AYE!!!
ぐるん
WHIRL
WHOOOOSH

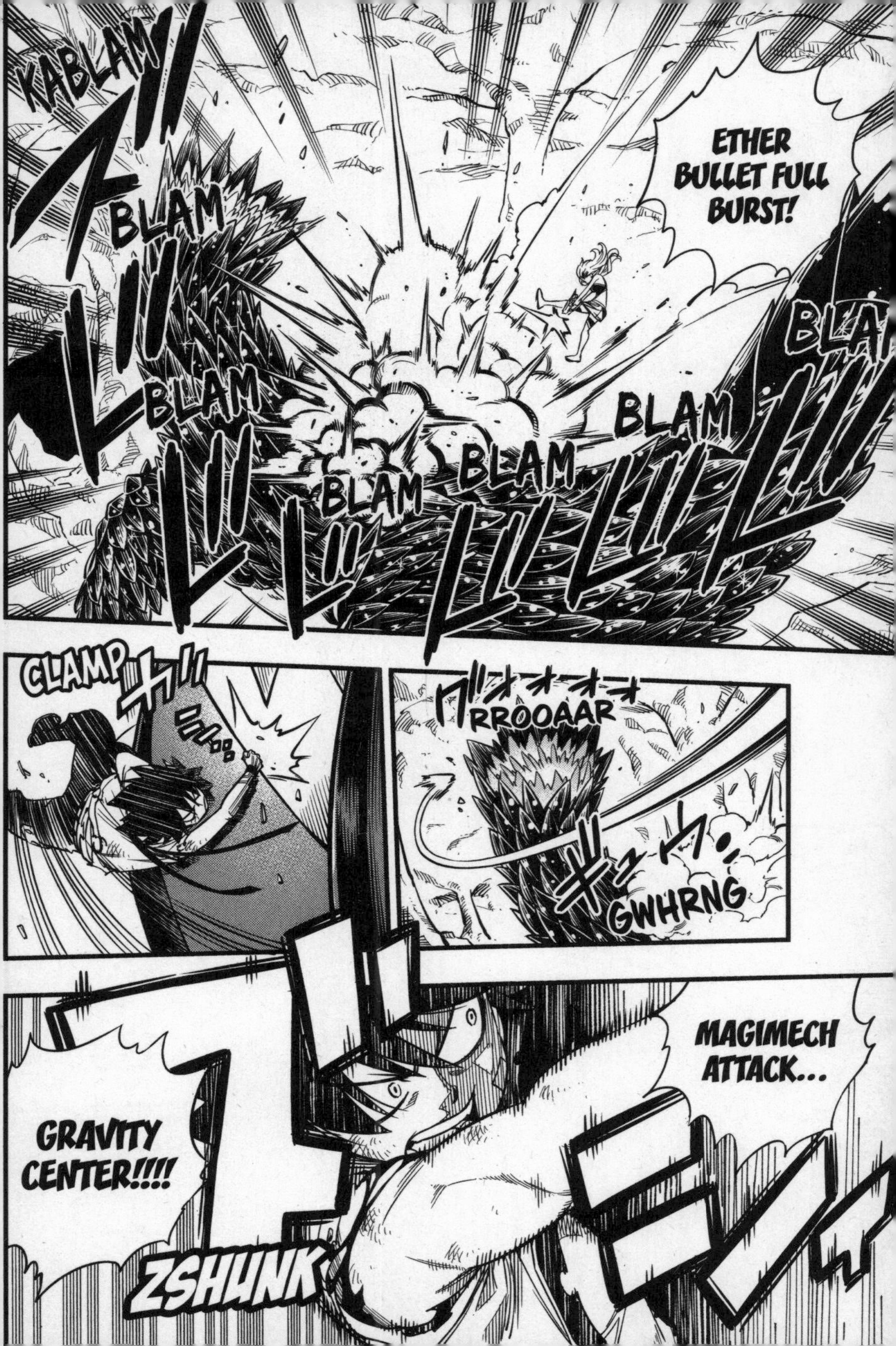
ETHER BULLET FULL BURST!
BLA
BLAM
BLAM
BLAM
BLAM
BLAM
KABLAM
RROOAAR
GWHRNG
CLAMP
MAGIMECH ATTACK...
GRAVITY CENTER!!!!
ZSHUNK

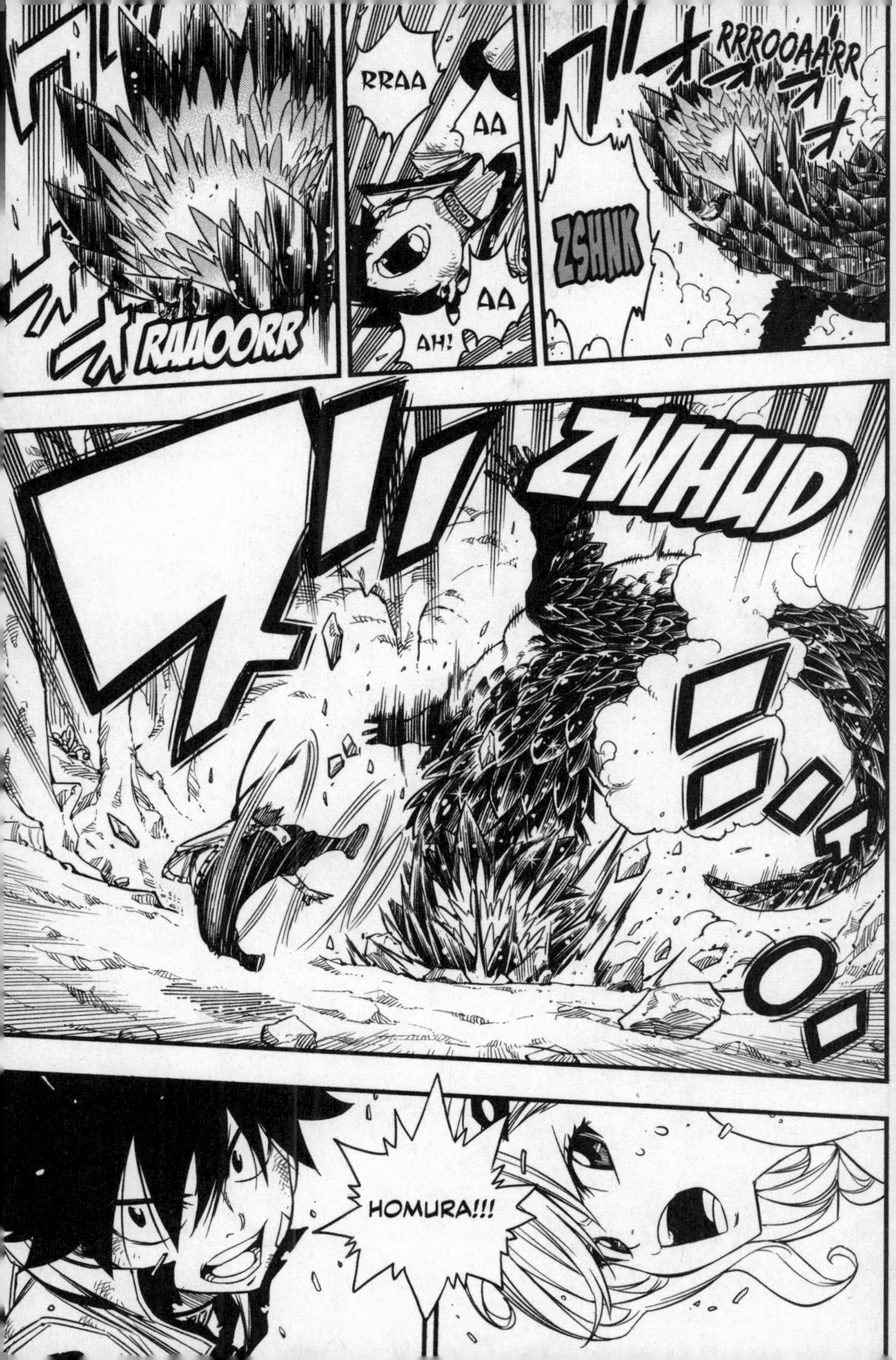
RRROOAARR
ZSHNK
RRAA
AA
AA
AH!
RAAAORR
ZWHUD
HOMURA!!!

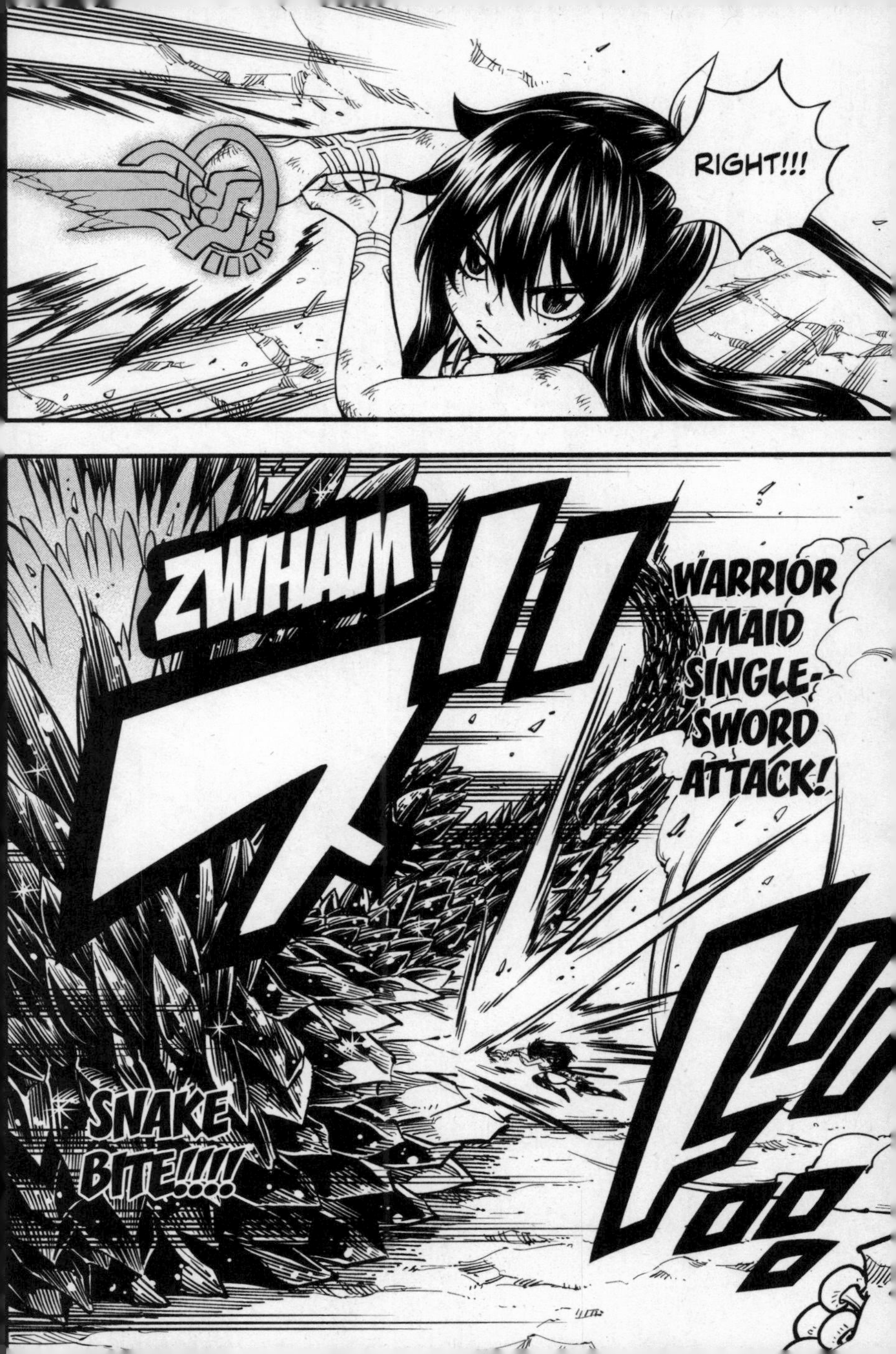
RIGHT!!!
WARRIOR MAID SINGLE-SWORD ATTACK!
ZWHAM
SNAKE BITE!!!!

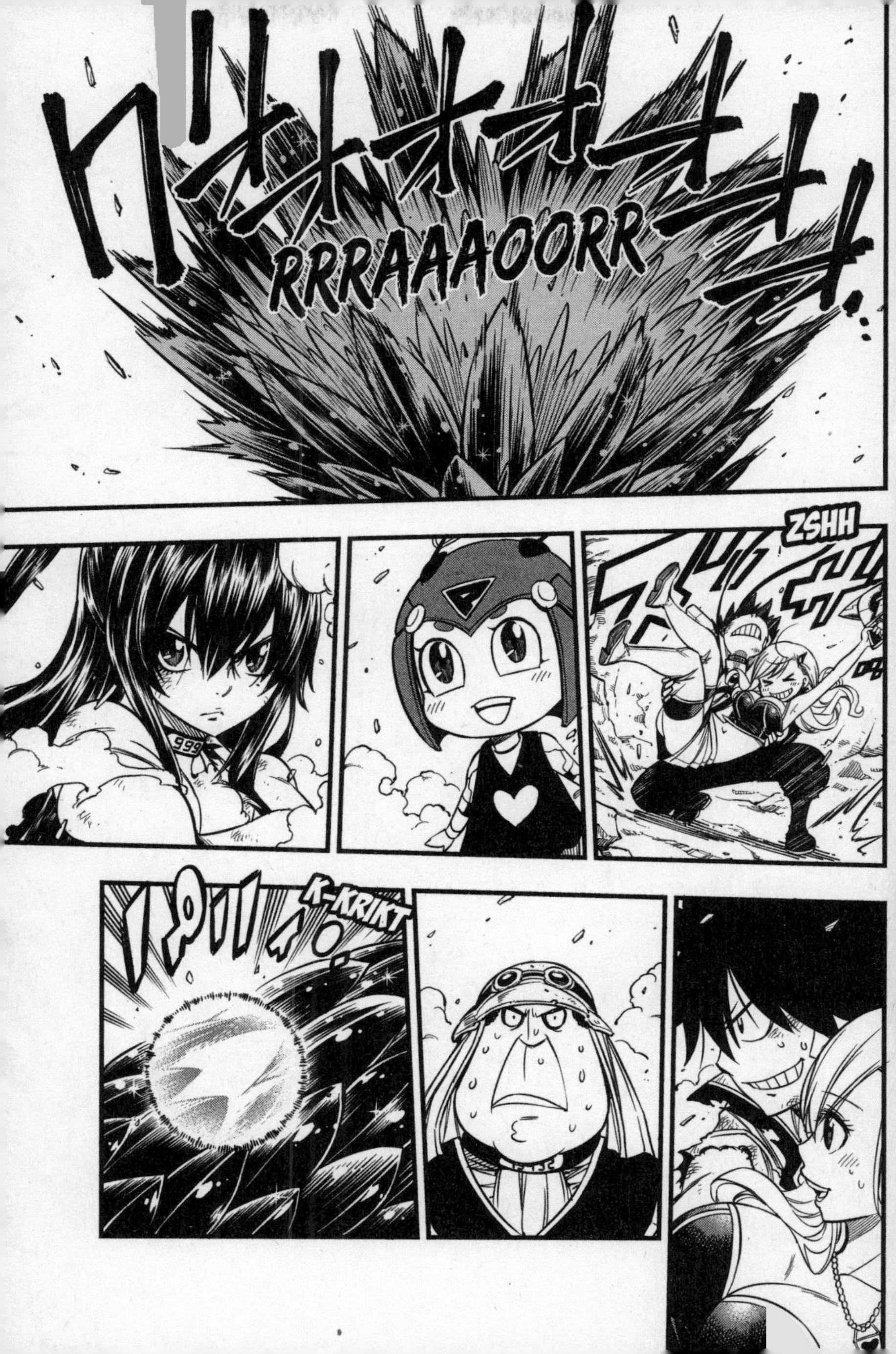
RRRAAAOORR
ZSHH
K-KRIKT

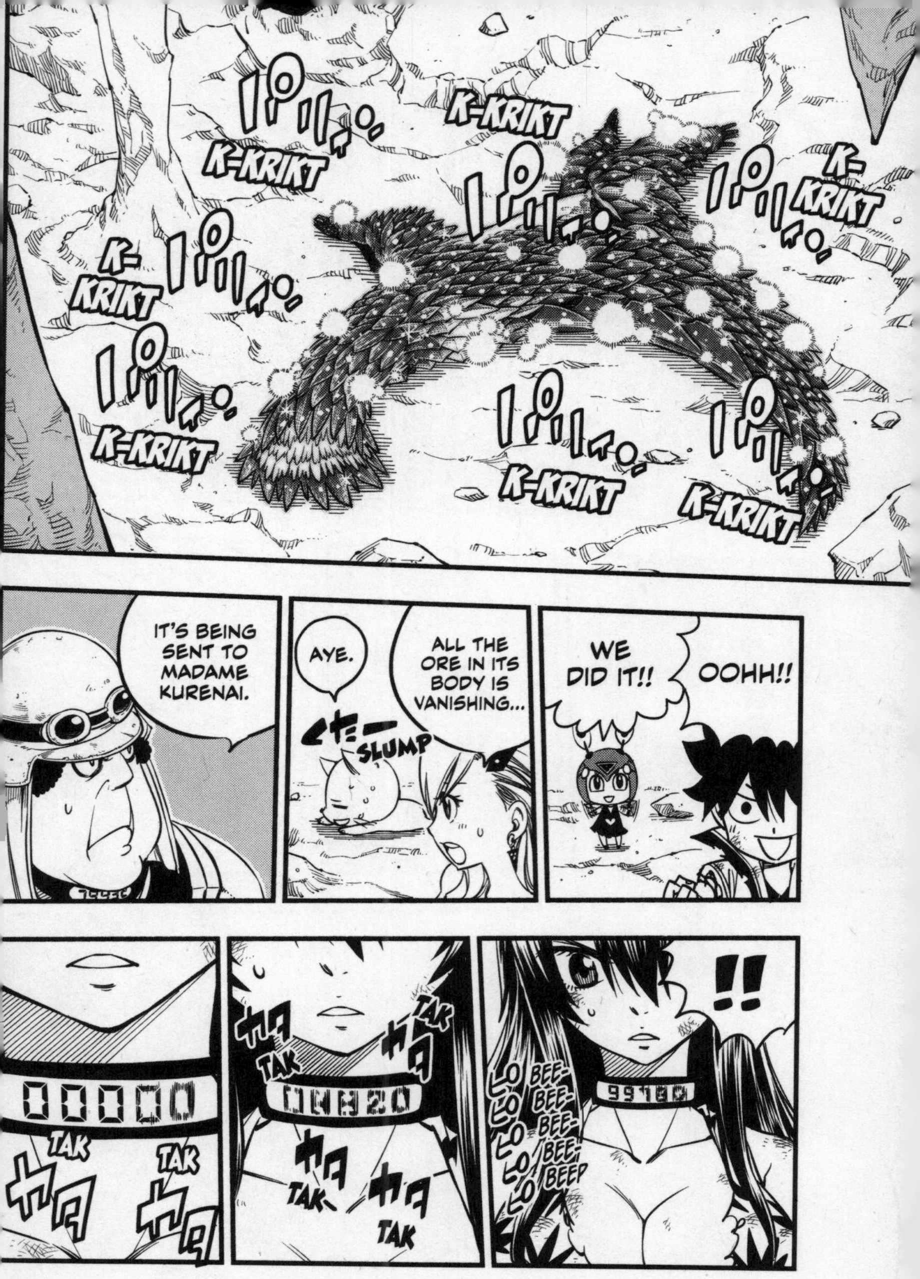
K-KRIKT
K-KRIKT
K-KRIKT
K-KRIKT
K-KRIKT
K-KRIKT
K-KRIKT
OOHH!!
WE DID IT!!
ALL THE ORE IN ITS BODY IS VANISHING...
AYE.
SLUMP
IT'S BEING SENT TO MADAME KURENAI.
!!
BEE-BEE-BEE-BEE-BEEP
TAK
TAK
TAK-
TAK
TAK
TAK

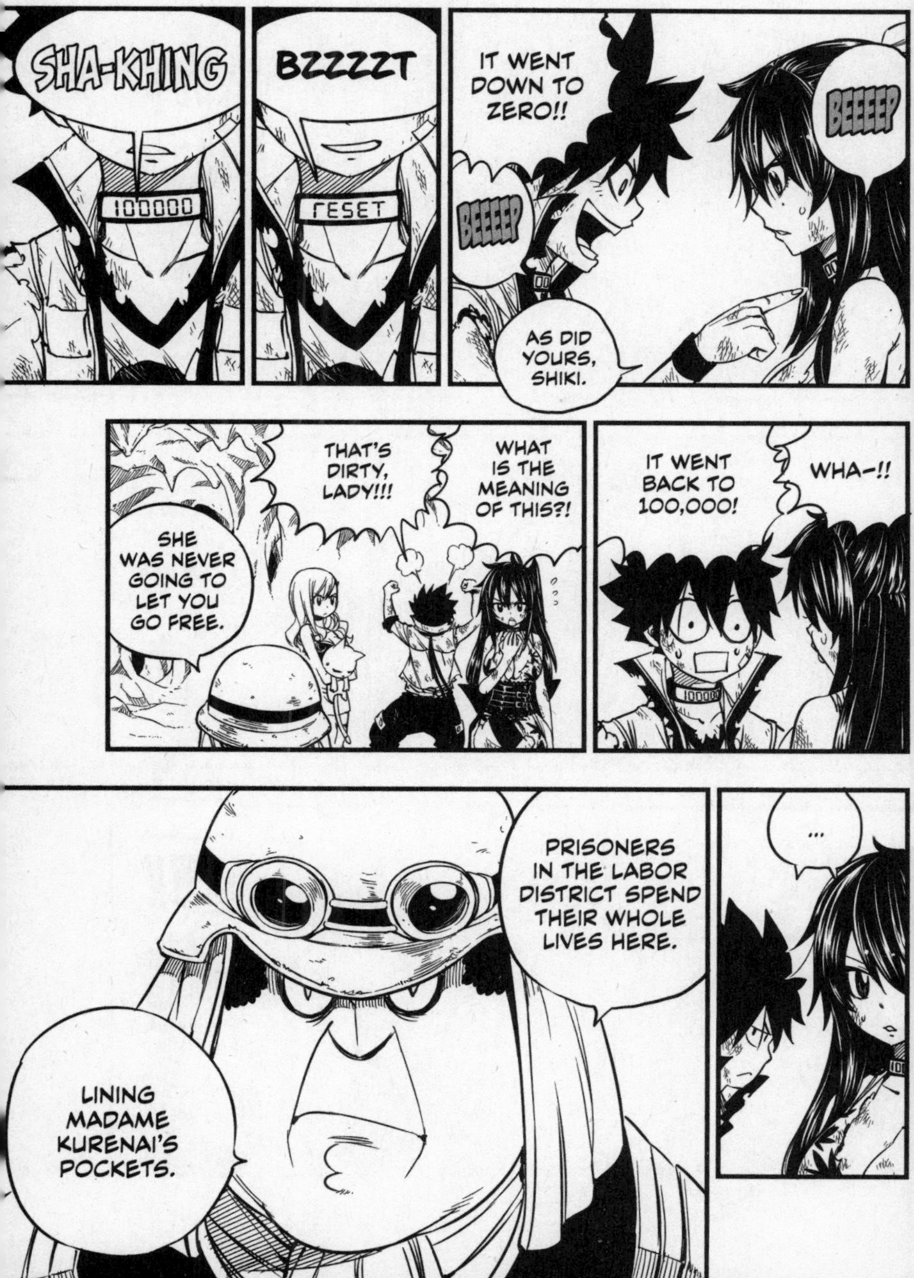
BEEEEP
IT WENT DOWN TO ZERO!!
BEEEEP
AS DID YOURS, SHIKI.
BZZZZZT
RESET
SHA-KHING
100000
WHA-!!
IT WENT BACK TO 100,000!
100000
WHAT IS THE MEANING OF THIS?!
THAT'S DIRTY, LADY!!!
SHE WAS NEVER GOING TO LET YOU GO FREE.
...
PRISONERS IN THE LABOR DISTRICT SPEND THEIR WHOLE LIVES HERE.
LINING MADAME KURENAI'S POCKETS.

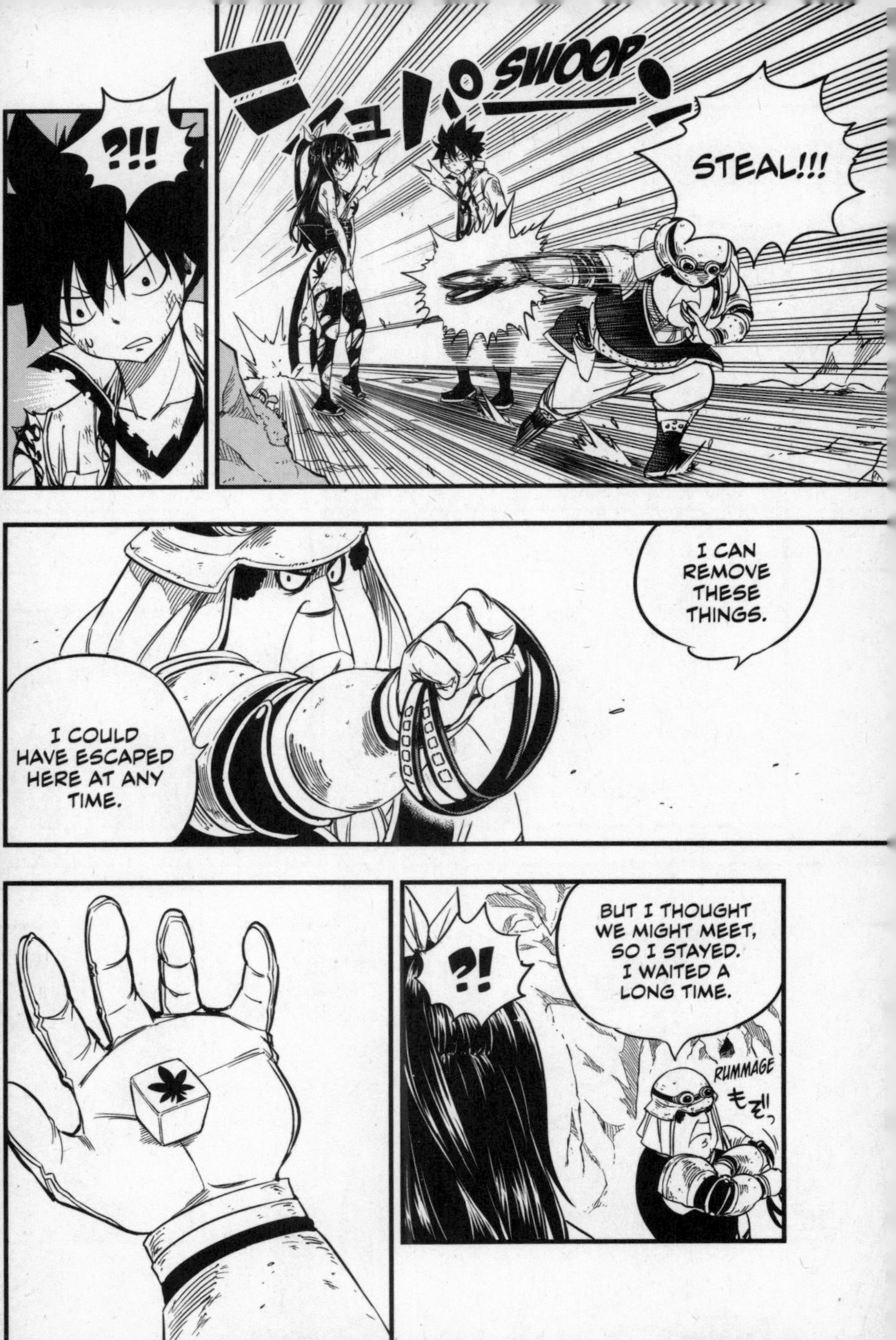
シュパーッ
SWOOP
STEAL!!!
?!!
I CAN REMOVE THESE THINGS.
I COULD HAVE ESCAPED HERE AT ANY TIME.
BUT I THOUGHT WE MIGHT MEET, SO I STAYED. I WAITED A LONG TIME.
?!
RUMMAGE
もぞっ

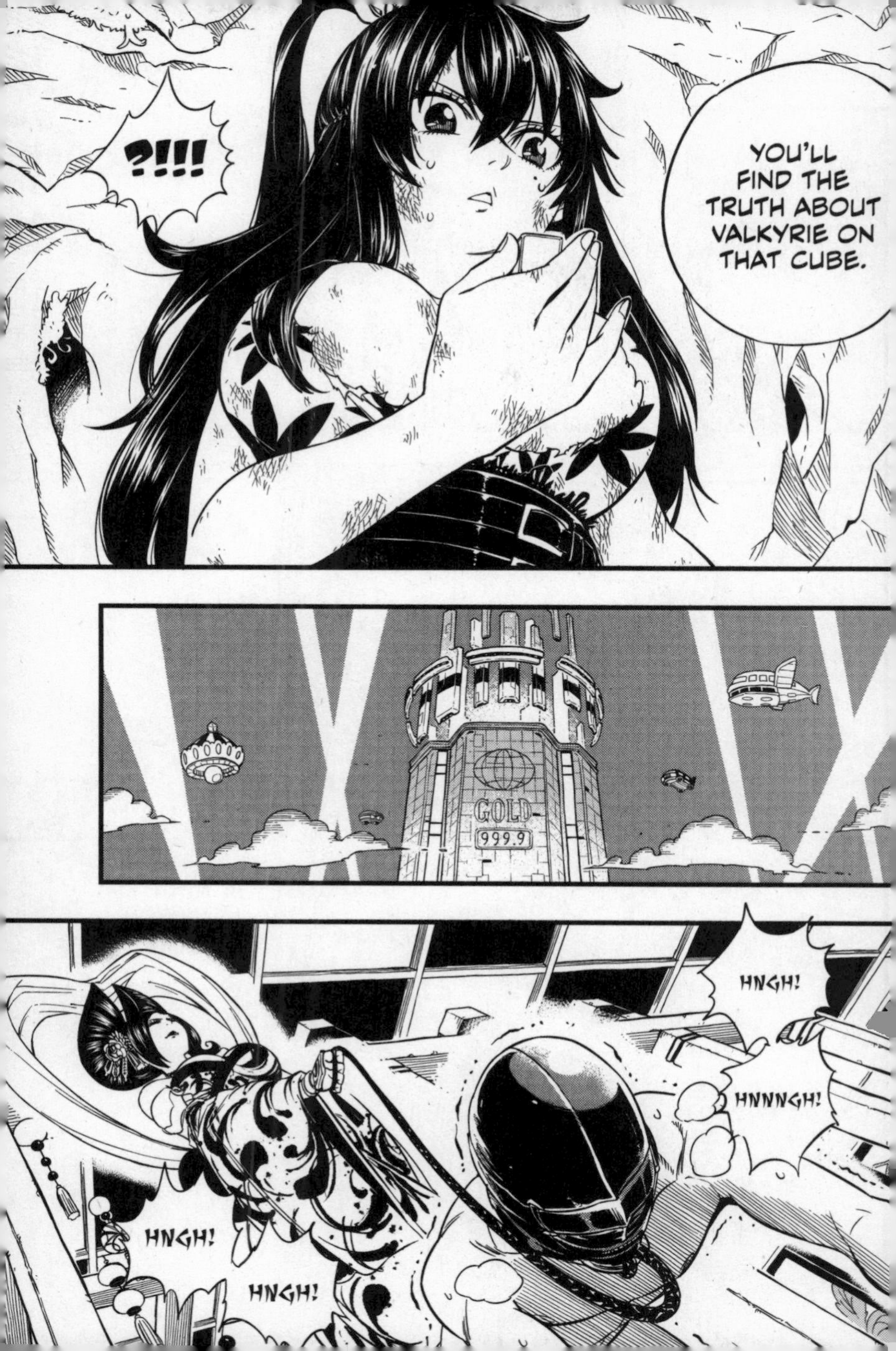
YOU'LL FIND THE TRUTH ABOUT VALKYRIE ON THAT CUBE.
?!!!!
GOLD
999.9
HNGH!
HNNNGH!
HNGH!
HNGH!

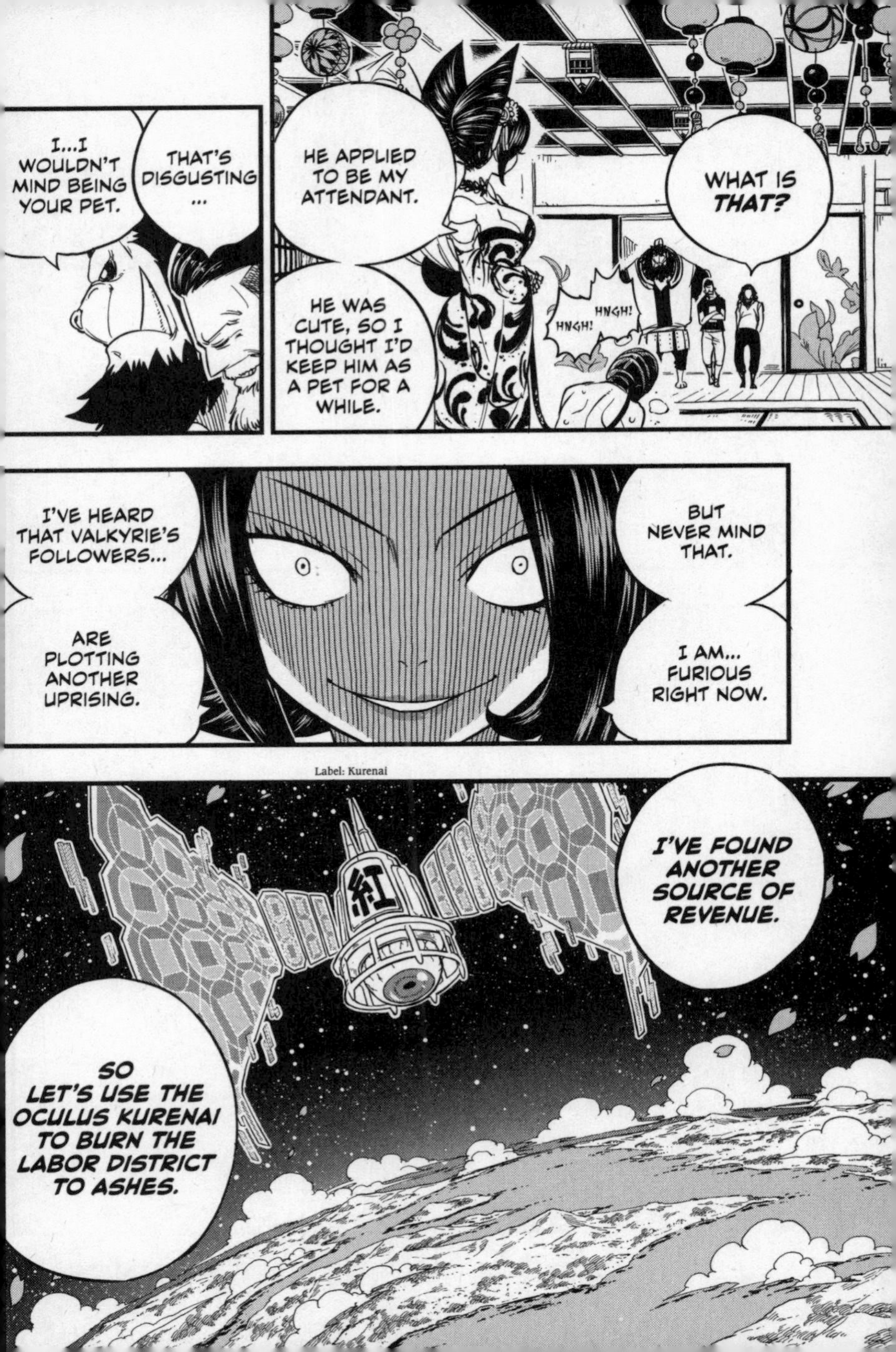
WHAT IS THAT?
HNGH! HNGH!
HE APPLIED TO BE MY ATTENDANT.
HE WAS CUTE, SO I THOUGHT I'D KEEP HIM AS A PET FOR A WHILE.
THAT'S DISGUSTING ...
I...I WOULDN'T MIND BEING YOUR PET.
BUT NEVER MIND THAT.
I AM... FURIOUS RIGHT NOW.
I'VE HEARD THAT VALKYRIE'S FOLLOWERS...
ARE PLOTTING ANOTHER UPRISING.
Label: Kurenai
紅
I'VE FOUND ANOTHER SOURCE OF REVENUE.
SO LET'S USE THE OCULUS KURENAI TO BURN THE LABOR DISTRICT TO ASHES.

EDENS ZERO

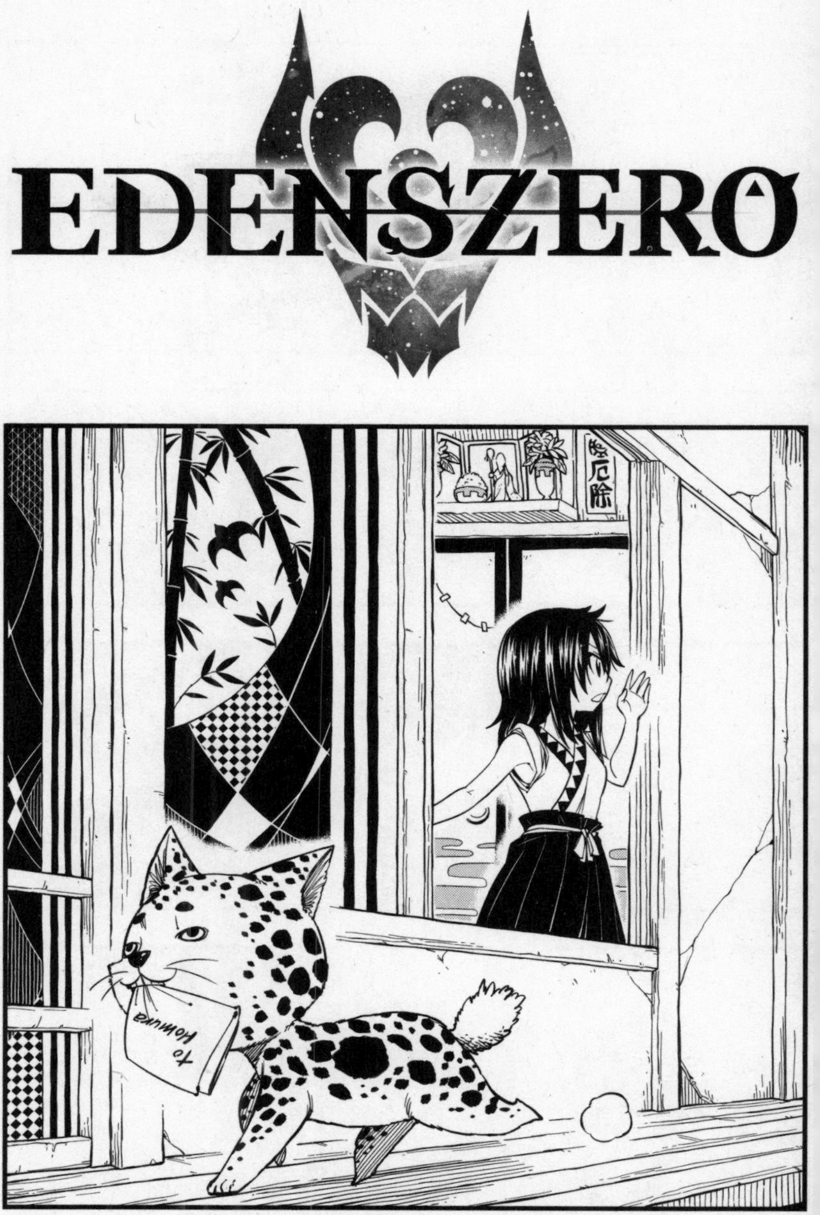
To Homura

CHAPTER 57: MY MOTHER'S A MACHINE

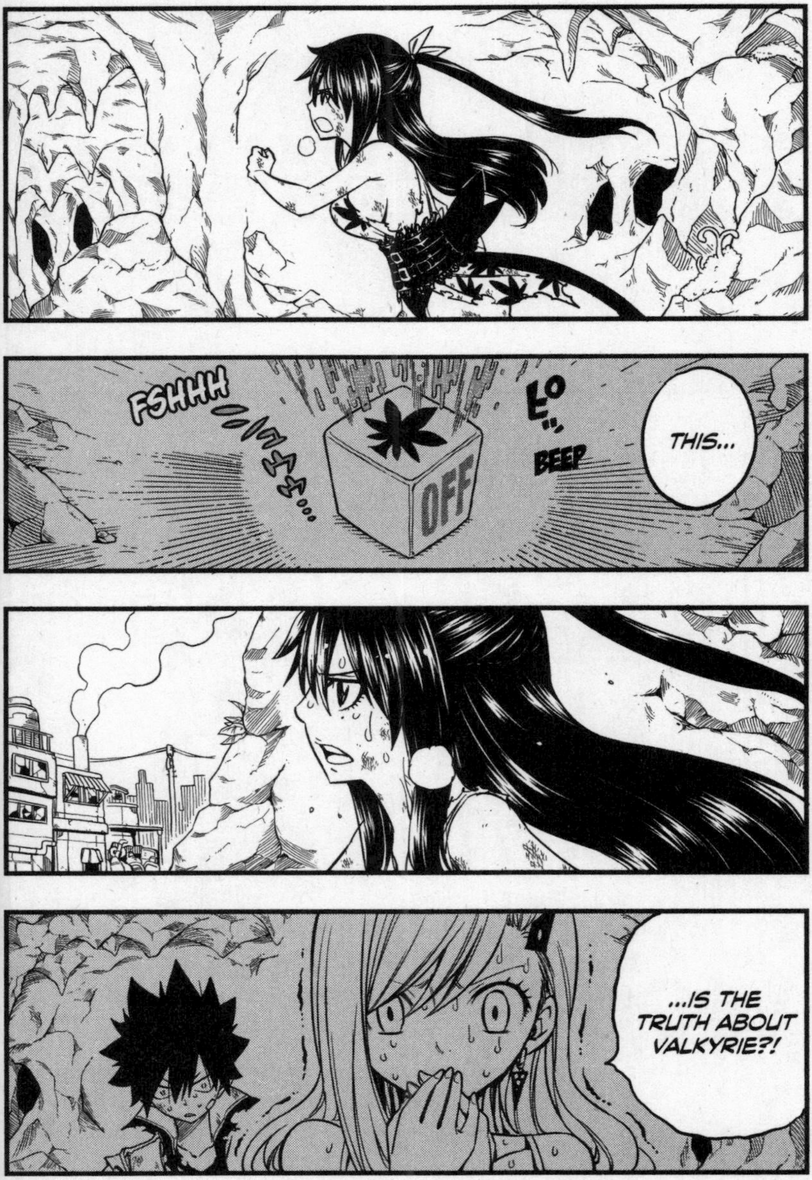
THIS...
BEEP
FSHHH
...IS THE TRUTH ABOUT VALKYRIE?!

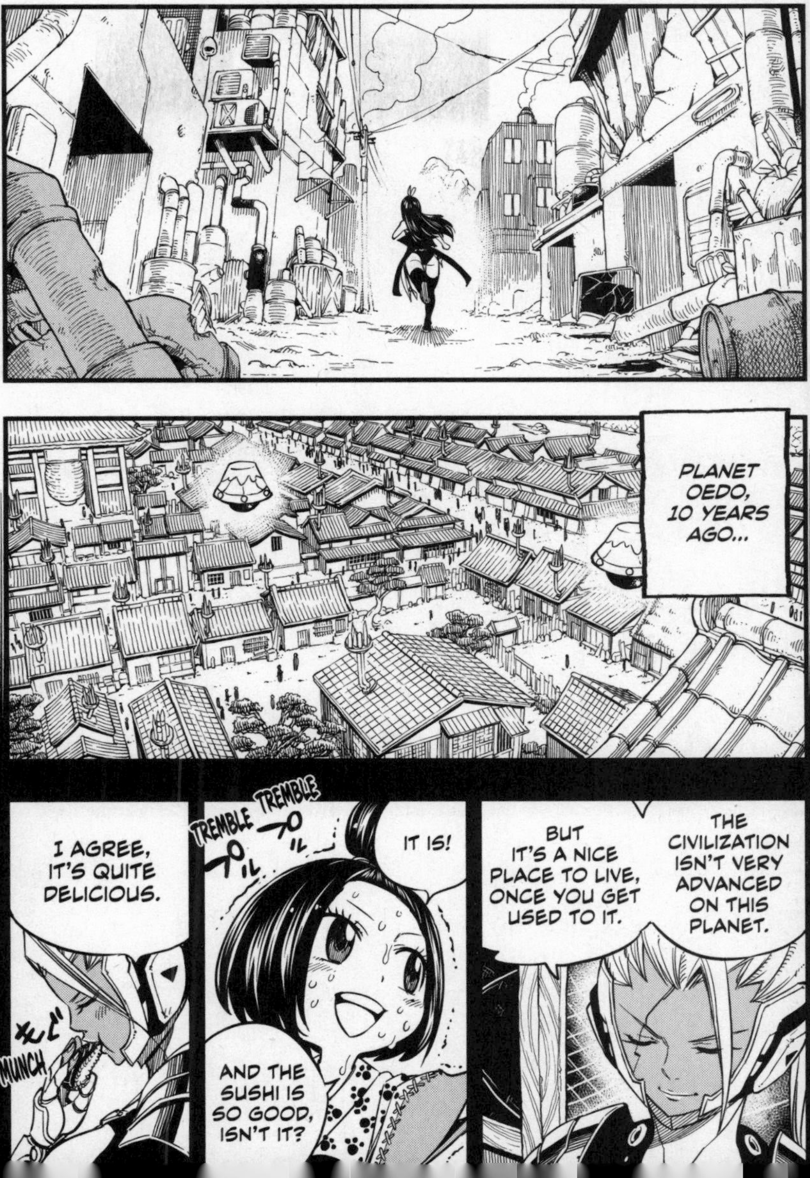
PLANET OEDO, 10 YEARS AGO...
THE CIVILIZATION ISN'T VERY ADVANCED ON THIS PLANET.
BUT IT'S A NICE PLACE TO LIVE, ONCE YOU GET USED TO IT.
IT IS!
TREMBLE TREMBLE
AND THE SUSHI IS SO GOOD, ISN'T IT?
I AGREE, IT'S QUITE DELICIOUS.
MUNCH

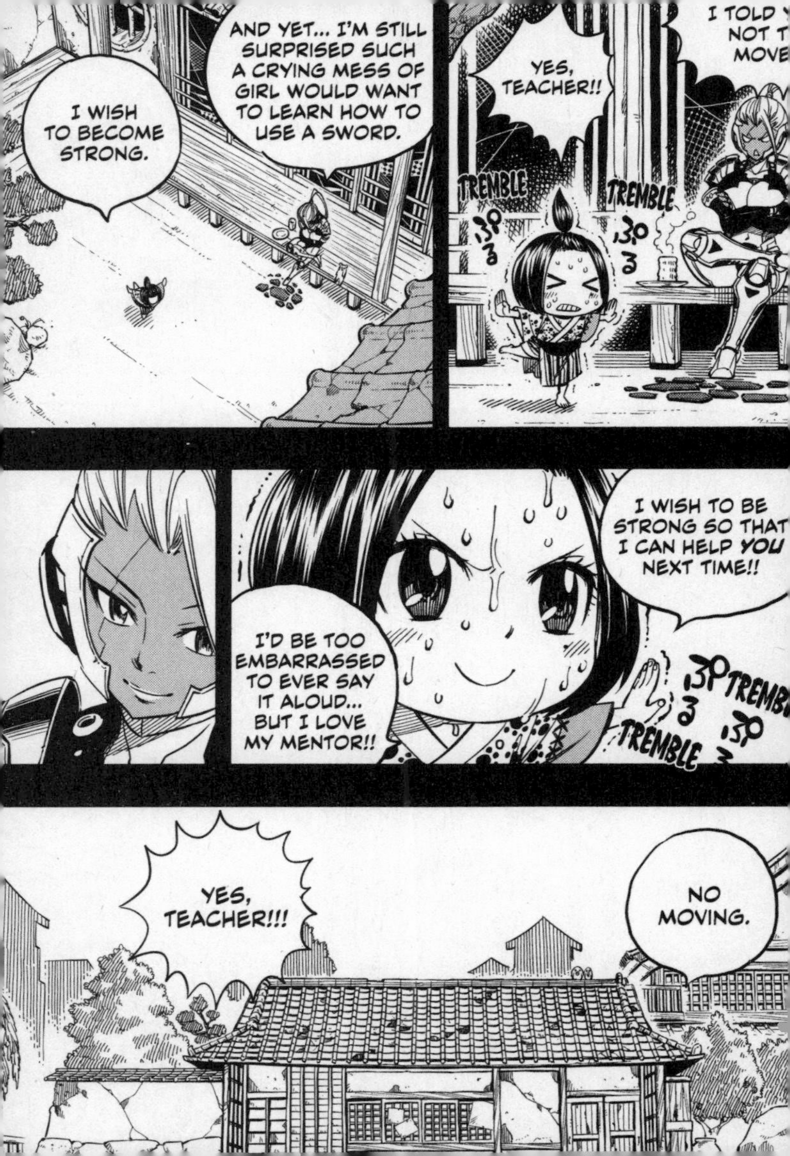
I TOLD
NOT T
MOVE
YES, TEACHER!!
TREMBLE
TREMBLE
AND YET... I'M STILL SURPRISED SUCH A CRYING MESS OF GIRL WOULD WANT TO LEARN HOW TO USE A SWORD.
I WISH TO BECOME STRONG.
I WISH TO BE STRONG SO THAT I CAN HELP *YOU* NEXT TIME!!
TREMBL
TREMBLE
I'D BE TOO EMBARRASSED TO EVER SAY IT ALOUD... BUT I LOVE MY MENTOR!!
NO MOVING.
YES, TEACHER!!!

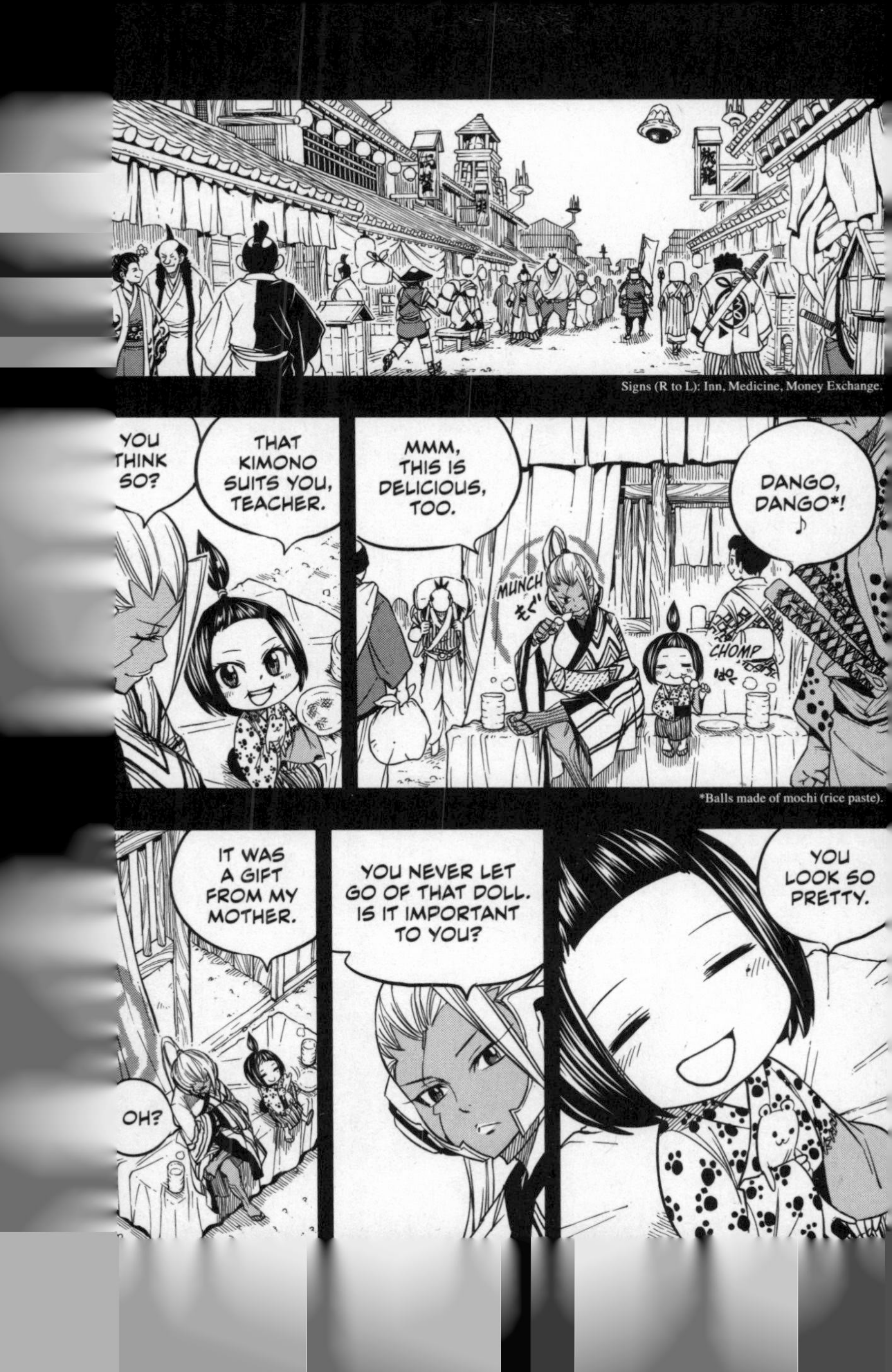
DANGO, DANGO*! ♪
MMM, THIS IS DELICIOUS, TOO.
MUNCH
CHOMP
THAT KIMONO SUITS YOU, TEACHER.
YOU THINK SO?
YOU LOOK SO PRETTY.
YOU NEVER LET GO OF THAT DOLL. IS IT IMPORTANT TO YOU?
IT WAS A GIFT FROM MY MOTHER.
OH?

Signs (R to L): Inn, Medicine, Money Exchange.

*Balls made of mochi (rice paste).

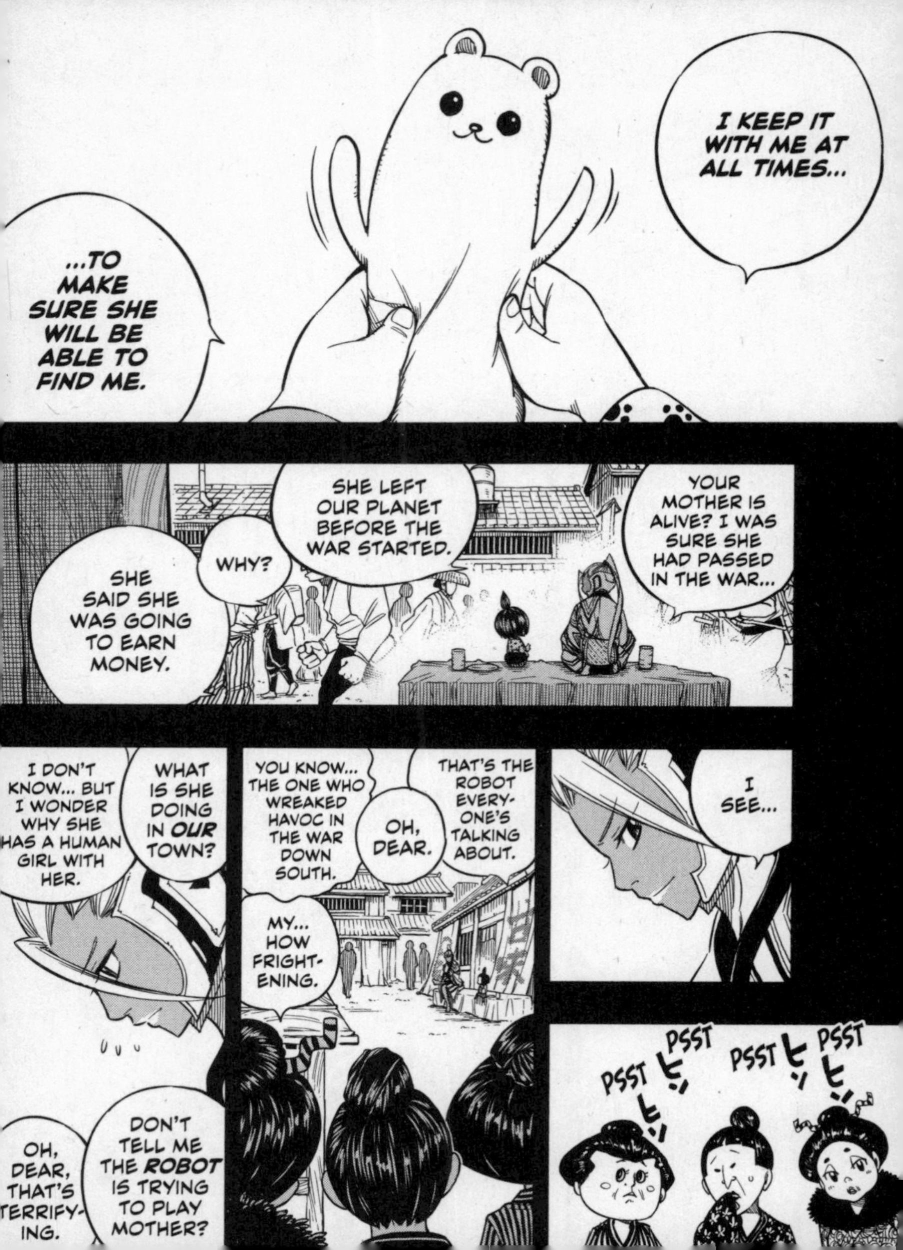
I KEEP IT WITH ME AT ALL TIMES...
...TO MAKE SURE SHE WILL BE ABLE TO FIND ME.
YOUR MOTHER IS ALIVE? I WAS SURE SHE HAD PASSED IN THE WAR...
SHE LEFT OUR PLANET BEFORE THE WAR STARTED.
WHY?
SHE SAID SHE WAS GOING TO EARN MONEY.
I SEE...
PSST
PSST
PSST
PSST
THAT'S THE ROBOT EVERYONE'S TALKING ABOUT.
OH, DEAR.
YOU KNOW... THE ONE WHO WREAKED HAVOC IN THE WAR DOWN SOUTH.
MY... HOW FRIGHTENING.
WHAT IS SHE DOING IN OUR TOWN?
I DON'T KNOW... BUT I WONDER WHY SHE HAS A HUMAN GIRL WITH HER.
DON'T TELL ME THE ROBOT IS TRYING TO PLAY MOTHER?
OH, DEAR, THAT'S TERRIFYING.

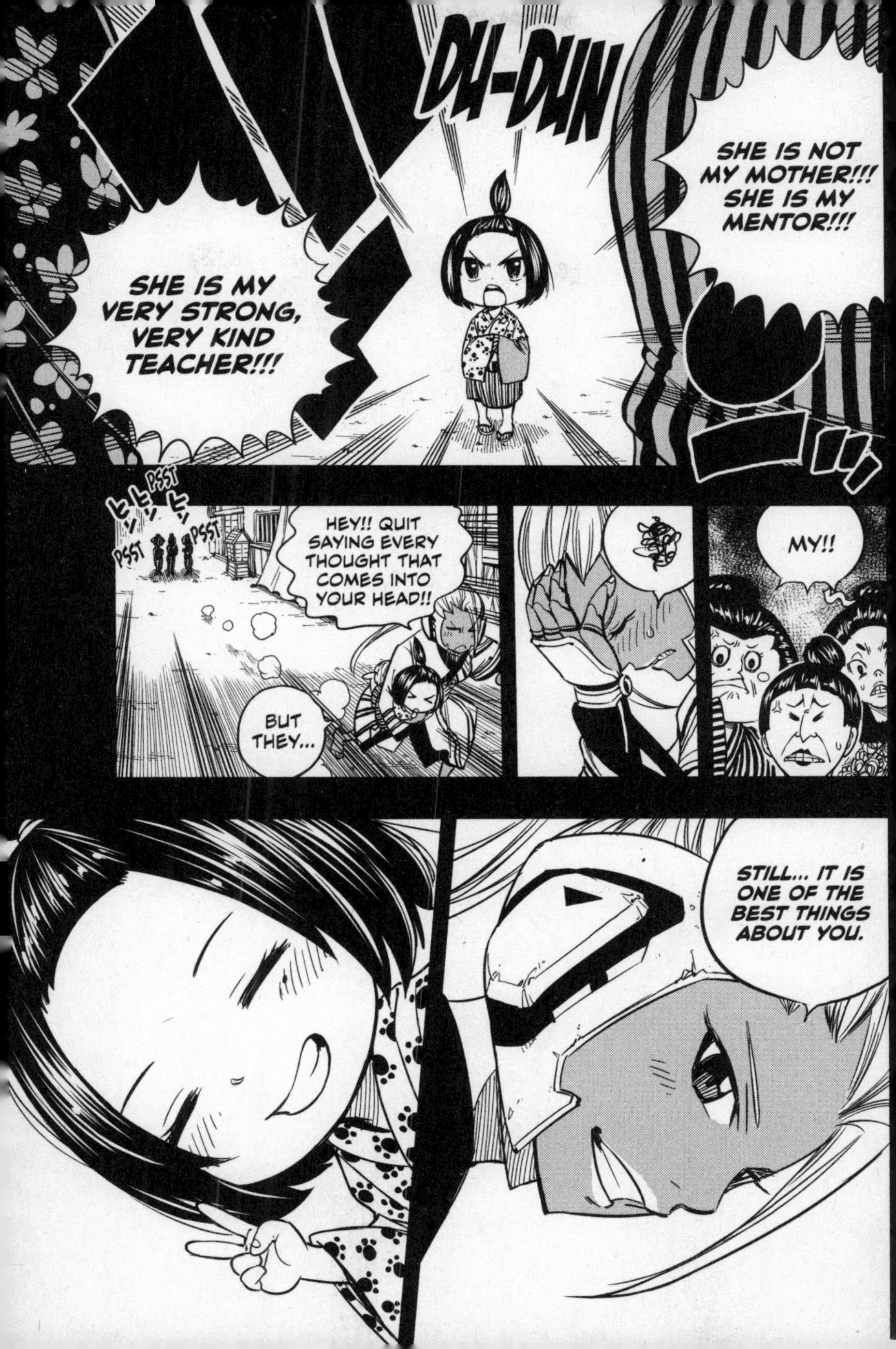
DU-DUN
SHE IS NOT MY MOTHER!!! SHE IS MY MENTOR!!!
SHE IS MY VERY STRONG, VERY KIND TEACHER!!!
MY!!
PSST PSST PSST
HEY!! QUIT SAYING EVERY THOUGHT THAT COMES INTO YOUR HEAD!!
BUT THEY...
STILL... IT IS ONE OF THE BEST THINGS ABOUT YOU.

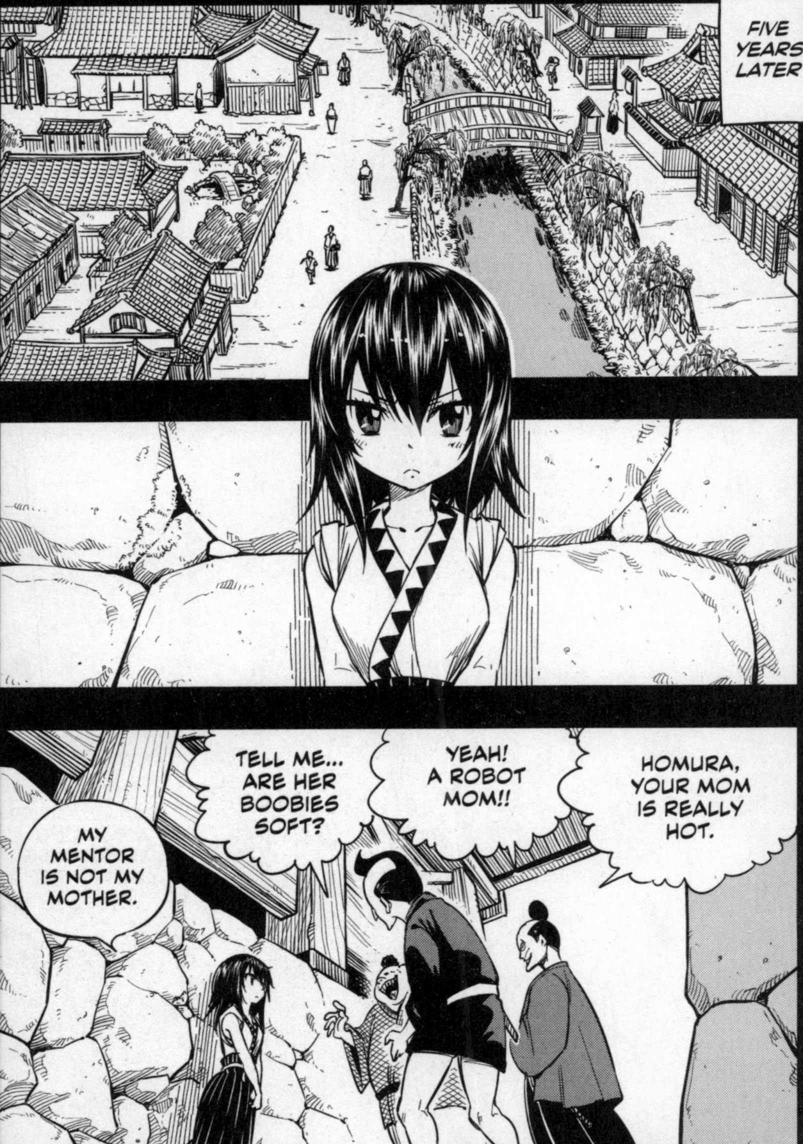
FIVE YEARS LATER
HOMURA, YOUR MOM IS REALLY HOT.
YEAH! A ROBOT MOM!!
TELL ME... ARE HER BOOBIES SOFT?
MY MENTOR IS NOT MY MOTHER.

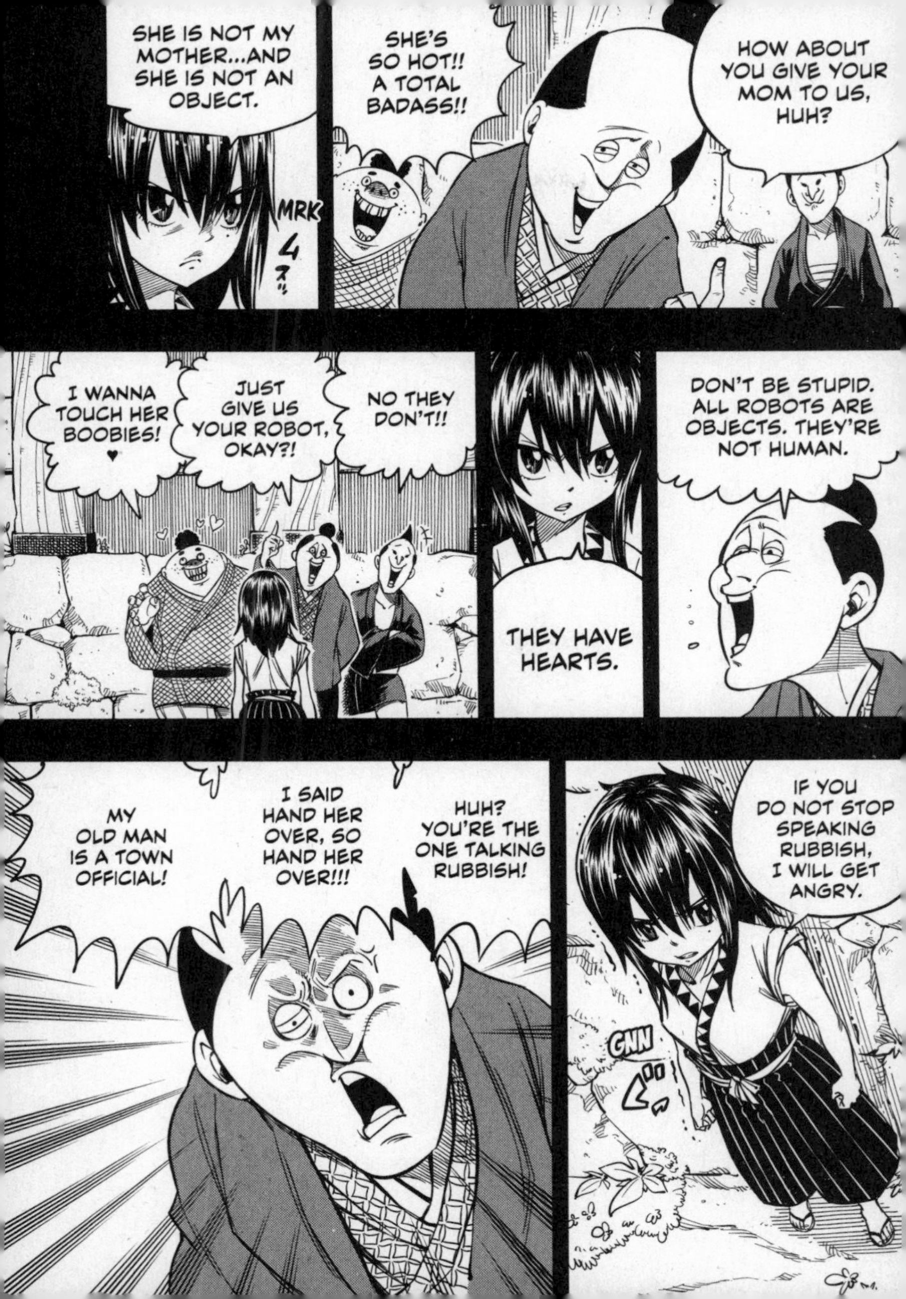
HOW ABOUT YOU GIVE YOUR MOM TO US, HUH?
SHE'S SO HOT!! A TOTAL BADASS!!
SHE IS NOT MY MOTHER...AND SHE IS NOT AN OBJECT.
MRK
DON'T BE STUPID. ALL ROBOTS ARE OBJECTS. THEY'RE NOT HUMAN.
THEY HAVE HEARTS.
NO THEY DON'T!!
JUST GIVE US YOUR ROBOT, OKAY?!
I WANNA TOUCH HER BOOBIES! ♥
IF YOU DO NOT STOP SPEAKING RUBBISH, I WILL GET ANGRY.
GNN
HUH? YOU'RE THE ONE TALKING RUBBISH!
I SAID HAND HER OVER, SO HAND HER OVER!!!
MY OLD MAN IS A TOWN OFFICIAL!

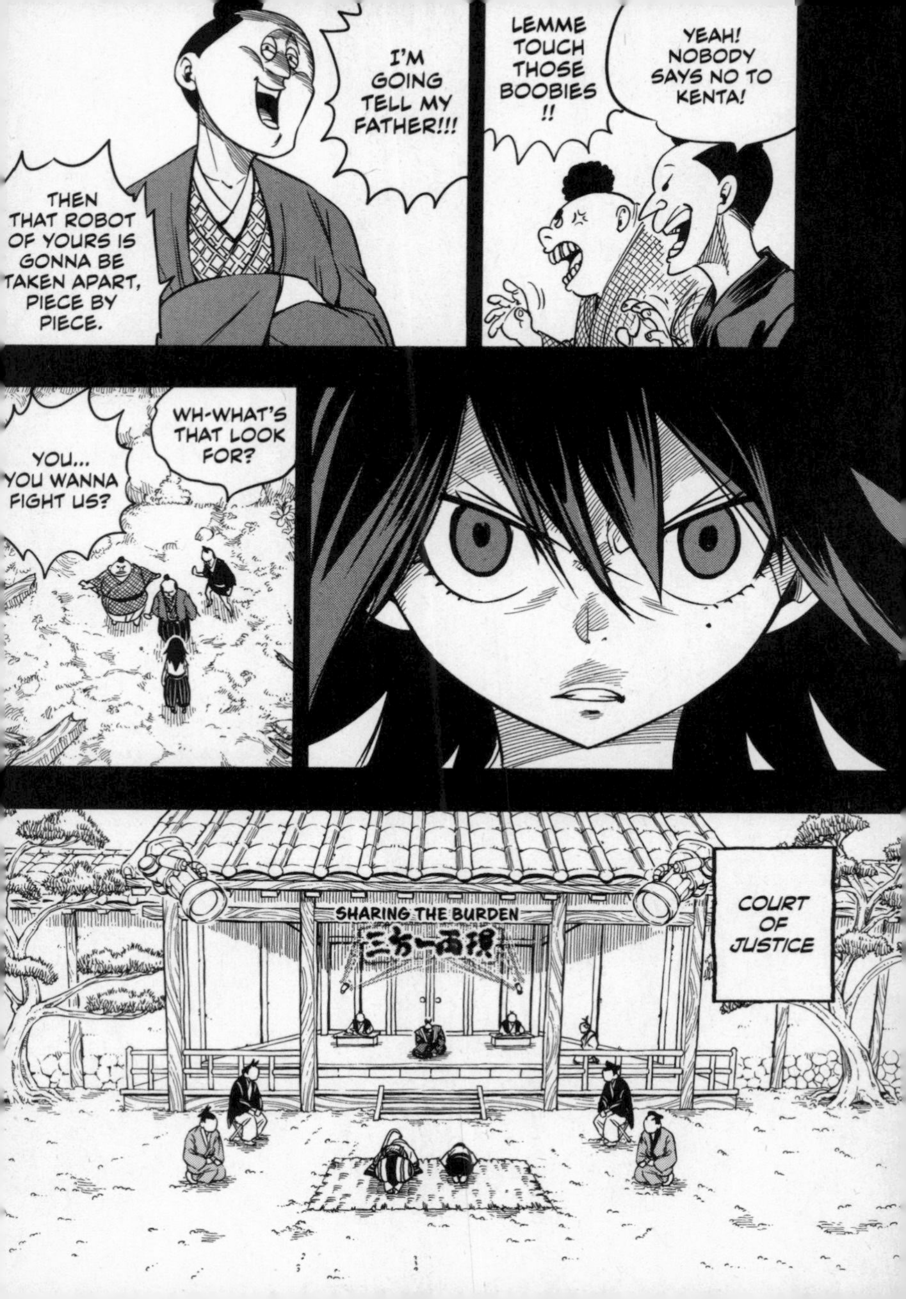
YEAH! NOBODY SAYS NO TO KENTA!
LEMME TOUCH THOSE BOOBIES !!
I'M GOING TELL MY FATHER!!!
THEN THAT ROBOT OF YOURS IS GONNA BE TAKEN APART, PIECE BY PIECE.
WH-WHAT'S THAT LOOK FOR?
YOU... YOU WANNA FIGHT US?
COURT OF JUSTICE
SHARING THE BURDEN

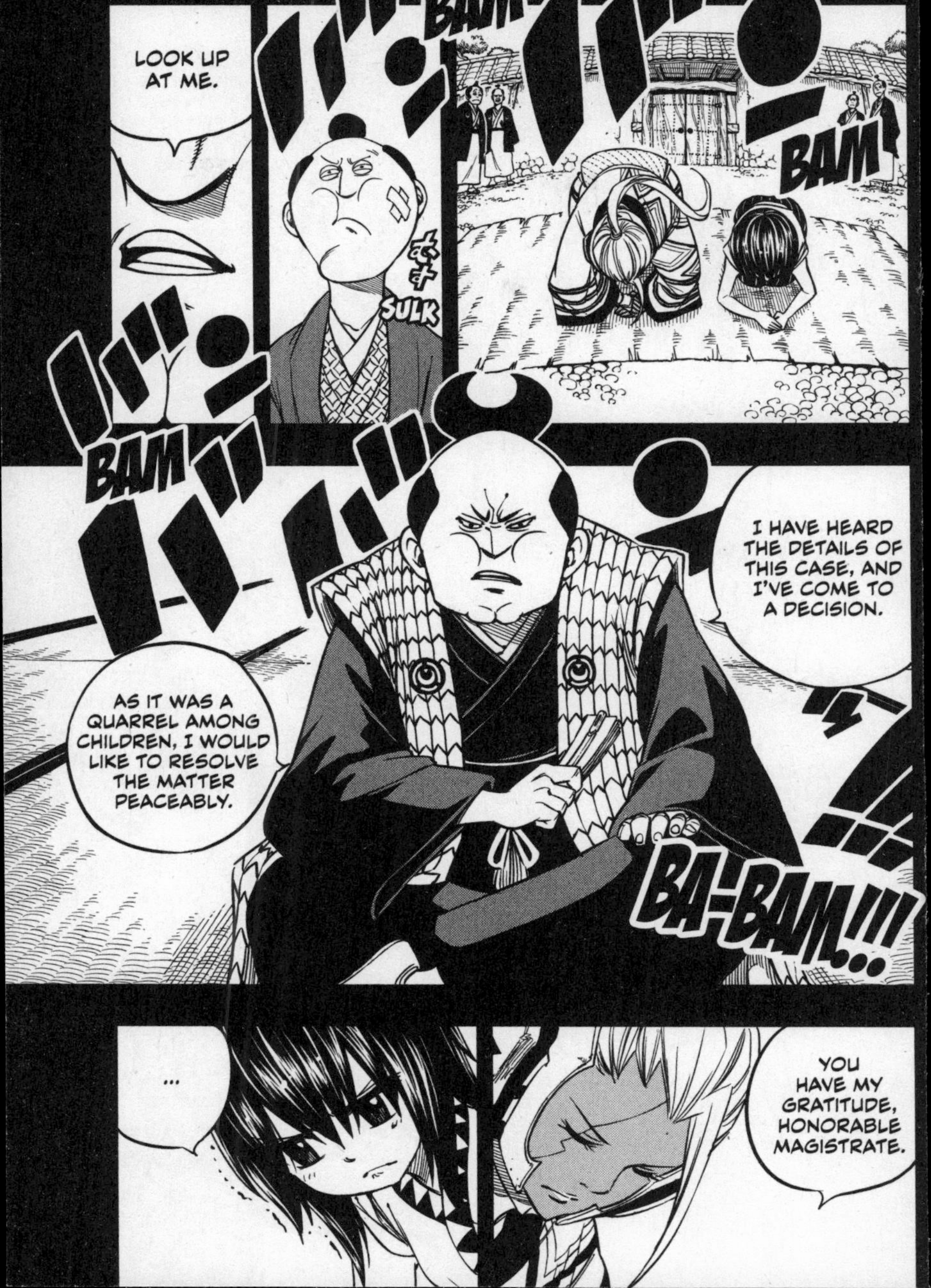
BAM
BAM
SULK
LOOK UP AT ME.
BAM
I HAVE HEARD THE DETAILS OF THIS CASE, AND I'VE COME TO A DECISION.
AS IT WAS A QUARREL AMONG CHILDREN, I WOULD LIKE TO RESOLVE THE MATTER PEACEABLY.
BA-BAM!!!
YOU HAVE MY GRATITUDE, HONORABLE MAGISTRATE.
...

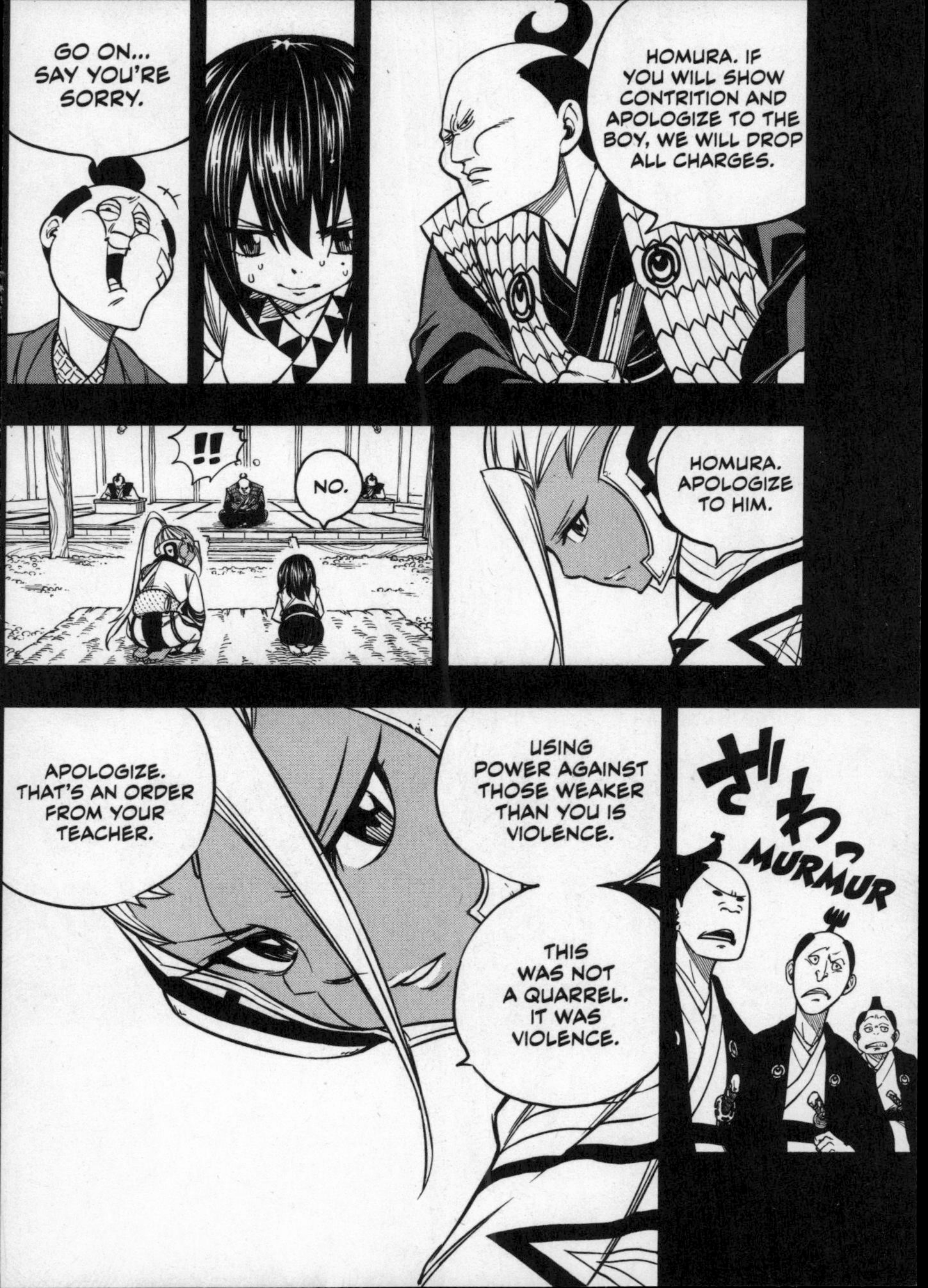
HOMURA. IF YOU WILL SHOW CONTRITION AND APOLOGIZE TO THE BOY, WE WILL DROP ALL CHARGES.
GO ON... SAY YOU'RE SORRY.
HOMURA. APOLOGIZE TO HIM.
!!
NO.
ざわっ
MURMUR
USING POWER AGAINST THOSE WEAKER THAN YOU IS VIOLENCE.
APOLOGIZE. THAT'S AN ORDER FROM YOUR TEACHER.
THIS WAS NOT A QUARREL. IT WAS VIOLENCE.

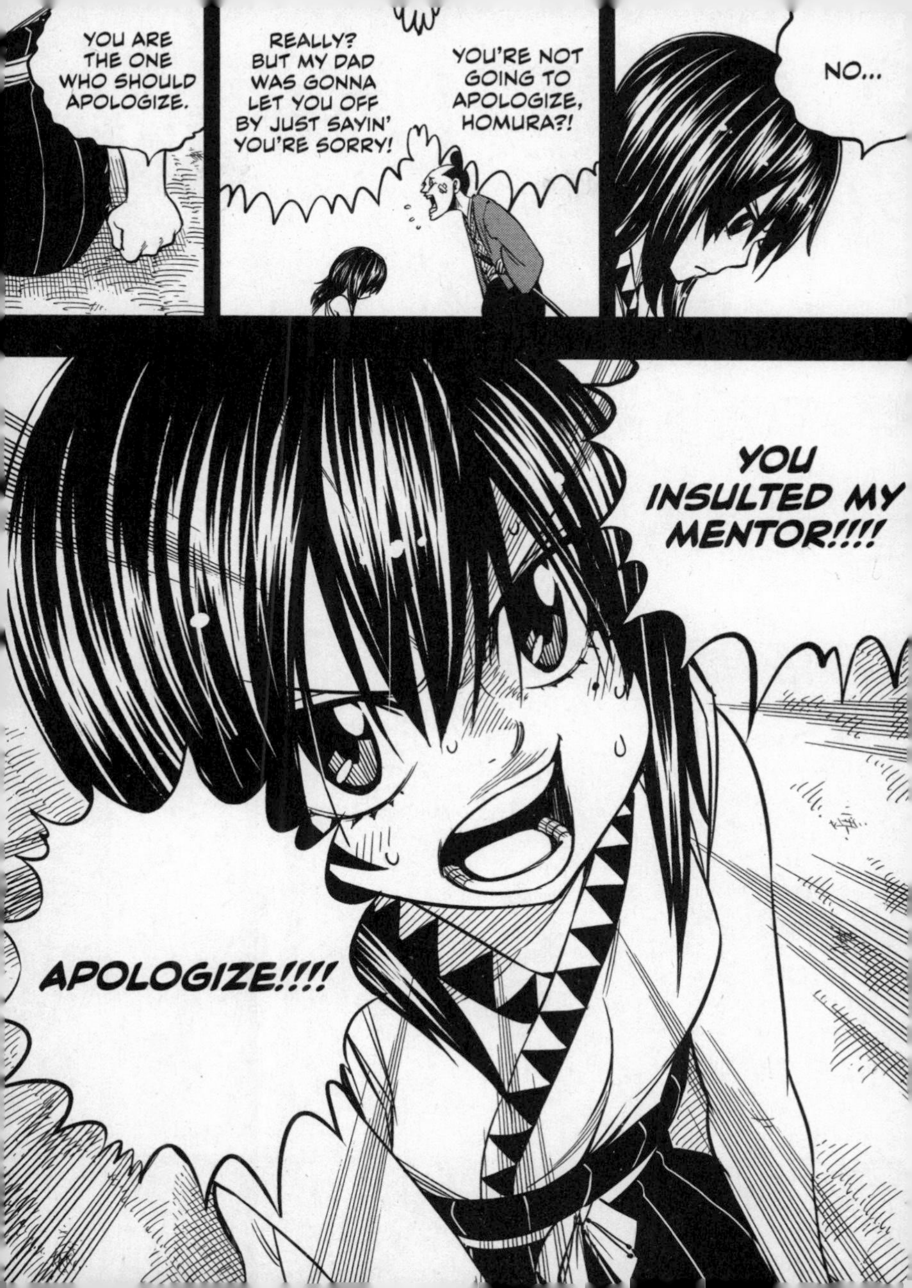
NO...
YOU'RE NOT GOING TO APOLOGIZE, HOMURA?!
REALLY? BUT MY DAD WAS GONNA LET YOU OFF BY JUST SAYIN' YOU'RE SORRY!
YOU ARE THE ONE WHO SHOULD APOLOGIZE.
YOU INSULTED MY MENTOR!!!!
APOLOGIZE!!!!

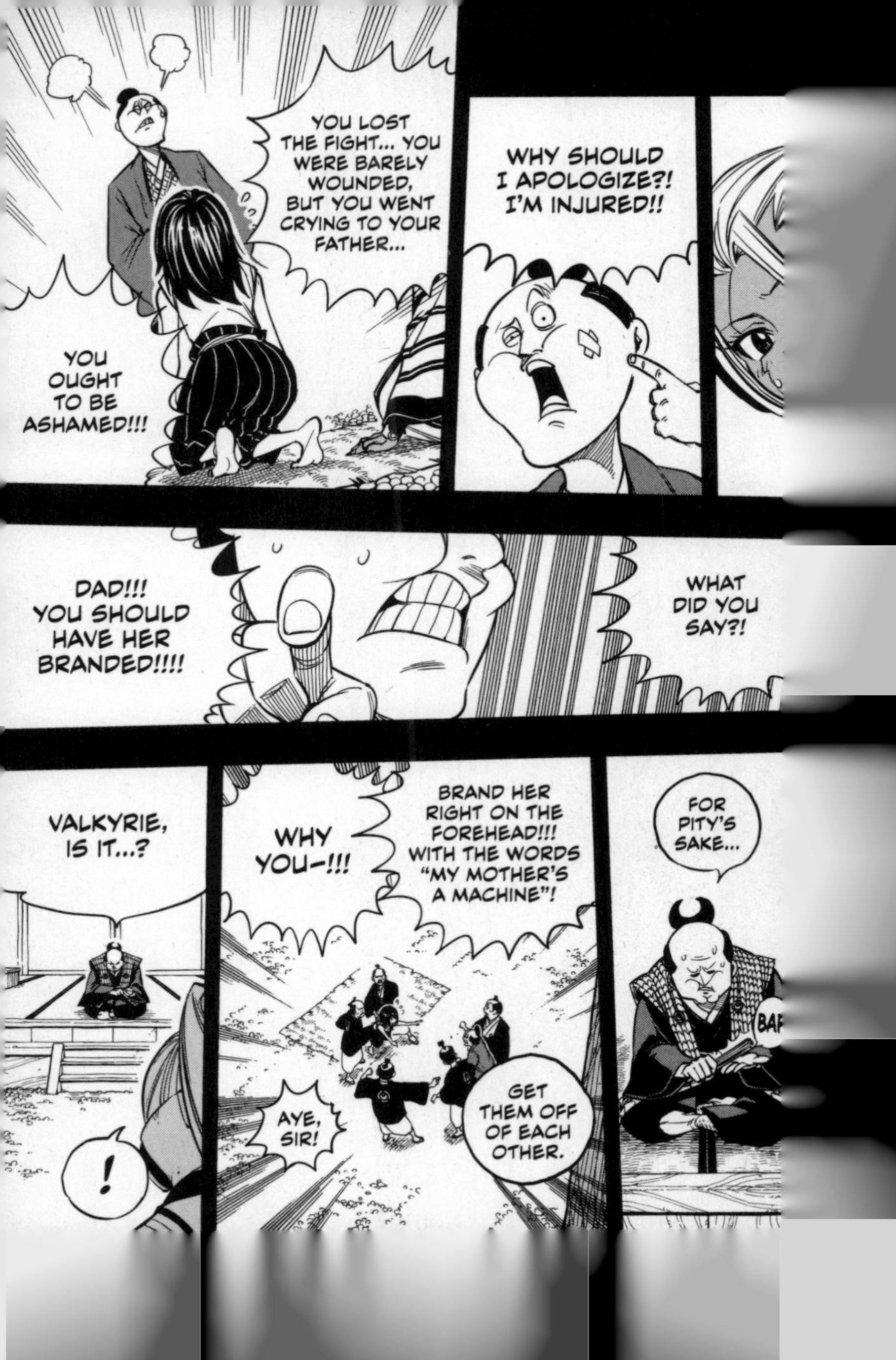
WHY SHOULD I APOLOGIZE?! I'M INJURED!!
YOU LOST THE FIGHT... YOU WERE BARELY WOUNDED, BUT YOU WENT CRYING TO YOUR FATHER...
YOU OUGHT TO BE ASHAMED!!!
WHAT DID YOU SAY?!
DAD!!! YOU SHOULD HAVE HER BRANDED!!!!
FOR PITY'S SAKE...
BRAND HER RIGHT ON THE FOREHEAD!!! WITH THE WORDS "MY MOTHER'S A MACHINE"!
WHY YOU-!!!
GET THEM OFF OF EACH OTHER.
AYE, SIR!
VALKYRIE, IS IT...?
!

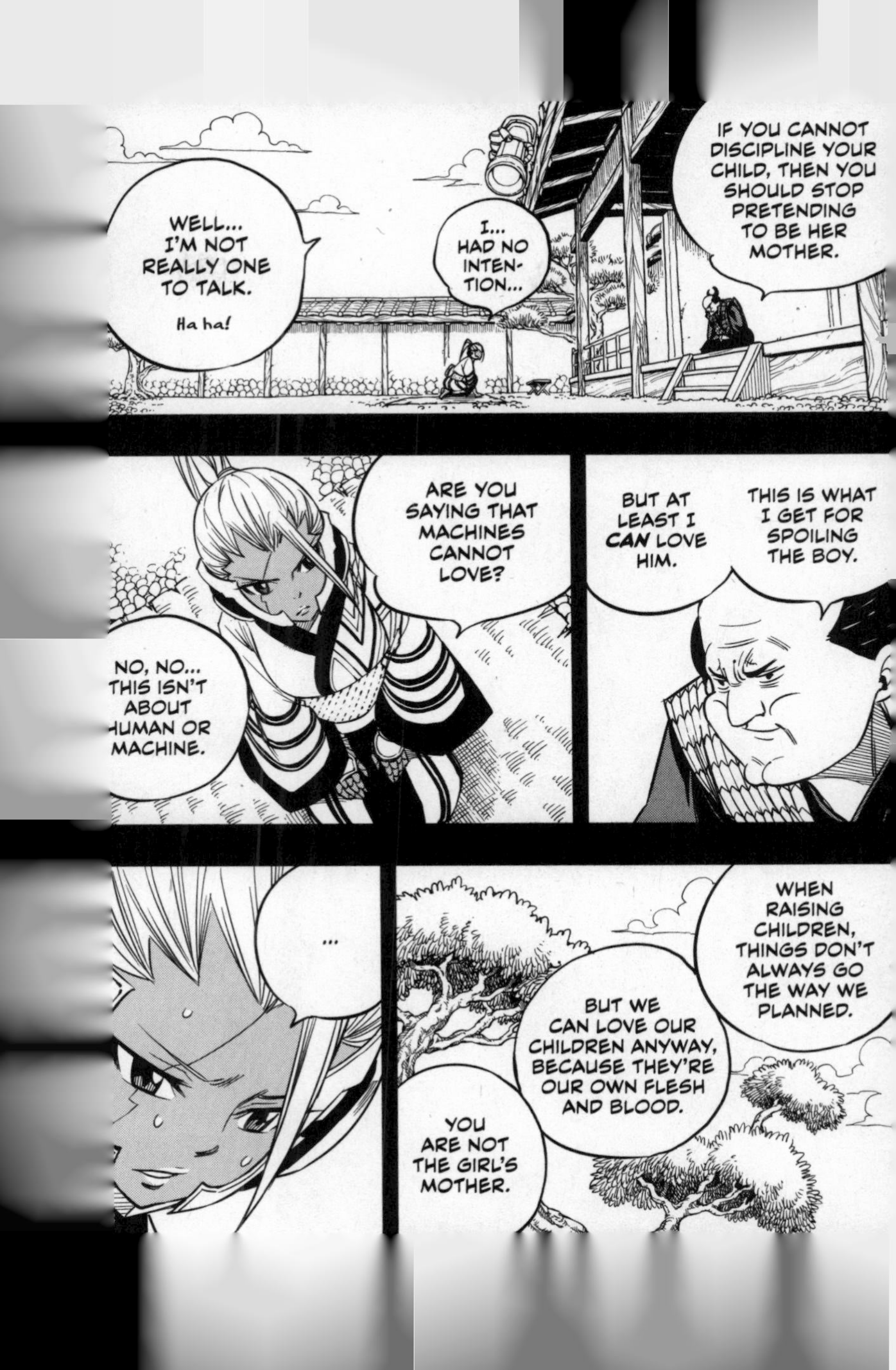
IF YOU CANNOT DISCIPLINE YOUR CHILD, THEN YOU SHOULD STOP PRETENDING TO BE HER MOTHER.
I... HAD NO INTENTION...
WELL... I'M NOT REALLY ONE TO TALK.
Ha ha!
THIS IS WHAT I GET FOR SPOILING THE BOY.
BUT AT LEAST I CAN LOVE HIM.
ARE YOU SAYING THAT MACHINES CANNOT LOVE?
NO, NO... THIS ISN'T ABOUT HUMAN OR MACHINE.
WHEN RAISING CHILDREN, THINGS DON'T ALWAYS GO THE WAY WE PLANNED.
BUT WE CAN LOVE OUR CHILDREN ANYWAY, BECAUSE THEY'RE OUR OWN FLESH AND BLOOD.
YOU ARE NOT THE GIRL'S MOTHER.
...

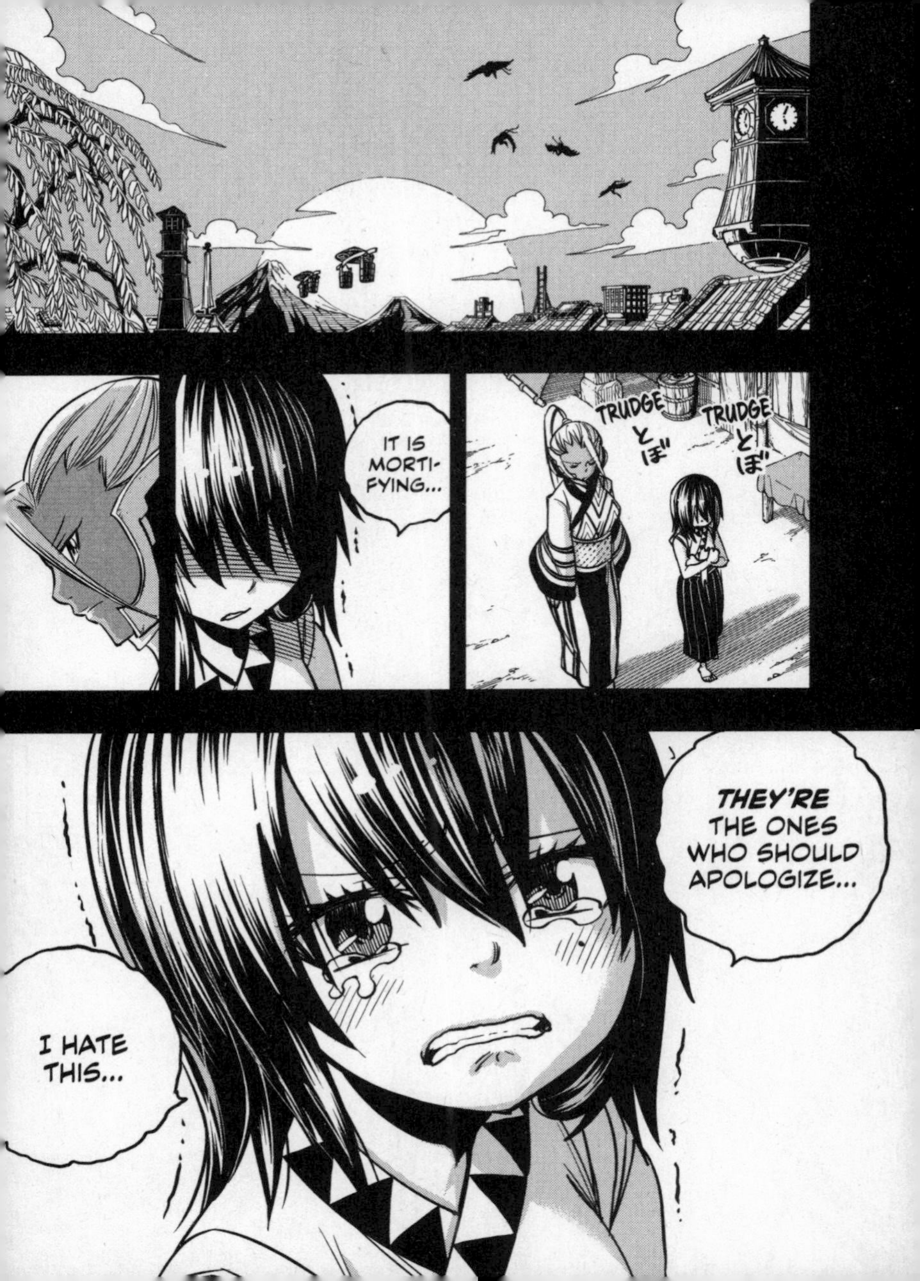
TRUDGE とぼ
TRUDGE とぼ
IT IS MORTI-FYING...
THEY'RE THE ONES WHO SHOULD APOLOGIZE...
I HATE THIS...

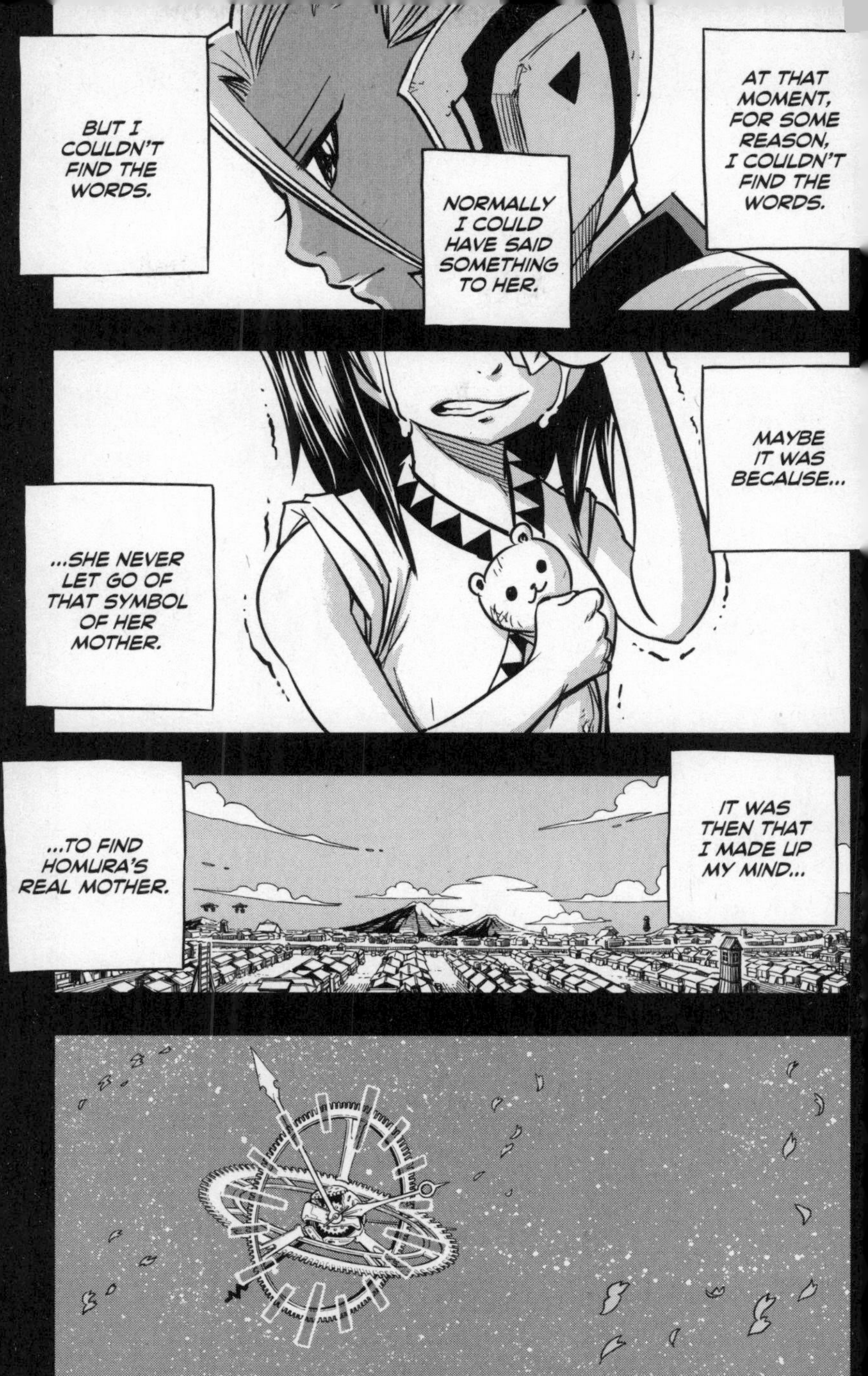
AT THAT MOMENT, FOR SOME REASON, I COULDN'T FIND THE WORDS.
NORMALLY I COULD HAVE SAID SOMETHING TO HER.
BUT I COULDN'T FIND THE WORDS.
MAYBE IT WAS BECAUSE...
...SHE NEVER LET GO OF THAT SYMBOL OF HER MOTHER.
IT WAS THEN THAT I MADE UP MY MIND...
...TO FIND HOMURA'S REAL MOTHER.

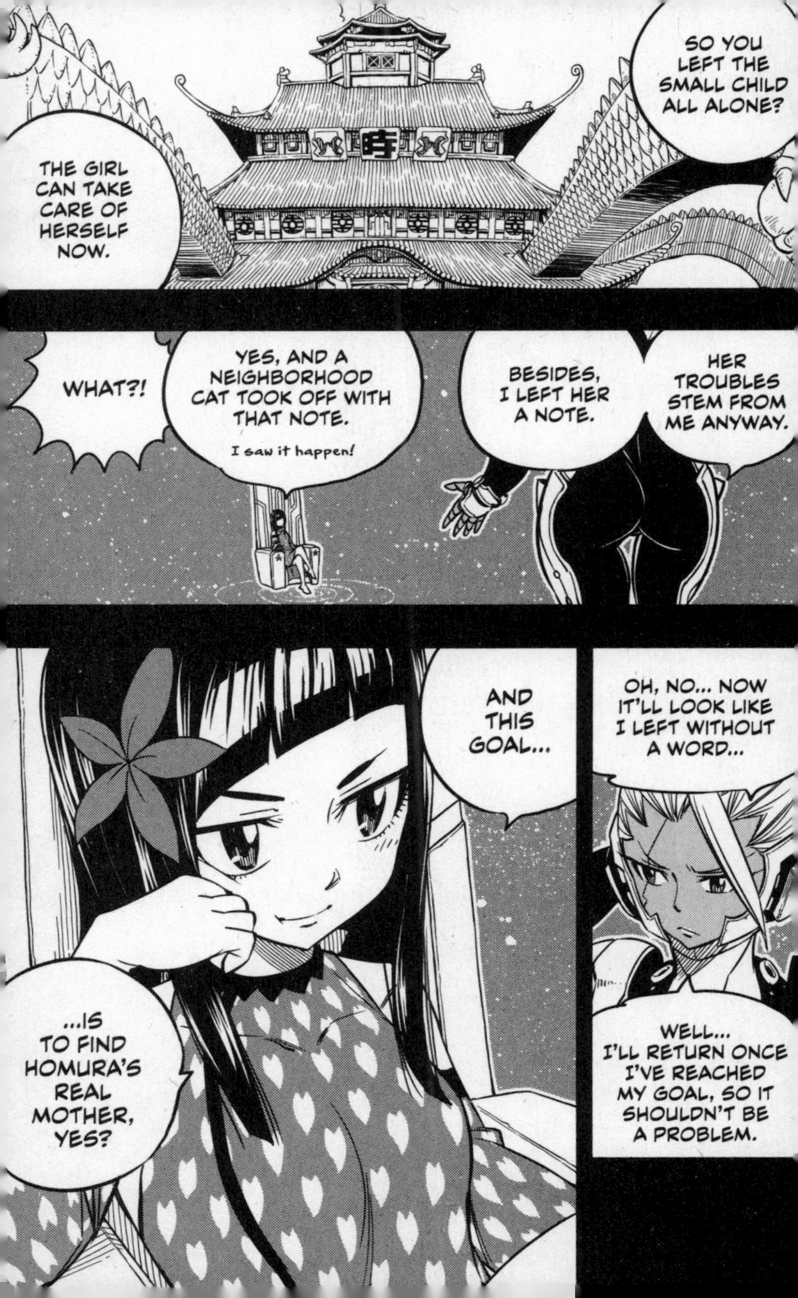
SO YOU LEFT THE SMALL CHILD ALL ALONE?
THE GIRL CAN TAKE CARE OF HERSELF NOW.
HER TROUBLES STEM FROM ME ANYWAY.
BESIDES, I LEFT HER A NOTE.
YES, AND A NEIGHBORHOOD CAT TOOK OFF WITH THAT NOTE.
I saw it happen!
WHAT?!
OH, NO... NOW IT'LL LOOK LIKE I LEFT WITHOUT A WORD...
WELL... I'LL RETURN ONCE I'VE REACHED MY GOAL, SO IT SHOULDN'T BE A PROBLEM.
AND THIS GOAL...
...IS TO FIND HOMURA'S REAL MOTHER, YES?

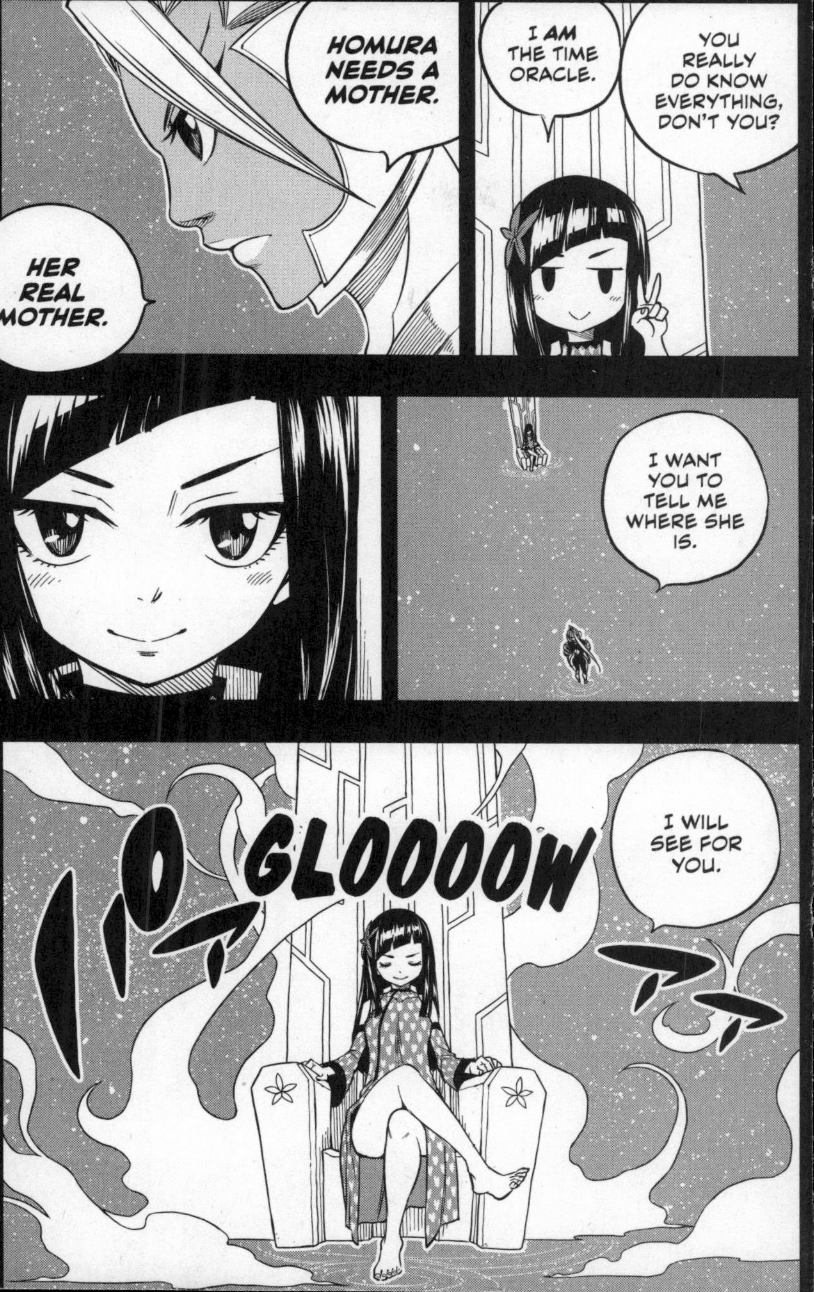
YOU REALLY DO KNOW EVERYTHING, DON'T YOU?
I AM THE TIME ORACLE.
HOMURA NEEDS A MOTHER.
HER REAL MOTHER.
I WANT YOU TO TELL ME WHERE SHE IS.
I WILL SEE FOR YOU.
GLOOOOOW

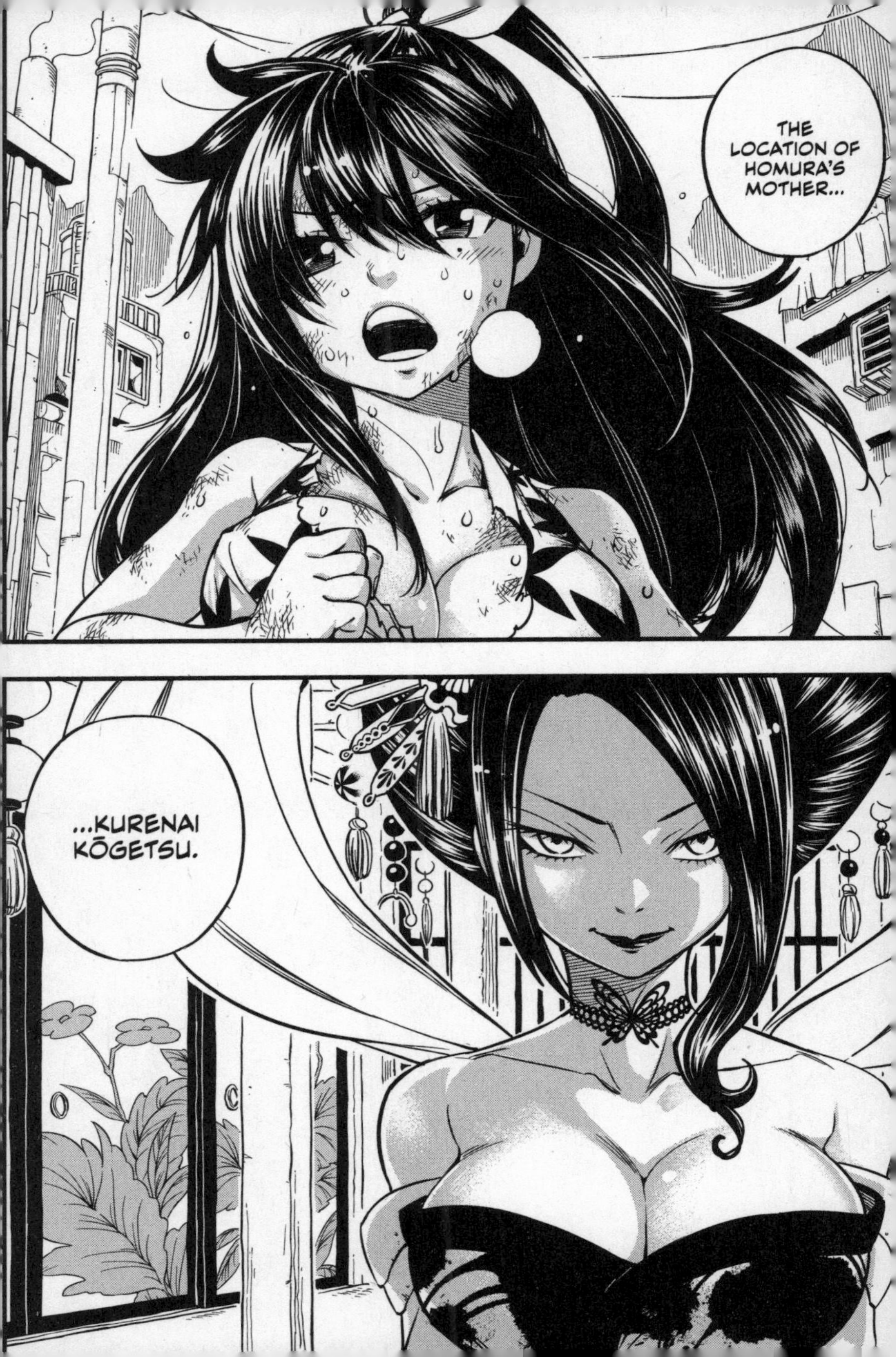
THE LOCATION OF HOMURA'S MOTHER...
...KURENAI KŌGETSU.

EDENS ZERO

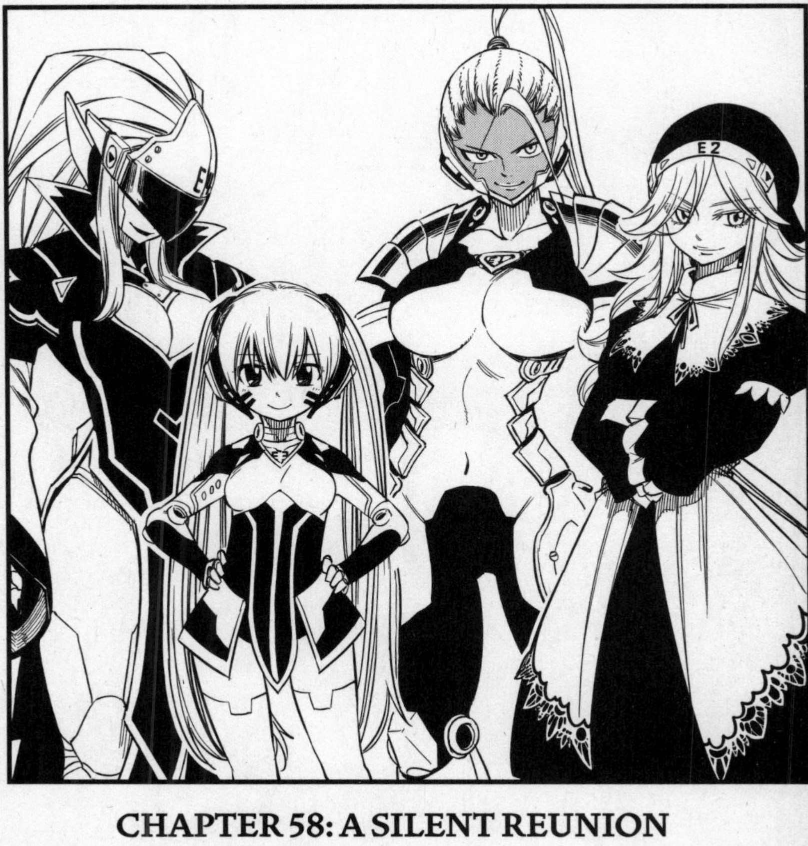

CHAPTER 58: A SILENT REUNION

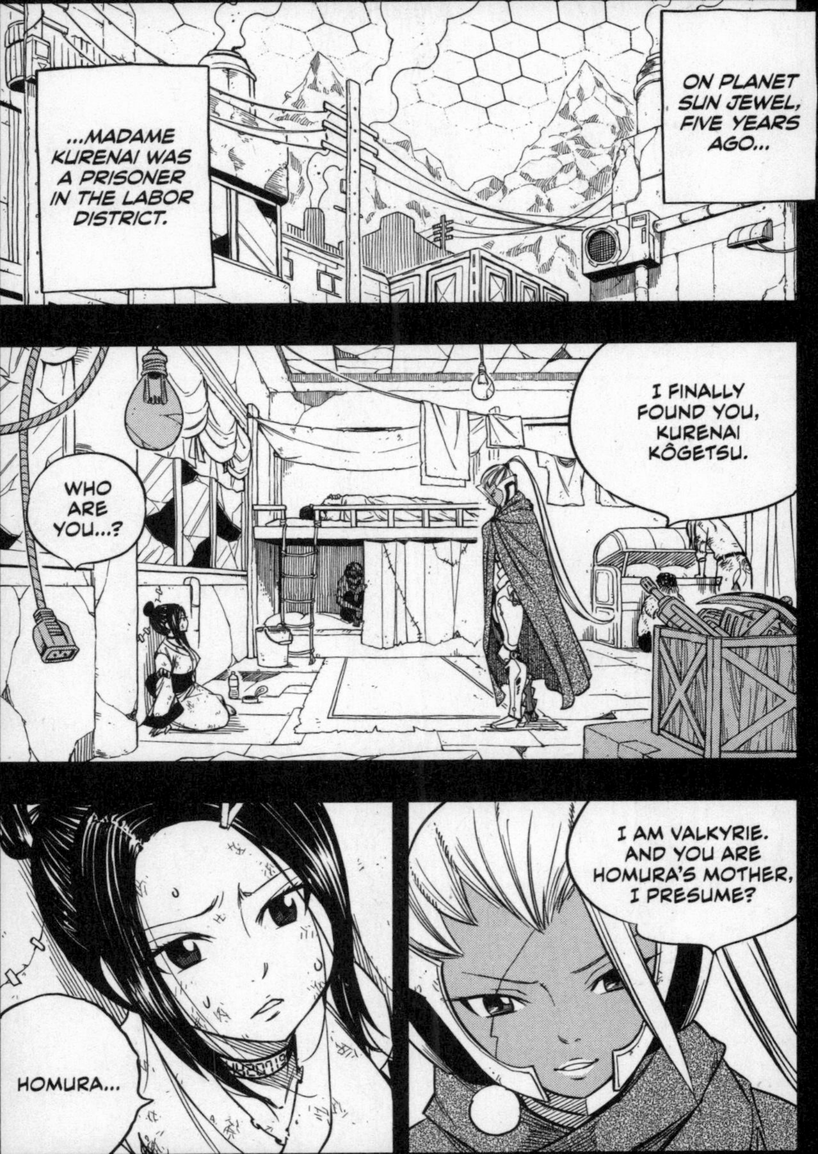
ON PLANET SUN JEWEL, FIVE YEARS AGO...
...MADAME KURENAI WAS A PRISONER IN THE LABOR DISTRICT.
I FINALLY FOUND YOU, KURENAI KÔGETSU.
WHO ARE YOU...?
I AM VALKYRIE. AND YOU ARE HOMURA'S MOTHER, I PRESUME?
HOMURA...

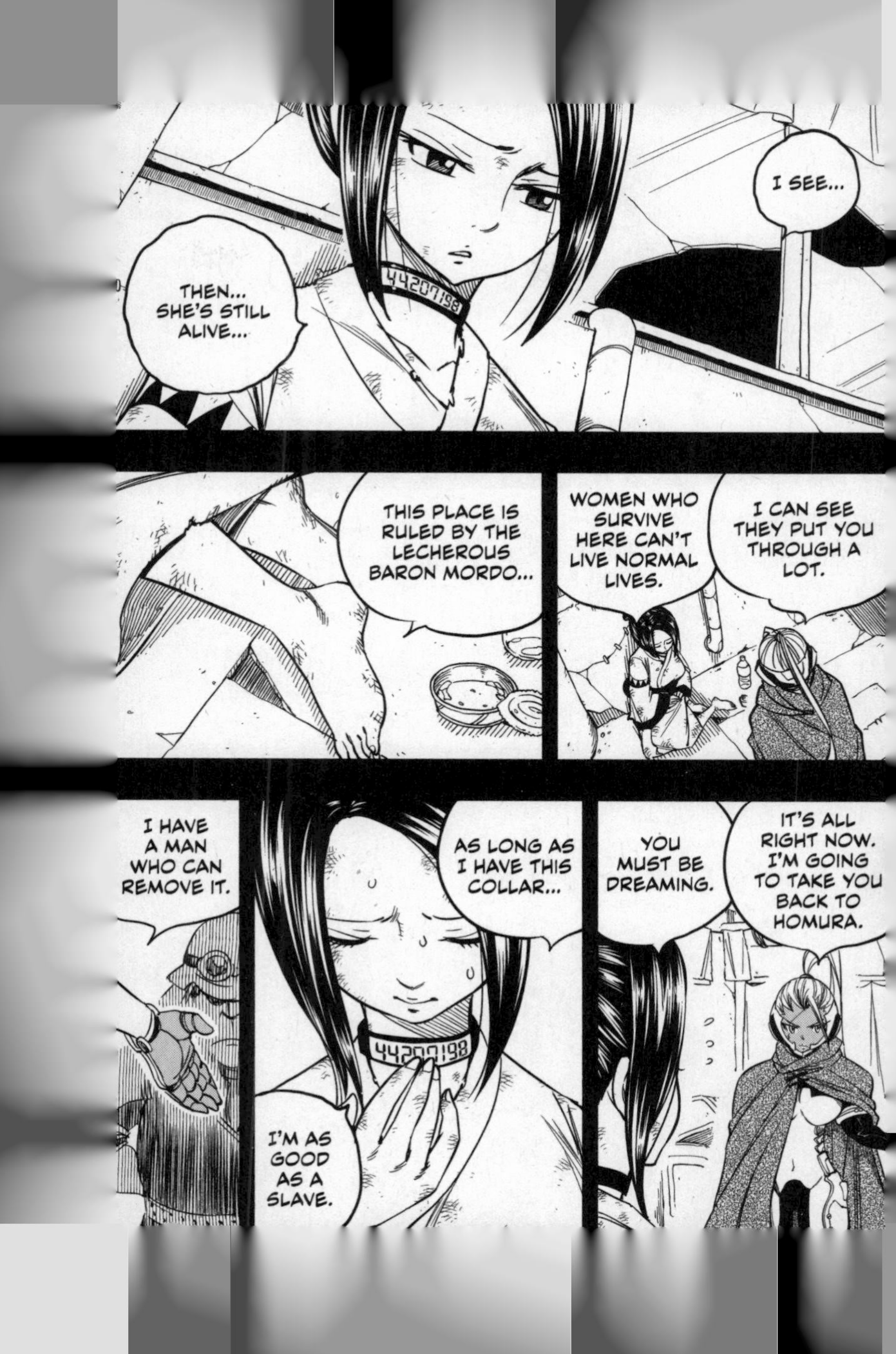
I SEE...
44207198
THEN... SHE'S STILL ALIVE...
I CAN SEE THEY PUT YOU THROUGH A LOT.
WOMEN WHO SURVIVE HERE CAN'T LIVE NORMAL LIVES.
THIS PLACE IS RULED BY THE LECHEROUS BARON MORDO...
IT'S ALL RIGHT NOW. I'M GOING TO TAKE YOU BACK TO HOMURA.
YOU MUST BE DREAMING.
AS LONG AS I HAVE THIS COLLAR...
44207198
I'M AS GOOD AS A SLAVE.
I HAVE A MAN WHO CAN REMOVE IT.

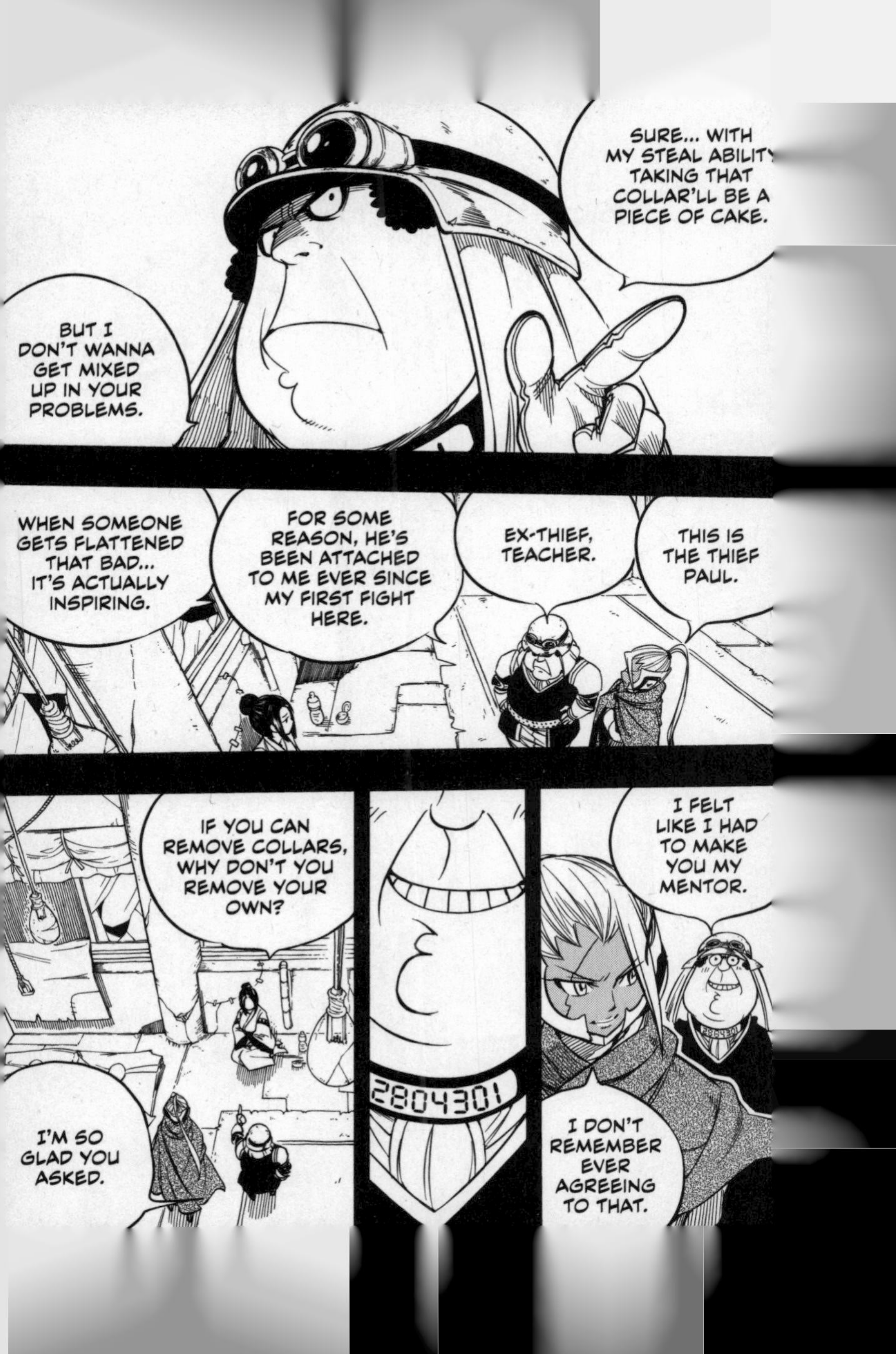
SURE... WITH MY STEAL ABILITY TAKING THAT COLLAR'LL BE A PIECE OF CAKE.
BUT I DON'T WANNA GET MIXED UP IN YOUR PROBLEMS.
THIS IS THE THIEF PAUL.
EX-THIEF, TEACHER.
FOR SOME REASON, HE'S BEEN ATTACHED TO ME EVER SINCE MY FIRST FIGHT HERE.
WHEN SOMEONE GETS FLATTENED THAT BAD... IT'S ACTUALLY INSPIRING.
I FELT LIKE I HAD TO MAKE YOU MY MENTOR.
I DON'T REMEMBER EVER AGREEING TO THAT.
2804301
IF YOU CAN REMOVE COLLARS, WHY DON'T YOU REMOVE YOUR OWN?
I'M SO GLAD YOU ASKED.

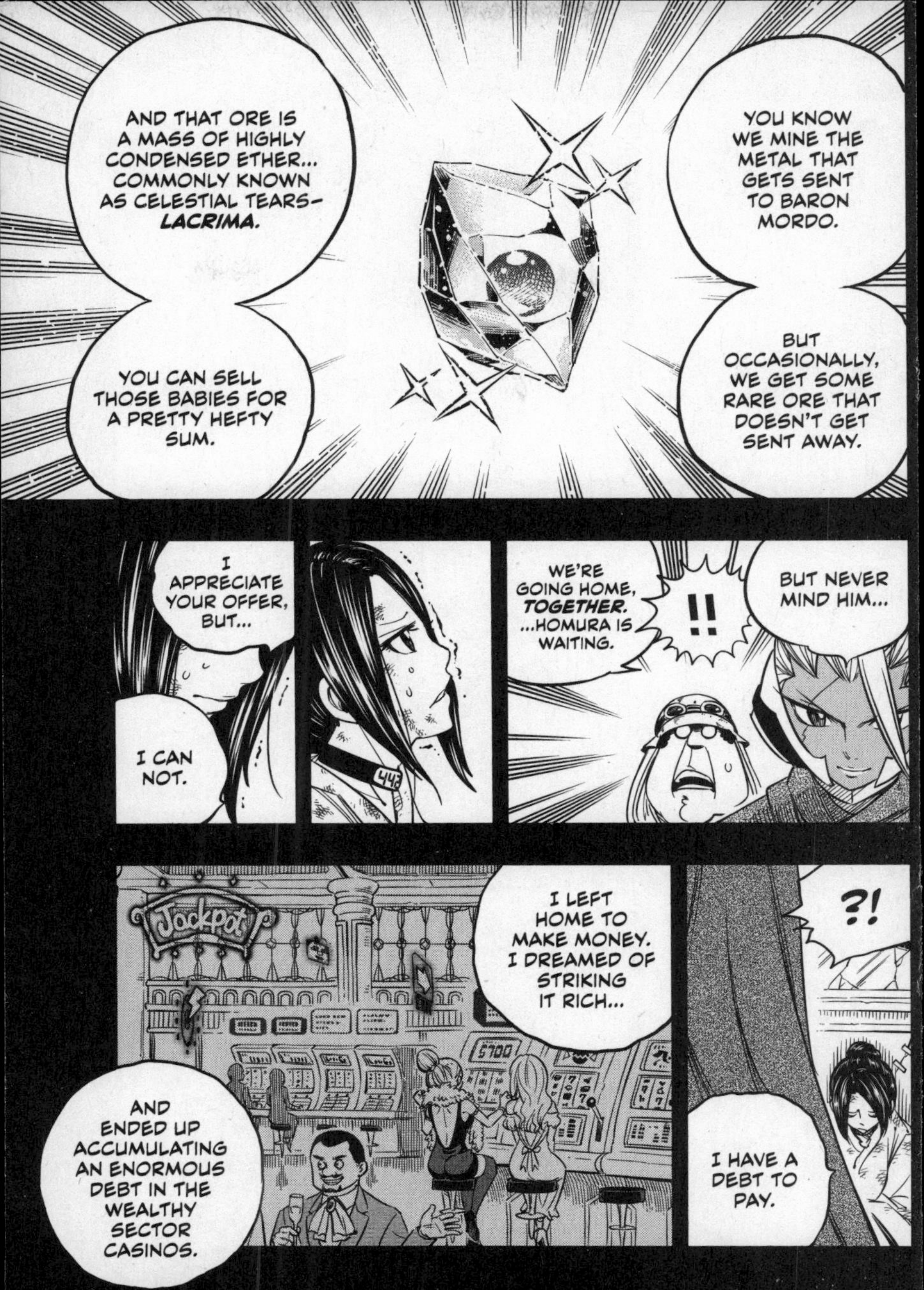
YOU KNOW WE MINE THE METAL THAT GETS SENT TO BARON MORDO.
BUT OCCASIONALLY, WE GET SOME RARE ORE THAT DOESN'T GET SENT AWAY.
AND THAT ORE IS A MASS OF HIGHLY CONDENSED ETHER... COMMONLY KNOWN AS CELESTIAL TEARS-*LACRIMA.*
YOU CAN SELL THOSE BABIES FOR A PRETTY HEFTY SUM.
BUT NEVER MIND HIM...
!!
WE'RE GOING HOME, ***TOGETHER.*** ...HOMURA IS WAITING.
442
I APPRECIATE YOUR OFFER, BUT...
I CAN NOT.
?!
I HAVE A DEBT TO PAY.
I LEFT HOME TO MAKE MONEY. I DREAMED OF STRIKING IT RICH...
Jackpot
5700
AND ENDED UP ACCUMULATING AN ENORMOUS DEBT IN THE WEALTHY SECTOR CASINOS.

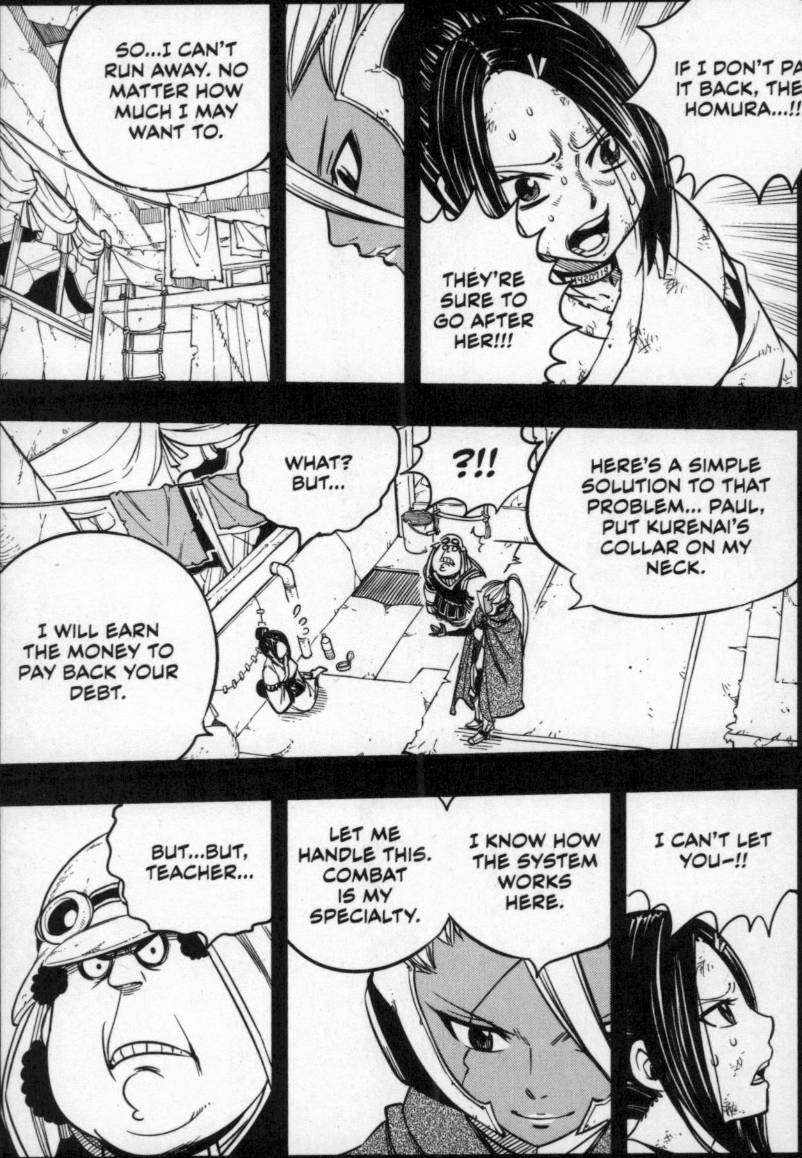
IF I DON'T PAY IT BACK, THEN HOMURA...!!!
THEY'RE SURE TO GO AFTER HER!!!
SO...I CAN'T RUN AWAY. NO MATTER HOW MUCH I MAY WANT TO.
HERE'S A SIMPLE SOLUTION TO THAT PROBLEM... PAUL, PUT KURENAI'S COLLAR ON MY NECK.
?!!
WHAT? BUT...
I WILL EARN THE MONEY TO PAY BACK YOUR DEBT.
I CAN'T LET YOU-!!
I KNOW HOW THE SYSTEM WORKS HERE.
LET ME HANDLE THIS. COMBAT IS MY SPECIALTY.
BUT...BUT, TEACHER...

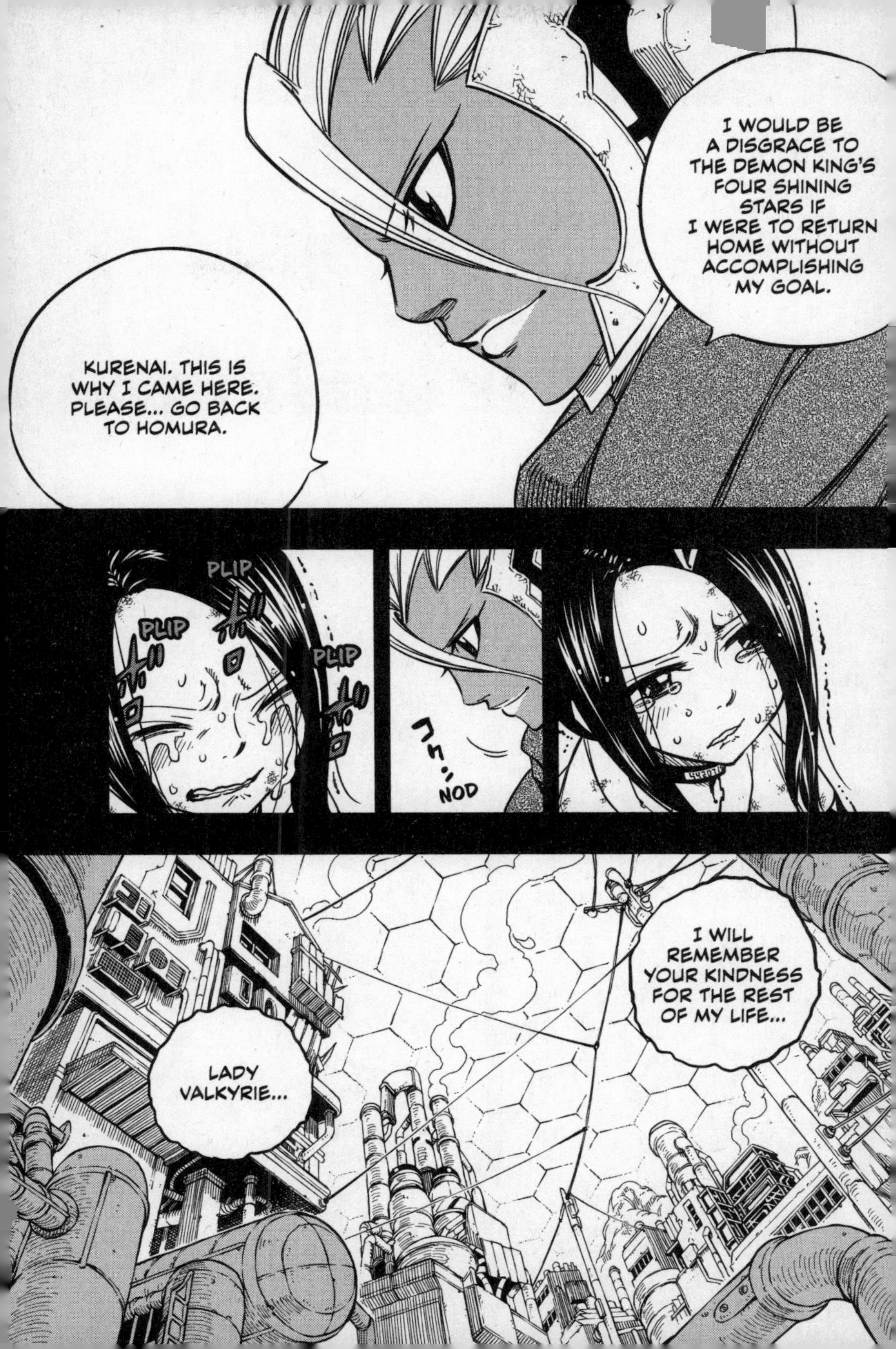
I WOULD BE A DISGRACE TO THE DEMON KING'S FOUR SHINING STARS IF I WERE TO RETURN HOME WITHOUT ACCOMPLISHING MY GOAL.
KURENAI. THIS IS WHY I CAME HERE. PLEASE... GO BACK TO HOMURA.
NOD
PLIP
PLIP
PLIP
I WILL REMEMBER YOUR KINDNESS FOR THE REST OF MY LIFE...
LADY VALKYRIE...

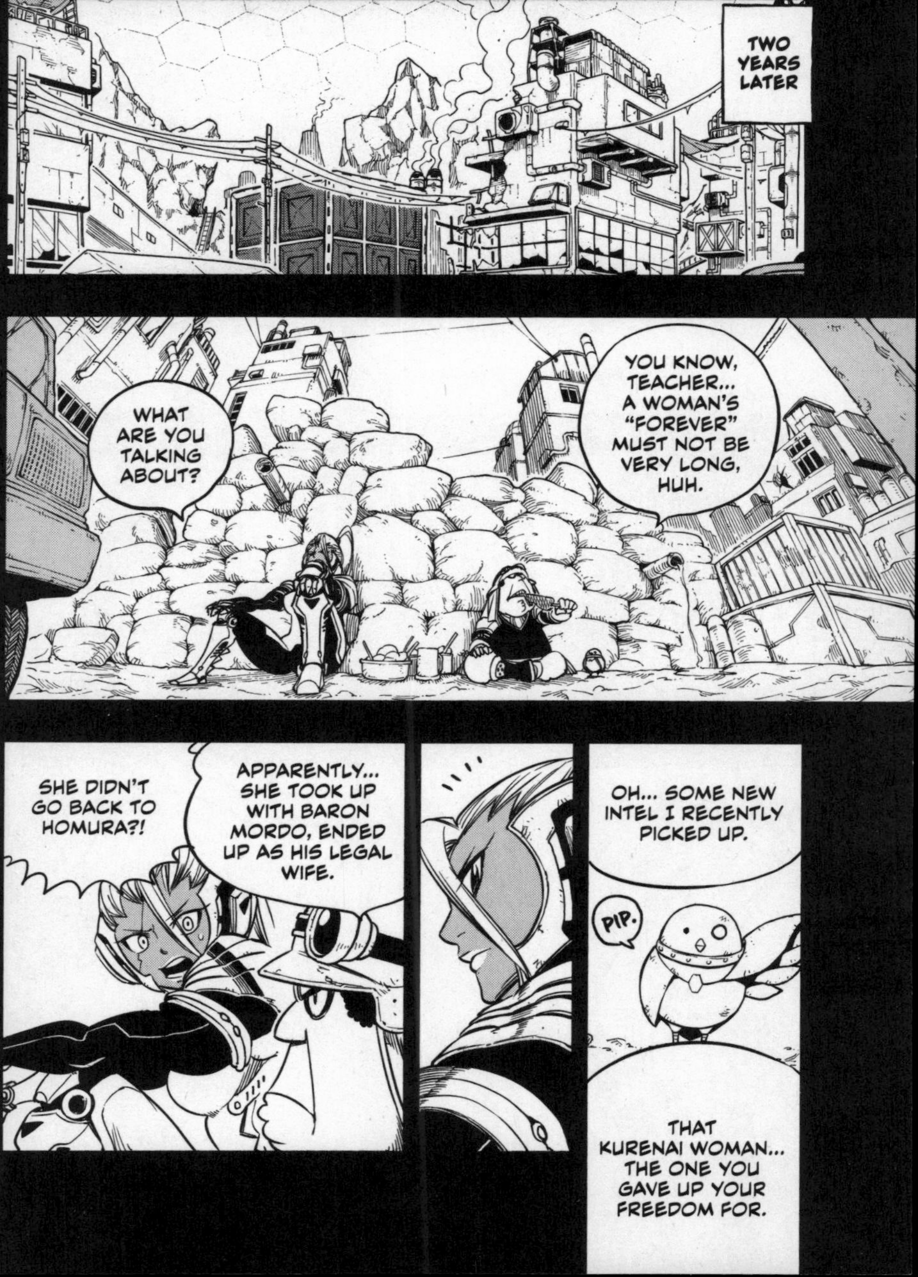
TWO YEARS LATER
YOU KNOW, TEACHER... A WOMAN'S "FOREVER" MUST NOT BE VERY LONG, HUH.
WHAT ARE YOU TALKING ABOUT?
OH... SOME NEW INTEL I RECENTLY PICKED UP.
PIP.
THAT KURENAI WOMAN... THE ONE YOU GAVE UP YOUR FREEDOM FOR.
APPARENTLY... SHE TOOK UP WITH BARON MORDO, ENDED UP AS HIS LEGAL WIFE.
SHE DIDN'T GO BACK TO HOMURA?!

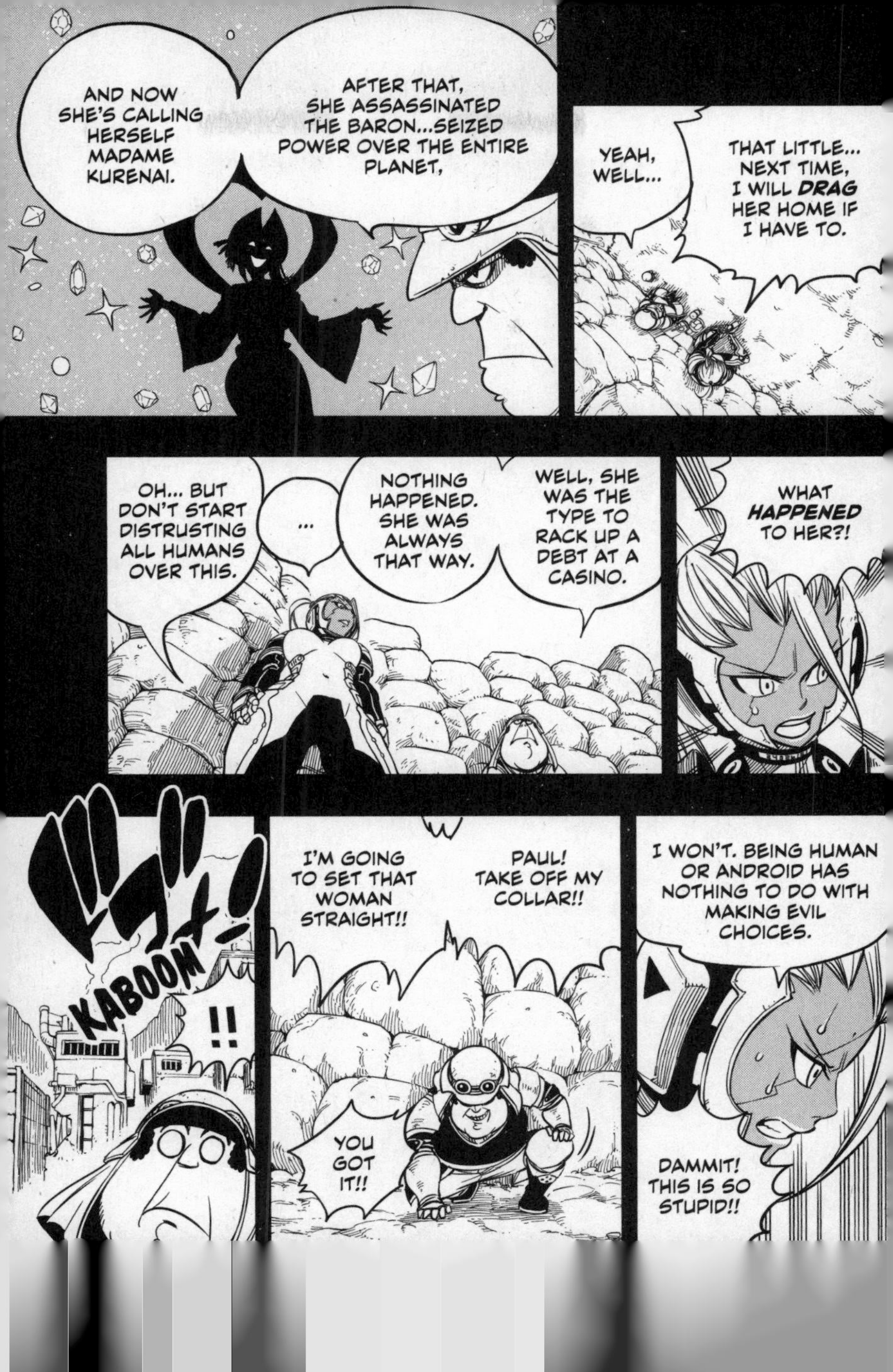
THAT LITTLE... NEXT TIME, I WILL **DRAG** HER HOME IF I HAVE TO.
YEAH, WELL...
AFTER THAT, SHE ASSASSINATED THE BARON...SEIZED POWER OVER THE ENTIRE PLANET,
AND NOW SHE'S CALLING HERSELF MADAME KURENAI.
WHAT **HAPPENED** TO HER?!
WELL, SHE WAS THE TYPE TO RACK UP A DEBT AT A CASINO.
NOTHING HAPPENED. SHE WAS ALWAYS THAT WAY.
...
OH... BUT DON'T START DISTRUSTING ALL HUMANS OVER THIS.
I WON'T. BEING HUMAN OR ANDROID HAS NOTHING TO DO WITH MAKING EVIL CHOICES.
DAMMIT! THIS IS SO STUPID!!
PAUL! TAKE OFF MY COLLAR!!
I'M GOING TO SET THAT WOMAN STRAIGHT!!
YOU GOT IT!!
KABOOM
!!

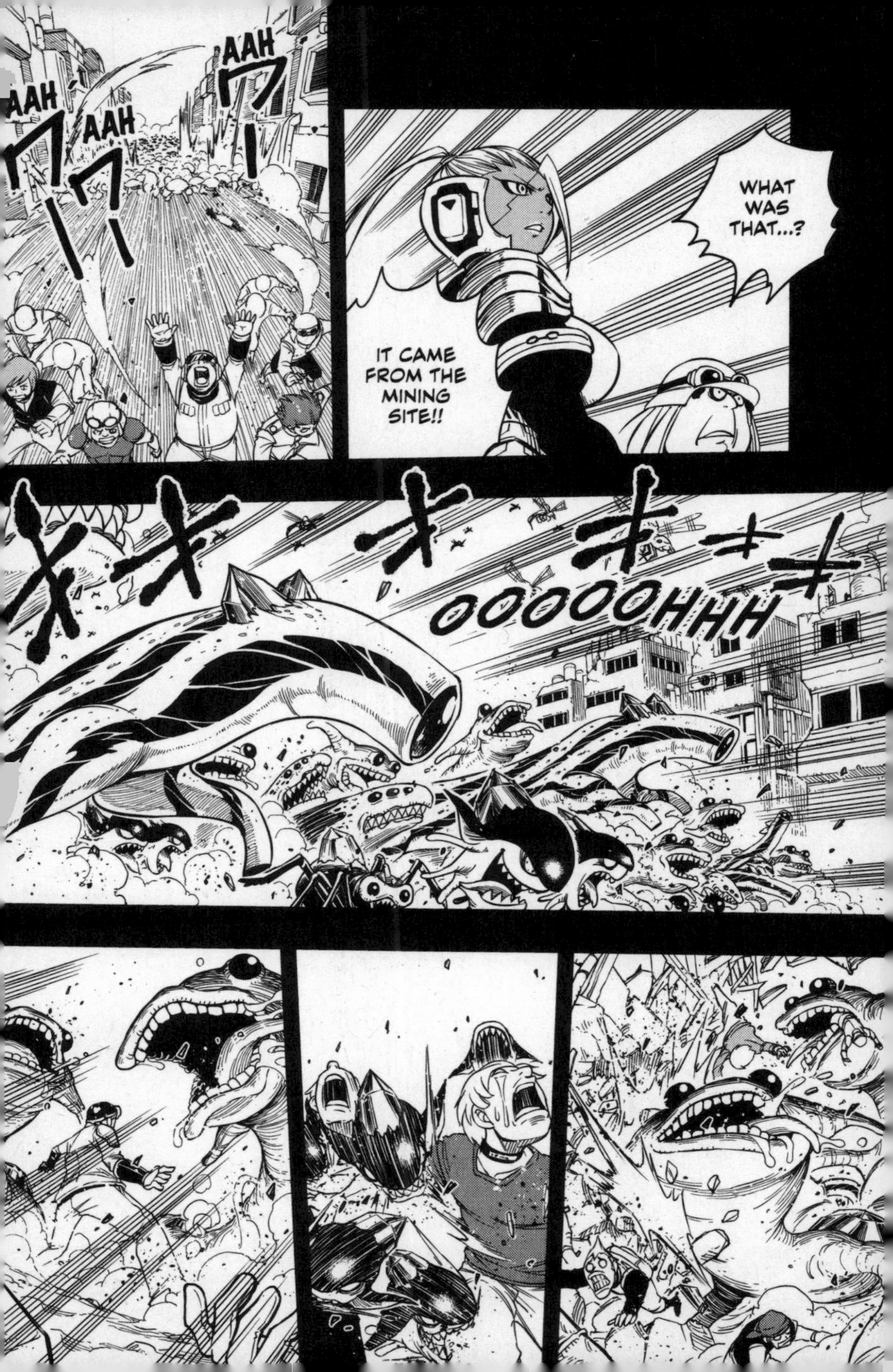
WHAT WAS THAT...?
IT CAME FROM THE MINING SITE!!
AAH
AAH
AAH
OOOOOOHHH

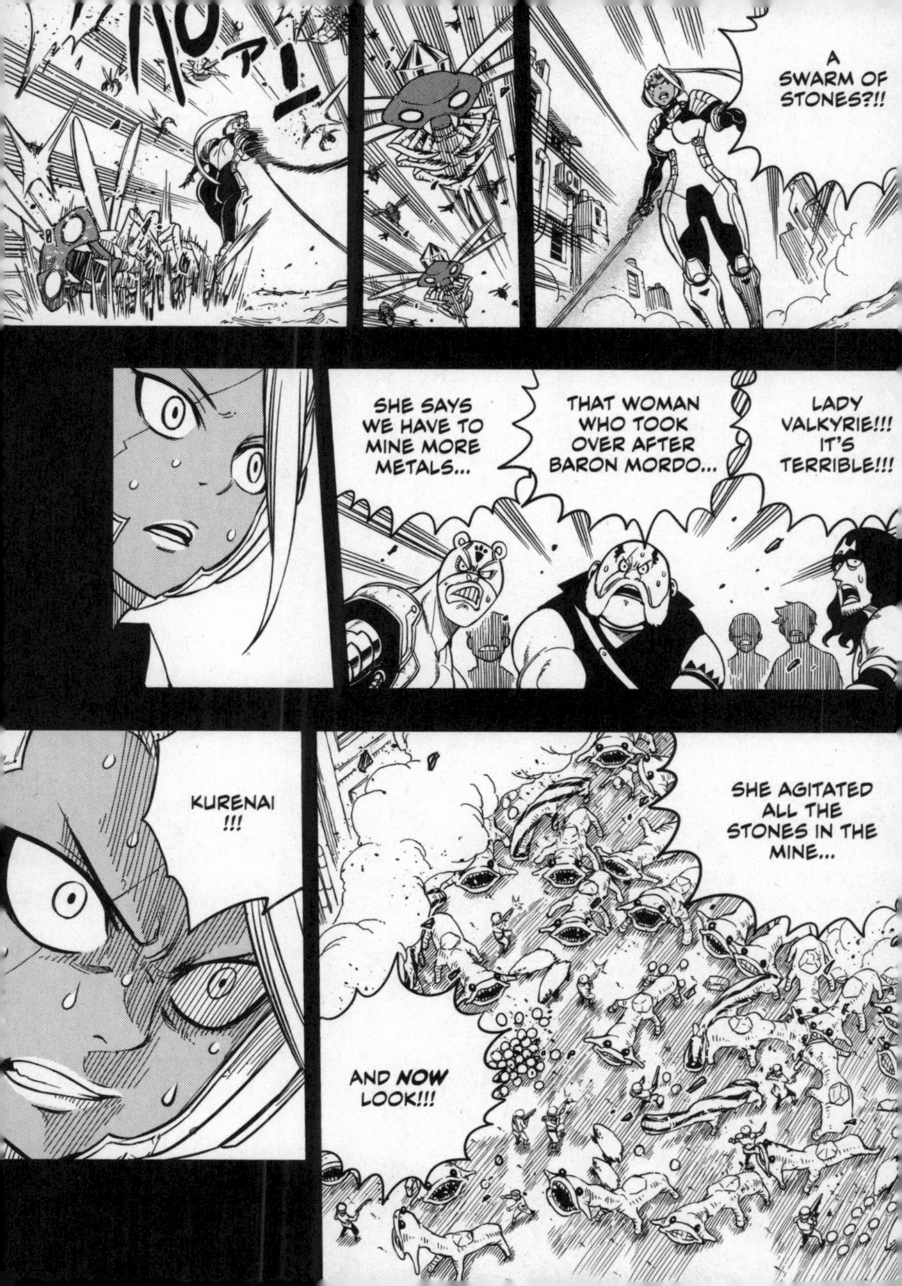
A SWARM OF STONES?!!
LADY VALKYRIE!!! IT'S TERRIBLE!!!
THAT WOMAN WHO TOOK OVER AFTER BARON MORDO...
SHE SAYS WE HAVE TO MINE MORE METALS...
SHE AGITATED ALL THE STONES IN THE MINE...
AND *NOW* LOOK!!!
KURENAI!!!

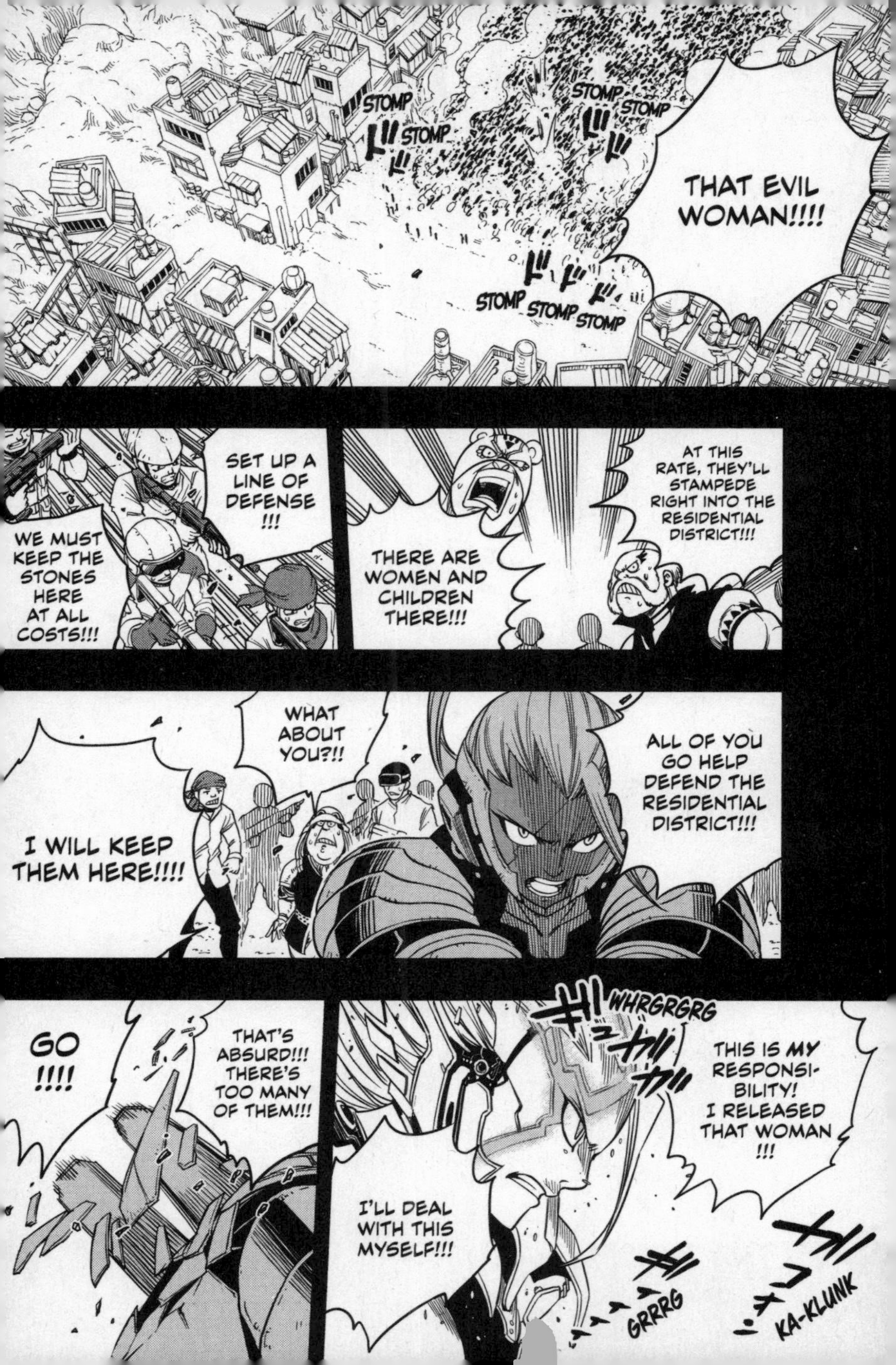
STOMP STOMP
STOMP STOMP
THAT EVIL WOMAN!!!!
STOMP STOMP STOMP
AT THIS RATE, THEY'LL STAMPEDE RIGHT INTO THE RESIDENTIAL DISTRICT!!!
THERE ARE WOMEN AND CHILDREN THERE!!!
SET UP A LINE OF DEFENSE!!!
WE MUST KEEP THE STONES HERE AT ALL COSTS!!!
ALL OF YOU GO HELP DEFEND THE RESIDENTIAL DISTRICT!!!
WHAT ABOUT YOU?!!
I WILL KEEP THEM HERE!!!!
WHRGRGRG
THIS IS MY RESPONSI-BILITY! I RELEASED THAT WOMAN!!!
I'LL DEAL WITH THIS MYSELF!!!
GRRRG
KA-KLUNK
THAT'S ABSURD!!! THERE'S TOO MANY OF THEM!!!
GO!!!!

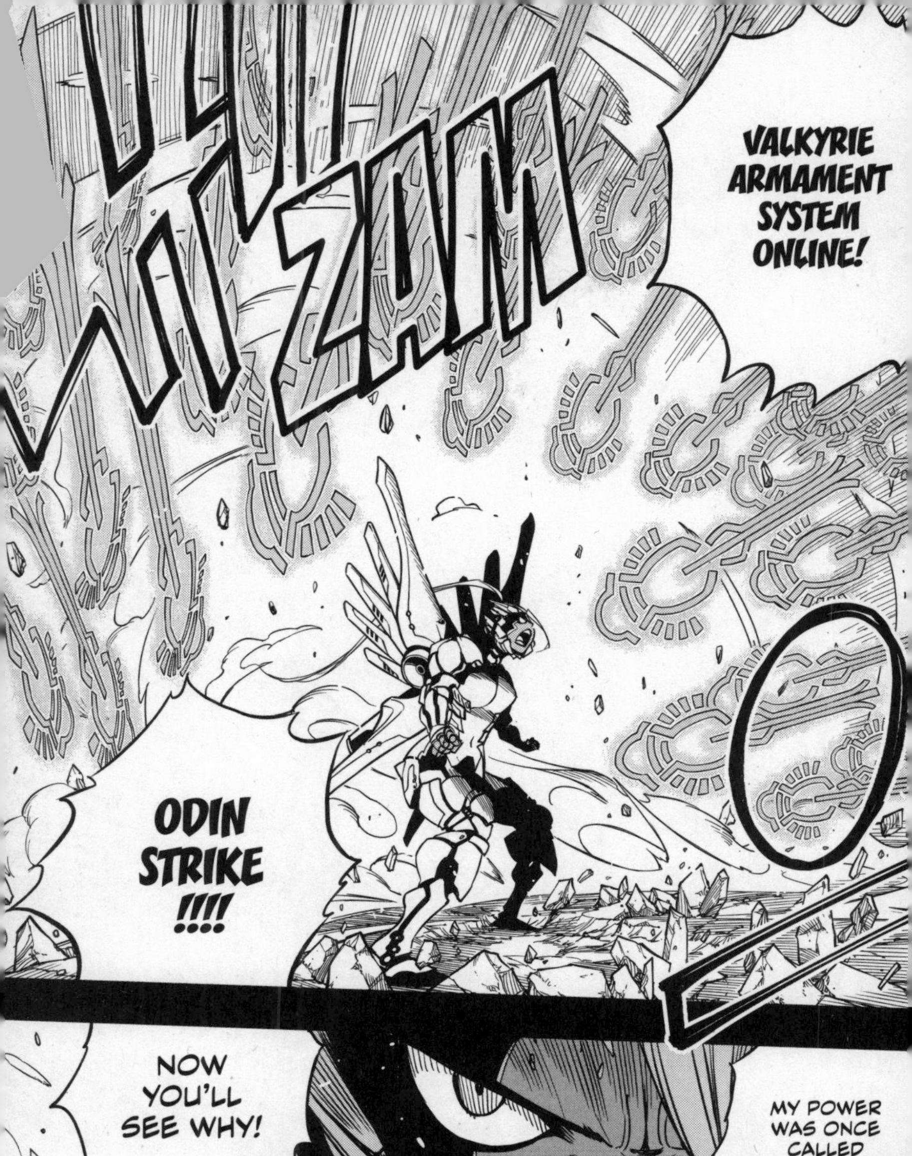
VALKYRIE ARMAMENT SYSTEM ONLINE!
ZAM
ODIN STRIKE !!!!
MY POWER WAS ONCE CALLED THE SWORD OF EDENS!
NOW YOU'LL SEE WHY!

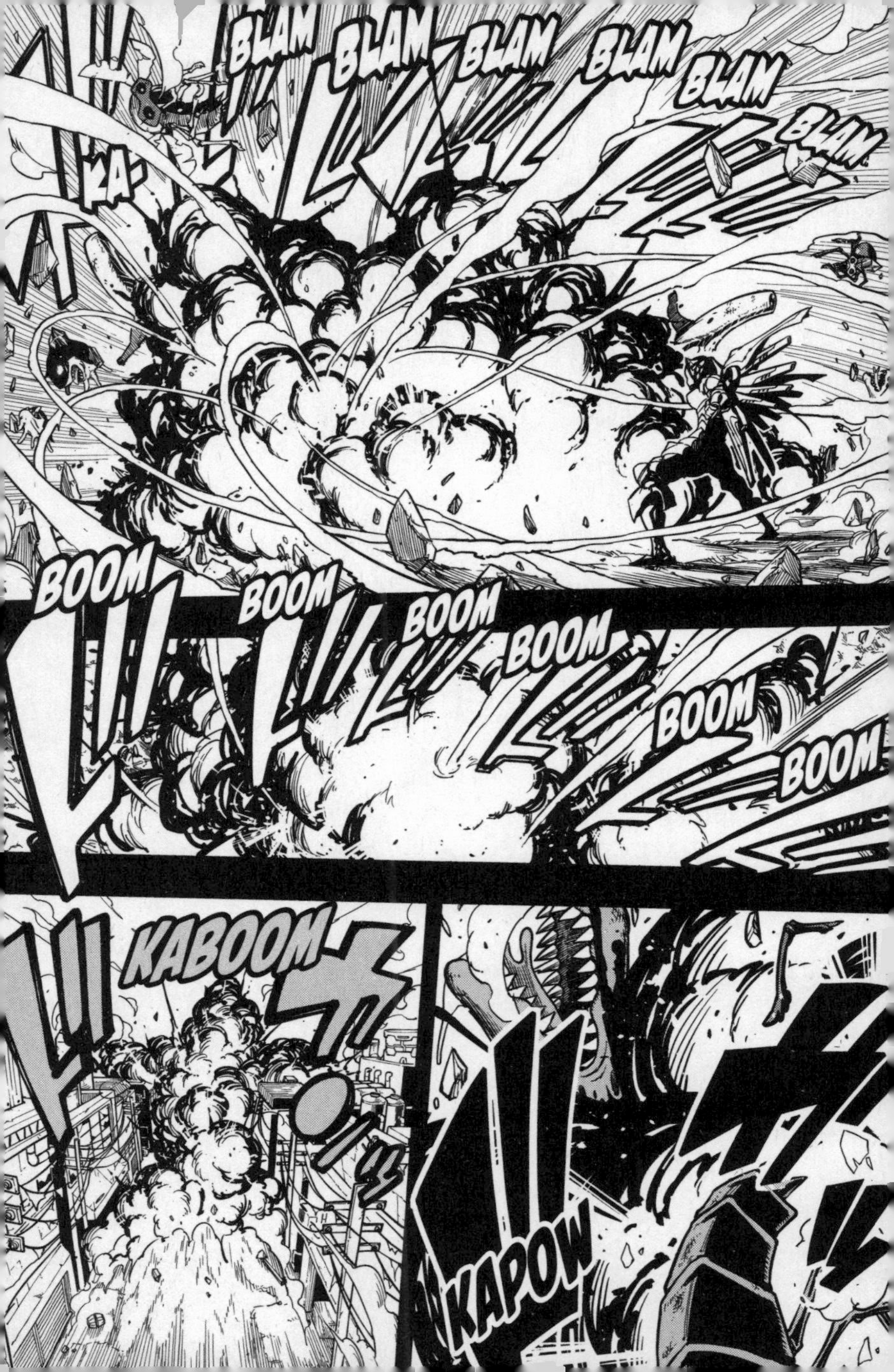
BLAM
BLAM
BLAM
BLAM
BLAM
BLAM
KA-
BOOM
BOOM
BOOM
BOOM
BOOM
BOOM
KAPOW
KABOOM

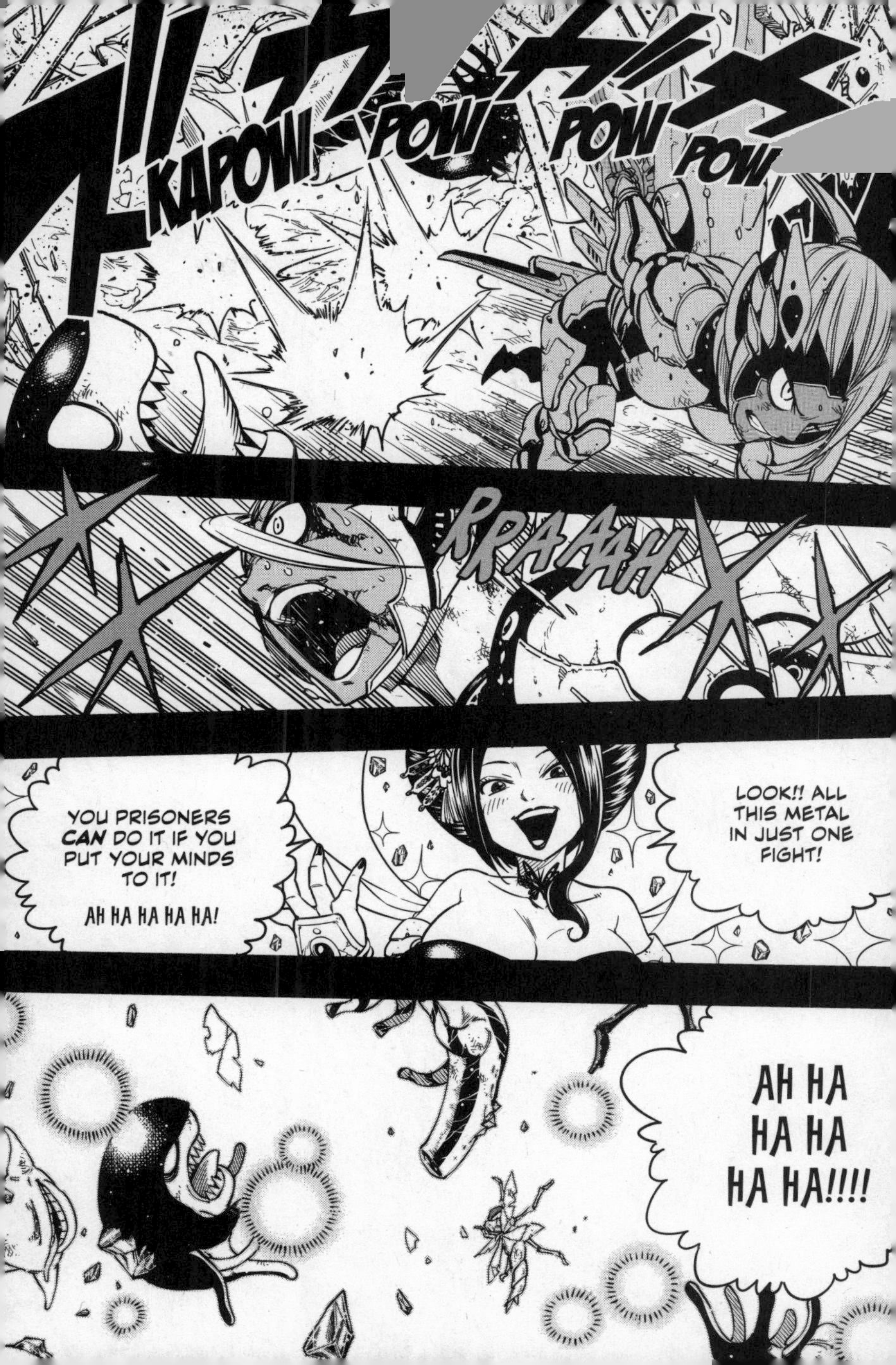
KAPOW POW POW POW
RRAAAH
LOOK!! ALL THIS METAL IN JUST ONE FIGHT!
YOU PRISONERS CAN DO IT IF YOU PUT YOUR MINDS TO IT!
AH HA HA HA HA!
AH HA HA HA HA HA!!!!

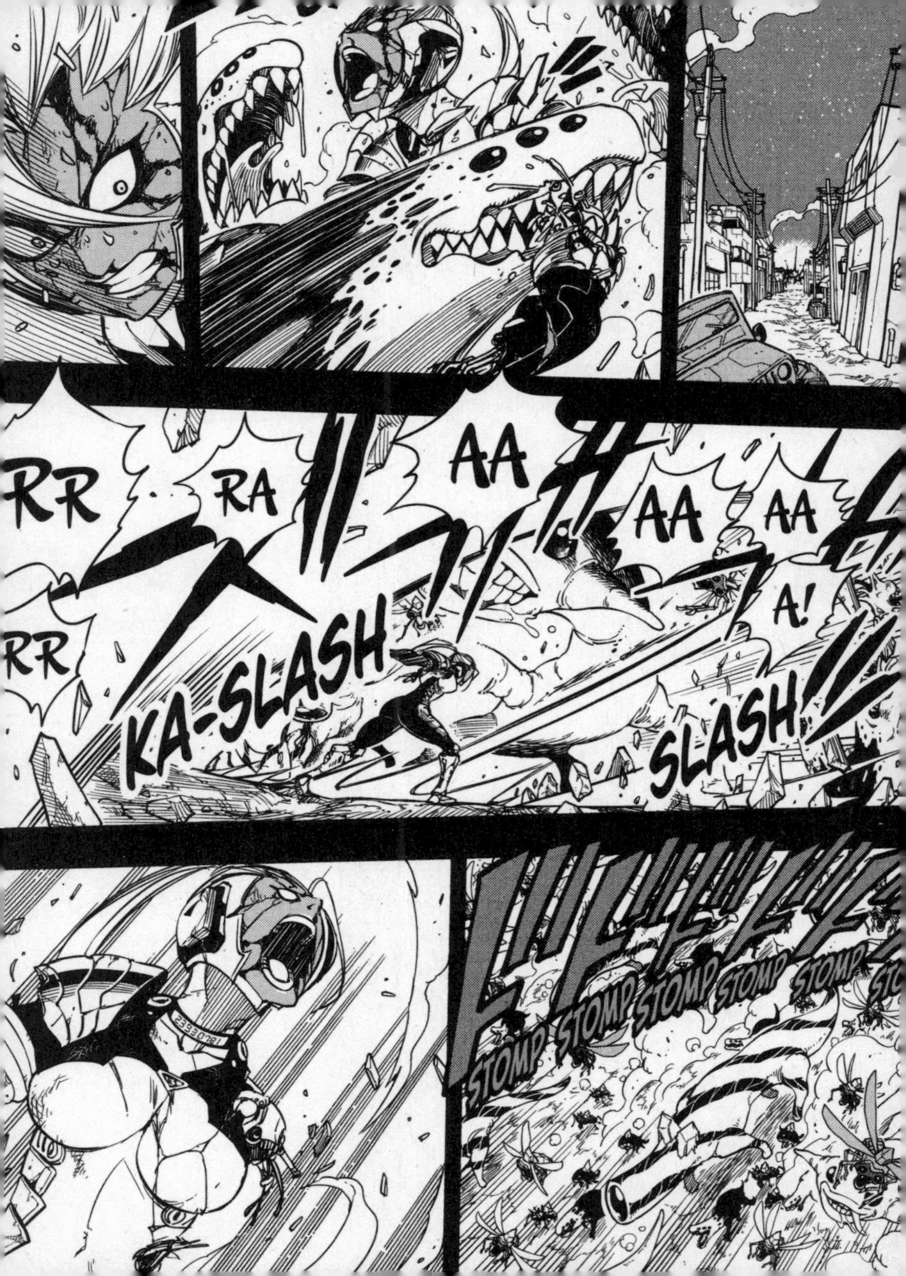
RR
RA
AA
AA
AA
A!
RR
SLASH!!
KA-SLASH
STOMP STOMP STOMP STOMP STOMP

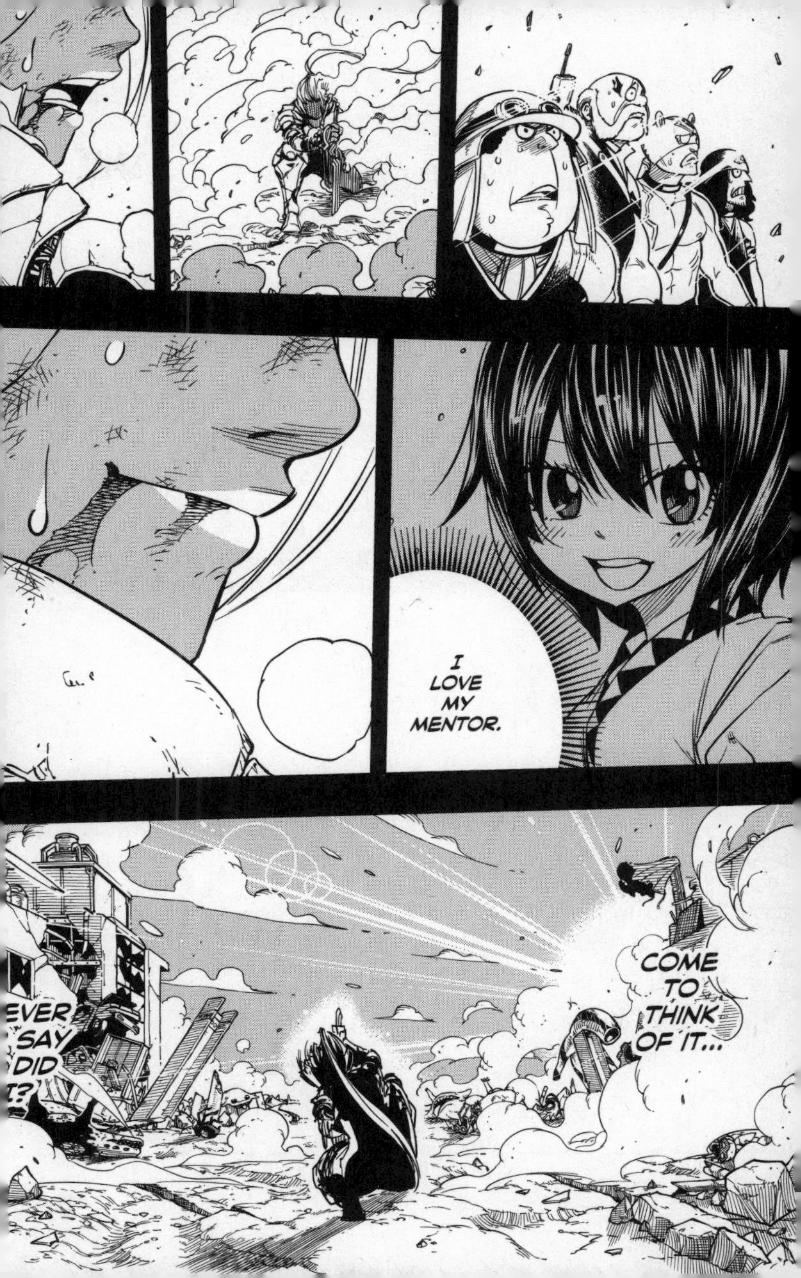
I LOVE MY MENTOR.
COME TO THINK OF IT...
EVER SAY DID

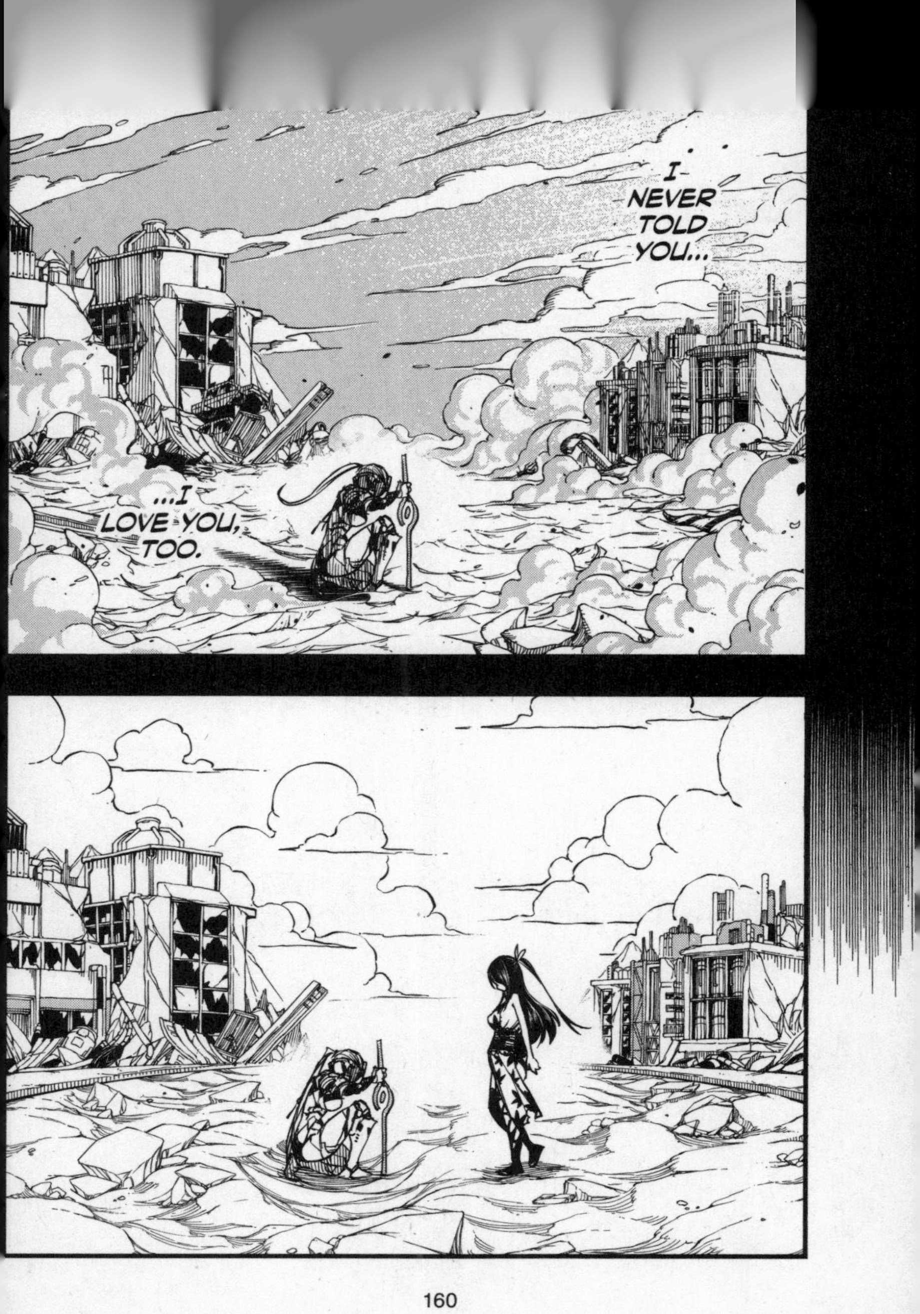
I- NEVER TOLD YOU...
...I LOVE YOU, TOO.

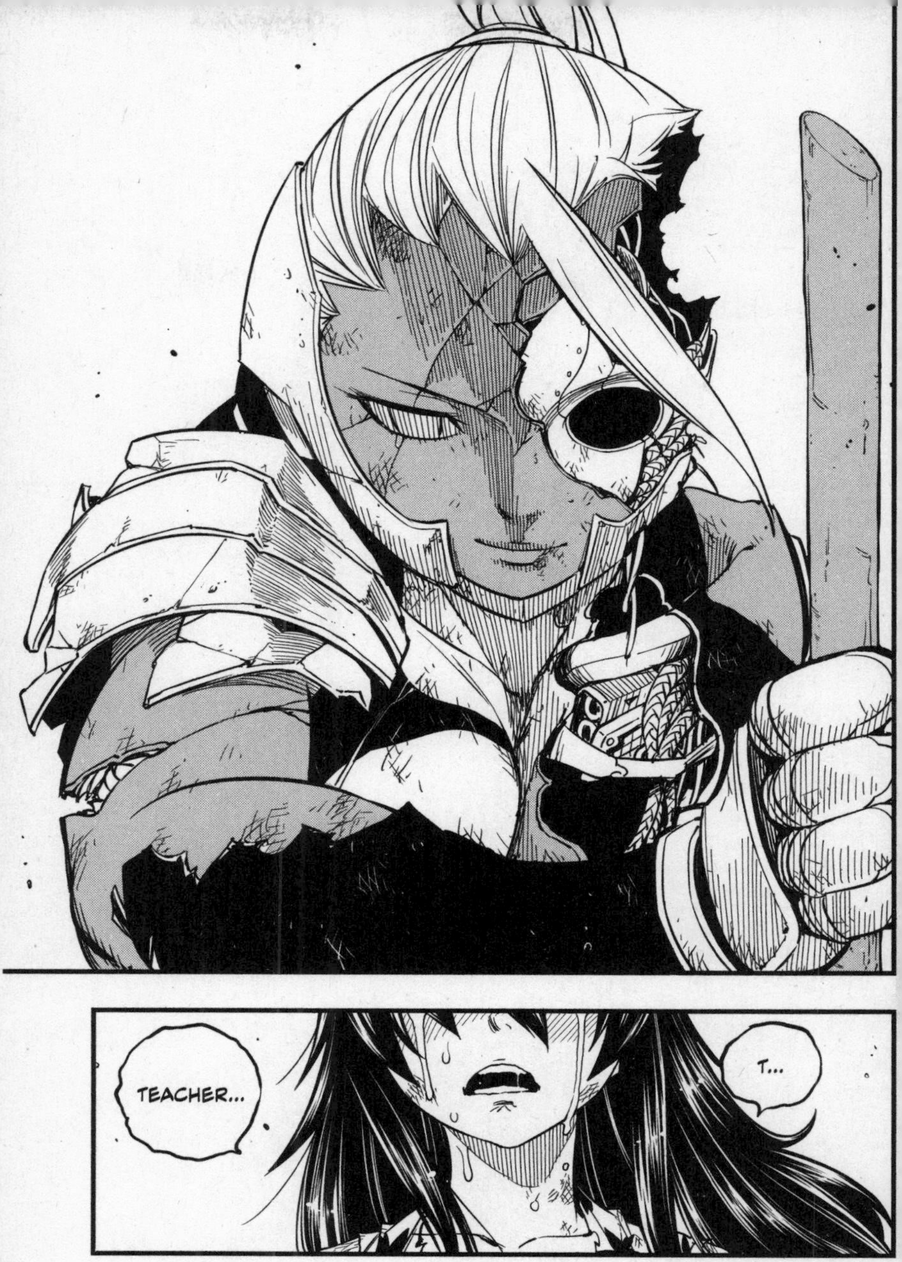
T...
TEACHER...

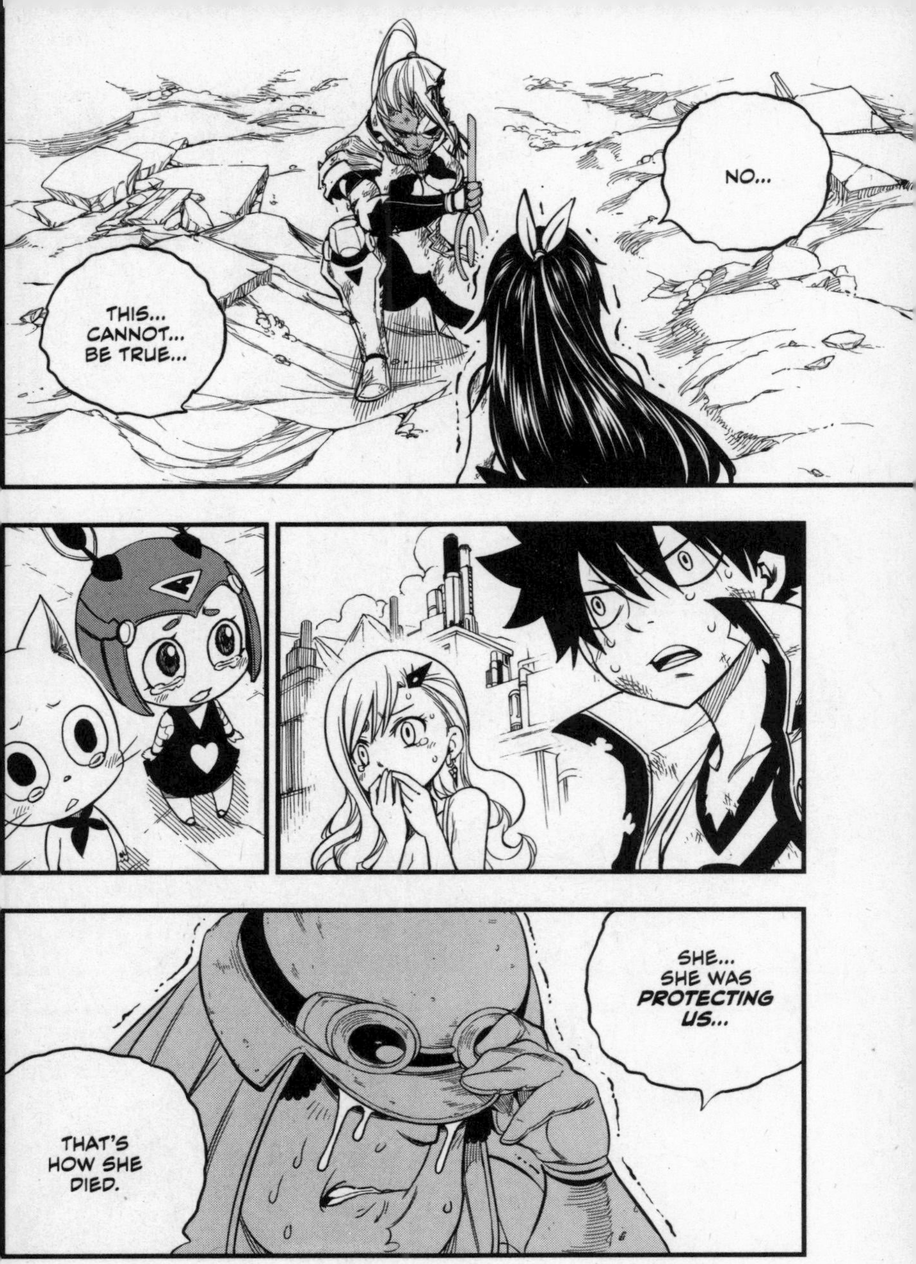
NO...
THIS... CANNOT... BE TRUE...
SHE... SHE WAS *PROTECTING US*...
THAT'S HOW SHE DIED.

EDENS ZERO

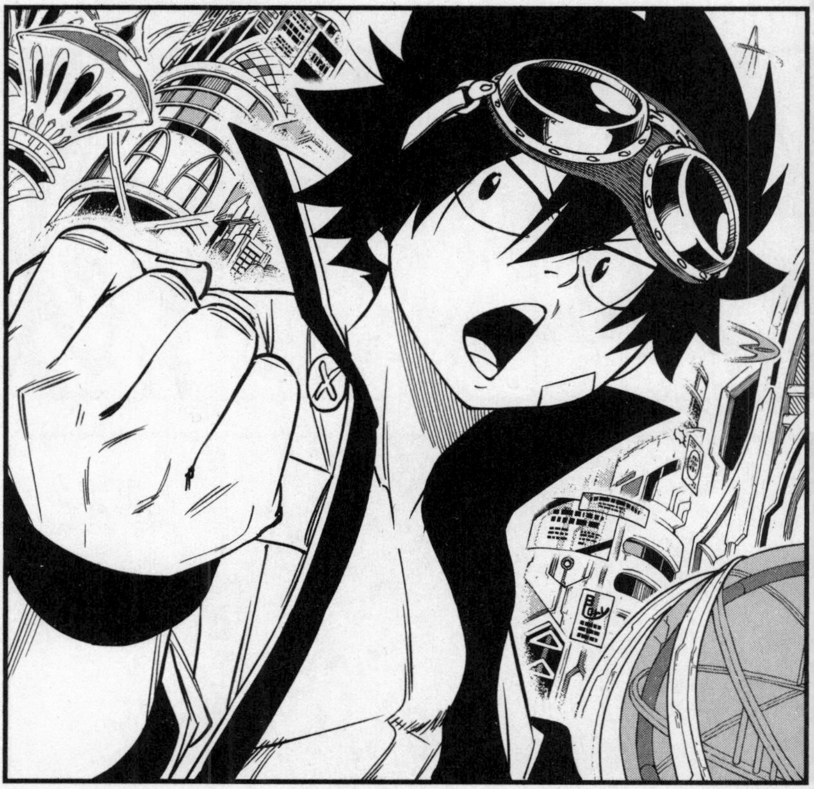

CHAPTER 59: I KNOW YOU CAN KEEP PRESSING ON

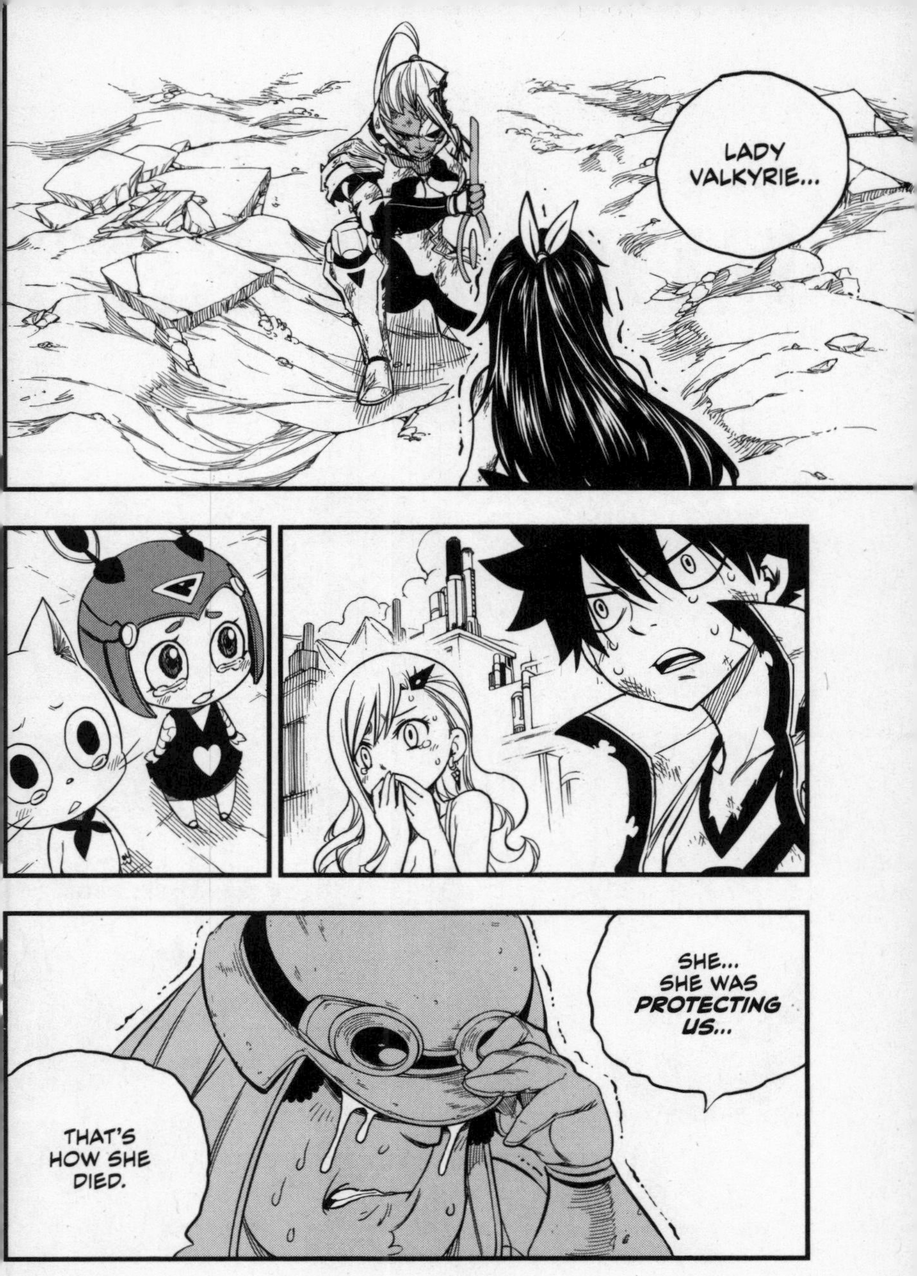
LADY VALKYRIE...
SHE... SHE WAS PROTECTING US...
THAT'S HOW SHE DIED.

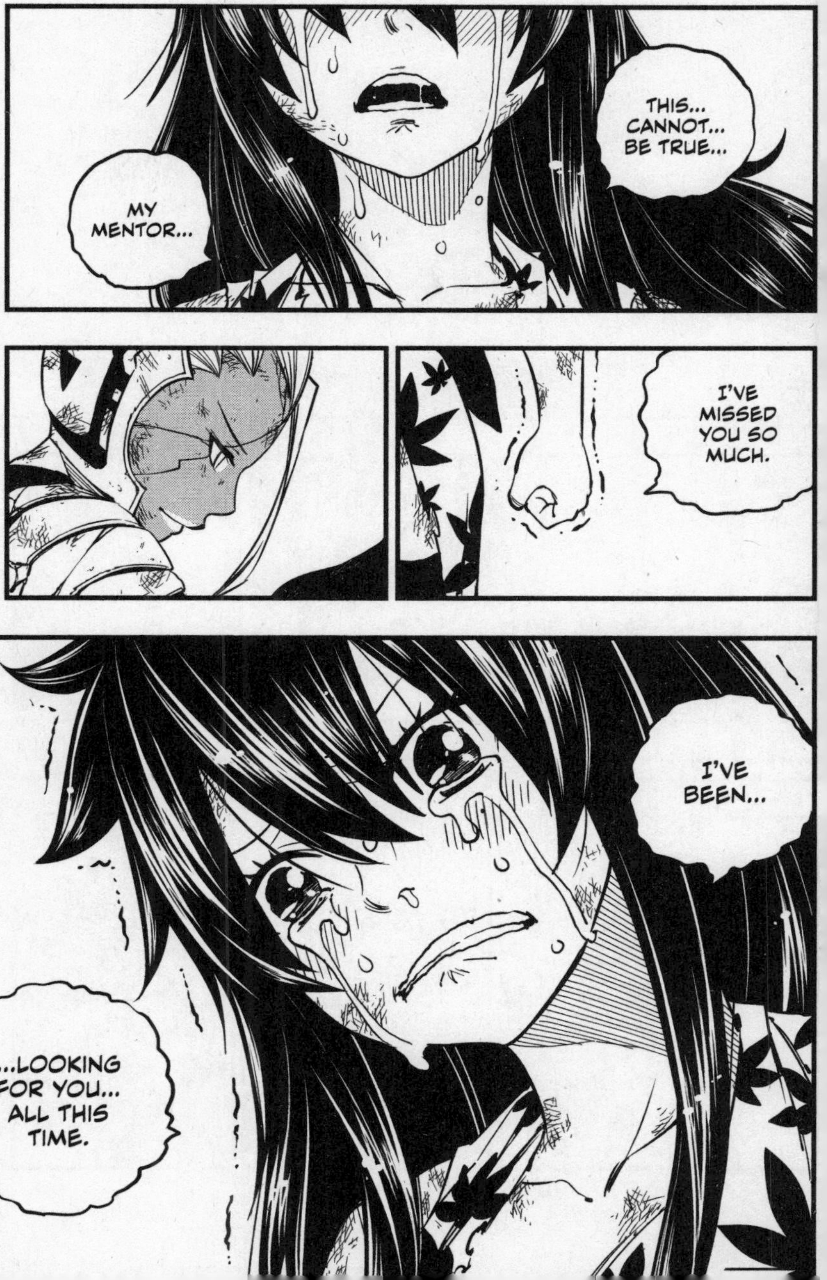
THIS... CANNOT... BE TRUE...
MY MENTOR...
I'VE MISSED YOU SO MUCH.
I'VE BEEN...
...LOOKING FOR YOU... ALL THIS TIME.

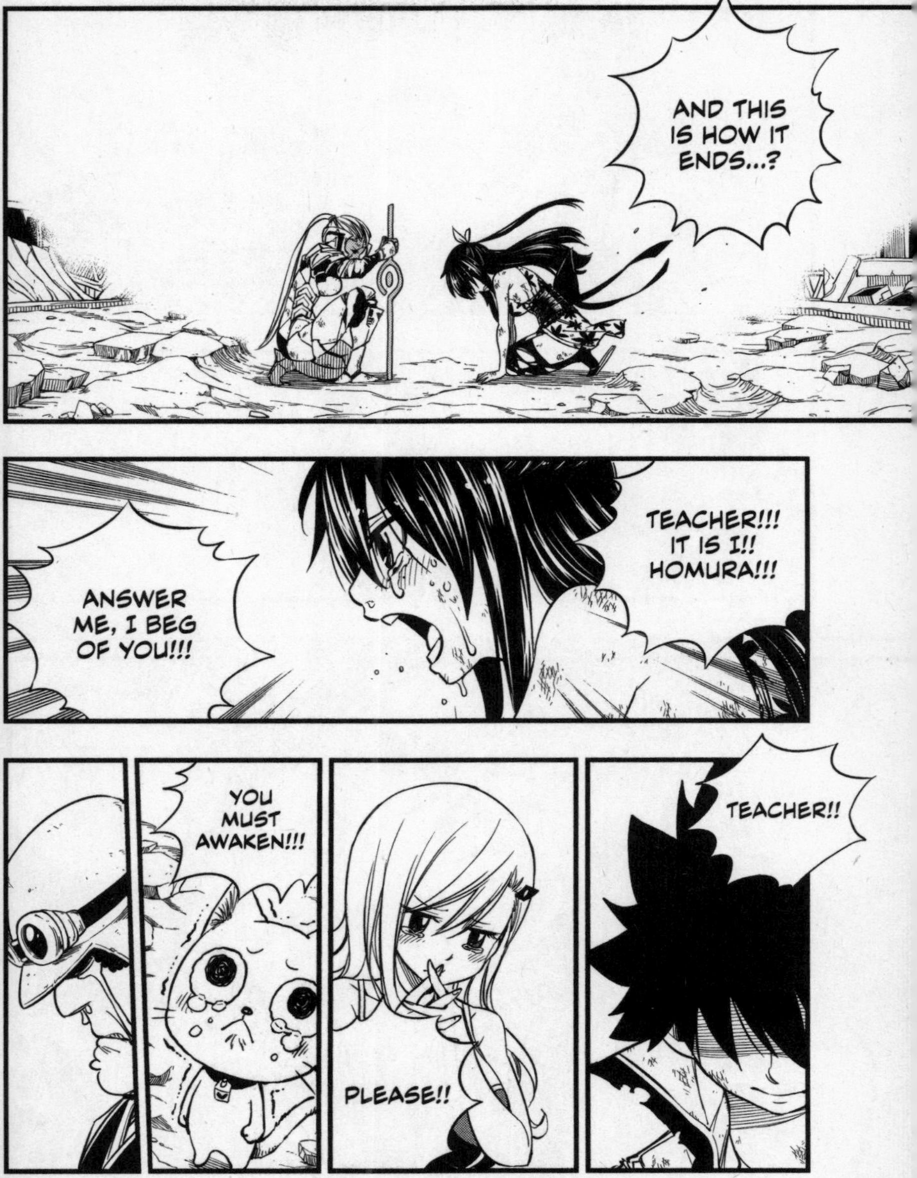
AND THIS IS HOW IT ENDS...?
TEACHER!!! IT IS I!! HOMURA!!!
ANSWER ME, I BEG OF YOU!!!
TEACHER!!
PLEASE!!
YOU MUST AWAKEN!!!

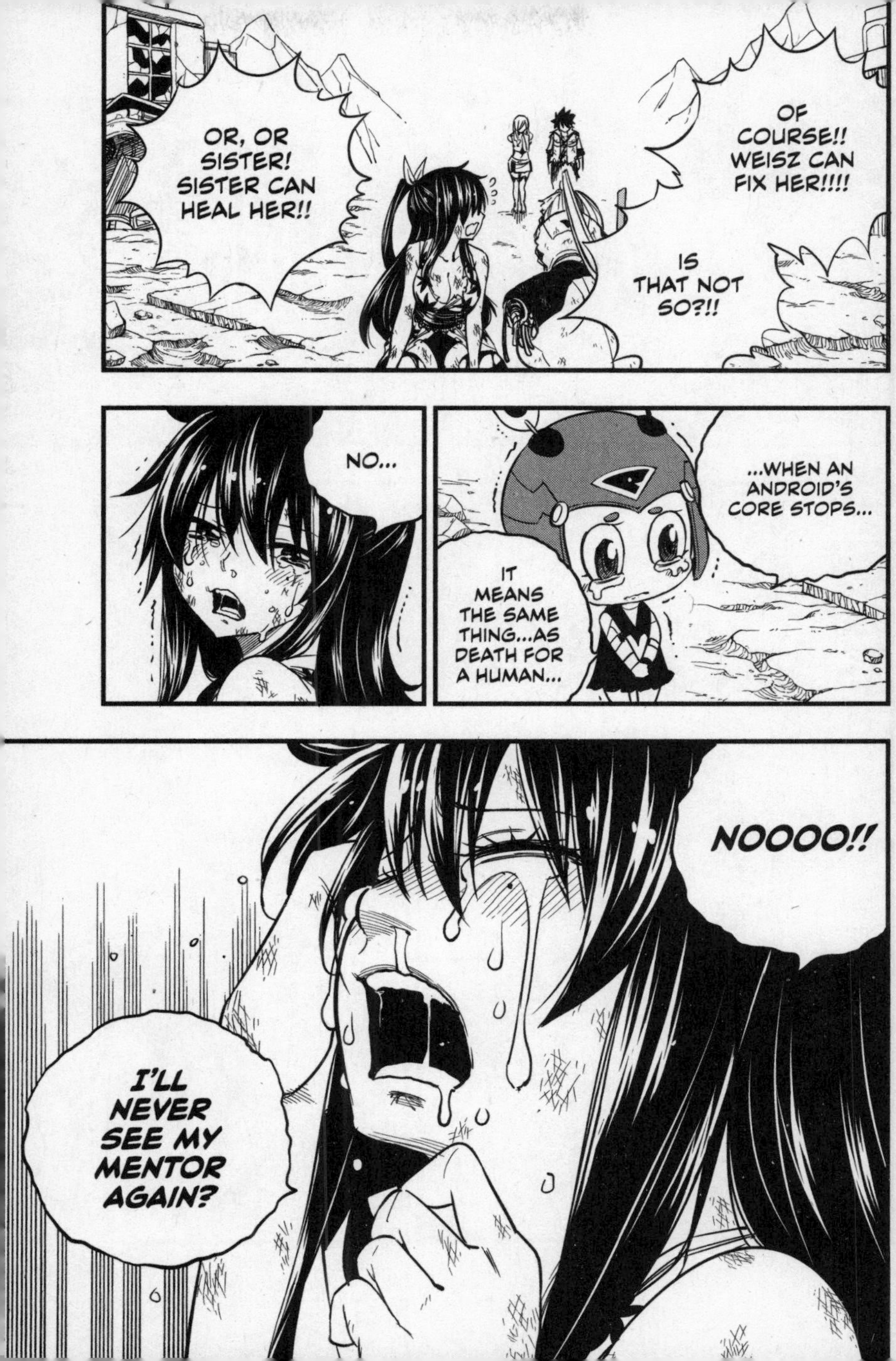
OF COURSE!! WEISZ CAN FIX HER!!!!
OR, OR SISTER! SISTER CAN HEAL HER!!
IS THAT NOT SO?!!
...WHEN AN ANDROID'S CORE STOPS...
IT MEANS THE SAME THING...AS DEATH FOR A HUMAN...
NO...
NOOOO!!
I'LL NEVER SEE MY MENTOR AGAIN?

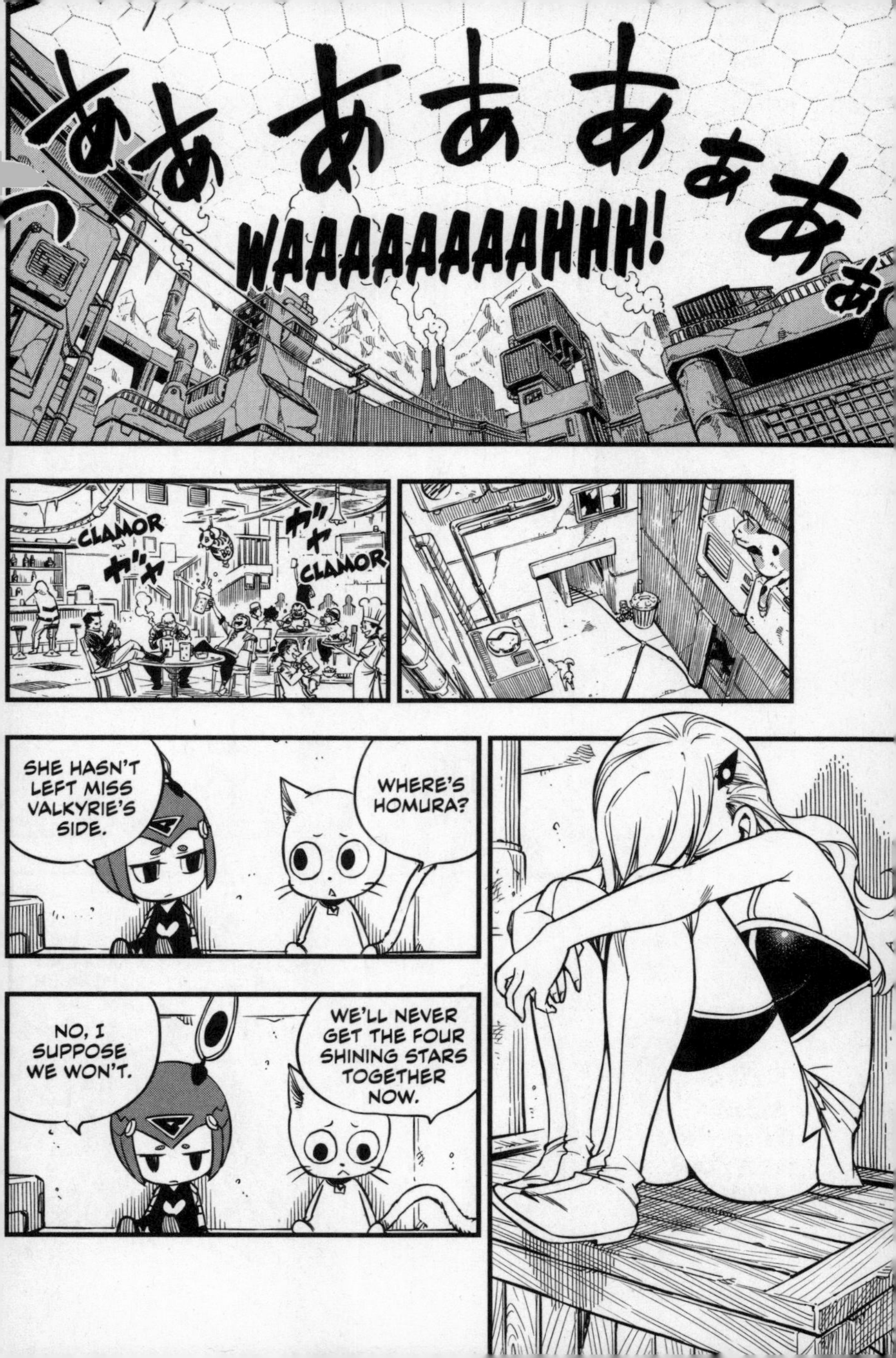

WAAAAAAAAHHH!
CLAMOR
CLAMOR
WHERE'S HOMURA?
SHE HASN'T LEFT MISS VALKYRIE'S SIDE.
WE'LL NEVER GET THE FOUR SHINING STARS TOGETHER NOW.
NO, I SUPPOSE WE WON'T.

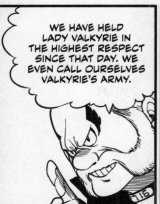

WHO WOULD'VE THOUGHT THAT GIRL WOULD BE HOMURA?
TALK ABOUT A COINCIDENCE.
WE HAVE HELD LADY VALKYRIE IN THE HIGHEST RESPECT SINCE THAT DAY. WE EVEN CALL OURSELVES VALKYRIE'S ARMY.
IF YOU RESPECT HER SO MUCH, WHY DID YOU LEAVE HER OUT THERE EXPOSED TO THE ELEMENTS?
IT'S NOT LIKE WE ABANDONED HER THERE!! WE LEFT HER THERE AS OUR BEACON!!!
IT'S *BECAUSE* OF HER THAT WE'VE BEEN ABLE TO KEEP GOING!!
AND BE-SIDES...
WE FELT LIKE WE SHOULDN'T TOUCH HER
UNTIL THE DAY HOMURA CAME TO FIND HER.
I SEE.
WE'VE BEEN PREPARING THE REBELLION AGAINST MADAME KURENAI FOR A LONG TIME.
YOU MIGHT CALL US THE RE-SISTANCE.

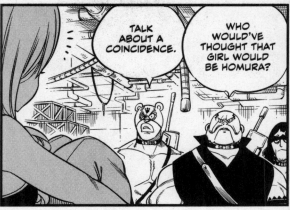

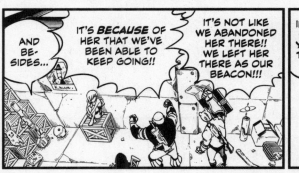

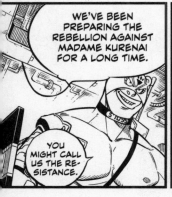

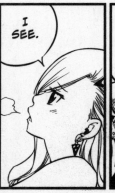

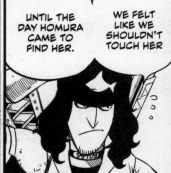

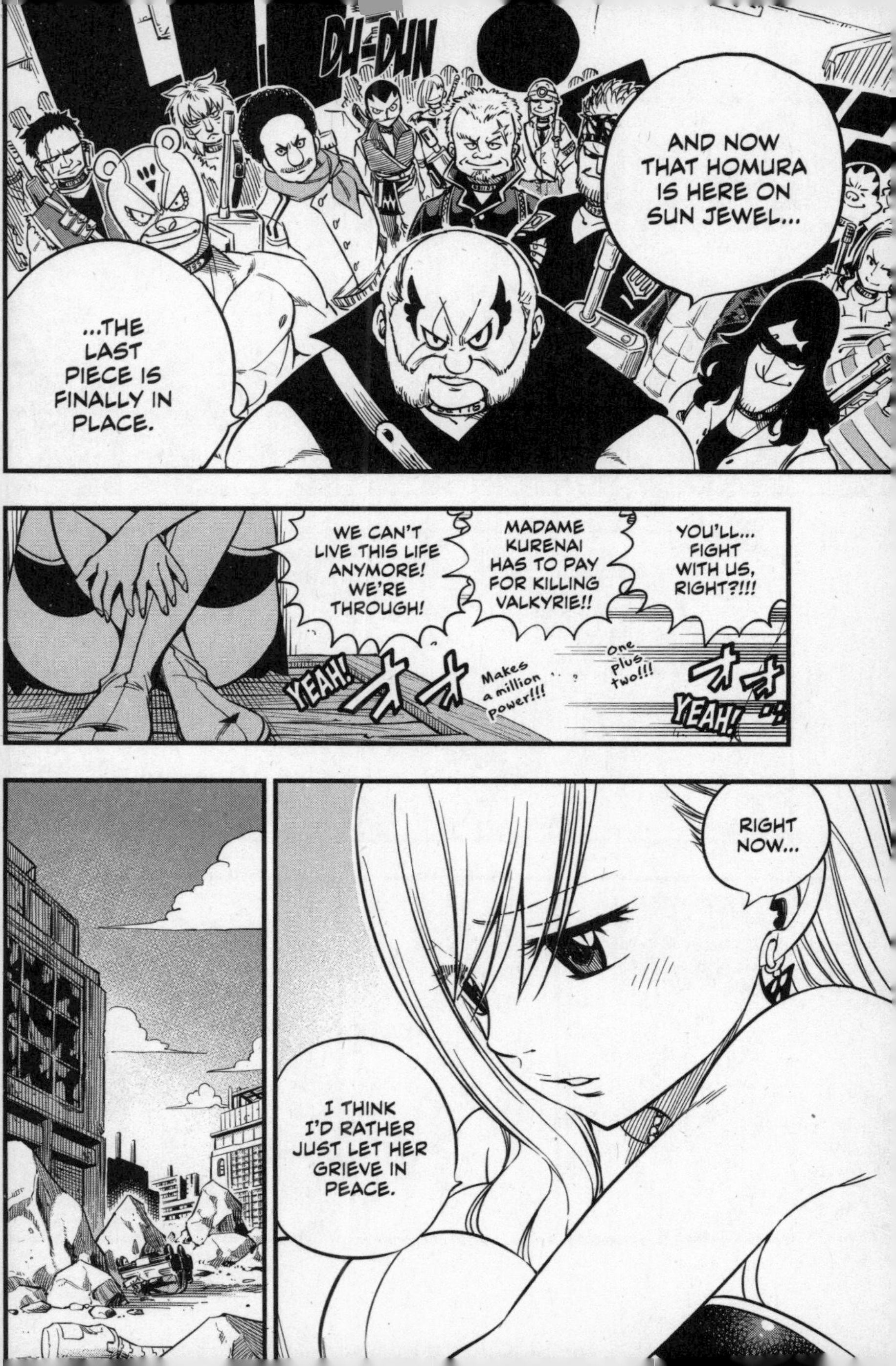
DU-DUN
AND NOW THAT HOMURA IS HERE ON SUN JEWEL...
...THE LAST PIECE IS FINALLY IN PLACE.
YOU'LL... FIGHT WITH US, RIGHT?!!!
MADAME KURENAI HAS TO PAY FOR KILLING VALKYRIE!!
WE CAN'T LIVE THIS LIFE ANYMORE! WE'RE THROUGH!
YEAH!
One plus two!!!
Makes a million power!!!
YEAH!
RIGHT NOW...
I THINK I'D RATHER JUST LET HER GRIEVE IN PEACE.

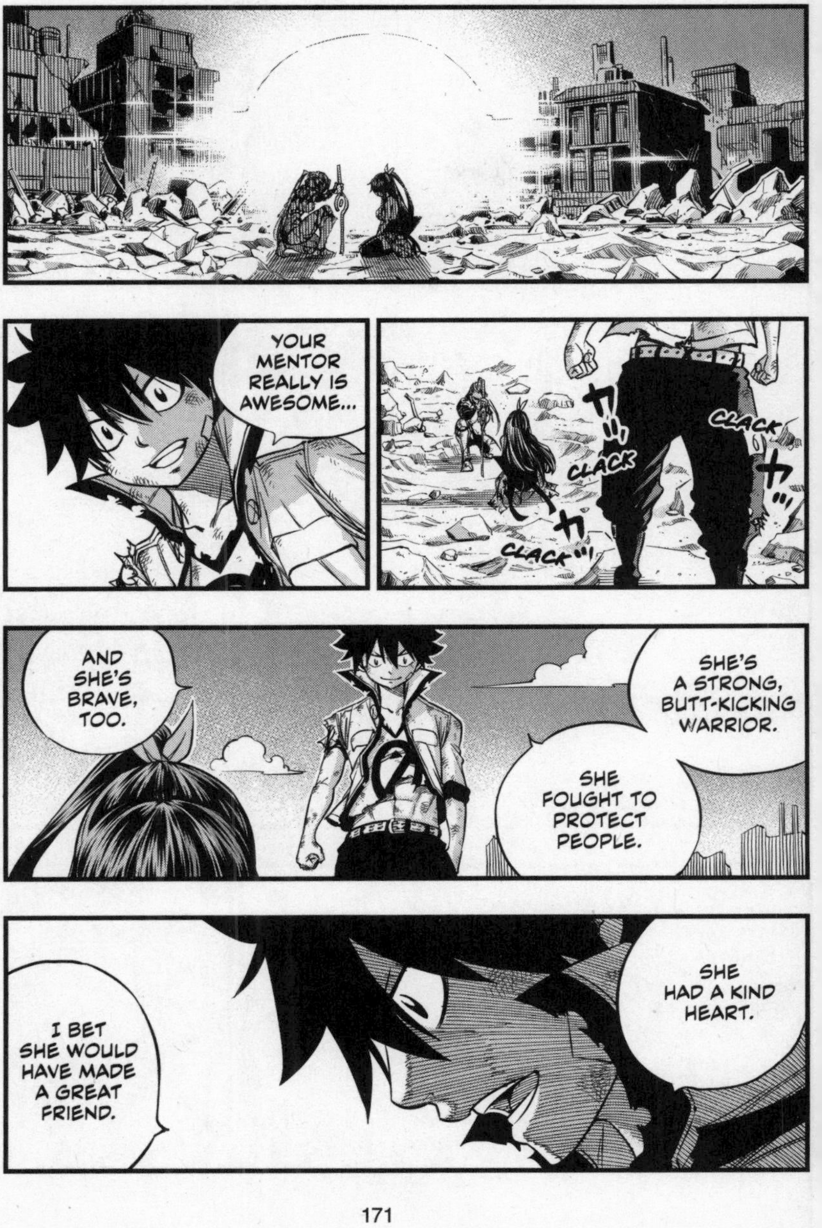
CLACK
CLACK
CLACK
YOUR MENTOR REALLY IS AWESOME...
SHE'S A STRONG, BUTT-KICKING WARRIOR.
SHE FOUGHT TO PROTECT PEOPLE.
AND SHE'S BRAVE, TOO.
SHE HAD A KIND HEART.
I BET SHE WOULD HAVE MADE A GREAT FRIEND.

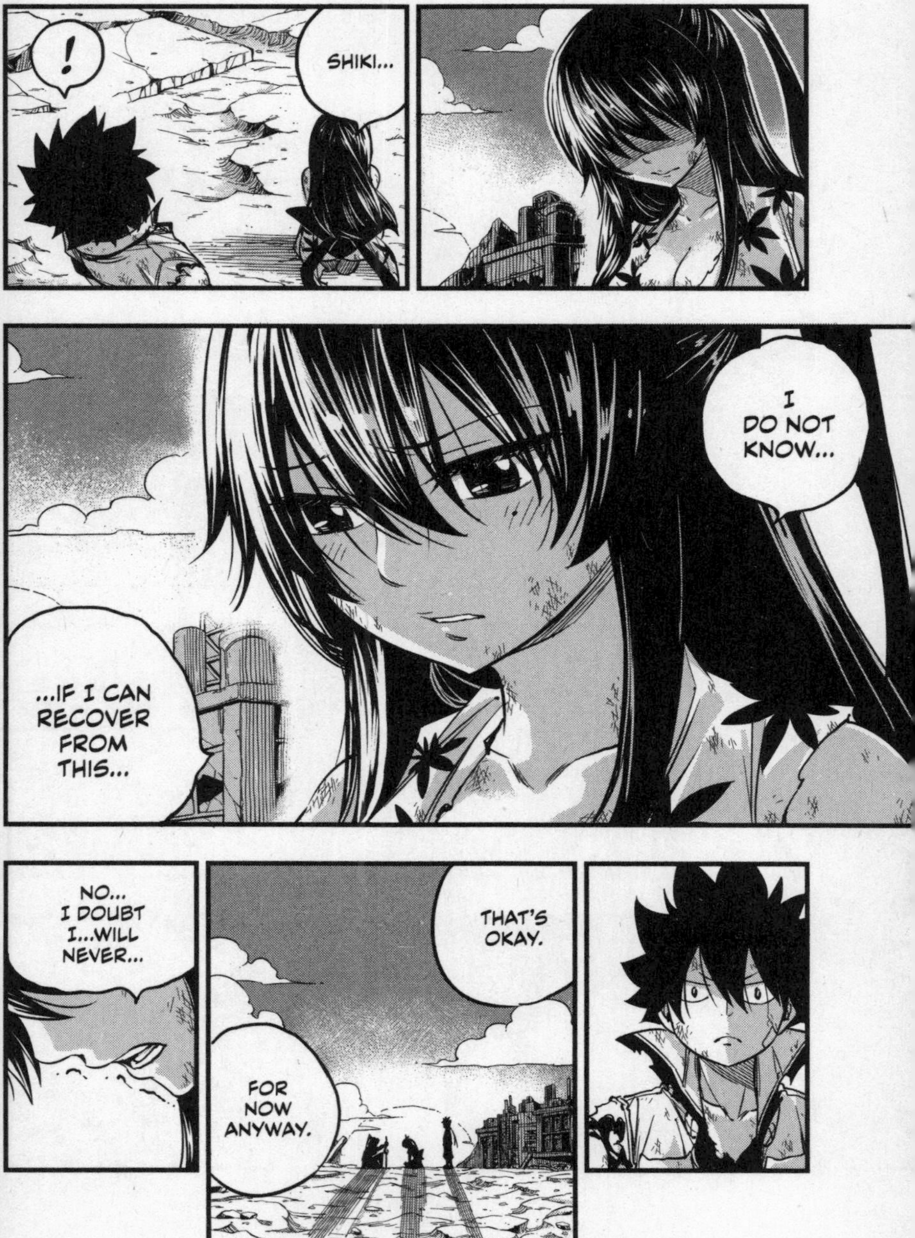
SHIKI...
!
I DO NOT KNOW...
...IF I CAN RECOVER FROM THIS...
THAT'S OKAY.
FOR NOW ANYWAY.
NO... I DOUBT I...WILL NEVER...

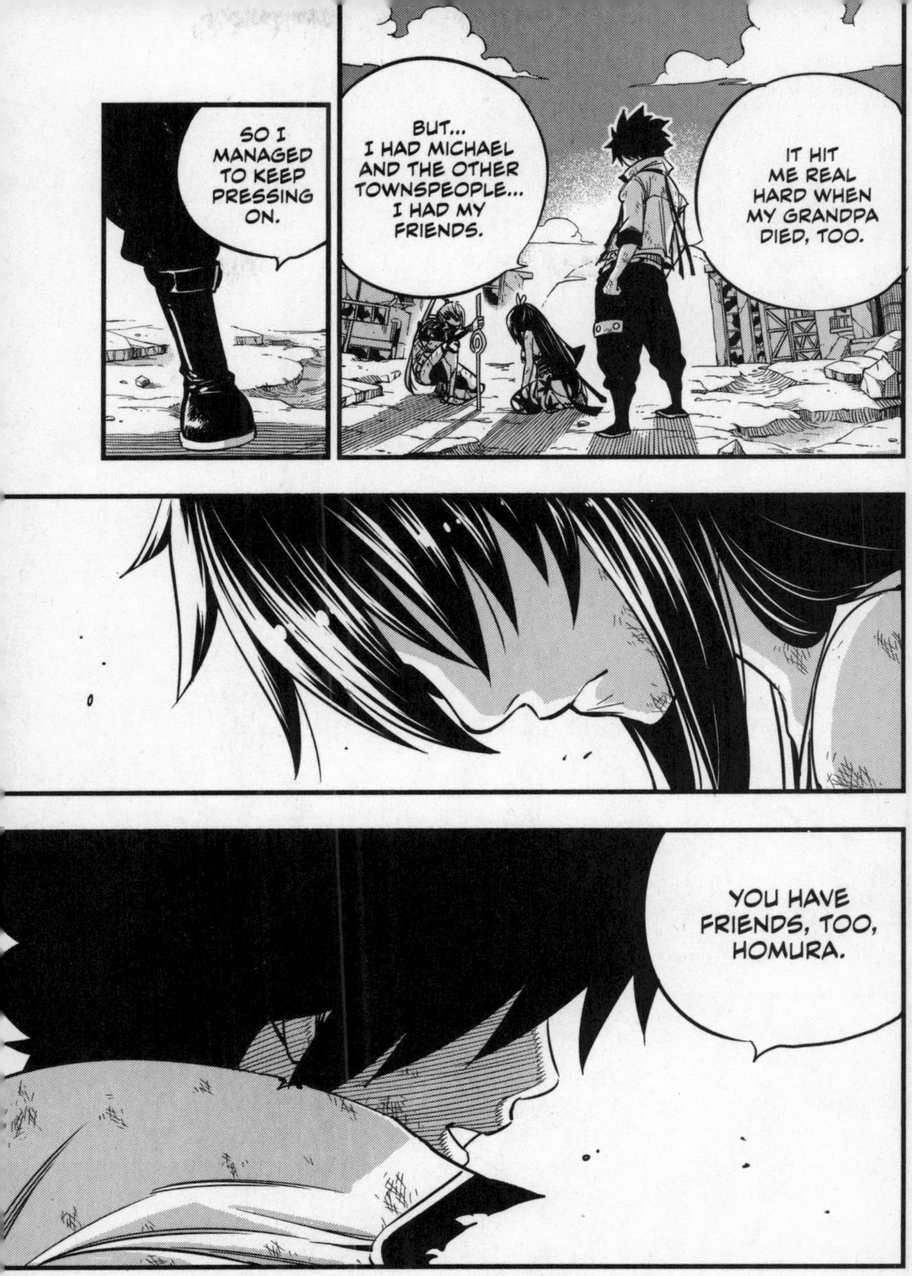
IT HIT ME REAL HARD WHEN MY GRANDPA DIED, TOO.
BUT... I HAD MICHAEL AND THE OTHER TOWNSPEOPLE... I HAD MY FRIENDS.
SO I MANAGED TO KEEP PRESSING ON.
YOU HAVE FRIENDS, TOO, HOMURA.

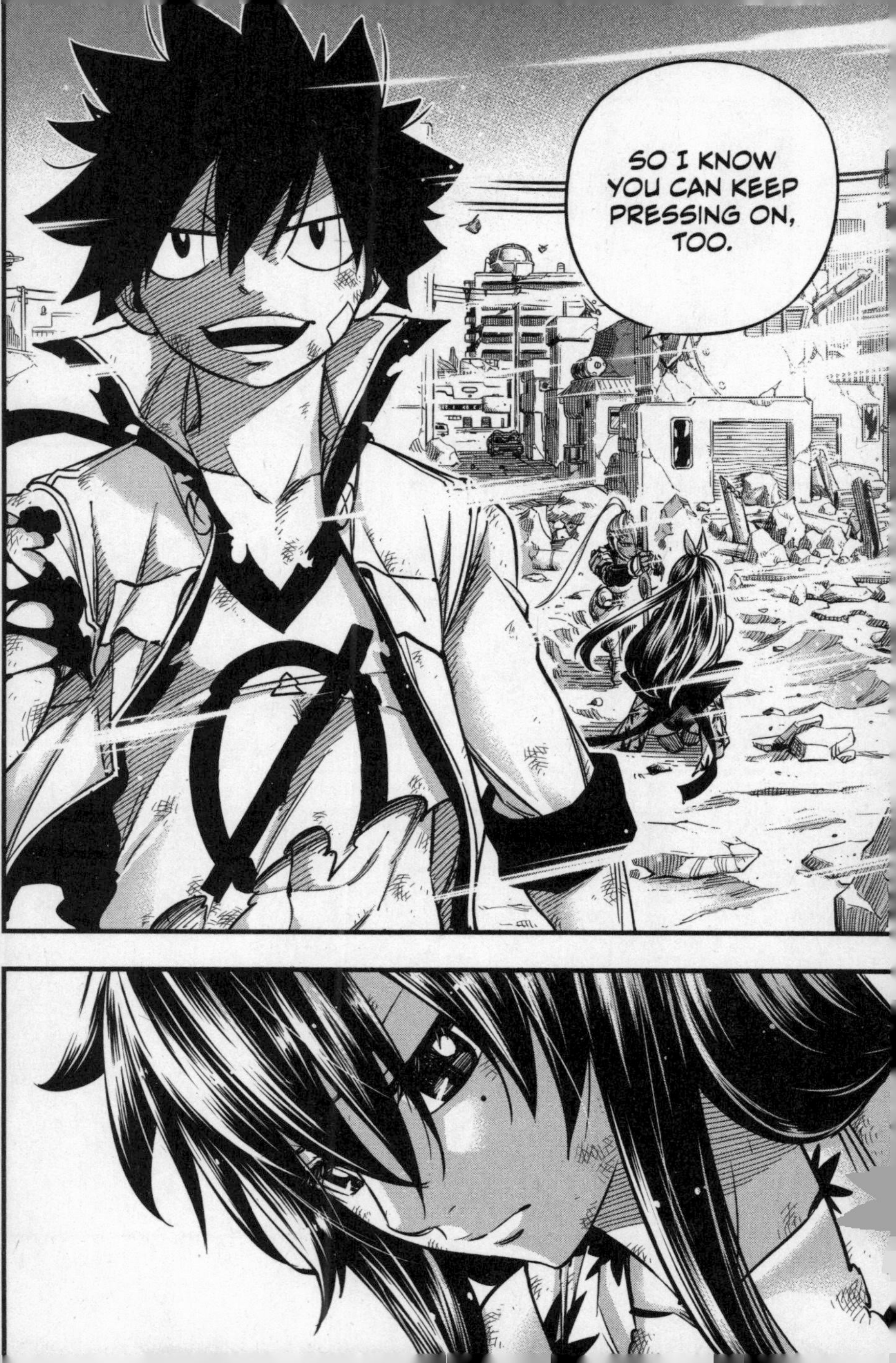
SO I KNOW YOU CAN KEEP PRESSING ON, TOO.

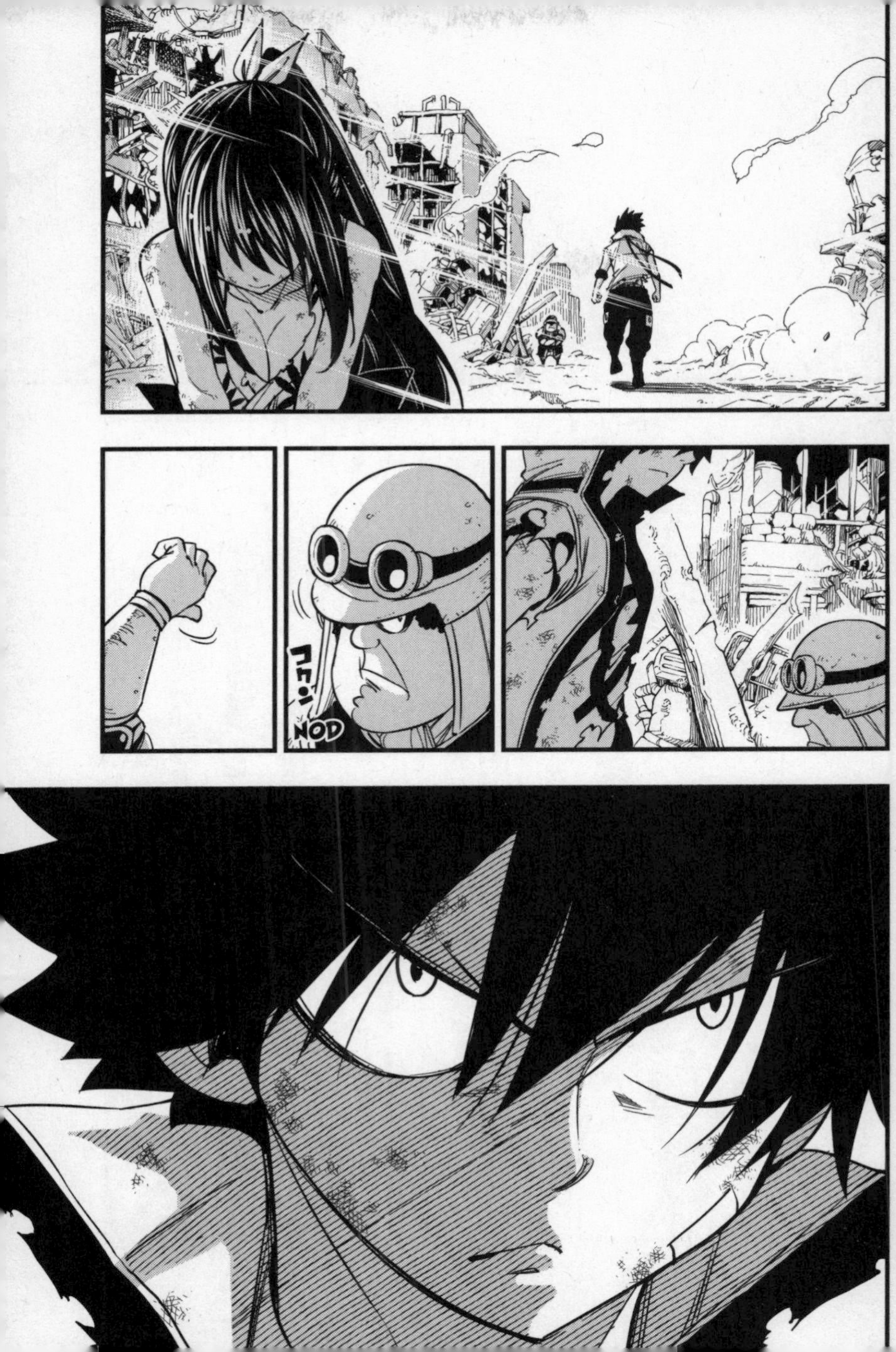
NOD

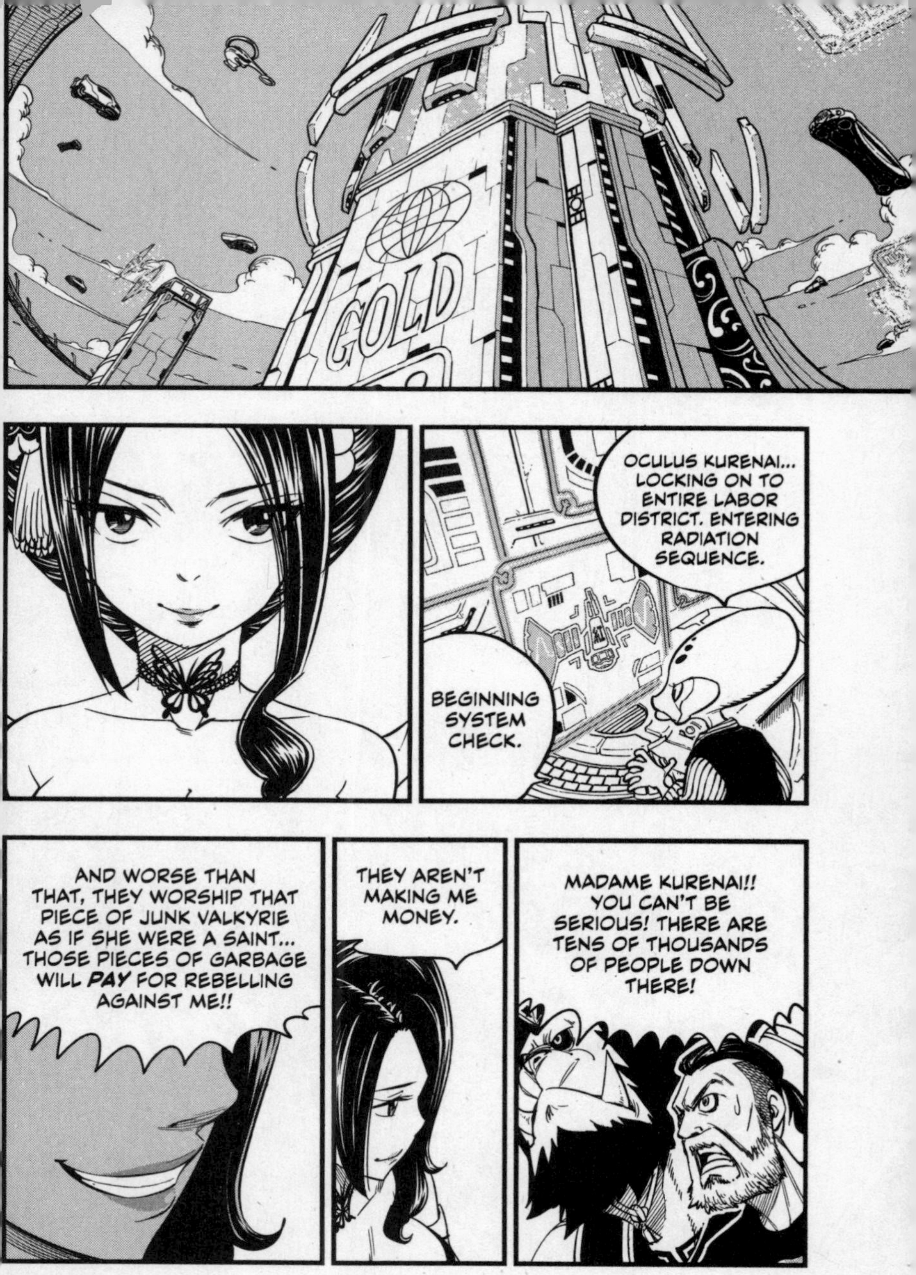
OCULUS KURENAI... LOCKING ON TO ENTIRE LABOR DISTRICT. ENTERING RADIATION SEQUENCE.
BEGINNING SYSTEM CHECK.
MADAME KURENAI!! YOU CAN'T BE SERIOUS! THERE ARE TENS OF THOUSANDS OF PEOPLE DOWN THERE!
THEY AREN'T MAKING ME MONEY.
AND WORSE THAN THAT, THEY WORSHIP THAT PIECE OF JUNK VALKYRIE AS IF SHE WERE A SAINT... THOSE PIECES OF GARBAGE WILL *PAY* FOR REBELLING AGAINST ME!!

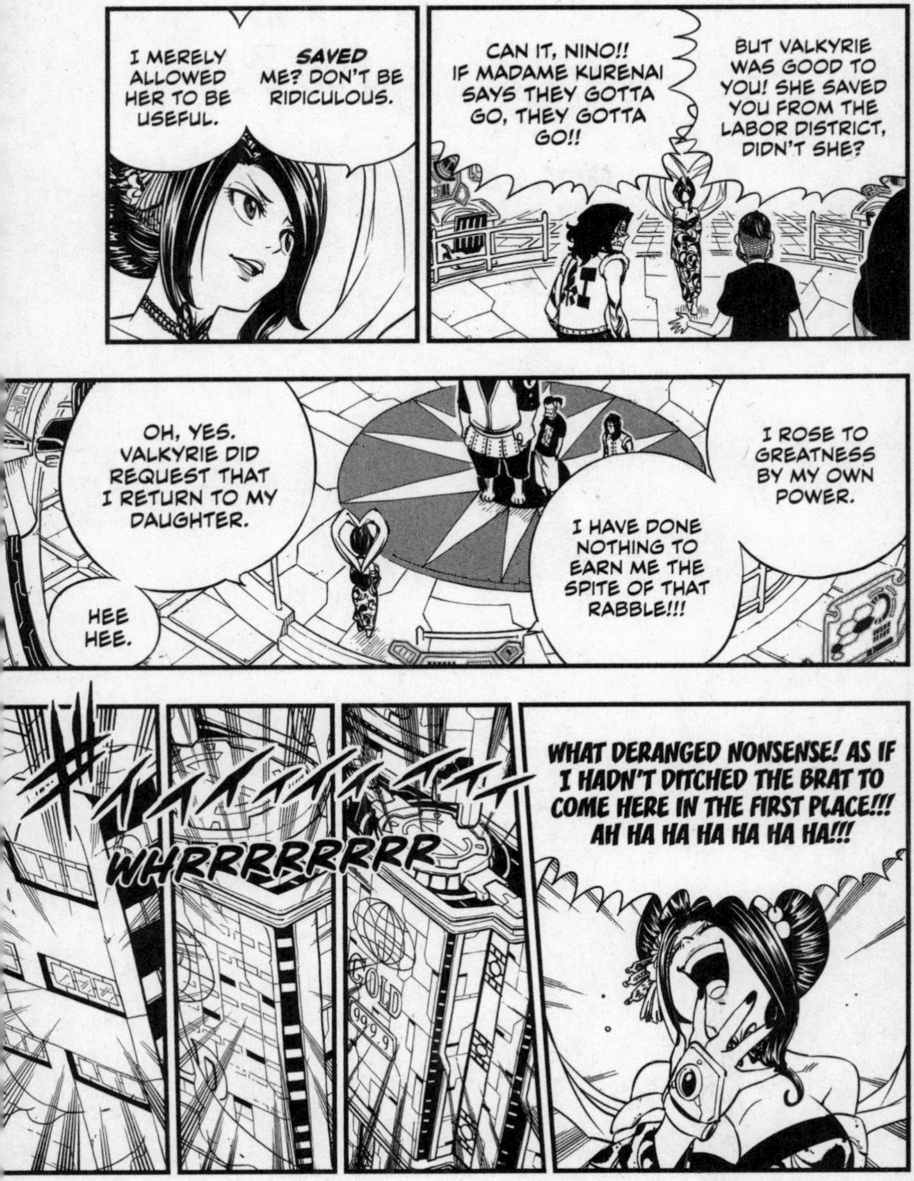
BUT VALKYRIE WAS GOOD TO YOU! SHE SAVED YOU FROM THE LABOR DISTRICT, DIDN'T SHE?
CAN IT, NINO!! IF MADAME KURENAI SAYS THEY GOTTA GO, THEY GOTTA GO!!
SAVED ME? DON'T BE RIDICULOUS.
I MERELY ALLOWED HER TO BE USEFUL.
I ROSE TO GREATNESS BY MY OWN POWER.
I HAVE DONE NOTHING TO EARN ME THE SPITE OF THAT RABBLE!!!
OH, YES. VALKYRIE DID REQUEST THAT I RETURN TO MY DAUGHTER.
HEE HEE.
WHAT DERANGED NONSENSE! AS IF I HADN'T DITCHED THE BRAT TO COME HERE IN THE FIRST PLACE!!! AH HA HA HA HA HA HA!!!
WHRRRRRRRR

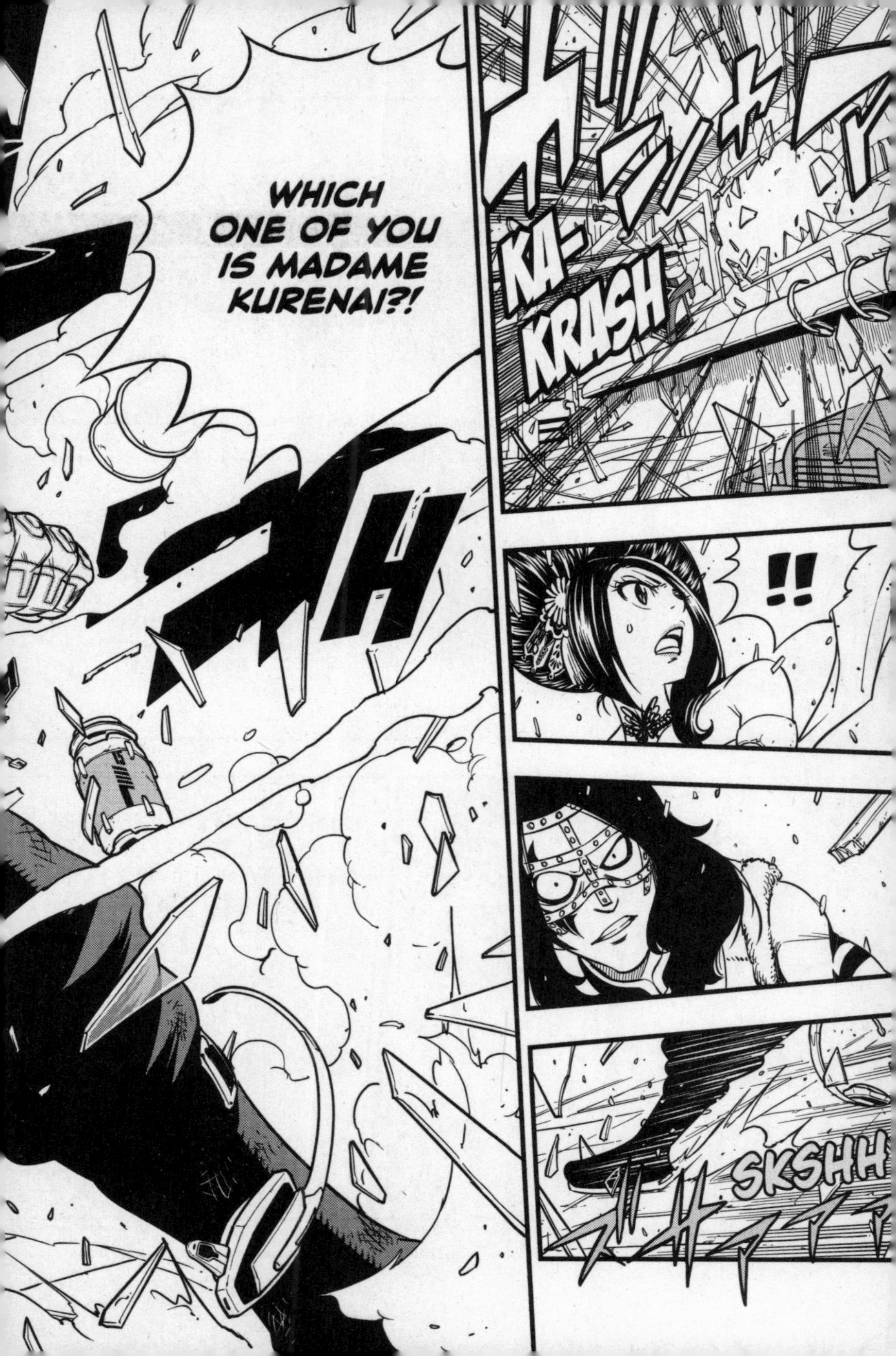
KA-
KRASH
!!
SKSHH
WHICH ONE OF YOU IS MADAME KURENAI?!

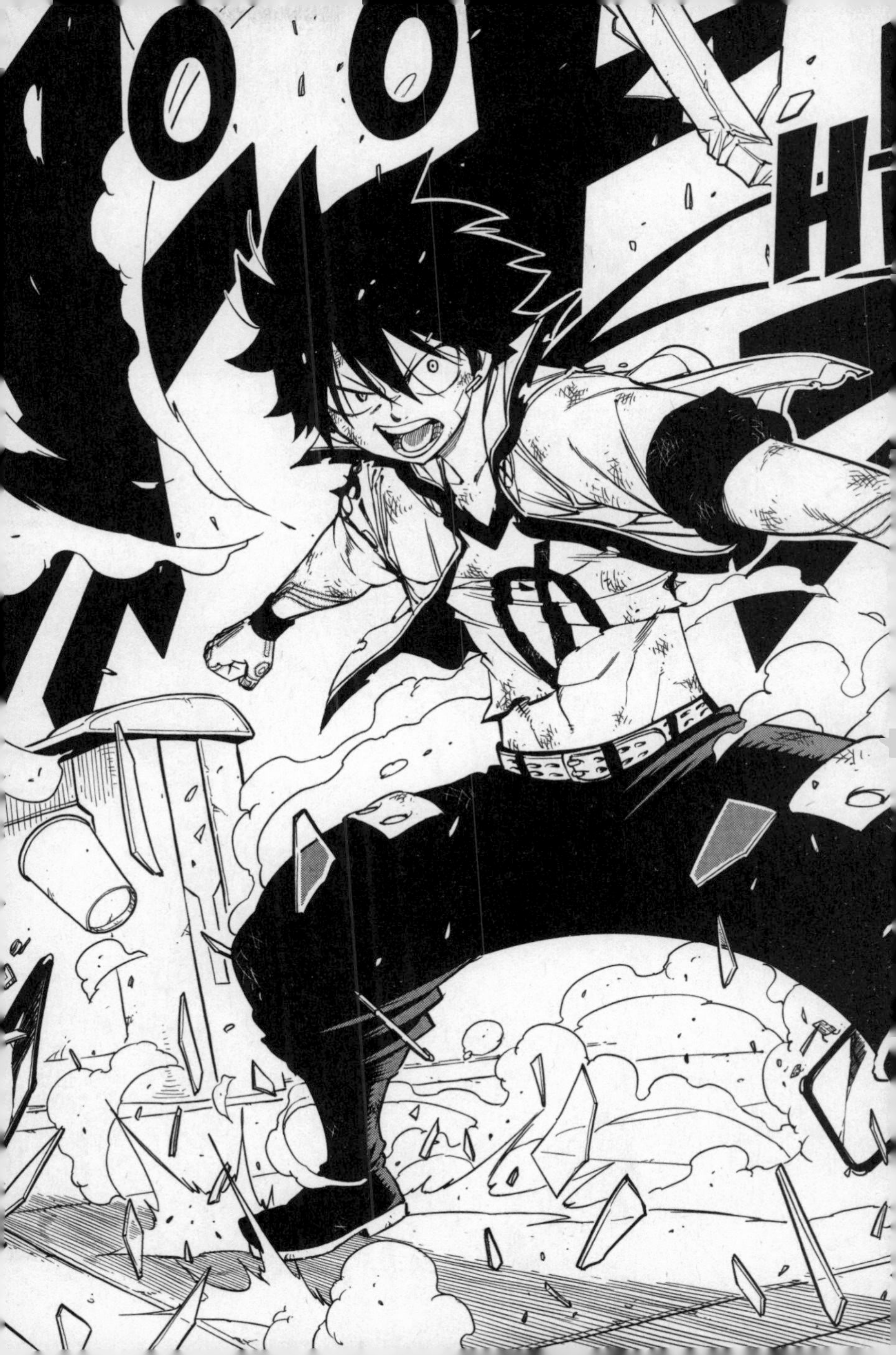

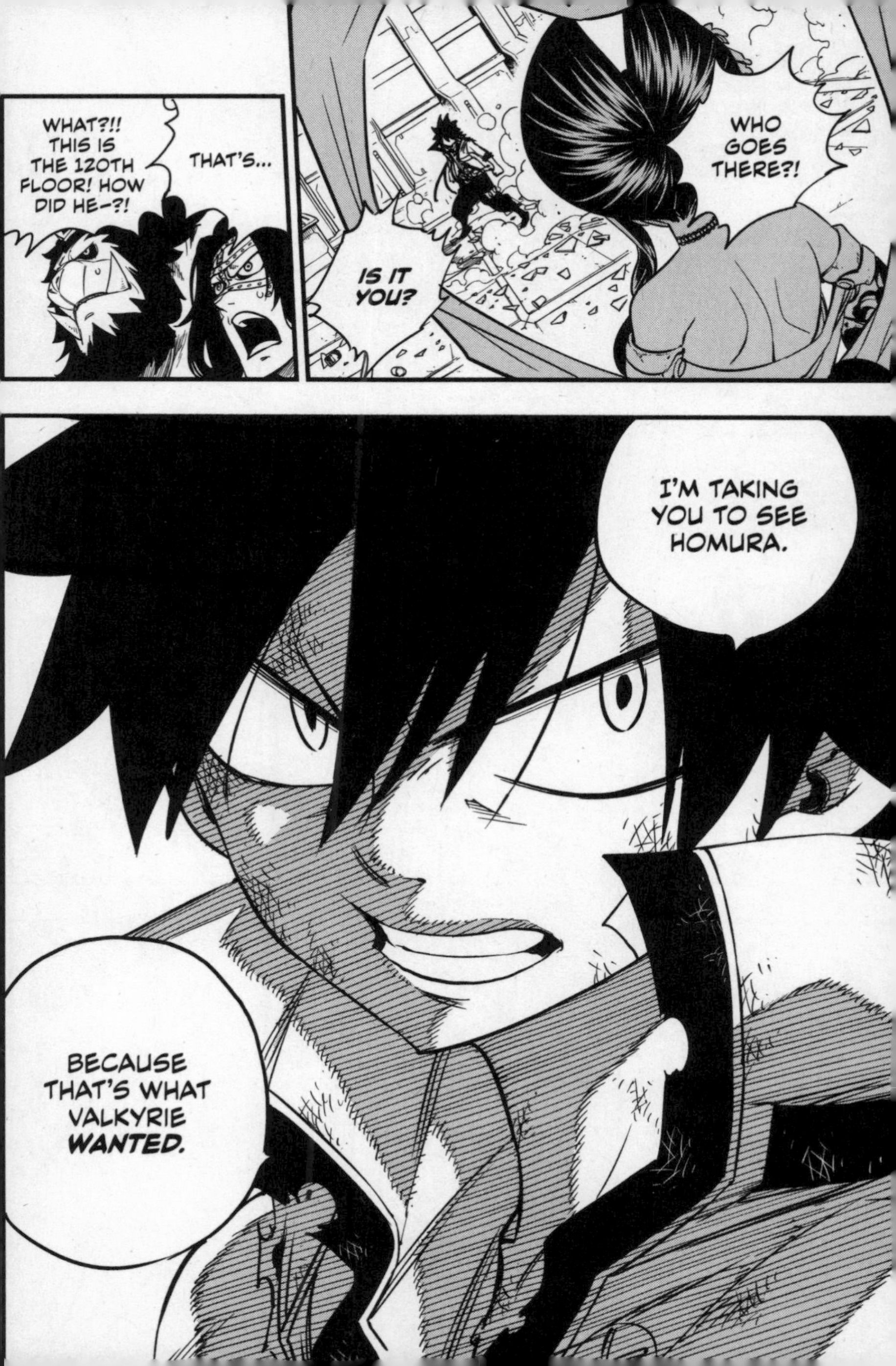
WHO GOES THERE?!
IS IT YOU?
THAT'S...
WHAT?!! THIS IS THE 120TH FLOOR! HOW DID HE-?!
I'M TAKING YOU TO SEE HOMURA.
BECAUSE THAT'S WHAT VALKYRIE ***WANTED.***

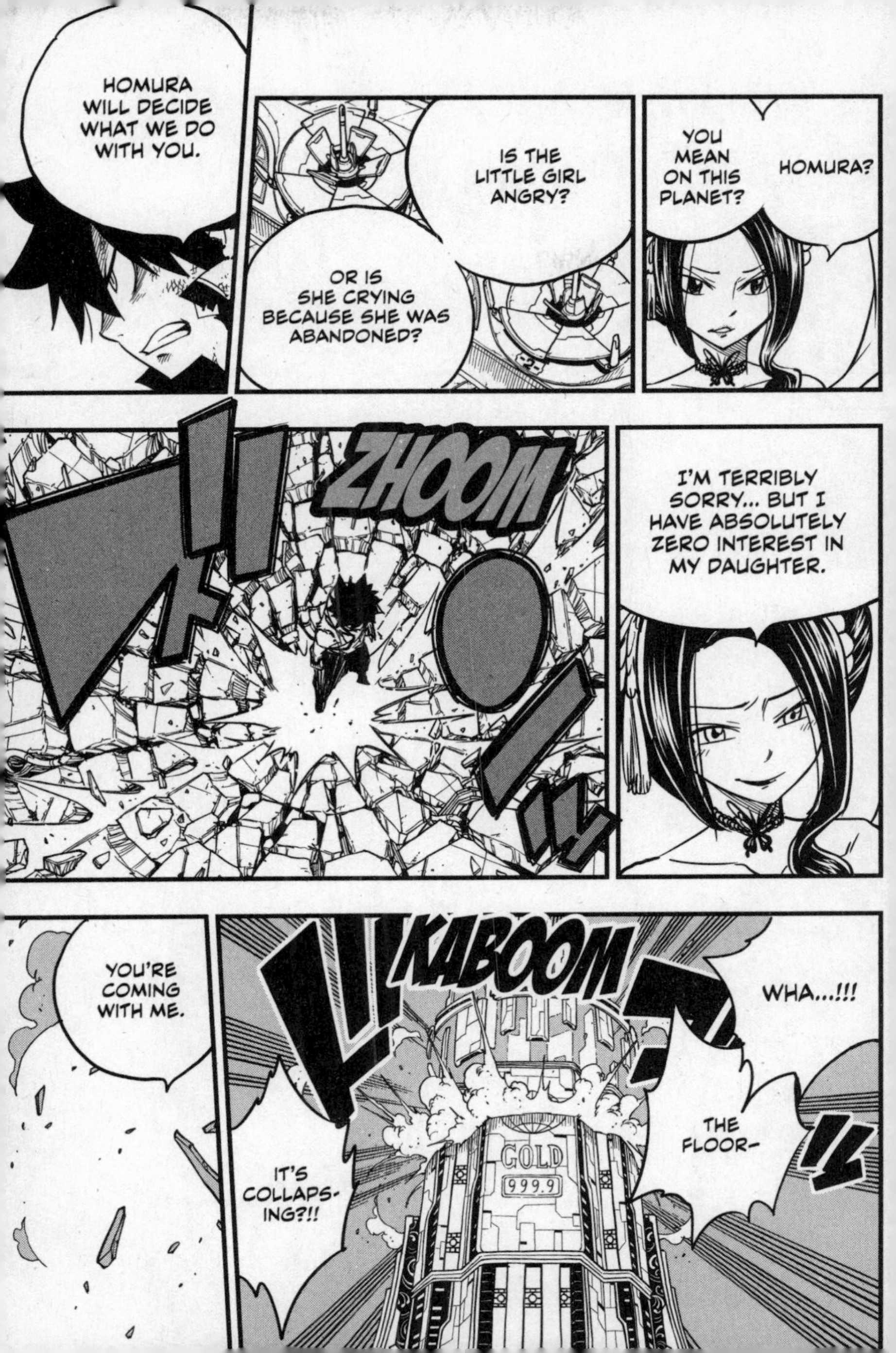

HOMURA?
YOU MEAN ON THIS PLANET?
IS THE LITTLE GIRL ANGRY?
OR IS SHE CRYING BECAUSE SHE WAS ABANDONED?
HOMURA WILL DECIDE WHAT WE DO WITH YOU.
I'M TERRIBLY SORRY... BUT I HAVE ABSOLUTELY ZERO INTEREST IN MY DAUGHTER.
ZHOOM
KABOOM
WHA...!!!
THE FLOOR-
GOLD
999.9
IT'S COLLAPSING?!!
YOU'RE COMING WITH ME.

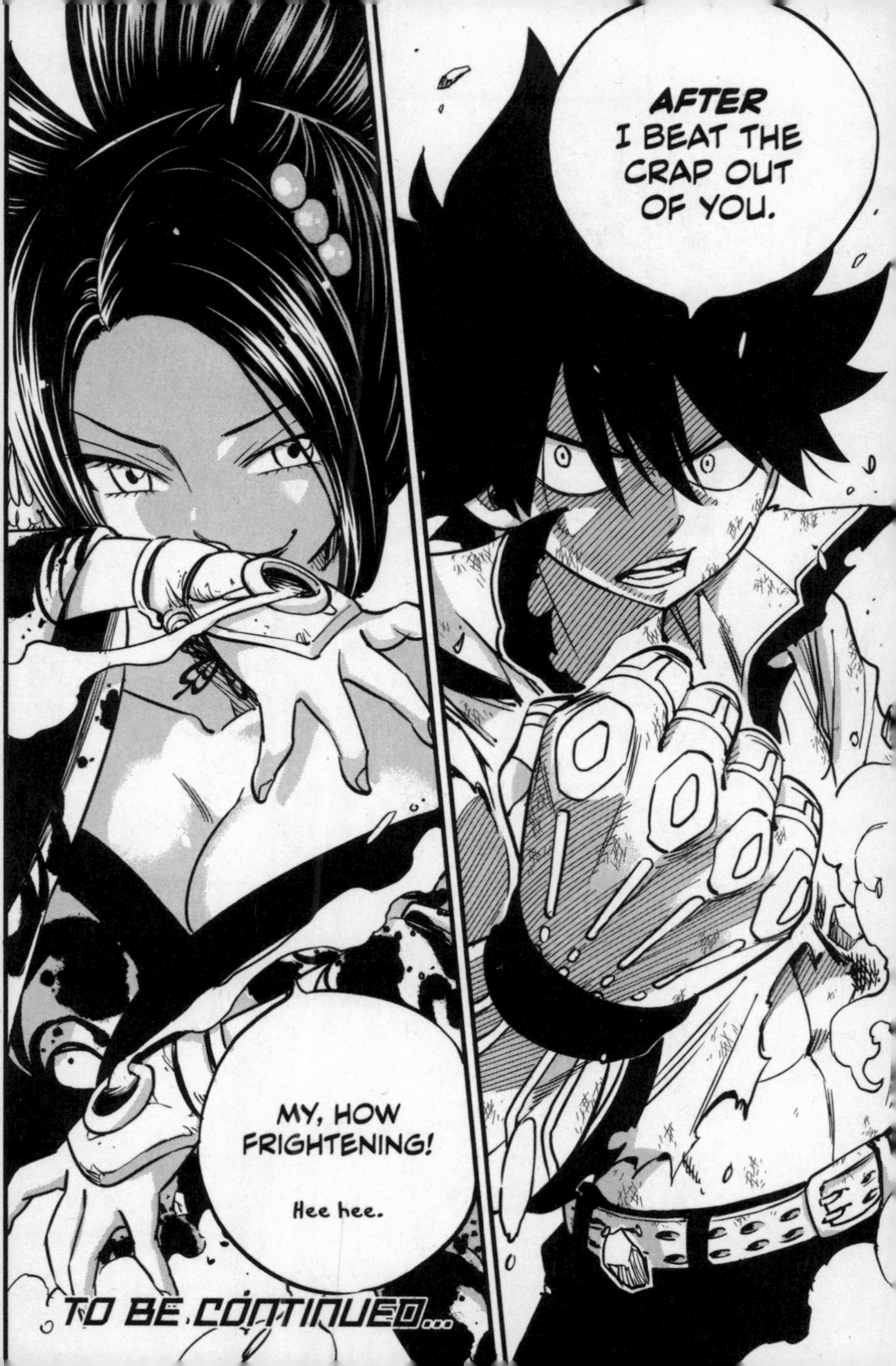
AFTER I BEAT THE CRAP OUT OF YOU.
MY, HOW FRIGHTENING!
Hee hee.
TO BE CONTINUED...

HAVE SUMORE BONUS PAGES

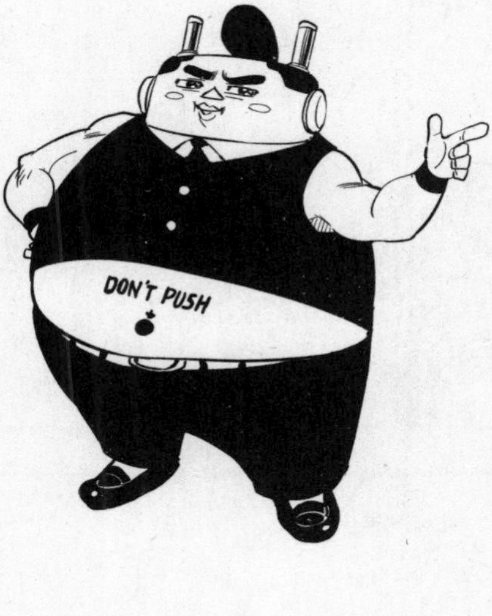
DON'T PUSH

BONUS MANGA
B-CUBER ROUND-TABLE TALK

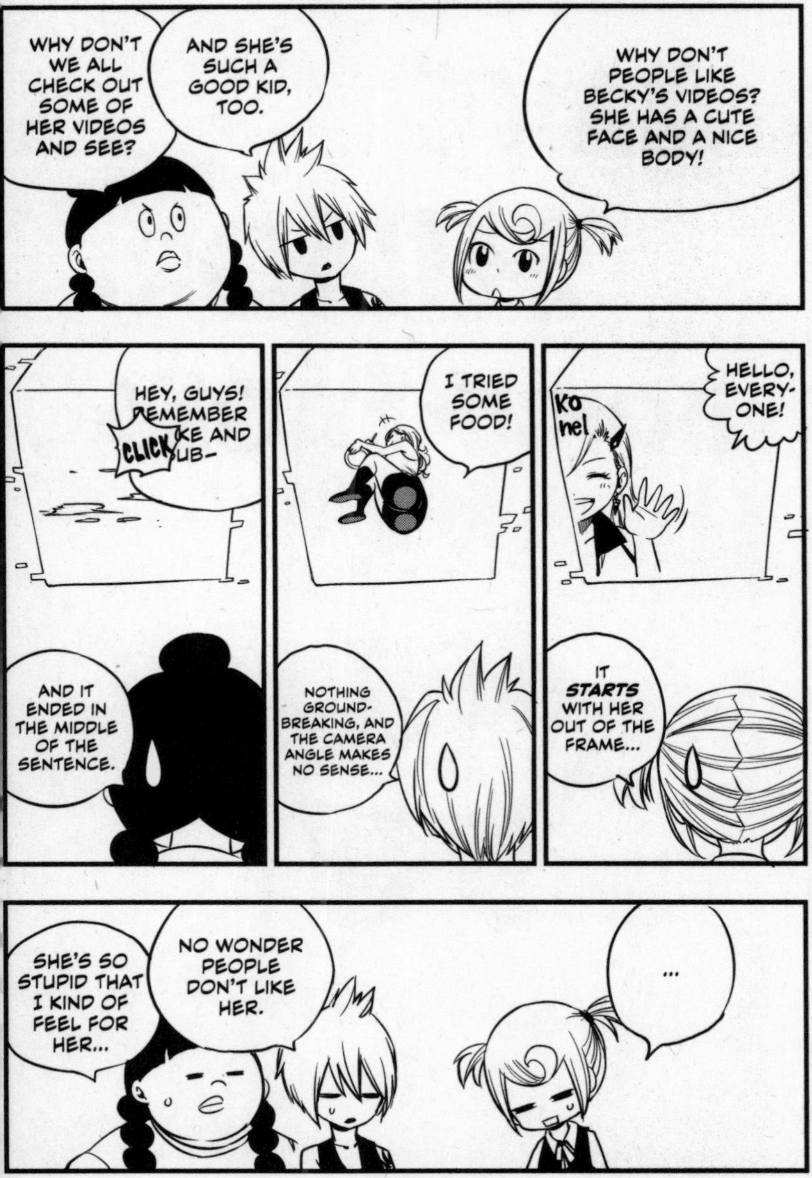
WHY DON'T PEOPLE LIKE BECKY'S VIDEOS? SHE HAS A CUTE FACE AND A NICE BODY!
AND SHE'S SUCH A GOOD KID, TOO.
WHY DON'T WE ALL CHECK OUT SOME OF HER VIDEOS AND SEE?
HELLO, EVERY-ONE!
Ko ne!
IT *STARTS* WITH HER OUT OF THE FRAME...
I TRIED SOME FOOD!
NOTHING GROUND-BREAKING, AND THE CAMERA ANGLE MAKES NO SENSE...
HEY, GUYS! REMEMBER KE AND UB-
CLICK
AND IT ENDED IN THE MIDDLE OF THE SENTENCE.
...
NO WONDER PEOPLE DON'T LIKE HER.
SHE'S SO STUPID THAT I KIND OF FEEL FOR HER...

SPOT THE DIFFERENCE

**Compare this picture to the title page
for Chapter 51 on page 3!
There are seven differences!
See if you can find them!!**

WELCOME TO THE NEXT INSTALLMENT OF...

(YUDETAMAGONZALEZ-SAN, OSAKA)

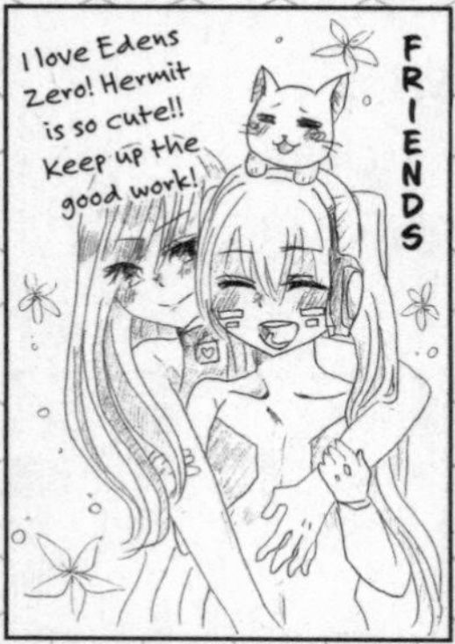
I love Edens Zero! Hermit is so cute!! Keep up the good work!
FRIENDS

▲ SEEING THOSE HEART-FELT SMILES REALLY WARMS THE HEART.

(SPLASH TOMATO-SAN, GIFU)

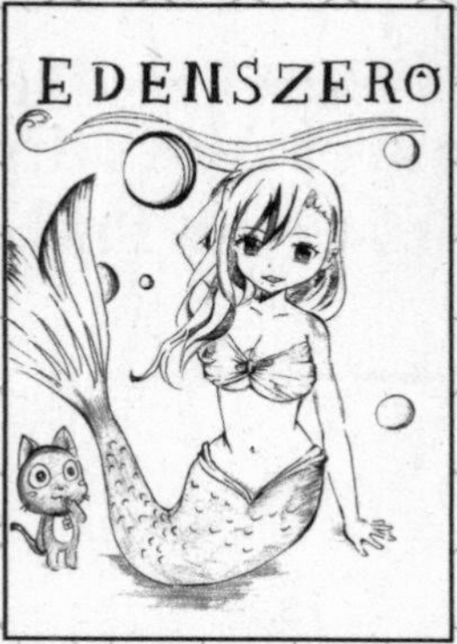
EDENSZERO

▲ SHE LOOKS BEAUTIFUL AS A MERMAID, BUT...I'M WORRIED ABOUT HAPPY!

(NON-SAN, TOCHIGI)

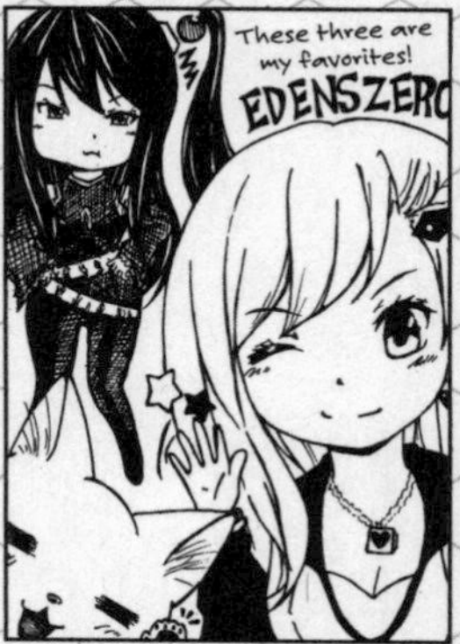
These three are my favorites!
EDENSZERO

▲ DRAWING LABILIA...YOU MUST LIKE TO TAKE THE PATH LEAST TRAVELED. GOOD JOB!

(MIKA-SAN, FUKUOKA)

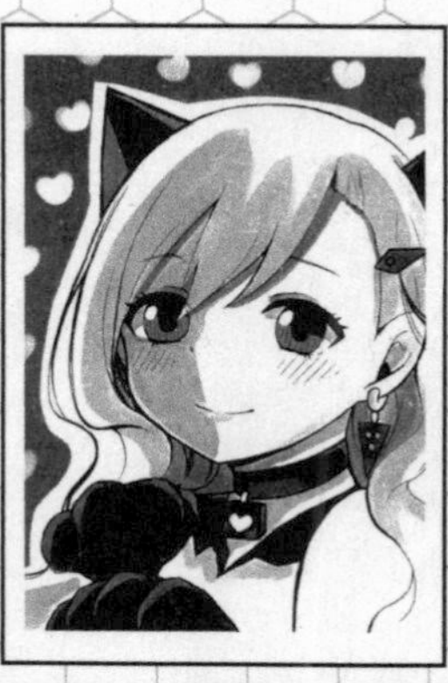

▲ ENNUI REBECCA. IT KIND OF MAKES ME THINK OF AUTUMN.

(MINORI CHIBA-SAN, SAITAMA)

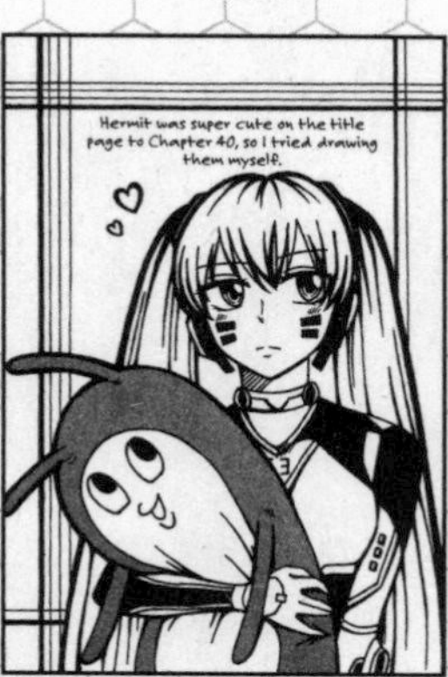
Hermit was super cute on the title page to Chapter 40, so I tried drawing them myself.

▲ THANK YOU. THE EXPRESSION AND THE PLUSHIE FROM CHAPTER 40 TURNED OUT PRETTY WELL.

EDITOR'S NOTE: SUBMISSIONS LIMITED TO JAPAN

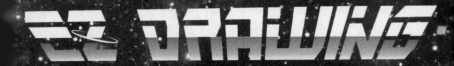

EZ DRAWING

(KUROBUTADON, KAGOSHIMA)

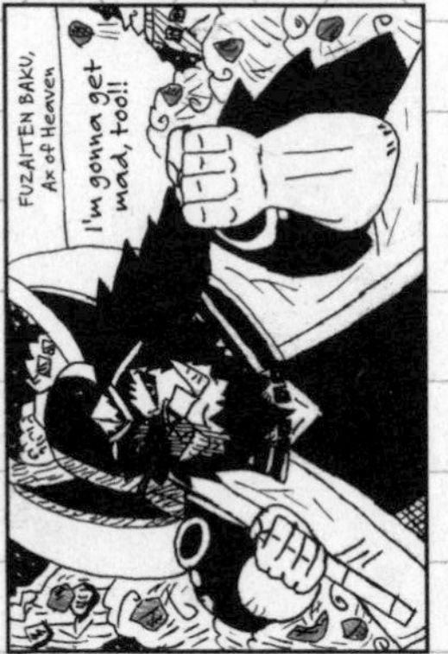
FUZAITEN BAKU, Ax of Heaven
I'm gonna get mad, too!!

▲ THANK YOU FOR MAKING HIM LOOK SO COOL. HE'S REALLY INTIMIDATING!

▲ THE DEMON KING'S FOUR SHINING STARS ASSEMBLED, PART ONE. WHICH OF THESE BEAUTIES IS YOUR FAVORITE?

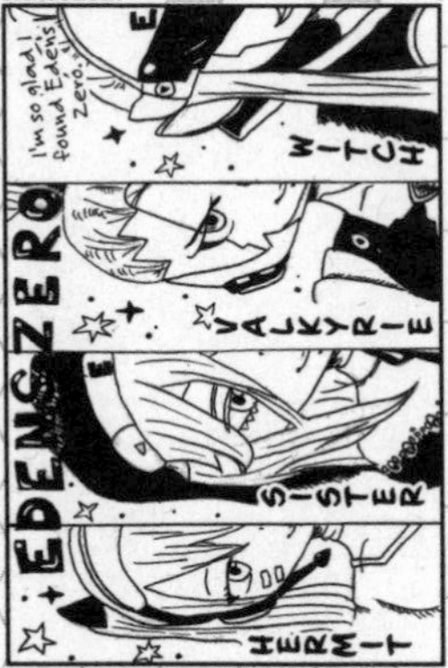
EDENS ZERO
I'm so glad I found Edens Zero.
WITCH
VALKYRIE
SISTER
HERMIT

(MEI-MEI-SAN, SHIZUOKA)

(YUTO YAMAMOTO-SAN, SHIZUOKA)

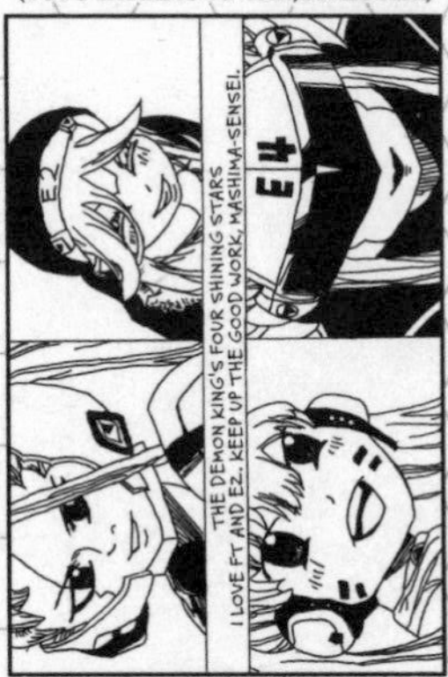
E2
E4
THE DEMON KING'S FOUR SHINING STARS
I LOVE FT AND EZ. KEEP UP THE GOOD WORK, MASHIMA-SENSEI.

▲ THE DEMON KING'S FOUR SHINING STARS ASSEMBLED, PART TWO. THANKS FOR DRAWING THEM IN NUMERICAL ORDER.

▲ SO IT'S SETTLED—THESE ARE THE THREE EDENS ZERO MASCOTS?! THOSE BIG ROUND EYES ARE SUPER CUTE.

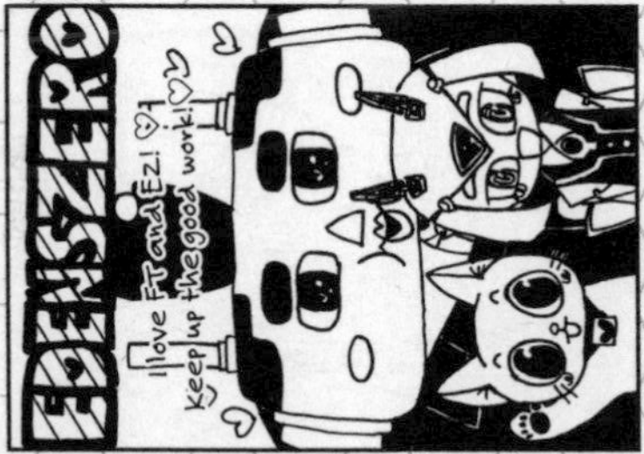
EDENS ZERO
I love FT and Ez!
Keep up the good work!

(HANA SAKAMOTO-SAN, CHIBA)

▲ THE SPACE NINJA LOOK REALLY DOES SUIT SHIKI. THE MINI CHARACTERS ARE ADORABLE.

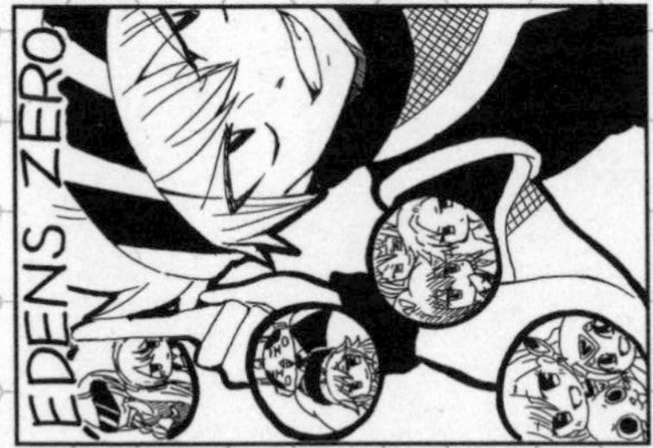
EDENS ZERO

(SHIINA-SAN, CHIBA)

EZ DRAWING extra

HERE ARE SOME UNIQUE EZ DRAWINGS FROM THE *EDENS ZERO* STAFF!!

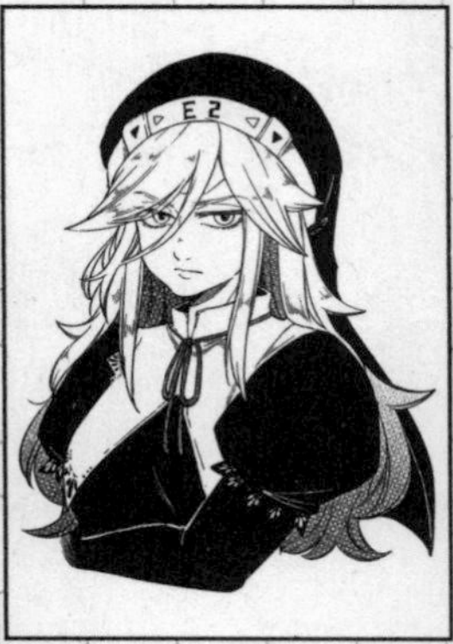

SAMABURU

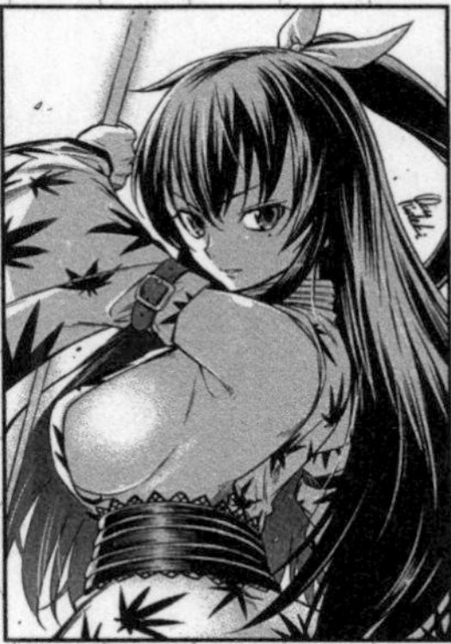

HIDEKI OKU

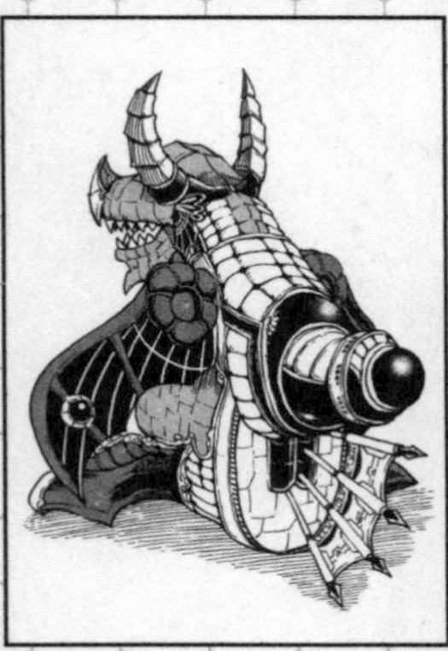

KOJI NAKAMURA

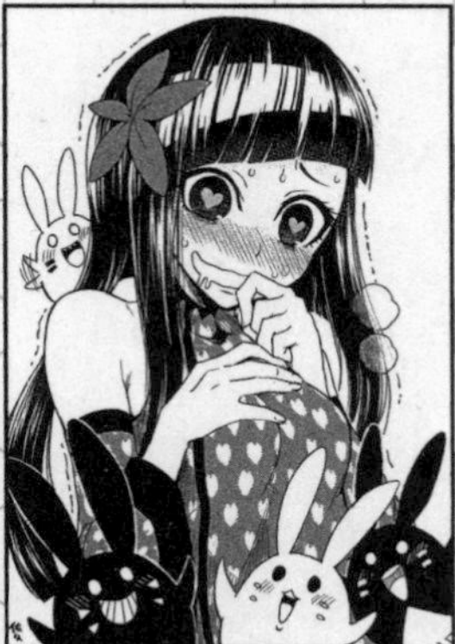

SAKU

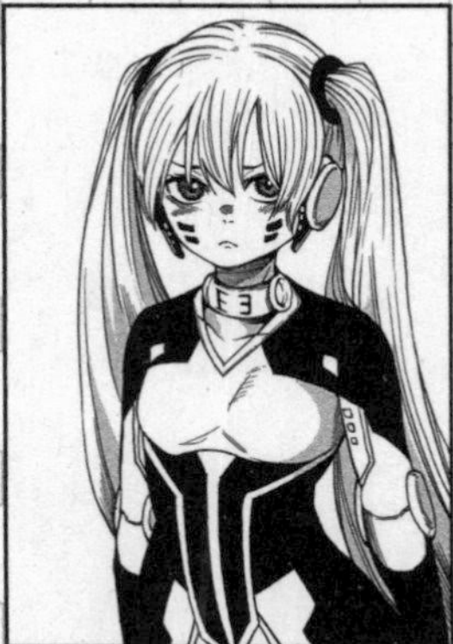

SHIZUYA SOMEYA

AFTERWORD

When my editors asked me, "Where does the name Madame Kurenai come from?" and I asked them, "Where do you think it came from?" their answers went something like this. My 40+year-old editor said, "Is it the rival character in a famous sports manga?" My 30+year-old editor said, "Is it the title of a song by a famous musician?" And my 20+year-old editor said, "I don't know, but it sounds really cool!"

The real answer is, Homura means "flame" (a name that makes you think of fire and the color red), so I named her mother Kurenai (meaning "crimson," another word that makes you think of fire and red). I don't remember where the Madame part came from; maybe I got it from some performer?

Now I'm going to talk about my editors a bit. Currently I have three of them. That's on the higher side for Kodansha's *Weekly Shonen Magazine*'s editorial department. I feel like normally, the majority of manga artists have one or two editors. But it's not like I've looked up the statistics or anything, so I don't know exactly. As for why I have three, it's simply because I have a lot of work. If we're just talking about manga planning meetings, in reality, one is enough. When there's a conflict of opinion, then having someone with a third perspective, to offer compromises or different solutions entirely, is even better. In my case, there are a lot of wide-scale, non-manga projects like anime, video games, merchandise, collabs, and international development to deal with, so one or two editors wouldn't be enough to cover it. Even with three, they seem really busy all year round. And this goes without saying, but my editors also edit other manga artists' works. I'm always thinking, "Wow, they have it rough," but I don't get a lot of chances to thank them directly, so I'd like to take this opportunity to say, "Thank you for everything."

Now, changing the subject, the character in this volume named Nino is modeled after a YouTuber I met in Germany. It started when I appeared on his channel, and I started talking about putting him in *EDENS ZERO*, and then I did. In the story, he's an enemy character, but in real life, he's a real nice, good-looking guy.

If I have the chance, I'd like to do more collaborations with some local YouTubers, too. Incidentally, a few of the YouTubers I know have already appeared in this manga.

Futaro Uesugi is a second-year in high school, scraping to get by and pay off his family's debt. The only thing he can do is study, so when Futaro receives a part-time job offer to tutor the five daughters of a wealthy businessman, he can't pass it up. Little does he know, these five beautiful sisters are quintuplets, but the only thing they have in common...is that they're all terrible at studying!

THE QUINTESSENTIAL QUINTUPLETS

negi haruba

ANIME OUT NOW!

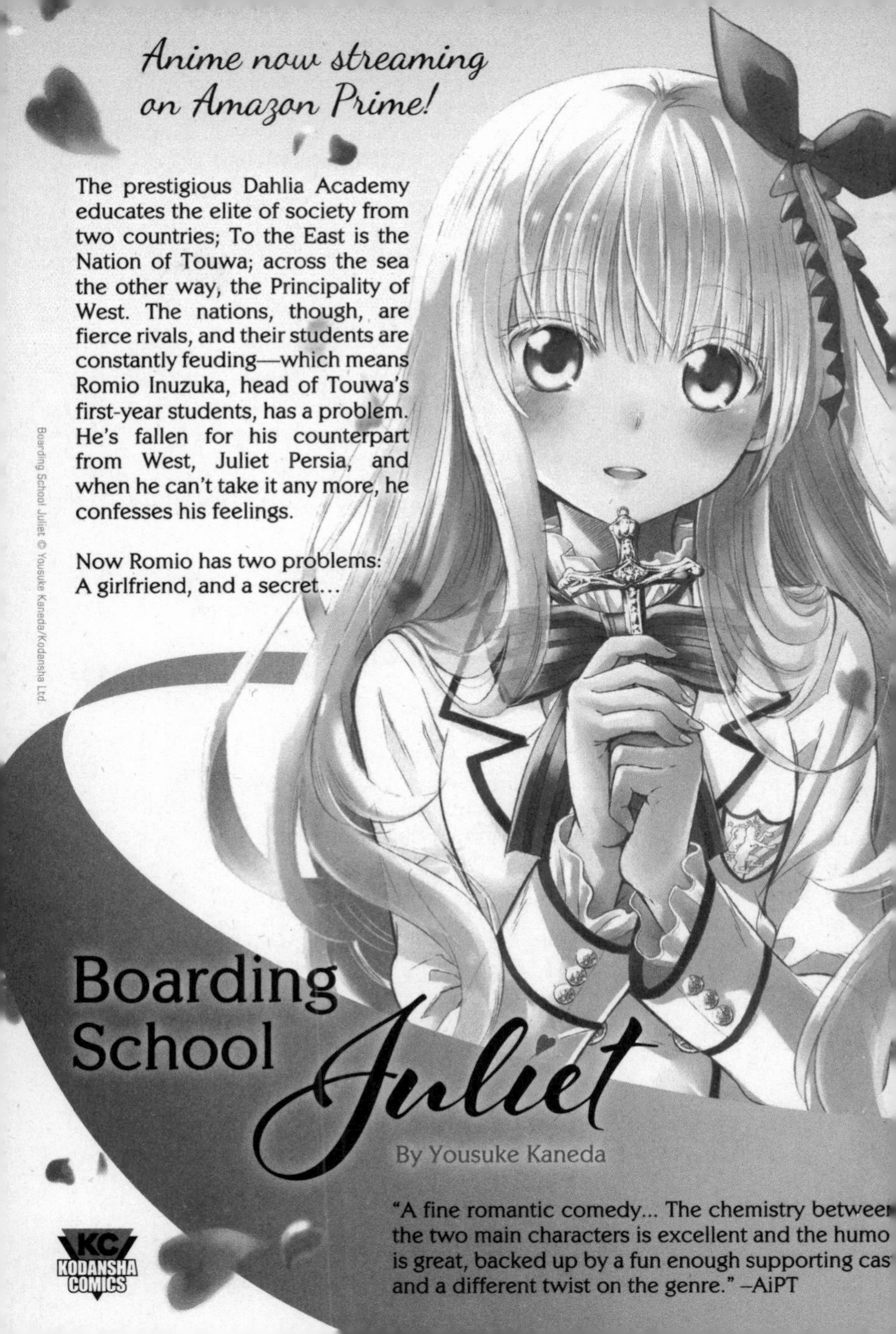
Anime now streaming on Amazon Prime!
The prestigious Dahlia Academy educates the elite of society from two countries; To the East is the Nation of Touwa; across the sea the other way, the Principality of West. The nations, though, are fierce rivals, and their students are constantly feuding—which means Romio Inuzuka, head of Touwa's first-year students, has a problem. He's fallen for his counterpart from West, Juliet Persia, and when he can't take it any more, he confesses his feelings.
Now Romio has two problems: A girlfriend, and a secret…
Boarding School Juliet
By Yousuke Kaneda
"A fine romantic comedy... The chemistry betwee the two main characters is excellent and the humo is great, backed up by a fun enough supporting cas and a different twist on the genre." –AiPT
KC KODANSHA COMICS
Boarding School Juliet © Yousuke Kaneda/Kodansha Ltd.

A Kodansha Comics Trade Paperback Original
EDENS ZERO 7 copyright © 2019 Hiro Mashima
English translation copyright © 2020 Hiro Mashima

All rights reserved.

Published in the United States by Kodansha Comics, an imprint of Kodansha USA Publishing, LLC, New York.

Publication rights for this English edition arranged through Kodansha Ltd., Tokyo.

First published in Japan in 2019 by Kodansha Ltd., Tokyo.

ISBN 978-1-63236-981-9

Original cover design by Narumi Miura (G x complex).

Printed in the United States of America.

www.kodanshacomics.com

9 8 7 6 5 4 3 2 1
Translation: Alethea Nibley & Athena Nibley
Lettering: AndWorld Design
Editing: Haruko Hashimoto
Kodansha Comics edition cover design by Phil Balsman

Publisher: Kiichiro Sugawara
Vice president of marketing & publicity: Naho Yamada

Director of publishing services: Ben Applegate
Associate director of operations: Stephen Pakula
Publishing services managing editor: Noelle Webster
Assistant production manager: Emi Lotto, Angela Zurlo